Ethnic Modernism

Ethnic Modernism

Werner Sollors

HARVARD UNIVERSITY PRESS
Cambridge, Massachusetts
London, England
2008

Copyright © 2002 by Cambridge University Press
Reprinted with permission
Originally published in *The Cambridge History of American Literature,* Volume 6: Prose Writing, 1910–1950, edited by Sacvan Bercovitch
Notes and Bibliography © 2008 by Werner Sollors
All rights reserved

First Harvard University Press paperback edition, 2008

Library of Congress Cataloging-in-Publication Data
Sollors, Werner.
    Ethnic modernism / Werner Sollors. — 1st Harvard University Press pbk. ed.
      p. cm.
    "Originally published in The Cambridge History of American Literature, volume 6 : Prose writing, 1910–1950, edited by Sacvan Bercovitch"—T.p. verso.
    Includes bibliographical references and index.
    ISBN-13: 978-0-674-03091-6 (alk. paper)
    1. American literature—20th century—History and criticism.
2. Modernism (Literature)—United States. 3. American literature—Minority authors—History and criticism. 4. American literature—African American authors—History and criticism. 5. Immigrants' writings, American—History and criticism. 6. Politics and literature—United States—History—20th century. 7. Ethnicity in literature.
8. Race in literature. 9. Immigrants in literature. I. Cambridge history of American literature. II. Title.
    PS228.M63S66 2008
      810.9'112—dc22   2008007143

For Alide

Contents

1	Introduction	*1*
2	Gertrude Stein and "Negro Sunshine"	*17*
3	Ethnic Lives and Lifelets	*35*
4	Ethnic Themes, Modern Themes	*59*
5	Mary Antin: Progressive Optimism against Odds	*65*
6	Who Is "American"?	*78*
7	American Languages	*85*
8	"All the past we leave behind"? Ole E. Rølvaag and the Immigrant Trilogy	*92*
9	Modernism, Ethnic Labeling, and the Quest for Wholeness: Jean Toomer's New American Race	*101*
10	Freud, Marx, Hard-Boiled	*113*
11	Hemingway Spoken Here	*128*
12	Henry Roth: Ethnicity, Modernity, and Modernism	*140*
13	*Brrrrrrriiiiiiiiiiiiiiiiiiiinng!* The Clock, the Salesman, and the Breast	*157*
14	Immigrant Literature and Totalitarianism	*183*

15	Was Modernism Antitotalitarian?	207
16	Facing the Extreme	219
17	Grand Central Terminal	235
	Chronology	243
	Notes	253
	Bibliography	283
	Acknowledgments	301
	Index	305

Ethnic Modernism

1

Introduction

The period from 1910 to 1950 was the age of modernism in literature, art, and music. James Joyce's *Ulysses,* T. S. Eliot's *Waste Land* (both published in 1922), and the experiments by Pablo Picasso, Duke Ellington, and Arnold Schönberg defined the aesthetic of the first half of the twentieth century in defiance of artistic developments from the Renaissance to nineteenth-century realism. The modernist emphasis was on "abstract" form rather than on theme and on a new nonlinearity rather than on traditional artistic development and execution. Artists and writers increasingly wished to represent the sense of speed and motion that trains, trolleys, automobiles, and other means of modern transportation made widely available. Modernists were also interested in adapting techniques of nonwestern art and of the new formal language of film. These trends supported the "experimental," detached, and often difficult quality of modernism that took different shape in the various movements (the many "isms") that emerged in the course of the century. Amazingly, what started as the fringe enterprise of a few radical artists at the beginning of the century who set out to "defamiliarize," to "alienate" their small audiences, and what appeared as if it would be replaced by a second wave of realism in the 1930s (when Gertrude Stein bought work by such painters as Christian Bérard, Pavel Tcheletchew, or Francis Rose), became the dominant expression of western art by the 1950s.

Looking back at modernism, the Harvard University critic Harry Levin marveled at the fact that "The Picasso" could have become the name of an apartment building in New York, and his Columbia University colleague Lionel Trilling wondered what had changed to make modernism teachable in so many colleges and schools around the United States. In the 1920s, Eda Lou Walton, an avant-garde professor of modern literature at New York University, had to smuggle a copy of *Ulysses* through U.S. customs in order to read and discuss it in her private boudoir, in unorthodox fashion, with adventurous young undergraduate boys. By the 1950s, Joyce could readily be assigned to coed students who had not yet reached the legal drinking age in many states. Gertrude Stein's famous device of "Rose is a rose is a rose is a rose" was enough of an irritant so that characters in Richard Wright's *Lawd Today* (finished in manuscript in 1937 under the title "Cesspool") would wonder about the "old white woman over in Paris" who had written it and then wouldn't tell what it meant; even Cab Calloway "ain't never said nothing that crazy."[1] In the second half of the century, Stein's line was milked for American Volkswagen commercials ("it runs and runs and runs").

At the beginning of the period, modernism may have still seemed foreign to many Americans. The public reactions were strong against the modernist paintings that were in the minority in the famous 1913 Armory Show, such as Marcel Duchamp's "Nude Descending a Staircase, No. 2" (1912), which was frequently ridiculed by cartoonists. Some saw in it the explosion of a tile factory. The New York *Evening Sun* parodied it, under the general heading "Seeing New York with a Cubist," as "The Rude Descending a Staircase (Rush hour at the Subway)."

Though William Carlos Williams said, "it was not until I clapped my eyes on Marcel Duchamp's Nude Descending a Staircase that I burst out laughing from the relief it brought me,"[2] Theodore Roosevelt published "A Layman's View of an Art Exhibition" in *Outlook* (March 22, 1913), in which he wrote:

> Take the picture which for some reason is called *A naked man going down stairs*. There is in my bath-room a really good Navajo rug which, on any proper interpretation of the Cubist theory, is a far more satisfactory and decorative picture. Now if, for some inscrutable reason, it suited somebody to call this rug a picture of, say, *A well-dressed man going up a ladder,* the name would fit the facts just about as well as in the case of the Cubist picture of the *Naked man going down stairs*. From the standpoint of terminology each name would have whatever merit inheres in a rather cheap straining after affect; and from the standpoint of decorative value, of sincerity, and of artistic merit, the Navajo rug is infinitely ahead of the picture.[3]

The opposition clearly had the upper hand, and the overwhelming majority of American works of art that were exhibited before World War II at the Venice Biennale, for example, were at first salon art, and later urban realist, regionalist, or social realist—or throughout the decades, recognizably detailed female nudes by hence forgotten painters—but they were not modernist. The single exception was the 1934 Biennale, for which Juliana Force of the brand-new Whitney Museum made the selections, and at which much American modernist work was shown, including Edward Hopper's *Early Sunday Morning*, Georgia O'Keeffe's *Mountains, New Mexico*, Max Weber's *Chinese Restaurant*, Reginald Marsh's *Why Not Use the "L"?*, and Walt Kuhn's *Blue Clown*. The exhibit was marred, however, by the central presence of a large and lifelike effigy of William Randolph Hearst's mistress, the glamorous silent-movie era comedienne Marion Davies (painted by the once famous celebrity portraitist Tadé Styka, the son of a Polish panorama artist) that Hearst's men had managed to sneak into the American pavilion without Force's knowledge; Force was unable to have it legally removed before the Biennale season ended. This much-commented-on installation (that still appeared in the centenary Biennale catalogue of 1995 as if it had been an official 1934 submission) seemed symbolic of the dominance of non-modernist art in the period, especially since Hearst's papers had given ample room to caricature modern paintings, comparing them to grandma's quilts or wondering whether the museums were hanging their modern artworks upside down. The conflict between Hearst and Force seemed ominously representative of the intensifying struggle between "fascist realism" and "democratic modernism," since Hearst had also published positive press reports on Mussolini, was on his way to meet Hitler, and knew Count Volpi di Misurata, the Fascist director of the Biennale, whereas Force was a democratic spirit and daring amateur who described modern American art in the 1934 Biennale catalogue in cosmopolitan terms as coming out of "the fusion of different races and nationalities which has given the U.S. a rare sensibility of being open to influences from around the world."[4]

When, in 1936, the not-yet-seven-year-old Museum of Modern Art in New York ran an all-European exhibition on *Cubism and Abstract Art* (its curator was Alfred H. Barr, Jr., who had pioneered in teaching modern art at Wellesley College from 1926–1929), the U.S. Customs Service determined that many of the sculptures (among them, those by Boccioni,

Miró, and Giacometti) were not "art" and subjected them to duties as imported materials (stone, wood, etc.). Under the headline "Furiously They Ask Once More: But Is It Art?" the *New York Times* gave lavish coverage to the show but also voiced the complaint that "these cliqued isms represent the flight from reality. Facing life as it is, they paint life as it isn't." In 1986, these facts were emphasized in the fiftieth-anniversary edition of the catalogue.[5]

The exhibitions in Alfred Stieglitz's Gallery 291 (1908–1917) reached only a relatively small group of intellectuals who were exposed to shows on African sculpture, Cézanne, Picasso, Braque, Matisse, and children's drawings (newly discovered as an art form). Stieglitz and his *Camera Work* (1903–1917) also appealed to a small circle of modernists who were eager to develop photography as art and to distinguish its aesthetic from that of painting. By 1938, this effort had not yet taken root, and photography received no mention in Harold Stearns's stocktaking collection *America Now* (1938), an updating of Stearns's earlier symposium *Civilization in the United States* (1922).

Antonín Dvořák had set the tone early for incorporating black American musical elements into modern music when he took the themes of black and Indian songs and made them part of his 1893 *Ninth Symphony* ("From the New World"). Yet ragtime and jazz were still regularly attacked in American newspapers in the 1920s, the so-called "jazz age." Even a calm academic, Walter Damrosch, found it necessary to address the Music Supervisors' national conference in 1928 with a worried and thoroughly derogatory comment on jazz, describing it as "a monotony of rhythm . . . without music and without soul" that "stifles the true musical instinct, turning away many of our talented young people from the persistent, continued study and execution of good music."[6] A few years before Duke Ellington launched his intricate musical experiment "Daybreak Express" (recorded in 1933), the *New York Times* still reported as a matter of fact the belief that "Jazz is quite unsatisfactory to any intelligent person" (April 17, 1928: 26). It is telling that music critic and CBS consultant Deems Taylor's contribution on "Music" to Harold Stearns's *America Now* (1938) makes no reference to jazz, but that Hearst paper columnist Louis Reid's entry on "Amusement: Radio and Movies" mentions that broadcasters were "primly-squeamish about recognizing jazz as such," yet they had unwittingly "accomplished the astounding service of making the whole world jazz-conscious."[7]

William Faulkner, ultimately the most significant American prose writer of the century, wrote his most important works from 1929 to 1942 to mixed reviews and, with the exception of *Sanctuary* (1931), reached only a relatively small audience.[8] It is symptomatic that literary critic John Chamberlain's contribution to Stearns's *America Now*, which discusses many major and minor writers of the 1930s, mentions Faulkner only once: "Erskine Caldwell and William Faulkner have their points, but they have not developed into major artists" (47). This sentence suggests the niche of sensationalist Southern gore within which Faulkner was still buried as a minor regionalist. The immigrant novelist and critic Ludwig Lewisohn held Faulkner in higher esteem as early as 1932, when he characterized him, in *Expression in America*, as the "most gifted" of contemporary "neo-naturalist writers" who, however, in "needlessly intricate and essentially confused books" "has preserved one active emotion, a very fruitful emotion for the naturalist: a fierce hatred for all that has given him pain."[9] (Was Quentin Compson's pained exclamation at the end of *Absalom, Absalom!* (1936), *"I dont hate it! I dont hate it!,"* also a response to Lewisohn?)

Even scholar and critic Alfred Kazin's influential interpretation of modern American prose literature, *On Native Grounds* (1942), which devotes more than ten pages to Faulkner, still concludes with the assessment that "Faulkner's corn-fed, tobacco-drooling phantoms are not the constituents of a representative American epic" and that "no writer ever made so much of his failure."[10] Reviewing *Go Down, Moses* in the *Nation* in the same year, Lionel Trilling took a more positive stance toward the book's Southern and racial themes, yet viewed Faulkner's "literary mannerisms" as "faults," found Faulkner's "reliance on the method of memory" "tiresome," his prose "irritating," and complained generally: "while I am sure that prose fiction may make great demands on our attention, it ought not to make these demands arbitrarily, and there is no reason why Mr. Faulkner cannot settle to whom the pronoun 'he' refers. Mr. Faulkner's new book is worth effort but not, I think, the kind of effort which I found necessary: I had to read it twice to get clear not only the finer shades of meaning but the simple primary intentions, and I had to construct an elaborate genealogical table to understand the family connections."[11] By 1945, virtually all of Faulkner's seventeen books had slipped out of print; even the plates had been recycled during the war years.[12]

At the beginning of the period, then, modern art seemed like a strange European invention, modern music and jazz had subcultural or popular, not national or artistic significance, and the best modernist literature had not found many sympathetic readers. American intellectuals could believe that modern art was not art, that modern music was not music or was merely entertainment, and that even the best modernist literature was simply an elaborately disguised failure. And on the level of "middlebrow readers"—a newly popular term located between the "highbrow" and "lowbrow" of critic Van Wyck Brooks's *America's Coming-of-Age* (1915)—the *Saturday Evening Post* expressed its hostility to modern art as alien to America in countless articles, often with the reassuringly homey realism of Norman Rockwell's cover art. It was also the *Saturday Evening Post* which serialized Mussolini's autobiography, a text ghostwritten by the anti-immigration and pro-deportation writer Richard Washburn Child, who had been U.S. ambassador to Italy during the fascist march on Rome in 1922.

By the mid-century, agencies of the United States government proudly adopted abstract art, modern jazz, and the 1950 Nobel prize winner William Faulkner (his works now partly available in Malcolm Cowley's thematically organized *Portable Faulkner* edition—with genealogies and a map) as true expressions of the American spirit that could be officially endorsed for export around the globe.[13] The fact that the remaining American opposition was shrilly xenophobic and right-wing only enhanced the development. Representative is a 1949 diatribe by Republican congressman George A. Dondero from Michigan who worried about the "intolerable situation" that "public schools, colleges, and universities . . . , invaded by a horde of foreign art manglers, are selling to our young men and women a subversive doctrine of 'isms.'" Dondero proclaimed in a thirty-minute address to Congress on August 16, 1949:

> All these isms are of foreign origin, and truly should have no place in American art. While not all are media of social or political protest, all are instruments and weapons of destruction. . . .
> Cubism aims to destroy by designed disorder.
> Futurism aims to destroy by the machine myth. . . .
> Dadaism aims to destroy by ridicule.
> Expressionism aims to destroy by aping the primitive and insane. . . .
> Abstractionism aims to destroy by the creation of brainstorms.
> Surrealism aims to destroy by the denial of reason. . . .

The artists of the "isms" change their designation as often and as readily as the Communist front organizations. Picasso, who is also a Dadaist, an abstractionist, or a surrealist, as unstable fancy dictates, is the hero of all the crackpots in so-called modern art.... But no matter what others call Picasso, he said of himself: "I am a Communist, and my painting is Communist painting."[14]

One of Dondero's deepest worries was that Kurt Seligmann, a Swiss surrealist, had been named as artistic judge by the Hallmark Company of Kansas City to determine the winner in their $30,000 Christmas card contest. What danger this represented to Christmas in America was obvious to Dondero, for surrealism "holds that our cultural heritage of religion is an obstacle to be overcome." Even Dondero had to concede, however, that "quite a few" sincere individuals now believed that "so-called modern or contemporary art cannot be Communist because art in Russia today is realistic."

Unfortunately for Dondero, President Dwight D. Eisenhower turned out to be one of those individuals, for on the occasion of the twenty-fifth anniversary of the Museum of Modern Art on February 19, 1954, he sent his "warm greetings"—tape-recorded—to all the museum's associates and friends. In this presidential message, which was played to the 2,500 assembled guests, Eisenhower called the MoMA a "great museum," stressed what he called the "important principle" that "freedom of the arts is a basic freedom, one of the pillars of liberty in our land," and said: "For our Republic to stay free, those among us with the rare gift of artistry must be able freely to use their talent." Equally important was that "our people must have unimpaired opportunity to see, to understand, to profit from our artists' work." He continued that "as long as artists are at liberty to feel with high personal intensity, as long as our artists are able to create with sincerity and conviction, there will be healthy controversy and progress in art. Only thus can there be opportunity for a genius to conceive and to produce a masterpiece for all mankind." Though General Eisenhower's own aesthetic sensibility was probably closer to Roosevelt's than their different assessments of modernism might suggest, Ike endorsed modern art as part of a Cold War logic, for such praise helped the anti-Communist objective of chastising the way in which modern art was either attacked by state propaganda or banned outright under totalitarian tyranny, the artists imprisoned or persecuted. "When artists are made the slaves and the tools of the state,"

Eisenhower argued, "when artists become chief propagandists of a cause, progress is arrested and creation and genius are destroyed." The president ended his greetings with a momentous resolution: "Let us resolve that this precious freedom of the arts, these precious freedoms of America, will, day by day, year by year, become ever stronger, ever brighter in our land."[15]

The *New York Times* described the event, at which such other speakers as New York's mayor and the secretary general of the United Nations also made addresses, under the headline "Eisenhower Links Art and Freedom." Dondero, however, simply could not understand Eisenhower's statements, and saw threatened his lifelong goal to "protect and preserve legitimate art as we have always known it in the United States."

Dondero notwithstanding, in the war and postwar years the tide was clearly turning toward an official acceptance of modernism. The American pavilion at the Biennale became more and more modernist each time, starting in 1948; and it began to include photographic art by Ben Shahn, Charles Sheeler, and Diane Arbus in its exhibits. On January 23, 1943, Duke Ellington's ambitious *Black, Brown, and Beige: A Tone Parallel to the History of the American Negro* opened at Carnegie Hall (presented as a benefit for Russian War Relief); and in 1956, the State Department (not being able to afford Louis Armstrong) sent Dizzy Gillespie on a tour of the Near and Middle East. Gillespie was only one of several jazz musicians who went on official government-sponsored tours to many countries, including ultimately the Soviet Union. (It would be hard to imagine Jelly Roll Morton on a Woodrow Wilson-sponsored tour abroad.) The officially financed Congress for Cultural Freedom promoted modern literature, art, and music in opposition to totalitarianism; at its Paris meeting in 1951 music by Arnold Schönberg was performed, and Jean Cocteau designed the stage set for a production of *Oedipus Rex* that was conducted by Igor Stravinsky.

College generation after generation was now being raised on modernism in literature and the arts (Dondero was right at least in this respect). In 1962, Warner Brothers released the animated musical feature film *Gay Purr-ee*, remarkably designed by Victor Haboush, in which "Mewsette," a cat with Judy Garland's voice, encounters all versions of modernist art in Paris, from van Gogh to Buffet; among the film's memorable song lines is "The chestnut, the willow, the colors of Utrillo." In the same year, even Norman Rockwell painted a modernist canvas for a

Saturday Evening Post cover (January 13) titled "The Connoisseur." The large Jackson Pollock-inspired painting in which abstract colors explode dramatically fills two-thirds of the image, but it is presented to the viewer behind (and partly obscured by) a realistically rendered, balding, conservatively dressed, and professorial-seeming gentleman, whose creased gray trousers, white hat, black umbrella, and shoes form a bland antithesis to the painting; he appears more skeptical observer than connoisseur. He also seems like an allegory of the professoriate's relationship to modernist art.

The United States was an intricate part of the development in the course of which modernism emerged as the dominant art form of the twentieth century. In fact, the U.S. became virtually identified with the culture of modernism by mid-century so that modernism now appeared as American as apple pie, the culture of modernism as an American "homemade world," and modern art as "the great American thing." The newly claimed and rapidly disseminated modernist American spirit received a literary genealogy that included proto-modernists like Herman Melville (rediscovered after 1919), among whose early advocates was the modern photographer and jazz supporter Carl Van Vechten. Edmund Wilson stressed, in *Axel's Castle* (1931), Edgar Allan Poe's significance as a "prophet of [French] symbolism." The important nineteenth-century poets were Walt Whitman and Emily Dickinson (in the newly restored unregularized edition published from 1951 to 1955) while Whittier, Longfellow, and Lowell moved into the distant background. The wish to view American culture as the prototypical modern one was pervasive by the 1950s. Thus the art critic Harold Rosenberg surprisingly cast the French pointillists in a tradition of popular American Currier and Ives lithographs when he wrote: "I have seen enlarged details of their New York scenes that are a match for Seurat."[16] However forced it seems in retrospect, the connection may have appeared natural enough at the moment.

The change in canonization and the new emphasis on American modernism coincided with the growing international reception of U.S. authors. In 1910, American literature was still of marginal significance outside of the borders of the United States. More American publishers were engaged in disseminating British authors than European houses were in reprinting the Americans. American literary culture lived from importing, not exporting works. After World War II, however, this changed remarkably—so much so that later in the twentieth century U.S. cultural products were second only to the weapons industry in achieving an export surplus, as the American entertainment industry had become a supplier of the whole world. From 1910 to 1950, the United States shifted from a country of consumers of European culture—"gondola guzzlers," as David Quixano, the hero of Israel Zangwill's play *The Melting-Pot* (1908) put it disparagingly—to a near-universal global "content provider" for all media, old and new.

This development went hand in hand with the dramatic changes brought about by new technological inventions like modern print techniques, records, sound movies, radio, and at the end of the period, television, all of which simplified dissemination and export. These inventions, and the continuing processes of urbanization, industrialization, secularization, and migration are often viewed as aspects of "modernism." In order to differentiate the sociological and technological developments from aesthetic movements, it may be helpful, however, to refer to the former as "modernity" and only the latter as modernism.

The changes from 1910 to 1950 coincided with a growing commercialization of literary production and publishing as part of a larger "entertainment industry," and with an unheard-of expansion of consumer culture. It was a development that changed the publication of literary texts dramatically by new features: there were tie-ins with film releases (e.g., the publishing of Anzia Yezierska's *Salome of the Tenements* on Thanksgiving Day 1922 when the moving picture based on her novel *Hungry Hearts* was also released), blanketing advertising campaigns for creating best-sellers (e.g., Claude McKay's *Home to Harlem* in 1928), and the presentation of authors as "celebrities" among the rich and famous. F. Scott Fitzgerald contributed an essay on the pressing question of "How to Live on $36,000 a Year" to the *Saturday Evening Post* in 1924; and Hemingway's mythical biographical persona became the embodiment of an American author of worldwide fame.

At the beginning of the century, ads began to interrupt serialized fiction in publications like Edward Bok's *Ladies' Home Journal*. After the middle of the century, the culture critic Paul Goodman suggested that television programming should properly be viewed as the interruption of commercials. George Horace Lorimer, the editor of the *Saturday Evening Post,* early on presented positively conceived images of the "businessman" and fought hard for expanding advertisements. Later he managed to choose appropriate content to accompany and reinforce advertising messages. By the mid-1920s, the *Post* contained more advertising than editorial matter (the back page alone selling for $15,000) and reached ten million readers and consumers. The development from a literary editor who sought business as a theme to a commercial entrepreneur who paid for content to accompany a journal's advertisements was well underway. In 1939 the then-Trotskyite *Partisan Review* sent out a questionnaire to writers—among them James Agee who incorporated it into *Let Us Now Praise Famous Men*—that included a question concerning the "corruption of the literary supplements by advertising" making difficult fair reviews of books.[17]

The very existence of competitive advertising signaled the presence of large, otherwise untapped readerships that could be reached, at least temporarily, through the organs that proliferated in the period. In 1920, John Dewey sensed that there was an enormous populace that was "constantly in transit," hence neither nationally American nor locally anchored and ideally suited as the readership for organs like the *Saturday Evening Post:* "They are just what they are—passengers. Hence the S—— E—— P—— and other journals expressly designed for this intermediate state of existence. . . . What becomes of all these periodicals? The man who answered this question would be the final authority on literature in America. Pending investigation, my hypothesis is that the brakeman, the Pullman porter, and those who clean out the street-cars inherit them."[18] The radical leftist Mike Gold called the *Saturday Evening Post* more vividly a "filthy lackeyrag, so fat, shiny, gorged with advertisements, putrid with prosperity like the bulky, diamonded duenna of a bawdy house," and in 1924, he found in the journal's pages "hired romanticists; hired liars about life; high salaried thimble-riggers, flim-flam men and circus fakers; Rolls Royce captains of fictional industry; sob sisters,"—an industrially produced and ever-expanding mass culture that was aesthetically and politically below contempt.[19]

The dramatic changes in the first half of the century were greatly enhanced by the two big wars in both of which the United States played a decisive role; the country asserted its military strength in World War I and its technological leadership by the first use of two nuclear bombs in World War II. The 1945 nuclear bombings of Hiroshima and Nagasaki were to remain the only two military uses of this quintessentially twentieth-century weapon, its only application in the "nuclear age" of the last century. The two World Wars made the period from 1910 to 1950 one of the most violent times in human history, claiming a total of at least sixty-five million human lives. Amidst all this violence, no battle or military action took place in the continental United States. However, partly as a consequence of the two World Wars, the U.S. moved from the periphery to the center of the world stage. Starting out as a minor player and debtor nation, it became one of the great world powers and creditor countries in the course of the first half of the century.

African Americans, European immigrants, and members of other minority groups were, *as* immigrants and ethnics, part of modernity, as they lived through such experiences of migration, ethnic identification, racialization, and alienation. In many ways, they also participated in, and significantly advanced, the course of modernism in the United States; Afro-American artists, including Fletcher Henderson, Louis Armstrong, Duke Ellington, and Charlie Parker, were central to the development of the new American music; modern composers Arnold Schönberg and Kurt Weill escaped to America from fascist Europe; immigrant and émigré artists like Joseph Stella, Max Weber, Ben Shahn, Man Ray, and Marcel Duchamp helped to establish modernist art; European exiles like Josef Albers were prominently active in such institutions as Black Mountain College while Hans Hoffmann taught the principles of modernist art and "abstract expressionism" in New York. Important modern-art collectors and curators such as Leo Stein, Etta Cone, Juliana Force, and Peggy Guggenheim were the children or grandchildren of immigrants.

Works of American "ethnic" prose literature, written by, about, or for persons who perceived themselves, or were perceived by others, as members of ethnic groups, are the central subject of these pages. Ethnic autobiographies, novels, short stories, and nonfiction works participated in the development of an American literary modernism that would carry the day only after World War II. The reception of some of these works resembled that of modernist art and literature in general. Jean Toomer's experimental book *Cane* (1923), a landmark of modernism, sold but a few hundred copies in the 1920s and then disappeared from view, only to reemerge as a Harper "perennial classic" in the 1960s and a mass-market Norton paperback since the 1970s; Henry Roth's novel *Call It Sleep* (1934) reached a couple of thousand readers in the 1930s, vanished, and reappeared as an Avon mass-market paperback in the 1960s, followed by a Farrar, Straus, and Giroux reprint. Both Toomer and Roth received prominent and positive *New York Times Book Review* coverage when they were reprinted, a rare occasion in an influential organ in which reprints are infrequently reviewed.[20]

While ethnic writers may have felt at home in modernism, they were not always equally at home in America—only in the utopian notion of what the country might become. In an age of racial definitions of U.S. citizenship, racist immigration restrictions, and eugenicist thought, ethnic writers often invoked America as an ideal, while the real United States was not yet claiming diversity in the spirit of multicultural pride that was to prevail only later. For the United States had yet to be reimagined as the "nation of nations" (that Walt Whitman had first proclaimed) rather than as England's stepchild.

The cultural work of recasting the United States as a multiethnic country was undertaken by American ethnic writers in the period, who like Abraham Cahan or Jessie Fauset were often fluent in other languages and well-versed in international debates about cosmopolitanism and art. American ethnic writers were increasingly drawn to ethnic pluralism or at least to a broader definition of the American "host culture" to which immigrants and minorities were to be "assimilated." Like the Russian-born Mary Antin or the Slovenian-American Louis Adamic, they may not have been in the forefront of aesthetic modernism, but they fought for a redefinition of America in the first half of the century though their vision took firmer public hold only in the second. Waldo Frank's manifesto *Our America* (1919) attempted to articulate the literary consequences of the new view of America when he demanded that American writers "study the cultures of the German, the Latin, the Celt, the Slav, the Anglo-Saxon and the African on the American continent: plot their reactions one upon the other, and their disappearance as integral worlds."[21] For Frank, Whitman doubled as the prophet of aesthetic modernism and of a multicultural view of America. Whitman's view of the United States as "nation of nations" was admired and echoed by many twentieth-century authors, as was his observation: "Thus far, impress'd by New England writers and schoolmasters, we tacitly abandon ourselves to the notion that our United States have been fashion'd from the British Islands only, and essentially form a second England only—which is a very great mistake." Ethnic writers tended to share Whitman's worry that Americans had not yet learned that their own antecedents were "ampler than has been supposed" and included many points of origin. (These intellectuals were less easily prepared to endorse Whitman's sentiment that English was "the dialect of common sense . . . , the chosen tongue to express growth faith self-esteem freedom justice equality friendliness amplitude prudence decision and courage." And they were probably unaware of Whitman's opposition to racial amalgamation—"Nature has set an impassable seal against it"—in an 1858 *Brooklyn Daily Times* editorial, followed by Whitman's rhetorical question, "Besides, is not America for the Whites? And is it not better so?")[22]

The period from 1910 to 1950 provided the United States with a new vocabulary that was needed for the multiethnic reimagining of the country—as well as for naming the fearful opposite of that vision. The radical New York critic Randolph Bourne was the first to advocate a "Trans-National America" in a 1916 landmark essay. Walter Lippmann gave currency to the term "stereotype" in 1922, a word that assumed a more sinister meaning in the 1930s and 1940s. In 1924 the phrasing "cultural pluralism" was coined by the immigrant philosopher and William James's student Horace M. Kallen, in opposition to the dominant ideology of ethnic assimilation; the significance of Kallen's coinage became palpable only decades later when it was more widely adopted. The word "ethnicity," which had been obsolete since the eighteenth century, was self-consciously revitalized by the anthropologist W. Lloyd Warner in 1941, at a time at which "race" had assumed too many charged connotations by its fascist use; and this usage also "took" only after the 1960s. The word "multicultural" was launched by Edward F. Haskell's little-known *Lance: A Novel about Multicultural Men* (1941). This American novel by an author who was the son of missionaries introduced the adjective "multicultural" to describe the pioneering quality of a few exceptional men who, in the modern age of transportation and communication transcend the confines of individual nation states, of one language, or of a single religion. The term "identity," omnipresent later in connection with the words "ethnic" and "national," goes back only to the immigrant psychologist Erik Erikson's attempt in *Childhood and Society* (1950) at offering a shortened English formula for Sigmund Freud's notion of "the secret familiarity of identical psychological construction," a notion Freud used to describe his sense of Jewishness that was not based on religious faith, national pride, or race.[23]

It is this vocabulary which has helped multiculturalism flourish by the end of the century. The terms began to circulate more widely as they provided an alternative to "racism," "totalitarianism," and "genocide." At first a positive term launched by fascists to describe the importance they assigned to race, the word "racism" came into general use only in the 1930s, and it acquired its pejorative sense when it became the central term to express intellectual critiques of Fascism. Magnus Hirschfeld's still remarkable antifascist book *Racism* (1938) marked the turning point. The same is true for "totalitarianism" which was launched in English in Luigi Sturzo's *Italy and Fascismo* (1926) and assumed its negative meaning only slowly, with Hannah Arendt's *Origins of Totalitarianism* (1951) marking the final point. "Genocide" was another English neologism introduced in a book by Polish émigré scholar and attorney Raphaël Lemkin, titled *Axis Rule in Occupied Europe* (1944). Lemkin coined the word by combining Greek *genos* (race, tribe) and Latin *cide* (killing), in analogy to tyrannicide or homicide, and suggested *ethnocide* as a synonym. Lemkin studied the new, eliminationist Nazi occupation policies (most especially toward Jews, but also toward other national groups in occupied countries) and found that these measures were genocidal because they intended to destroy "the essential foundations of the life of national groups, with the aim of annihilating the groups themselves." Lemkin's coinage was disseminated more widely when the United Nations adopted the term in a 1945 indictment of Nazi leaders for having "conducted deliberate and systematic genocide—namely, the extermination of racial and national groups."[24]

This newly coined twentieth-century vocabulary reflected, and helped to shape, a new emphasis on ethnic identity and on cultural pluralism in modern democratic societies, which were, after World War II and the Holocaust, more unambiguously defined against the fascist trajectory from racist stereotype to genocide.

The ascent of aesthetic modernism, the expansion and dominance of commercialism and mass culture, the growing international importance of the United States in a very violent period of world history, and the changing ethnic and developing multicultural definition of "America" mark a dramatic transformation, and American literature participated in these developments.

The remaining question is what made such enormous changes possible. The attempt to address it, at least in its cultural components, will take us to the cultural policies of the great ideological challenges to bourgeois democracy that were active in the twentieth century—Communism and Fascism. It will take us to the complicated negotiations of ethnic and national identities at the peak of the assertion of the power of nation states to assimilate, to ignore, to mistreat, or to exclude its minorities. And it will take us to a variety of works of American literature—a small number of them read very closely—in which the tensions of ethnicity, modernity, and modernism are present, and are often central.

2

Gertrude Stein and "Negro Sunshine"

There may be no better beginning for the story of ethnic modernism in American prose literature than the ending of Gertrude Stein's "Melanctha: Each One as She May." This story, which forms the central part of *Three Lives,* an important book that was first published in 1909, ends:

> But Melanctha Herbert never really killed herself because she was so blue, though often she thought this would be really the best way for her to do. Melanctha never killed herself, she only got a bad fever and went into the hospital where they took good care of her and cured her.
>
> When Melanctha was very well again, she took a place and began to work and to live regular. Then Melanctha got very sick again, she began to cough and sweat and be so weak she could not stand to do her work.
>
> Melanctha went back to the hospital, and there the Doctor told her that she had consumption, and before long she would surely die. They sent her where she would be taken care of, a home for poor consumptives, and there Melanctha stayed until she died.
>
> FINIS[1]

Readers who are used to nineteenth-century aesthetic conventions—one only has to think of Little Eva in *Uncle Tom's Cabin* or of Mimi in *La Bohème*—will be startled by the coldness of this "detached" death scene of Stein's heroine. No effort is undertaken to draw on the reader's sympathy or to develop the narrative in a way that would sustain emotional engagement and identification. There is no protracted agony and suffering, there are no tears of near and dear ones, and no last words are spoken. Instead, Stein "comforts" the reader with the information that Melanctha did not commit suicide but "only" got ill; then she immediately reports that Melanctha got well, refusing to build momentum toward a death scene. Abruptly, the heroine's one-sentence recuperation gives way to a relapse that leads to her quick death within two further sentences, before the reader fully realizes what has happened. The doctor's emphatically noneuphemistic statement "that she had consumption, and before long she would surely die" seems inappropriately colloquial; and the simple language and repetitions in this passage do not create a feeling of familiarity but rather instill a sense of distance from Melanctha in readers. The "FINIS" is not the climactic conclusion to the protracted death struggle of a consumptive heroine, but a sudden interruption of the reading process. In many ways, the understated ending of "Melanctha" marks an end of established narrative conventions and readers' expectations.

This effect is reinforced as the other two stories included in *Three Lives* end similarly. "The Good Anna" leaves the reader with the sentences: "Then they did the operation, and then the good Anna with her strong, strained, worn-out body died" (56). "The Gentle Lena" concludes: "When it was all over Lena had died, too, and nobody knew just how it had happened to her" (200). Stein's *Three Lives* is thus a book about the deaths of three working-class women; and no web of feeling or meaning surrounds the abruptness and finality of death.

Stein's death scenes are not without precedent—but they go well beyond Gustave Flaubert's "Un Coeur Simple," a tale Stein translated while she was writing *Three Lives*. Stein's scenes are part of a whole arsenal of modern strategies that she employs and that make her stand out among contemporaries Willa Cather, Theodore Dreiser, and Jack London. Such strategies also separated *Three Lives* from the format of the ethnic life story and from Stein's earlier autobiographically inspired materials (nobody dies in the popular ethnic life stories of the period or in Stein's earlier *Q.E.D.; or, Things as They Are*), making way for a new, unforgettable, and also cold and rather reader-unfriendly style. The themes of searching for love, of triangles, and of jealousy are rendered no more engagingly than are the death scenes. This is a typical passage about Dr. Jeff Campbell, who finds out that Melanctha is unfaithful:

> Now Jeff began to have always a strong feeling that Melanctha could no longer stand it, with all her bad suffering, to let him fight out with himself what was right for him to be doing. Now he felt he must not, when she was there with him, keep on, with this kind of fighting that was always going on inside him. Jeff Campbell never knew yet, what he

thought was the right way, for himself and for all the colored people to be living. Jeff was coming always each time closer to be really understanding, but now Melanctha was so bad in her suffering with him, that he knew she could not any longer have him with her while he was always showing that he never really yet was sure what it was, the right way, for them to be really loving. (114)

The features of Stein's literary style include a strange predilection for the unexpected and enigmatic use of the word "always," which is also among the most popular words, appearing a total of 745 times in "Melanctha" alone, and, in general relentless repetitions of a relatively simple vocabulary, the pervasive -ing form (appearing nine times in the brief cited excerpt alone) and the dependent adverbial clause, a meandering narration, and no attempt at differentiating distinct voices so that narrator, characters, and even the letters they write all sound alike, assuming a stylized or stilted, self-conscious, pseudo-colloquial voice. When the narrator asks, "What was it that now really happened to them?" (109), this is not the pleasant intervention of an omniscient narrator who addresses the reader in the way in which Harriet Beecher Stowe would have asked rhetorical questions such as "Who is to blame?" For Stowe, the obvious answer ("you, sir!") could be given by any reader. Stein's interventions raise real questions, and simple though they may seem, they tend to be unanswerable.

There are some minimalist sentences; descriptive "literary" adjectives are usually avoided in favor of flat, "childlike," nonspecific yet strangely evaluative ones (like "good" or "fine"); and there are also long and sprawling sentences generated by repetitions and variations in which the reader desperately tries to recognize a pattern. But the sentences are the essential element of Stein's prose, as she herself put it in *The Autobiography of Alice B. Toklas* (1933): "Sentences not only words but sentences and always sentences have been Gertrude Stein's life long passion."[2] The text of *Three Lives* interrupts, it disturbs, it thwarts expectations; Stein's writing is formal and calls attention to itself. The deadpan, detached narrator avoids grand emotions and all feelings—except maybe those generated by the composition itself.

Form was becoming the central theme of a work of prose fiction. And it would remain the central theme of work after work Stein produced, culminating early in her massive "novel" *The Making of Americans* (finished by 1911 and published in 1925), in which the meandering narration that was present in *Three Lives* takes on a new proportion because of the epic possibilities of variation and repetition. When, in *The Making of Americans,* Stein makes observations about repetition, she articulates even these observations repetitively: "Repeating is the whole of living and by repeating comes understanding, and understanding is to some the most important part of living. Repeating is the whole of living, and it makes of living a thing always more familiar to each one and so we have old men's and women's wisdom, and repeating, simple repeating is the whole of them."[3] And so forth. Carl Van Doren assessed *The Making of Americans* in 1940: "Often praised, this huge novel has seldom been read, nor will it ever be except by enthusiasts who tolerate its tedious, mannered repetitions because of the pleasure they take in the delicate and intricate variety of its sentences."[4] Edmund Wilson voiced a similar sentiment in a famous quip on *The Making of Americans:* "I confess that I have not read this book all through, and I do not know whether it is possible to do so."[5]

It is doubtful that any reader has imagined that being stranded on an island with only a set of Stein's complete works would be an unambiguously exciting and pleasant experience. It is hardly surprising that Stein never became a popular author—excepting only her somewhat more conciliatory *Autobiography of Alice B. Toklas* in which Stein states disarmingly that the newspapers "always say . . . that my writing is appalling but they always quote it and what is more, they quote it correctly, and those they say they admire they do not quote" (86–87). No wonder that Stein "did not believe that anyone could read anything she wrote and be interested" (63). Yet with her strange sense of humor, she continued to contribute to the creation of herself as the enigmatic mother of all American modernists. When Harold Loeb, the editor of the little magazine *Broom,* asked her for something that was as fine as "Melanctha," she sent him a piece entitled "As Fine as Melanctha" (1923).

How did Stein arrive at her experimental mode, in which losing the general reader was part of the program? Perhaps it was merely a matter of Stein's temper, character, and of her willful idiosyncrasies. Yet her appeal to other writers suggests that it was also the result of other historical and cultural factors that were related to the rise of modernism.

Central was the field of modern psychology and its interest in unconscious processes. As a student at the Harvard Annex, later Radcliffe College, Stein participated in Hugo Münsterberg's experiments in automatism, and her very first publication was an essay on the topic of automatic writing. Undertaken jointly with Leon M. Solomons, this study of "Normal Motor Automatism" for the *Harvard Psychological Laboratory* of 1896 describes various experiments in producing automatic writing. To stimulate it, Stein and Solomons note, "dialect stories do not go well at all." Among the observations they made were the following: "Miss Stein found it sufficient distraction often to simply read what her arm wrote, but following three or four words behind her pencil." And: "The stuff written was grammatical, and the words and phrases fitted together right, but there was not much connected thought." The specimen sentences Solomons and Stein cite include "When he could not be the longest and thus to be, and thus to be, the strongest" and "This long time when he did this best time, and he could thus have been bound, and in this long time, when he could be this to first use of this long time. . . ."[6] "It is very interesting to read," Stein writes of these early experiments in retrospect in *The Autobiography of Alice B. Toklas*, "because the method of writing to be afterwards developed in Three Lives and Making of Americans already shows itself" (86). She ascribed her interest in representing unconscious processes to her psychological training and to her work with William James who had coined the term "stream of thought" in his *Principles of Psychology* (1890), who called for an examination of the "hidden self," and who claimed that a *"comparative study of trances and sub-conscious states* is . . . of the most urgent importance for the comprehension of our nature."[7] In the section entitled "The Stream of Consciousness" that forms part of James's *Talks to Teachers on Psychology: and to Students on Some of Life's Ideals* (1905), he further called attention to the "succession of states, or waves, or fields . . . of knowledge, of feeling, of desire, of deliberation, etc., that constantly pass and repass, and that constitute our inner life" and found the process by which one state "dissolves into another" often very gradual.[8]

Stein represented the unconscious in the nonlinear and repetitious forms in which it seemed to articulate itself. In this sense Stein's modernism can also be seen as an extension of psychological realism. "Henry James in his later writing had had a dim feeling that this was what he knew he should do," as Stein put it.[9] Though in *The Autobiography of Alice B. Toklas* she claimed not to have read him in her student years, she "quite definitely" considered him "as her forerunner" (86). From the point of view of modern psychology, realism was somewhat incomplete.

Realism did not represent the characters' meandering thought processes accurately; modern prose writers wished to correct that (as did the dramatists around the Provincetown Playhouse).

American realism often understated the importance—or at least ignored some physical details—of sexuality in literary representation, and some modernists set out to correct that emphatically. Frankness in sexual matters was, of course, one reason why modern novels from *Ulysses* (1922) and D. H. Lawrence's *Lady Chatterley's Lover* (1928) to William Burroughs's *Naked Lunch* (1959) had difficulties with censors and government agencies, which suspected such books of being pornographic. However, if Stein was one of these modern authors, her unique style probably did little to stimulate, even among suspicious censors, pornographic readings of such sentences as "Feeling or for it, as feeling or for it, came in or come in, or come out of there or feeling as feeling or feeling as for it," written in her "erotic" work *As a Wife Has a Cow: A Love Story* (1926).[10]

Stein did not produce automatic writing in the Harvard psychology experiments or in her later literary output, as she stressed in *Everybody's Autobiography* (1937). Stein stylized very consciously, whether she was writing about thought processes or attempting dialogue in fiction, whether the genre was poetry, drama, opera, or public lecturing. In her prose writings she avoided the conventional distinction of narrator and character and the differentiation between characters, not just in the name of a higher realism but in the name of a new and unmistakable style. It was this intimidating and forbidding "Steinian" style that put off even friends and supporters who had a well-established interest in unconscious processes. Thus William James apologized to his former student Gertrude Stein for never having finished reading *Three Lives*. He wrote her that it was the kind of book about which one says to oneself, "I will go at it carefully when just the right mood comes." He added, "But apparently the right mood never came."[11]

If modern psychology was one element in Stein's literary experimentation, then the development of modernist painting at the beginning of the century formed another important inspiration. As the children of a well-to-do businessman who had invested in the booming streetcar business in Oakland, Gertrude Stein and her brother Leo became art collectors, connected with Bernard Berenson and Daniel-Henry Kahnweiler. In Paris, Stein was part of the circle of most illustrious modern artists. She sat for famous Picasso and Francis Picabia portraits and for Jacques

Lipchitz and Jo Davidson sculptures, she knew Matisse and Cézanne well, and Juan Gris illustrated her *As a Wife Has a Cow*. She introduced Matisse and Picasso to American audiences in articles for Alfred Stieglitz's *Camera Work* (in 1912, one year before the Armory Show). The guest list of visitors to the apartment she shared with Alice B. Toklas at 27, rue de Fleurus in Paris resembles a dictionary of modern art. Although she included the ironic disclaimer in *The Autobiography of Alice B. Toklas* that she "was not at any time interested in african sculpture," she witnessed, and participated in, the interest in African masks and the beginnings of cubism (79). The art collector Etta Cone typed a manuscript of *Three Lives*. The list goes on. It is thus helpful to regard Stein as a writer among visual artists, and to see her style in connection with movements from cubism to fauvism. Mabel Dodge, who ran a radical salon off Eighth Street in Greenwich Village attended by Emma Goldman, Mike Gold, and Jean Toomer at various times, commented in 1913 that "in a large studio in Paris, hung with paintings by Renoir, Matisse and Picasso, Gertrude Stein is doing with words what Picasso is doing with paint. She is impelling language to induce new states of consciousness, and in doing so language becomes with her a creative art rather than a mirror of history."[12] And a review of *Three Lives* for the *Philadelphia Public Ledger*, entitled "A Futurist Novel" found that "the blur which this futurist in writing at first creates cannot be cleared until we are willing to bring the thought and intelligence to its interpretation which we needed when examining *The Nude Descending the Stairs*."[13] The analogy to visual modernism is all the more justified since modern artists may have played down the continuities that linked their work to a long tradition of ornamental and decorative art which was generally nonrepresentational, tended to suggest flatness rather than depth, and practiced repetition to the point of serial appearance—qualities that were as present in modern paintings as they were in Stein's writing.

Stein also took a strong interest in modern photography, and she kept in touch with Stieglitz and Man Ray. In *Lectures in America* (1935), she also compared her method of repetition with variation to the language of film. "In a cinema picture no two pictures are exactly alike each one is just that much different from the one before."[14] This analogy, phrased in a sentence that provides a formal equivalent for its statement, is all the more interesting since Stein's onetime mentor Hugo Münsterberg also became one of the pioneers of film theory with his book *The Photoplay* (1915).

Similarly, though not as deeply, Stein was connected with modern music. She commented on the aesthetic effect of Richard Strauss's *Electra*; and she collaborated with Virgil Thomson on the opera *Four Saints in Three Acts,* produced by an organization called "The Friends and Enemies of Modern Music" in 1934, with an all-black cast, tan-faced and in cellophane costumes. "There is a Difference Between Steinse and Nonsteinse," the *New York Times* subtitled its review of the Hartford opening, adding, "What Difference." And the article points out that Stein "apparently uses words for sound instead of meaning."[15] The *sounds* of Stein's words do matter, and the principles of repetition and variation resemble fugues or the musical leitmotif technique, even in texts that are not librettos. Stein also described jazz bands, in *Lectures in America,* as engaged in the difference between the thing seen and the thing felt that causes nervousness in the theater: "The jazz bands made of this thing [. . .] an end in itself. They made of this different tempo a something that was nothing but a difference in tempo between anybody and everybody including all those doing it and all those hearing and seeing it" (95).

Stein was attracted to the developments of modern psychology, art, photography, film, and music because she liked to adopt a simple and direct literary voice that was "objective" rather than confessional. This aspect of her work becomes clearer when one compares *Three Lives* with its more straightforwardly autobiographic precursor *Q.E.D.,* an early and still somewhat confessional work (written in 1903 and published posthumously) which centers on a love triangle among women. Stein's own projection figure is Adele who loves the unfaithful Helen. Interestingly, some of the exact wording was adopted by Stein for "Melanctha," only that the theme of same-sex love relations among white women became predominantly heterosexual and black, with Stein's voice turning into Jeff Campbell's, and Helen's into Melanctha's. But in the process of sexual and ethnic transformation, confession gives way to principles of composition, as the style changes and becomes more experimental and Steinian. Stein's modernist language may thus also have been a mask, a protection against emotional vulnerability, or at the very least an objectification and stylization of the memory of a painful experience. The ethnic mask seemed particularly suited to deflect from the confessional.

No matter how idiosyncratic and difficult it was, Stein's writing—together with Joyce's, Eliot's, Ezra Pound's, and Virginia Woolf's—set a standard to which many twentieth-century English-language writers aspired and against which they measured themselves and each other. Stein's particular emphasis on the sentence as the most important unit of even long works of prose inspired many authors. Once the modernist style existed as a new code of literary representation, it constituted a challenge to modern writers. Especially after World War I, which signaled the violent end of an era, more and more writers tried to live up to that challenge. It is poetically just that it was Stein who coined the phrase "Lost Generation," brought into wide circulation as the famous epigraph to Ernest Hemingway's novel *The Sun Also Rises* (1926): "'You are all a lost generation.'—GERTRUDE STEIN *in conversation.*" Two and a half decades later, Delmore Schwartz wrote in "The Grapes of Crisis" (1951) that victory in World War II was supposed to bring about the end of all totalitarian regimes: "'We are all the last generation,' Adolf Hitler might have remarked to Gertrude Stein or Pablo Picasso in Paris in May, 1940."[16] And a decade and a half after Stein's death, the City Lights Books editors of the *Beatitude Anthology* (1960) ascribed to Stein, tongue-in-cheek, the statement: "'You are all a Beat Generation.'—Gertrude Stein in conversation with Jack Kerouac."[17] Stein's influence on writers like Sherwood Anderson is well known. And William Faulkner could have won a Stein-soundalike competition with sentences like the following from *Absalom, Absalom!* (1936):

> All of a sudden he discovered, not what he wanted to do but what he just had to do, had to do whether he wanted to or not, because if he did not do it he knew that he could never live with himself for the rest of his life, never live with what all the men and women that had died to make him had left inside of him for him to pass on, with all the dead ones waiting and watching to see if he was going to do it right, fix things right so that he would be able to look in the face not only of the old dead ones but all the living ones that would come after him when he would be one of the dead.[18]

(That novel also contains what is probably the longest single sentence in a twentieth-century American novel.)

Of course, modern writers took many paths toward modernism. In Claude McKay's *Home to Harlem* (1928), for example, Ray, the Haitian-born protagonist and counterpart to African-American Jake, explains how "the great mass carnage in Europe and the great mass revolution in Russia" had given him the sense of having lived through "the end of an era" and how he felt that this experience required new "dreams of patterns of words achieving form." He mentions Joyce, Sherwood Anderson, D. H. Lawrence, and Henri Barbusse, and he observes that "only the Russians of the late era seemed to stand up like giants in the new. Gogol, Dostoievski, Tolstoy, Chekhov, Turgeniev."[19] But he does not refer to Gertrude Stein in his quest for literary models that would offer a formal equivalent to the experience of World War I. Stein was, after all, only *one* model of the pervasive trend toward modernism.

The literary modernism of Stein's *Three Lives* developed a specific focus on ethnicity. The book's heroines are not only working class, but also ethnically marked. Lena and Anna are German-American, and Melanctha is mixed-race African American. Stein's family had German-American household help, and she stressed in *The Autobiography of Alice B. Toklas* that her interest in blacks originated when she was at Johns Hopkins Medical School. "It was then that she had to take her turn in the delivering of babies and it was at that time that she noticed the negroes and the places that she afterwards used in the second of the Three Lives stories, Melanctha Herbert, the story that was the beginning of her revolutionary work" (90).

Stein's merging of modernist style and ethnic subject matter was what made her writing particularly relevant to American ethnic authors who had specific reasons to go beyond realism and who felt that Stein's dismantling of the "old" was a freeing experience. The realistic mode of narration had included conventions (such as local-color dialect writing) and tags that were often negatively charged ethnic stereotypes—and compared to that legacy, Stein's writing seemed perhaps not "realistic" in the sense of the dominant nineteenth-century aesthetic but "convincing" and "truthful," worthy to be upheld as a model and to be adopted, imitated, and varied upon. Strangely enough then, "Melanctha"—which was, as we have seen, the partial result of a transracial projection—came to be perceived as a white American author's particularly humane representation of a black character.

Hutchins Hapgood, whose book *The Spirit of the Ghetto: Studies of the Jewish Quarter of New York* (1902) had established him as an ethnic specialist, read *Three Lives* in manuscript and wrote Stein a genuinely enthusiastic letter, praising the stories for their "reality, truth, unconventionality," and singling out "Melanctha" as "the very best thing on the subject of the Negro that I have ever read."[20] Carl Van Vechten, Stein's close friend, lifelong correspondent, and literary executor who also promoted Harlem Renaissance literature, photographed the most famous black intellectuals of the period, and authored the novel *Nigger Heaven* (1926), claimed that "Melanctha" was "perhaps the first American story in which the negro is regarded [...] not as an object for condescending compassion or derision."[21] This interpretation was indirectly shared even by Wyndham Lewis, the English modernist painter and writer living in Paris who vehemently opposed populist tendencies in literature. Lewis deplored the "monstrous, desperate soggy *lengths* of primitive mass life" that he sensed in Stein's work, "undoubtedly intended as an epic contribution to the present mass-democracy." "In adopting the simplicity, the illiterateness, of the mass-average of the Melancthas and Annas, Miss Stein gives proof of all the false 'revolutionary' propagandist *plainmanism* of her time." What Van Vechten found admirable in Stein, Lewis considered deplorable; he diagnosed her prose as cold, "composed of dead and inanimate material."[22]

Stein also had detractors on the left. In *Change the World!* (1934), Mike Gold, the second-generation immigrant author of the book *Jews Without Money* (1930) and advocate of proletarian fiction (who had Americanized his original name Itzok Granich) wrote that Stein's work was "an example of the most extreme subjectivism of the contemporary bourgeois artist, and a reflection of the ideological anarchy into which the whole of bourgeois literature has fallen.... When one reads her work it appears to resemble the monotonous gibberings of paranoiacs in the private wards of asylums. It appears to be a deliberate irrationality, a deliberate infantilism."[23] Gold claimed that "Stein did not care to communicate because essentially there was nothing to communicate," and he concluded with the strong proclamation that Marxists

> see in the work of Gertrude Stein extreme symptoms of the decay of capitalist culture. They view her work as the completed attempt to annihilate all relations between the artist and the society in which he lives.... The literary idiocy of Gertrude Stein only reflects the madness of the whole system of capitalist values. It is part of the signs of doom that are written largely everywhere on the walls of bourgeois society. (210–211)

Was Stein an ethnic populist and "plainmanist" who shouted the people's howl and was particularly sensitive to black and immigrant character portrayal, or was she an example of bourgeois decadence and idiocy whose works unwittingly were the writing on the wall that spelled doom for capitalist power relations? Precisely because of the style that so annoyed Mike Gold, many black and white ethnic writers took the former position, and praised Stein for the "populist"-seeming side of her modernism that Wyndham Lewis so detested.

When, after World War II, the African-American radical Richard Wright reviewed Stein's *Wars I Have Seen* (1945), he famously defended Stein against Gold's attack. Wright claimed that in order to "gauge the degree to which Miss Stein's prose was tainted with the spirit of counter-revolution" he read "Melanctha" aloud in a Black Belt basement to "a group of semi-literate black stock-yard workers—'basic proletarians with an instinct for revolution'" (as Wright echoes Gold ironically). And what was the result, according to Wright? "They understood every word. Enthralled, they slapped their thighs, howled, laughed, stomped, and interrupted me constantly to comment upon the characters. My fondness for Steinian prose never distressed me after that."[24] Wright thus conferred upon Stein's prose both proletarian and racial credentials. He also held up Stein's "Melanctha" as the best modern prose piece in the collection *I Wish I'd Written That* (1946) and argued, echoing Van Vechten, that it was "the first long serious literary treatment of Negro life in the United States."[25] Wright's love for Stein's "good story, even though slightly screwy,"[26] was based on Stein's language, in which he believed he heard his own grandmother's "deep, pure Negro dialect."[27] "While turning the pages of 'Melanctha,' I suddenly began to *hear* the English *language* for the first time in my life! . . . English as Negroes spoke it: simple, melodious, tolling, rolling, rough, infectious, subjective, laughing, cutting."[28] Wright also admired Stein's *What Are Masterpieces* (1940); he wrote a blurb for, and reviewed, *Brewsie and Willie* (1946); and in "The Horror and the Glory," the second part of his autobiography *Black Boy* (set in galleys in 1945 but published only posthumously under the title *American Hunger* in 1977), Wright described how, under the influence of Stein's *Three Lives*, he composed such "disconnected sentences for the sheer love of words" as the following:

> "The soft melting hunk of butter trickled in gold down the stringy grooves of the split yam."
> Or:
> "The child's clumsy fingers fumbled in sleep, feeling vainly for the wish of its dream."
> "The old man huddled in the dark doorway, his bony face lit by the burning yellow in the window of distant skyscrapers."[29]

Stein's and Wright's temperamental difference is apparent even in the few examples Wright summons to suggest similarity. Nonetheless, Stein returned Wright's compliments when she said about his autobiography *Black Boy* (1945): "I do not think there has been anything done like it since I wrote *Three Lives*."[30]

Sounding somewhat like Wright's version of Stein, James T. Farrell's Irish-American trilogy *Studs Lonigan* (completed in 1935) includes sentences like "He sucked malted milk through a straw, and watched the soda jerkers hustle orders amid the noise and clatter of the buzz of the electric malted-milk shakers."[31] And when Italian-American Jerre Mangione returned many years later to his ethnic neighborhood in Rochester that he had evoked in *Mount Allegro* (1943) and found only a 22-acre Coca-Cola bottling plant, he commented with Stein's proverbial phrasing about Oakland: "When you get there, there's no there there."[32] In Zora Neale Hurston's *Dust Tracks on a Road: An Autobiography* (1942), which also contains sentences that resemble Wright's Stein imitations, the case against racial generalizations is formulated in the familiar way: "There is no *The Negro* here." Faulkner was not alone in the occasional wish to sound like Stein; and, for beginning ethnic writers, being in awe of Stein was so pervasive as to be recognized as a danger. The young Armenian-American writer William Saroyan who had "read around in *Three Lives*" in the San Francisco Public Library, wrote Stein a virtual fan letter on the occasion of Stein's visit to the United States in 1934 in which he stated, in a Steinian fashion:

> Some critics say I have to be careful and not notice the writings of Gertrude Stein but I think they are fooling themselves when they pretend any American writing that is American and is writing is not partly the consequence of the writing of Gertrude Stein and as the saying is they don't seem to know the war is over.[33]

On the strength of the letter, Stein met with Saroyan in San Francisco. Jack Dunphy's little remembered but very stylishly written Philadelphia Irish-American novel *John Fury* (1946) places much emphasis on sentences ("Katie looked down Market Street at the trolley swaying as it came along from side to side like a great happy caterpillar with one round yellow eye"), and each chapter is divided into blocks of prose-poemlike paragraphs in which repetitions and variations are common. When asked about how he came to write the novel, Dunphy said:

"Started reading Gertrude Stein's *Making of Americans* but gave it up to write a novel of my own. Gave that up too . . . Finally started (and finished) *John Fury*."[34]

The admiration and support for Gertrude Stein among twentieth-century African-American writers was particularly strong. It seems that among the most important figures only Claude McKay was explicitly critical of Stein, accusing her pointedly, in his autobiography *A Long Way from Home* (1937), of being able to see only "black as black and white as white, without any shades." He did not like the cult around Stein and reported that when he examined "Melanctha" he "could not see wherein intrinsically it was what it was cracked up to be."[35]

Most African-American writers' views differed from McKay's. In his column "What to Read" for *The Crisis* (December 1910), W. E. B. Du Bois included Stein's *Three Lives* in a short list of the most noteworthy books. James Weldon Johnson believed that with "Melanctha" Stein had established herself as the first "white writer to write a story of love between a Negro man and woman and deal with them as normal members of the human family."[36] Jean Toomer's *Cane* (1923), which includes some Steinian sentences, opens with a "Melanctha"-inspired section titled "Karintha." Nella Larsen's novels *Quicksand* (1928) and *Passing* (1929) employed some loosely Steinian modernisms; and at Van Vechten's suggestion, Larsen sent an advance copy of *Quicksand* to Stein, together with a note in which she praised Stein's "Melanctha" as a "truly great story" she had read "many times": "I never cease to wonder how you came to write it," Larsen wrote to Stein, "and just why you and not one of us should so accurately have caught the spirit of this race of mine."[37] In 1937, the poet and critic Sterling Brown thought that "Melanctha," though "not realistic in the usual sense, [. . .] gives a convincing portrait of a mysterious, uncertain girl, 'wandering in her ways,' doomed to tragedy, a Negro Madame Bovary or Esther Waters," and judged that "Stein broke the white American literary tradition of portraying black characters as subhuman or as fools."[38] And though the experimental novelist Clarence Major "did not 'hear' the same tonal qualities Wright heard," he still concluded in 1979: "When the speech of Jeff and Melanctha is compared to the speech of Negro characters created by Paul Laurence Dunbar, Joel Chandler Harris, Mark Twain, and even Melville, and Stein's contemporary, Sherwood Anderson, the characters Jeff and Melanctha do seem exceedingly convincing in the way they talk."[39]

It is difficult to see how this could be the case with dialogues like the following: "I certainly do understand Dr. Campbell that you mean you don't believe it's right to love anybody." "Why sure no, yes I do Miss Melanctha. I certainly do believe strong in loving, and in being good to everybody, and trying to understand what they all need, to help them" (85–86). What in Stein's language had the freeing effect that American writers, and especially immigrant and black authors, reported?

It was certainly not Stein's delicate avoidance of racial stereotypes. On the contrary, she seemed to cherish ethnic tags, and she used them consciously and with great gusto. The word "german" (lower case, as Stein at times likes to render her ethnic adjectives) is repeated endlessly in "The Gentle Lena," a character of "unexpectant and unsuffering german patience" (171). In *The Autobiography of Alice B. Toklas,* we find such passages as the following: "She did not like the stranger's looks. Who is that, said she to Alfy. I didn't bring him, said Alfy. He looks like a Jew, said Gertrude Stein, he is worse than that, says Alfy" (13). And "french," "german," and "spanish" qualities are abundantly claimed. In *Three Lives,* in "As Fine as Melanctha," and in letters to Van Vechten, Stein uses the word "nigger." Rose Johnson may have been inspired by the minstrel song "Coal Black Rose." In *The Autobiography of Alice B. Toklas,* one can read how Stein reacted to the "quantities of negroes" that Carl Van Vechten sent: "Gertrude Stein concluded that negroes were not suffering from persecution, they were suffering from nothingness" (292). For her, "the african is not primitive, he has a very ancient but a very narrow culture and there it remains. Consequently nothing does or can happen." McKay quipped that not long after Stein published this, "something was happening: Negro Americans were rendering her opera *Four Saints in Three Acts.*" Stein's term "nothingness" has been considered a precursor to Ralph Ellison's concept of "invisibility" (and in praising John Kouwenhoven's *The Beer Can by the Highway* Ellison wrote, "A can is a can is a can").[40] Yet "nothingness" was also enough of a provocation for the black modernist poet Melvin Tolson to ask ironically in *Harlem Gallery* (1965): "Listen, Black Boy. / Did the High Priestess at 27 rue de Fleurus / assert, 'The Negro suffers from nothingness'?"[41] The "Black Boy" addressed may here allude to Richard Wright. Stein also advised Paul Robeson ("as soon as another person came into the room he became definitely a negro") not to claim spirituals: "Gertrude Stein did not like hearing him sing spirituals. They do not belong to you any more than anything else, so why claim them, she said. He did not answer."[42] In letters to Carl Van Vechten, Stein praised the addressee for his good taste in friends, called Robeson "a dear," and reported the beginning of her conversation with him as follows: "why you like niggers so much Robeson." McKay faulted Stein for taking Robeson as "*the* representative of Negro culture," but reported that Robeson told him after his encounter with Stein "that she was all right" and that McKay should also seek her out; and Van Vechten wrote Stein that Robeson "adores you."

Perhaps it was Stein's very directness that made the difference. In her fiction, her explicit and programmatic use of stereotypic adjectives and ethnic tags, coupled with her love for repetition, at times seems to deplete racist language of its traditional weight. This is the case with the repetition of the phrase "negro sunshine" throughout "Melanctha." Sterling Brown noticed that "Gertrude Stein speaks of 'the wide abandoned laughter that gives the broad glow to negro sunshine,' but her major characters do not have it."[43] It is true that in the tale, Rose Johnson "had not the wide, abandoned laughter that makes the warm broad glow to negro sunshine" (59–60), and James Herbert "had never had the wide abandoned laughter that gives the broad glow to negro sunshine" (64). However, Dr. Jefferson Campbell does: "He sang when he was happy, and he laughed, and his was the free abandoned laughter that gives the warm broad glow to negro sunshine" (77). By this point in the story, however, the stereotypical quality of "negro sunshine" that so few characters seem to possess has already eroded. The next time, Jeff has "a warm broad glow, like southern sunshine" (96). And after that substitution by a regional adjective, the ethnic metaphor turns into a literal weather report: "It was summer now, and they had warm sunshine to wander" (108). A tag became a word again, one might say; and it appeared to have shed much of its hurtful baggage in the process. It is also significant that in *Q.E.D.* Adele was associated with "warm sunshine" (208)—well before the racial transformation of the story into "Melanctha" was to take place.

Stein's dismantling of a sinister linguistic feature by repetition speaks to another reward Stein's prose held for writers who came to regard her as a model. Many ethnic stories were painful stories; so how could they be told without making the storytellers vulnerable? In "Melanctha," Stein had taken a tale of personal suffering and turned it into a prose experiment in which the biographical sources were both revealed and hidden. Would this not make a good method for other authors who wanted to give expression to pain? What Ludwig Lewisohn described as a reason for Sherwood Anderson's "instinctive submission to the influence of Gertrude Stein" may thus be particularly applicable to minority and immigrant writers: "In her," Lewisohn writes about Anderson, "he found a writer driven to utter her secret yet constantly inhibited from doing so and feigning, as a defensive rationalization, that one could no more utter oneself through human speech until that speech was shattered into meaninglessness and the communication at once needed but neurotically inhibited could no longer take place." What made this model all the more attractive was that writers did not have to go to Stein's extremes or, as Lewisohn put it, "follow Miss Stein the whole way to sheer babbling."[44]

What furthermore may have attracted some writers to Stein was the fact that she did not differentiate between a standard-English narrator and dialect-speaking characters. She thus avoided a procedure that, some writers felt, only dramatized racial hierarchies. This lack of differentiation helped to universalize by putting characters and narrator on an equal footing; of course, it also generalized as it took away the specific sound patterns that could be associated with ethnic location. It deserves to be remembered that Claude McKay found that Stein only "reproduced a number of the common phrases relating to Negroes," among them "abandoned laughter" and "Negro sunshine," "all prettily framed in a tricked-out style." In the "telling of the story," he found "nothing striking or informative about Negro life" and noted that "Melanctha, the mulattress, might have been a Jewess."[45]

Whatever the ultimate reasons, there clearly were aspects of Stein's writing that made her work surprisingly congenial for ethnics who tended to be skeptical of American local color and race-differentiated dialect writing and who—like Sterling Brown—were otherwise quick to denounce ethnic stereotyping in literature, for authors who wanted to reveal pain without doubling the pain in the telling, and for writers who realized the benefit of going part of the way into Stein's direction.

Richard Wright's claims about the stockyard workers' reactions notwithstanding, Stein's writing defamiliarized and alienated its readers, whereas so much ethnic writing rested on making ethnic outsiders seem familiar to "general American" readers—in part by stereotyping minority characters, whether for progressive or reactionary motives. *Three Lives* may thus be viewed both as an aesthetic departure from the genre of the ethnic life story and as an example of it.

What was noticeably absent in the appreciation was the attempt to read Stein as an "ethnic" writer. Stein was a second-generation German-Jewish immigrant child and an American expatriate who returned to the United States only once between 1903 and the time of her death in 1946; she was an outsider to prevailing American sexual norms, as Hemingway made sure to remind readers even after his death, and long after hers, in his authorized posthumous publication of *A Moveable Feast* (1964). There Hemingway spoke of Stein's "strong German-Jewish face" and reported to a mass audience that "Miss Stein and her friend" had forgiven Hemingway and his wife "for being in love and being married." Hemingway insisted on revealing that Stein had told him that male homosexuals commit "ugly and repugnant" acts, then are "disgusted with themselves" and drink, take drugs, and always change partners, but that the situation of female homosexuals was the opposite: "They do nothing that they are disgusted by and nothing that is repulsive and afterwards they are happy and they can lead happy lives together."[46] This sounds suspiciously like Jake Barnes's definition of immorality in *The Sun Also Rises* as "things that make you disgusted afterward." In a July 1956 letter to Harvey Breit, Hemingway wrote bluntly: "Stein was a nice woman until she had change of life and opted for fags and fags alone."[47]

In *Three Lives* Gertrude Stein had set up a model for literature that would be both "ethnic" and "modernist." Yet *Three Lives* was not read for the author's ethnicity in a manner that differentiated Stein as a supposed "insider" writing about German-American women Lena and Anna and as a white "outsider" depicting mixed-race Melanctha and Jeff Campbell. It was not Stein's ethnobiographical persona (was she "ethnic"?), her gender (did she write "women's literature"?), her sexual orientation (did she write "as a Lesbian"?), or her possible ethnic bias (how did she really feel about black, mixed-race, Jewish, or German Americans?) but her style that mattered most to minority writers who were her contemporaries. Her innovations in writing seemed too important to be read in the light of social categories that otherwise may have defined her existence. If the need for biographical material arose, it was filled not with ethnic genealogies but with intellectual party scenes of Stein and Toklas among the painters and artworks at the mythical rue de Fleurus in Paris.

3

Ethnic Lives and Lifelets

When Gertrude Stein's "Gentle Lena" realizes that her marriage plans have failed, she goes home alone in a streetcar crying, and the conductor and the other passengers empathize with her: "And everybody in the car was sorry for poor Lena." The conductor kindly promises her, "You'll get a real man yet, one that will be better for you," and Lena feels slightly better (185). Stein may have thwarted the reader's expectation to express empathy in the brief death scenes of *Three Lives,* but she did represent the kindness of strangers in the streetcar setting of her modern city of "Bridgepoint." In Stein's *Q.E.D.* Helen, wandering about Boston, "revelled in the American street-car crowd with its ready intercourse, free comments and airy persiflage all without double meanings which created an atmosphere that never suggested for a moment the need to be on guard" (239).

Streetcars are a prototypical modern symbol that the reader often encounters in literature of the first half of the twentieth century. Henry James, returning to America in 1904–1905 after a very long absence, found in the electric cars that had arrived in New York in 1887 the concentrated presence of new immigrants: "The carful, again and again, is a foreign carful; a row of faces, up and down, testifying, without exception, to alienism unmistakable, alienism undisguised and unashamed," he writes in *The American Scene* (1907).[1] Streetcar settings—as well as scenes on subways, trains, buses, and other means of public transportation—may provide local background, may bring friendly, hostile, or indifferent strangers together, may inspire a hero to seek a revelation on the tracks, or may serve as a formal inspiration to convey the sense of movement, speed, or electric power. One only has to think of Ezra Pound's "In a Station of the Metro" ("The apparition of these faces in the crowd; / Petals on a wet, black bough."). "Trams and dusty trees" (the line that opens the song of one of the Wagnerian Thames daughters) in T. S. Eliot's *Waste Land* also suggests the intimate connection between this theme and literary modernism. Eliot's line is not only a version of contrasting machine and garden but also juxtaposes the tramway of modernity with trees, the ultimate image of rootedness, though the trees are dusty in this cityscape. There are also numerous representations of trolleys in modern art. Examples include Mary Stevenson Cassatt's *In the Omnibus (The Tramway)* (1891), the Italian Carlo Carrà's futurist painting *What the Street-Car Told Me* (1910–1911), the Russian Kazimir Malevich, who did an oil canvas entitled *Lady in a Tram* (1913) just before he moved toward the pure abstraction of suprematism, the German Nikolaus Braun's primitivist *Berliner Straßenszene* (1921), and the Canadian Miller Gore Brittain's Hopper-like *Two Waitresses on a Streetcar Crossing the Reversing Falls* (1940). Numerous modern works of art represent subways and trains, including Max Weber, *Grand Central Terminal* (1915), Edward Hopper, *Night on the El Train* (1920), Reginald Marsh, *Why Not Use the "L"?* (1930), and George Tooker's *The Subway* (1950). In 1920, John Dewey thought that train and streetcar passengers were the ideal readers of periodicals that seemed "designed" for the mobile passengers' "intermediate state of existence."[2] Streetcar scenes are especially interesting in retrospect since electric streetcars, once a prime symbol of modernity, have now assumed an aura of nostalgic quaintness after their literal disappearance from most American cities in the course of the twentieth century.

At about the same time that Stein was working on her *Three Lives*, the New York *Independent*, the *Outlook*, and several other American newspapers and periodicals ran brief life stories which aimed, as the editor of the *Independent* put it, to "typify the life of the average worker in some particular vocation, and to make each story the genuine experience of a real person." One of the autobiographic contributions to the *Independent* was entitled "The Race Problem—An Autobiography by a Southern Colored Woman" (March 17, 1904). Its anonymous author relates a visit to "a Southern city where" she did not know "the 'Jim Crow' law is enforced." On boarding an electric car, she takes the most convenient seat.

The conductor yelled, "What do you mean? Niggers don't sit with white folks down here. You must have come from 'way up yonder. I'm not Roosevelt. We don't sit with niggers, much less eat with them."

I was astonished and said, "I am a stranger and did not know of your law." His answer was: "Well, no back talk now; that's what I'm here for—to tell niggers their places when they don't know them."

Every white man, woman and child was in a titter of laughter by this time at what they considered the conductor's wit.[3]

The southern colored woman is refused full participation in those means of transportation that seem to embody modernity: shortly afterward she is denied entrance to an elevator in a skyscraper and is sent instead to the freight lift. The modern settings serve as a contrast to the inhuman treatment the autobiographer receives; and, unlike in "The Gentle Lena," empathy is a stranger to the story of the southern colored woman.

Who were the "white people" on the colored woman's streetcar? Did they include immigrants from Europe who were here benefiting from "whiteness"? It is telling that the conductor justifies segregation by alluding to Theodore Roosevelt's famous lunch with Booker T. Washington in the White House on October 18, 1901, that caused a public stir against interracial meals, with some white voices professing "horror that a white gentleman can entertain a colored one at his table." The day after the meal, the *Baltimore Sun* published the somewhat misleading front-page headline, "The Black Man to Be Put on Top of the White Man," editorializing that this association on the basis of "social equality" was unacceptable to the South because the "inevitable result of this association is the intermarriage between black men and white women and white men and black women." The interracial Roosevelt lunch was a central public event in the age of the color line. It was enough of a theme to form the basis of a paranoid novel, Robert Lee Durham's *The Call of the South* (1908), a book actually premised on the assumption that the daughter of a president who had invited black leaders for lunch would herself fall in love with and tragically marry a man who had an African great-grandfather—with the most disastrous consequences for the president and his daughter. Readers of the *Independent* were obviously expected to catch the Roosevelt allusion.

Touchiness about interracial dining was only one symptom of the tense and explosive volatility of race relations. American ethnic heterogeneity at the beginning of the twentieth century was intensely debated and conflict-ridden. The color line between black and white marked the deepest divide, but there were many other ethnic fault lines. The United States had grown from a small, rural, provincial, and British-dominated country into a large, modern, polyethnic, and increasingly urban nation. In 1910 there were ninety-two million Americans (a fourfold growth from only twenty-three million before the Civil War); among them nearly ten million blacks (up from three and a half million in 1850) and only 280,000 Indians. Immigration had reached impressive proportions: More than thirteen million of those counted in 1910 were foreign-born, mostly in Europe; the number increases to over thirty-two million if one includes the second-generation children of foreign-born Americans that the Census then counted under the category "total foreign white stock." Two and a half million had come from Germany, more than a million and a half from Russia, and more than a million each from Ireland, Italy, Austria, Scandinavia, and Great Britain. The majority of the newcomers were arriving during the "new immigration," the wave that peaked between the 1880s and the 1920s. There were twenty-three thousand Japanese, eighty-five thousand Chinese immigrants (their number declined once Chinese exclusion took effect), and many people of Spanish and some of French descent who had been incorporated into the United States by annexation and territorial expansion. Large-scale internal migration from the South to the North and from the countryside to cities added to the changing composition of American cities starting with World War I. For example, while in 1910 approximately a quarter of all African-Americans lived in cities, by 1950 more than half of a new total of about fifteen million did.[4]

The chance to establish a sense of multiethnic American nationhood that would include cross-cultural and interracial empathy seemed slim in this period when the ideal of the homogeneous nation state was at its peak. Ethnic and linguistic heterogeneity were successfully portrayed as political dynamite and as the serious cultural danger of "balkanizing" the United States and transforming it into a "house divided" or a new "Babel." Proponents of continued immigration often viewed assimilation into Anglo-America as the best method of integrating newcomers, while opponents (who doubted that assimilation was ever possible for heterogeneous "racial stocks") opted for restriction and exclusion. The Americanization movement of World War I was accompanied by language bans and the Anglicization of foreign words and names. Walter Lippmann observed in 1929 that the Americanization movement "in some of its public manifestations has as much resemblance to patriotism as the rape of the Sabine women had to the love of Dante for Beatrice."[5] And after 1920 immigration was legislated to decline dramatically from the nearly ten million who came between 1910 and 1930 to a mere million and a half who arrived between 1930 and 1950—exactly when millions would have needed asylum. (By comparison, in the year 1907 alone, more than one and a quarter of a million immigrants had come to the United States.) In 1910, more than one in seven Americans was foreign-born; by 1950 the percentage had dropped by more than half, for then only one fifteenth of a total of one hundred and fifty million Americans was foreign-born. Immigration restrictions, often fueled by racial prejudice, were part of many social expressions of a growing white American conservatism that was particularly hostile to the made-up social category of "nonwhites."

The further curtailment of African-American rights and advancement of racial segregation, the terror of lynching and white mob violence euphemistically referred to as "race riots" (in East St. Louis and Tulsa), the expansion of bans on racial intermarriage, and the passing of eugenicist-inspired and explicitly racist laws like the Virginia *Act to Preserve Racial Purity* (1924), a dramatic change in American Indian policy from coercive assimilation to the *Indian Reorganization Act* (1934) which enforced tribal organization, the severe discriminative framework surrounding Asian immigrants, and a more pervasive dissemination of an aggressive white "race consciousness" all found support among American citizens and intellectuals at least until World War II. In short, it was not a very comfortable time for ethnic minorities in the United States, for the pressures of the fiercely asserted hegemony of "whiteness" and of Anglo-American assimilation were enormous.

The published output of ethnic prose writing in the decades from 1910 to 1950, however, was truly impressive; literature of American ethnic minorities moved from the margins toward the center of American literature in those years. Black America saw the flourishing of the Harlem Renaissance, and strong literary production of fiction continued through the 1930s and 1940s, paving the way for the full entrance into American mainstream literature marked by the book-of-the-month-club selection of Richard Wright's *Native Son* (1940) and the winning of the National Book Award by Ralph Ellison's *Invisible Man* (1952). American

Jewish prose writers offered strong works from the still-marginalized beginnings with Abraham Cahan, Anzia Yezierska, Samuel Ornitz, and Daniel Fuchs to the high point of Saul Bellow's National Book Award–winning *Adventures of Augie March* (1953), and on to the fullest possible public recognition signaled by the conferral of the Nobel Prize for literature to Saul Bellow in 1976 and to Isaac Bashevis Singer in 1978. Immigrant and ethnic autobiography and fiction represented the lives of many different groups, ranging from Syrian (Salom Rizk) to Jamaican (Claude McKay), from Irish (Mary Doyle Curran) to Italian (John Fante), and from Slovak (Thomas Bell) to Slovene (Louis Adamic). Ethnic writers benefited—as did many American authors—from new institutions: Rosenwald and Guggenheim fellowships permitted uninterrupted writing time, writers' centers like Yaddo or Taos provided congenial settings, and many journals supported modern fiction writers. Whit Burnett and Martha Foley's *Story Magazine* (1931–1953) published and awarded such "new" writers as Nelson Algren, William Saroyan, Zora Neale Hurston, James T. Farrell, and Richard Wright; the annually published volumes *Best Short Stories* (1915–1932) and *Best American Short Stories* (1942–1977) helped many short-fiction writers—among them Konrad Bercovici, Nelson Algren, Saul Bellow, Leo Surmelian, and Carlos Bulosan as well as Vladimir Nabokov and Lionel Trilling—to reach a wider national audience. Louis Adamic's journal *Common Ground* (published from 1940 to 1949 by the Common Council for American Unity) and Edwin Seaver's *Cross Section* anthologies (1944–1948) specifically aimed for a polyethnic representation among contemporary American authors. Most important, the Works Progress Administration (WPA) gave support to many artists and authors who would later become famous. From 1935 to 1943 the Federal Writers' Project (FWP) helped to employ writers of diverse backgrounds, created a wide forum for exchanges of opinions (such as theaters, journals, and conventions), and involved authors in a large-scale, government-sponsored enterprise of taking stock of America, which included interesting historical or social science research projects such as the background work for, and writing of, the Writers' Guide Series, interviews with many ex-slaves, and the collecting of rural and urban folklore. The fact that on June 14, 1939, during his work on the Federal Writers Project in Harlem, Ralph Ellison heard and recorded the black tale of Sweet-the-monkey who "could make hisself invisible" is suggestive of the importance of the FWP in the development of American literature. As time went on, writers would also be more and more likely to teach "creative writing" in colleges throughout the United States.

While the hostility to languages other than English that was fomented in the World War I years, in a powerful mix of Anglo-American ethnocentrism and political reasoning, had a dampening effect on American ethnic literature in languages apart from English, the publication of non-English-language prose writing in the United States continued. The surveillance of all foreign-language papers from 1917 into the 1920s by the vast translation supervision enterprise of the postmaster general affected two thousand American periodicals written in Ruthenian, Syrian, Bohemian, "Spanish-Jewish" (Ladino), Tagalog-Visayan, Romanian, and many other languages, as well as bi- and trilingual journals in Polish-Latin, Danish-Norwegian-Swedish, or German-Hungarian. Yet just a few years later, *I de dage* (In Those Days, 1924) and *Riket grundlægges* (Founding the Kingdom, 1925), the first two volumes of Ole E. Rølvaag's Norwegian-language immigrant saga, a high point of non-English literature of the United States, were received with great enthusiasm in Lincoln Colcord's English translation under the title *Giants in the Earth: A Saga of the Prairie* (1927).

The foundations for modern multicultural literature were being laid in those decades. Not only did Oliver LaFarge's widely read *Laughing Boy* (1929) include a prayer ("House made of dawn light, House made of evening light") to which N. Scott Momaday's novel *House Made of Dawn* (1968) would later allude, but the first important modern novels by American Indians, John Joseph Mathews, *Sundown* (1934) and D'Arcy McNickle, *The Surrounded* (1936), were also published then. Asian-American fiction and autobiography began to take off with Sui Sin Far's sophisticated story collection, *Mrs. Spring Fragrance* (1912), as well as with Younghill Kang's *East Goes West: The Making of an Oriental Yankee* (1937), Pardee Lowe's *Father and Glorious Descendant* (1942), Carlos Bulosan's *America Is in the Heart: A Personal History* (1946), Toshio Mori's *Yokohama, California*, and Hisaye Yamamoto's "Seventeen Syllables" (both published in 1949). The first use of the word "Chicano" (derived from "mexicano") appeared in Mario Suárez's short story "Señor Garza" (1947) which anticipated features of the later Chicano literary movement that would begin, after 1950, with John Rechy's sketches, such as "El Paso del Norte" (1958), and with José Antonio Villareal's novel *Pocho* (1959).

The difficulties ethnic writers faced affected their literary production. Legislative changes were accompanied by an intense debate about the future of the country and the nature of various ethnic groups. In such contexts, ethnoautobiographic literature was an eminently political genre, as it seemed to provide information for the general reading public about the "desirability," potential "assimilability," or "compatibility" of whole groups of people. While American authors who were not ethnically marked often extolled freestanding individualism, ethnic writers operated under a system that has been called "compulsive representation," for they were often read as informants about the collectivities they were believed to embody. It is hardly surprising, then, that English-language American ethnic autobiography has, with some important exceptions, tended to present a positively conceived collective self and curbed too candidly self-critical individual representation that might be held against the authors *and* their groups, turning literary revelation into a "debit to the race." A negatively shaped self-portrait, as in Richard Wright's autobiography *Black Boy* (1945), was a strategic ploy, intended to show the terrible effects of racial segregation on human consciousness—though, despite this anti-segregationist political purpose, Wright was often taken to task for not offering a more positive representation of African-American life in *Black Boy*.

As debate raged about who should and should not be included in the category "American," the ethnic writers' answer often was, "We *are* Americans." In the very titles of their books they pronounced their compatibility with the culture and the political system of the United States where their presence had become so questionable. Jacob Riis set the tone with his autobiography *The Making of an American* (1901), a title Mary Antin later wished had still been available to her when she was writing her autobiography; she ultimately chose the title *The Promised Land* (1912) for what became a truly representative work of the genre. Other writers who adopted "American" titles were Edward Steiner, *From Alien to Citizen* (1914); Marcus Ravage, *An American in the Making* (1917); Horace Bridges, *On Becoming an American* (1919); Edward Bok, *The Americanization of Edward Bok*, (1920); Louis Adamic, *My America* (1938); and Salom Rizk, *Syrian Yankee* (1943). The title of Gertrude Stein's *The Making of Americans* was thus also a response to a flourishing genre.

Whereas immigration restrictionists and liberal reformers alike discussed ethnic heterogeneity in terms of the problems posed by crime, health, housing conditions, and poverty, the representative ethnic texts of the period were typically written by American immigrants and their descendants and by members of minorities who not only claimed America but also stressed that they had "made it." Following such famous titles as Booker T. Washington's autobiography *Up From Slavery* (1901, partly ghostwritten by Max Bennett Thrasher), the Irish immigrant Alexander Irvine gave his autobiography the telling title *From the Bottom Up* (1910), anticipating the slogan of American social historians in the 1960s. Other titles in this vein included Michael Pupin, *From Immigrant to Inventor* (1923) and Richard Bartholdt, *From Steerage to Congress* (1930). In the manner of the American uplift saga "from log cabin to White House," ethnic autobiographers attempted to include immigrants and minorities in tales of educational and economic upward mobility, transforming their marginality into a version of the typical American story. The illustrations that accompanied some of the autobiographies often supported this message, as the reader who just leafs through these volumes is taken from images of modest beginnings like Alexander Irvine's and S. S. McClure's birthplaces in Northern Ireland, or Mary Antin's grandfather's house in Polotzk, to encounters with famous Anglo-American or English people (for Jacob Riis and Edward Bok, Theodore Roosevelt; for Mary Antin, Edward Everett Hale; for Alexander Irvine, Jack London; for S. S. McClure, Robert Louis Stevenson), and to an arrival in an enviable American residence such as shown in the full-page photographs of "'Happy Hollow,' Mr. Irvine's Present Home Near Peekskill, New York" or of "Edward Bok's Present Home 'Swastika' (named by Rudyard Kipling), at Merion, Pennsylvania."

Part of the ethnic writer's perceived task was to go against commonly held ethnic stereotypes: Mike Gold's *Jews Without Money* (1930) announces this strategy in its title, and the narrator is indignant when he reports that his teacher called him "Little Kike."[6] (A nice counterpoint would be to read Myra Kelly's chapter "H. R. H. The Prince of Hester Street" in *Little Citizens: The Humour of School Life* [1904] which tells stories about Lower East Side schools from the Irish-American teacher Constance Bailey's point of view, including an episode in which Isidore Belchatosky "with growing fluency...cursed and swore and blasphemed; using words of whose existence Teacher had never heard or known and at whose meaning she could but faintly guess.")⁷ The Jamaican immigrant Claude McKay includes much stereotype-questioning in his autobiography *A Long Way From Home* (1937): for example, when a Russian poet's wife asks McKay to "dance a jazz" with her, he obliges, but ironically adds that he probably did not "measure up to the standard of Aframerican choreography."⁸ Thomas Bell's Slovak-American steel-mill workers' novel *Out of this Furnace* (1941) was viewed by the author as an "answer to all those unthinking people who look down on the Slovaks," stereotyping them as "Hunkies."⁹ Jerre Mangione's autobiographically inspired *Mount Allegro* (1943) describes the young protagonist Gerlando Amoroso's attempts to convince his teachers that, though Italian, he was neither talented as a singer nor as a painter; on a more serious note, he was taught that as a male of Sicilian parentage, he ought never to be seen publicly holding a knife.¹⁰ It could be difficult to become in the eyes of others the cliché of the knife-wielding Sicilian. Ironically, this stereotype-confronting tendency has led to the strange fact that a reader who searches for ethnic stereotypes against a given group is most likely to encounter them in literature by members of that group—who often tried to name, attack, and refute these clichéd notions. As the narrator of John Fante's short story "The Odyssey of a Wop" (1933, 1940) puts it: "As I grow older, I find out that Italians use Wop and Dago much more than Americans." Yet he also reports an incident when, working as a waiter, he is taunted so much by the chef that he actually becomes the knife-wielding "Wop" stereotype for a moment: "I am not thinking of throwing it, but since he says I won't, I do. It goes over his head and strikes the wall and drops with a clatter to the floor."¹¹

American ethnic autobiographers sensed that the stakes were high, for a "general reader" might judge the merit of a writer's ethnic group on the basis of reading a single book. Thus ethnic authors tended to flash their accomplishments, identifying their achievement and upward mobility with the respective ethnic group as a whole and with America, instead of revealing their individual perversions, nightmares, fears, or human failings. They often made a particular case for their own ethnic group by arguing for a special connection, an early historical link, a blood sacrifice, or a shared destiny with America. This claim of a special affinity has been called "homemaking myth," and many ethnic groups have made themselves at home in America by emphasizing an early arrival in the New World, a linguistic connection, a shared war experience, a "gift" or an ideological relationship, or any other element suited to establish the putative unity of the respective group culture and the dominant culture of the United States. Ethnic heroes—among them the autobiographers themselves—were sometimes the living symbols of such homemaking myths.[12]

Immigrants and members of minority groups also made their case by testifying against other ethnic groups. The representation of Italian boys in Gold's *Jews Without Money,* of the Irish neighbors in Ole Rølvaag's *Giants of the Earth* (1927), and of Polish farmers in Edna Ferber's *American Beauty* (1931) are just a few examples of this common strategy. In Anzia Yezierska's *Salome of the Tenements* (1922), the Jewish heroine Sonya Vrunsky finds in her Anglo-American beloved John Manning "the Anglo-Saxon coldness, its centuries of solid ice that all the suns of the sky can't melt." Yet Yezierska's narrator balances this cliché with quite unironic and rather anti-Semitic-sounding descriptions of her heroine: "The eternal urge of her race to rise—to rise—to transmute failure, heartbreak and despair into a driving will to conquer—swept her up to the heights of hope again."[13] As if in direct opposition to Jerre Mangione, a butcher's wife in Henry Roth's *Call It Sleep* (1934) warns her husband: "Do you oppose an Italian? Don't you know they carry knives—all of them?"[14] In short, the lives narrated by outsiders, marginals, immigrants, and ethnics could easily play a problematic role in affirming ethnic stereotypes. Even when ethnic writers included social criticism and an attack on specific laws and customs, on bigotry, racism, or on narrow notions of Americanness, they could also be more upbeat than, and just as biased as, certain authors from then dominant groups.

An offbeat contribution to the immigration debate was made by *The Sieve; or, Revelations of the Man Mill* (1921), an unusual narrative by the immigrant Feri Felix Weiss, who arrived in the United States in 1892 (apparently from Hungary) and became an immigration inspector. He writes almost nothing about his own life and past, focusing instead on his difficult work of sorting out bad aliens from desirable ones. Latvian anarchists, stowaways from many lands, a trachoma-infected Armenian girl (whose case as "the girl without a country" goes all the way to the Supreme Court), young European girls lured away from their parents by Mormon missionaries and headed for a fate of polygamy in Utah, Italian picture brides, smuggled-in Chinese, and legal immigrants from many countries who come with near-unintelligible information about their destination in the United States—these are some of the problem cases that cause "leaks in the sieve" that Weiss tries to mend with the conviction of a believer in "the Religion of Eugenics." His book makes a telling counterpoint to the many immigrant narratives with arrival scenes. Yet despite his cautiously restrictionist outlook, Weiss saw his job as a contribution to the rededication of Plymouth Rock and proudly ended his book with his participation at an immigrant education conference in Plymouth on the occasion of the tercentenary of the Pilgrims' journey.[15]

As a balancing element to strategies of ethno-American compatibility, ethnic literature also tended to include positive references to country-of-origin communities and their character traits that were *not* "American." In such references often lay a point of subtle resistance to, or overt critique of, America. This was the case even in the most pro-American and apparently assimilationist works. *The Americanization of Edward Bok: The Autobiography of a Dutch Boy Fifty Years After* (1920), written in the third person, was a model of the cheery quality of the genre of the success story, and it celebrated the joys of progress and acquisition. Yet near the end of his autobiography even Bok, the famed editor of the *Ladies' Home Journal,* included a section entitled "Where America Fell Short With Me." There Bok remembers how wasteful America appeared to him upon his arrival: "it was an easy calculation that what was thrown away in a week's time from Brooklyn homes would feed the poor of the Netherlands." He attacks such "infernal Americanisms" as the phrase "That will do," for preventing Americans from aspiring to thoroughness and excellence.[16] (A quarter of a century earlier Abraham Cahan had seen the adoption of the phrase as a symptom of shallow Americanization when a character in his *Yekl: A Tale of the New York Ghetto* [1896] says: "America for a country and *'dod'll do'* [that'll do] for a language.")[17] Bok also criticizes the popular movement to Americanize immigrants, claiming boldly that the Americanizers themselves needed Americanization. And he wonders "whether, after all, the foreign-born does not make in some sense a better American—whether he is not able to get a truer perspective; whether his is not the deeper desire to see America greater; whether he is not less content to let its faulty institutions be as they are; whether in seeing faults he does not make a more decided effort to have America reach those ideals or those fundamentals of his own land which he feels are in his nature, and the best of which he is anxious to graft into the character of his adopted land?" (451). The reason Bok gives for his decision to retire from the editorship of the *Ladies' Home Journal* at age fifty-six comes as no surprise: "After all, he was still Dutch; he held on to the lesson which his people had learned years ago; [. . .] that the Great Adventure of Life was something more than material work, and that the time to go is while the going is good!" (425). Ironically then, Bok argued that it was being and remaining Dutch that made him a better American. Amazingly, he said so at the peak of the Americanization movement, and with Roosevelt's explicit endorsement.

The possibilities and constraints of American ethnic autobiography and prose fiction are apparent in the short life stories that were published in the *Independent,* and of which the southern colored woman was an example. More than seventy such life stories appeared in the *Independent* before World War I, and the labor-and-reform-oriented Progressive editor Hamilton Holt perceived the potential of these "lifelets" (as they were called by Edwin E. Slosson)[18] to form a collective image of the new polyethnic America. Holt's idea of collecting such life stories for *The Independent* was carried out with the help of several professional writers, including Sydney Reid, the already-mentioned Irish-American Alexander Irvine, and the Princeton-trained writer Ernest Poole who had also helped Upton Sinclair to find sources for *The Jungle* and was the author of the novel *The Voice of the Street* (1906), a book about New York's Lower East Side, to be followed by *The Harbor* (1915), and *Millions* (1922). In 1925 Holt became the president of Rollins College in Winter Park, Florida, where he instituted educational reforms and attracted an illustrious faculty, some of whose members, after a serious crisis in 1933, left Rollins only to found the even more experimental (and more famous) Black Mountain College—one of the seedbeds of American aesthetic modernism.

Holt collected sixteen lives in a book entitled *The Life Stories of Undistinguished Americans as Told by Themselves* (1906). The programmatic title suggested that everyone in the world could be American and that being "undistinguished" could be a mark of distinction. The collection opens with the story of Antanas Kaztauskis, a Lithuanian refugee from Russian oppression who works in the brutal Chicago stockyard and joins a union (there are similarities with Upton Sinclair's *The Jungle,* published in the same year). The machinery of death becomes chillingly real in this practical account of a world of profit:

> My job was in the cattle killing room. I pushed the blood along the gutter. Some people think these jobs make men bad. I do not think so. The men who do the killing are not as bad as the ladies with fine clothes who come every day to look at it, because they have to do it. The cattle do not suffer. They are knocked senseless with a big hammer and are dead before they wake up. This is done not to spare them pain, but because if they got hot and sweating with fear and pain the meat would not be so good. I soon saw that every job in the room was done like this—so as to save everything and make money. One Lithuanian who worked with me, said, "They get all the blood out of those cattle and all the work out of us men." (16)

The volume ends with a Chinese merchant's wish to return from New York's Chinatown to his native village in China: Lee Chew even draws a floor plan of his father's house (176). In the book, the American Indian Ah-nen-la-de-ni is prevented at his Pennsylvania school from expressing himself in the only language he knows, and the unnamed African American experiences the hell of a Georgia peon camp. A farmer's wife in Illinois has to struggle against an overwhelming work load, and her own husband, in order to follow her calling as a writer, and an itinerant Southern Methodist minister pursues his career against the physical handicap of his defective eyesight. The Italian bootblack Rocco Corresca and the Swedish farmer Axel Jarlson build their lives in New York and Minnesota. A Japanese servant describes how California employers have humiliated him. Nothing is more telling than the Polish sweatshop worker Sadie Frowne's understated and almost casual remark: "Where the needle goes through the nail it makes a sore finger, or where it splinters a bone it does much harm. Sometimes a finger has to come off. Generally, though, one can be cured by a salve" (27). This destructive side of industrial labor gives a serious dimension to her naively comic premodern account of always arriving very early at work because she does not believe in the existence of alarm clocks: "I have heard that there is a sort of clock that calls you at the very time you want to get up, but I can't believe that because I don't see how the clock would know" (26). A Greek peddler misses the flavor of Greek fruit in America and mentions a 10 percent return migration rate to Greece; the French dressmaker Amelia des Moulins knows that there is only one Paris and is looking forward to the voyage that will take her back to France. The German nurse girl Agnes describes the ups and downs of her work and looks forward to getting married to a grocery store assistant. The pro-Turkish Syrian Church sentences the Syrian journalist L. J. A. to death for having published critical articles on the Armenian massacres in New York's Arab-language press.

Some of the immigrant stories include arrival scenes at the Statue of Liberty. Sadie Frowne noted that upon arriving in New York she "saw the beautiful bay and the big woman with the spikes on her head and the lamp that is lighted at night in her hand (Goddess of Liberty) (22)"; and the Syrian journalist mentions that he "passed close by the grand Statue of Liberty and saw in the distance the beautiful white bridge a way up in the blue sky and the big buildings towering up like our own mountain peaks" (154). Such descriptions belong to the long series of texts starting with Emma Lazarus's poem "The New Colossus" (1883) which reinterpreted the Statue of Liberty, officially designated as embodying Franco-American friendship, as a symbol of welcome to immigrants. Some lifelets contain interesting misreadings of the symbol. Thus Mike Trudics, the Hungarian peon, describes the statue's torch as a broom: "A well dressed man who spoke our language told us that the big iron woman in the harbor was a goddess that gave out liberty freely and without cost to everybody. He said the thing in her hand that looked like a broom was light—that it was to give us light and liberty too. [...] [H]e told us a man could stand inside the broom" (201).

The stories portray fun and leisure, and we hear of fortune-tellers, cafés, the theater, picnics, or concerts, and, again and again, of Coney Island—where, however, the Igorrote chief Fomoaley Ponci is on display, brought to America from the recently conquered Philippines. He serves as a reminder of the stark inequality that is pervasive in the New World, and present even in the world of entertainment. Interestingly, the *Independent* published Russian writer Maxim Gorky's contemporary critique of Coney Island as a "paying business, as a means to extract their earnings from the pockets of the people" who experience "boredom" (the title of the essay) as a result of their monotonous jobs.[19] Coney Island is not the only site of social tension among the various Americans who speak in the *Life Stories:* they belong to different classes, so much so that just a part of the Greek peddler's income could have completely saved the African American from his fate of peonage. The volume as a whole suggests the broadening of the term "American" that its editor intended. Yet it also revealed the problems and conflicts of a multiethnic society in which great riches and dramatic poverty coexist.

Ethnic tensions are as widespread as class inequality. Because of their differences in culture, religion, and language, the undistinguished Americans measure each other by incompatible yardsticks and at times look at each other with skeptical and biased eyes—as "foreigners" or "devils," "red-haired savages" or "infidels." When the Irish cook learns that her American employers are Jewish, she packs her bags and says, "I beg your pardon, ma'am, but I can't eat the bread of them as crucified the Saviour" (90). The lady's answer that Christ also was a Jew only confirms the maid in her decision to quit. The Chinese businessman maintains that, "No one would hire an Irishman, German, Englishman or Italian when he could get a Chinese, because our countrymen are so much more honest, industrious, steady, sober and painstaking" (184). Each life story develops a sympathetic and individualized view of the group it represents, while many propagate "stereotypes" of other groups. Thus the Italian bootblack can say: "He was Irish, but a good man" (35). The Swedish farmer notes that his French-Canadian friend "was part Indian, and yet was laughing all the time" (53) whereas he found that the steerage passengers "were Swedes and very pleasant and friendly" (52). The feature of viewing one's own group in positive terms and members of other groups as types was pervasive in American ethnic literature. One novel of the period, Jessie Fauset's *Plum Bun* (1929), explicitly lets its heroine become self-conscious of this general trait. In *Plum Bun*, the mixed-race artist Angela Murray recognizes that her award-winning project of creating a great painting of "Fourteenth Street types" at New York's Union Square is flawed because Angela herself would also be nothing but a social "type" to others. As her wisdom and her sympathy with the down-and-outs grow, she comes to understand "how fiercely she would have rebelled had anyone from a superior social plane taken her for copy!"[20]

What were the common denominators of an increasingly polyethnic country? One person's utopia could be another person's hell. This makes a widely shared expression of nostalgia for one particular sacred past difficult. Religion, for example, could mean unpredictably diverse things for different Americans: the Lithuanian does not often go to church in the New World because he finds religious service "too slow" in America

(19). The Italian bootblack notes that there are "here plenty of Protestants who are heretics, but they have a religion, too" and that their churches "have no saints and no altars, which seems strange" (37). The Jewish garment worker comments that in America, unlike in Poland, only men go to synagogue (23); and compared to China, Lee Chew writes, America is a country where people pay no regards to the precepts of Kong-foo-tsze (Confucius) and the Sages (177).

For the people who speak in this collection there is no agreed-upon "sacred" realm that is being secularized. In this respect they are representative of Americans. To whose religious past can a polyethnic society dream of returning? Christianity? (Catholicism? Protestantism? Greek or Maronite Orthodoxy?) Islam? Judaism? Hinduism? Confucianism? or nature worship? The inhabitants of this book have left many different sacred and secular pasts behind—yet they continue to view the modern through the lenses provided by these various pasts. Is "secularization" merely a convenient metaphor in such a state of affairs, leaving open the issue of which specific form of sacredness is to be left behind and focusing instead on the shared process of becoming "modern" and secularized? Might not a rhetoric of "making it new" create the hope for a unity to emerge in the future—so that Americans, in Lee Chew's grandfather's critical words, are "constantly showing disrespect for their ancestors by getting new things to take the place of the old" (178)? Would not specific forms of religious fundamentalism, of precisely defined "faith-based values," or of a single dogmatically designated meaning of the civil-religion formula "In God We Trust" simply have to be exclusionary and divisive in a society of many past and present creeds?

The problem of heterogeneity also affects expectations for the future. While the majority of the life-story subjects imagine a better future in America, there are those who will go back to a country of origin, those who only dream of return emigration, those who have no country to which they can return, and those who have little hope for a future anywhere. (In representing the theme of return migration, the *Life Stories* reflected the fact that more than thirty of each hundred immigrants returned to their country of origin between 1910 and 1930.) When the French dressmaker announces that she is going back to Paris, she is embracing a past to which no other undistinguished American could hope to return. This highlights a problem with many "back to . . ." movements in the modern United States—unless what followed was a mere abstraction, a vague generalization that could then be fleshed out in the most heterogeneous fashion. It was a problem that stood out in an era when nation-states cherished myths of homogeneity, shared origins, and a common destiny.

Even the constitution of individual ethnic identity could be the result of complex interethnic interaction and negotiation. The Indian describes his first encounter with the generalization "Mohawk" to which he supposedly belonged but also a name in which he senses an insult (he was right since the name means "cannibal" or "coward" in Algonquin); the Greek peddler alternates between a description of Greeks as "they" and as "we," as does the Syrian when he speaks about "his" people. Axel Jarlson may say "with us" and mean "in Sweden" but he also uses the phrase "this country" to refer to the United States; whereas "Americans or even Swedes who live in America" do not command the narrator's use of the pronoun "we," which most often refers to personally known groupings of family and friends of any nationality.

These ethnic issues and interethnic differences are not only recognizable in hindsight. Some undistinguished Americans directly responded to the lifelets of others. The southern colored woman wrote the *Independent* in response to other first-person stories that had appeared in it before hers. She explicitly addresses two of the other autobiographers.

> I would be contented and happy if I, an American citizen, could say as Axel Jarlson (the Swedish emigrant, whose story appeared in THE INDEPENDENT of January 8th, 1903) says, "There are no aristocrats to push him down and say that he is not worthy because his father was poor." There are "aristocrats" to push me and mine down and say we are not worthy because we are colored. The Chinaman, Lee Chew, ends his article in THE INDEPENDENT of February 19th, 1903, by saying, "Under the circumstances how can I call this my home, and how can any one blame me if I take my money and go back to my village in China?"
>
> Happy Chinaman! Fortunate Lee Chew! You can go back to your village and enjoy your money. This is my village, my home, yet I am an outcast! (220)

The various lifelets add up to a polyethnic panorama, a "complete picture of America in all its strata," and for the book Holt selected those stories that would best typify what he thought of as "the five great races" and a series of representative professions (xxix). More than that, these life stories suggest the global interconnectedness of working-class Americans at the beginning of the century. They also make vivid the difficulty of associating a single "type" with the word "American," and of taking for granted a historical sense of a widely shared past among a heterogeneous populace.

What could the Founding Fathers, or the American nineteenth century, or most any aspect of American history mean to so many ethnic Americans? The slim output by English-writing ethnic authors of the otherwise so popular genre of historical fiction is symptomatic of this problem. An example of minor contributions to the genre is provided by Frances Winwar. Born "Vinciguerra" in Taormina, Sicily, she adopted her Anglicized pen name, an exact translation of her Italian name, when she published *The Ardent Flame* (1927), a thirteenth-century romance based on the tale of Francesca di Rimini; she also wrote an American historical novel about the hysteria of the Salem witchcraft trials, *Gallows Hill* (1937). Yet only one single African-American historical novel was published between 1910 and 1950, Arna Bontemps's *Black Thunder* (1936); and Henry Roth's attempt at completing a second novel in the 1930s failed precisely because he could not imagine what the historical memory of the Civil War could have meant to a twentieth-century native-born American radical.

In many ways, the short autobiographical sketches, presented from the point of view of a liberal reformer, represent the more general tensions in ethnic autobiography in the first half of the century, though *The Life Stories of Undistinguished Americans* do not reveal much of the subjects' psychology. The social questionnaire that the storytellers answered or anticipated and addressed implicitly did not provide much of an opening for such revelations. "Where do you come from? Why, when, and how did you come to America? Are you better off now? Where do you work? How much money do you make? Where do you live? How do you spend your day? What is the role of the family in your group?" The authors or informants were busy answering the cluster of direct or implied questions that surrounded the debates about immigration and race. Their lives seemed to be interesting to the extent that they were socially representative for the groups they "typified," a fact the titles or subtitles of many life stories made clear. (One only has to think of "The Race Problem—an Autobiography by a Southern Colored Woman.") The narrators conveyed social meaning and found little time for introspection. After all, such short "lifelets" may not be the appropriate place for laying bare one's inner soul. They were a popular genre with American readers, and Ernest Poole followed Holt's lead, authoring such first-person stories as "Up from the Ghetto: From a Dweller to a Speculator in Slums" and "Getting That Home: Told by Jan, the Big Polish Laborer," even for the anti-immigration *Saturday Evening Post* (1906).

Numerous "authentic" and "inauthentic" ethnic autobiographies followed, and the borderline between "real" and "fake" is more difficult to draw than one might think, as the genre of ethnic autobiographies written by impersonators suggests. Now, if one sees a nonrepresentational, modernist painting and learns that the artist was Jewish, that fact alone does not necessarily add anything to the understanding or enjoyment of the work. Only fascists, nativists, or racists believed that Jews were determined to paint *as* Jews; hence the revelation that a painter was Jewish could have enormous consequences in a fascist world. Outside of racist paranoia, there might only be a mild recognition of kinship, group pride, or of very subtle difference that would not necessarily have a bearing on the appreciation of the work itself. Similarly, if we were then told that the first ascription had been false and that the artist actually was not Jewish but Anglo-American, that information would just result in an unemotional correction process in our brains.

These rules do not apply to American ethnic autobiography (or to much ethnic literature in general). For better or worse, ethnic literature has often been read as social evidence; and the "ethnic authenticity" of the work in question (which largely depended on the ethnic background of the author) was therefore a crucial element for ethnic advocates and detractors alike. This issue can be traced back at least to the early abolitionists who, like Richard Hildreth in his immensely popular *The Slave; or, Memoirs of Archy Moore* (1836), had created the fake slave narrative and were challenged for it by southerners. Reading texts for an author's ethnicity was also not uncommon in discussions of American literature that tried to excise some parts of that literature as too foreign. The University of Illinois literary historian Stuart P. Sherman, for example, attacked Theodore Dreiser in the *Nation* in 1915 for his "barbaric naturalism" that was representative of "a new note in American literature, coming from the 'ethnic' element of our mixed population." Dreiser's ethnic background, Sherman implied, seemed to make him less of an "American," less of a "main stream" writer.[21]

Yet even a casual survey of American ethnic autobiography shows a great variety of forms that complicate a reading process which aims for clear ethnic boundaries on which inclusion or exclusion, appreciation or dismissal could be based. As in the case of the *Life Stories,* the borderline between "authentic," "as told to," ghostwritten, and fabricated texts is fluid.

Some autobiographies were published by an ethnic author who was identified by name, and they were narrated in the first-person singular. Mary Antin's *The Promised Land* (1912) is representative, but it begins with the warning, "I am absolutely other than the person whose story I have to tell."[22] Antin proposed to her publisher the use of two different names for her past and present self throughout the book. Other ethnic autobiographies were published under the author's name and were narrated in the third person. *The Americanization of Edward Bok* (1920) is a good example, yet the use of the third person here is universal only for the Edward of the past, whereas the Bok of the present uses the first person to describe his current views and opinions. Thus, one chapter is entitled "A Bewildered Bok," another one, "What I Owe to America." The confusion of pronouns in the *Life Stories* was merely an example of a more widespread phenomenon. Gertrude Stein was to be the master at confusing pronouns in *The Autobiography of Alice B. Toklas;* it was an "autobiography" ostensibly written in Toklas's voice which logically referred to Gertrude Stein in the third person (and always by her full name). Yet at the very end of the book this fiction is surprisingly given up: "About six weeks ago Gertrude Stein said, it does not look to me as if you were ever going to write that autobiography. You know what I am going to do. I am going to write it for you. I am going to write it as simply as Defoe did the autobiography of Robinson Crusoe. And she has and this is it."[23]

Some writers adopted pen names that would make the reader expect "ethnic" works. In the nineteenth century, Henry Harland had published Jewish romances under the name "Sidney Luska"; and after the end of our period Daniel James published a Chicano book under the ethnically more appropriate pseudonym "Danny Santiago." The story of the Eaton sisters Winifred and Edith Maude constitutes an interesting example of the complicated boundaries between literary fiction and ethnic authenticity. The daughters of an interracial Anglo-Chinese couple, Edith chose the Chinese-American identity of "Sui Sin Far" and published "Leaves from the Mental Portfolio of an Eurasian," an autobiographic lifelet for

Holt's *Independent* (1909), whereas the younger Winifred concealed her partly Chinese origins and opted for the Japanese pen name "Onoto Watanna" and wrote geisha romances such as *Miss Nume of Japan: A Japanese-American Romance* (1899), some of which made it to Hollywood. At first glance, one sister would seem to be "authentic" and the other "fake," yet both had to work at imagining and sustaining the divergent Asian images they wished to project. And books by both sisters were lavishly designed in an "oriental" manner.

Anonymous publication also permitted full fictionalization of the genre expectation, as in the case of the first-person-singular *Autobiography of an Ex-Colored Man* (1912), taken to be a confession by a man of partly black ancestry who had passed for white and was now revealing the secrets of race relations by drawing aside the "veil," although the book was really a novel written by James Weldon Johnson. The immigrant intellectual Abraham Cahan's first-person novel *The Rise of David Levinsky* (1917), praised by Carl Van Doren as "the most important of all immigrant novels" before 1920, was first published in partial serialization in *McClure's Magazine,* illustrated, and under the title "The Autobiography of an American Jew" (1913).[24] Originally, Samuel Ornitz's novel *Haunch, Paunch and Jowl* (1923) was published anonymously, advertised by its publisher Boni and Liveright with a big question mark instead of an author's photograph, and classified by the philosopher Horace Kallen as a "pseudo-autobiography."[25] Sylvester C. Long's *Long Lance* (1928) was published as an American Indian autobiography, and though the author lived as a Native American, his claim of Indian ancestry is now often considered invalid. When the editors of *Esquire* wanted to accept the story "Christ in Concrete" (1937) by the Italian-American bricklayer Pietro di Donato they were worried that they might have fallen for a "Union Square or Greenwich Village gag" and they sent Jewish-American writer Meyer Levin to "look up, and over, Mr. di Donato and confirm or deny our cynical suspicion." Fortunately, Levin found di Donato to be the real article; Levin reported that the young Italian-American writer was "indeed a bricklayer, and apparently a very good one" who furthermore looked "like young Dante."[26] Elizabeth Stern's works *My Mother and I* (1917, introduced by Theodore Roosevelt) and *I Am a Woman— And a Jew* (1926), long read as authentic autobiographic expressions by an American Jewish woman, were later dismantled by Stern's own son who claimed that Stern had made up her Jewish birth. The dispute around these dramatically conflicting claims has not yet been resolved.[27]

Other autobiographies were published under an ethnic author's name, but were commissioned and ghostwritten, or resulted from different degrees of collaboration. Thus *My Autobiography* (1914), the Irish immigrant memoir "by S. S. McClure" was in reality ghostwritten by Willa Cather. McClure, a powerful editor who had invented syndicated writing, had control over his text, but the ethnic subjects whose life stories were published in "as told to" format (among them, several of Holt's *Life Stories* and many of the first-person lifelets published in American magazines) had no such power. The growing phenomenon of ghostwriting affected both "celebrities" (a concept that has been on the ascent since the 1920s) and the truly poor (who often had little or no control over the shaping or the thrust of their published autobiographies). Various euphemisms were used to describe the relationship of subject and writer, such as "in collaboration with," "given by," "reported by," "with," and even "directed by" (in a 1928 *Saturday Evening Post* life story about the actor Harold Lloyd). Past and present self, first and third person, and authorized and spoken-for subjects have populated the books with alternating genre ascription, yet all were often read for the "ethnic character"—however problematically it may have been constituted.

There was considerable confusion about the literary genres of ethnic writing. Louis Adamic began writing *Laughing in the Jungle: The Autobiography of an Immigrant in America* (1931) as a novel, but then augmented it with previously published essays as well as new first-person materials about the author's Slovenian childhood in the province of Carniola and emigration to America in 1914, so that the subtitle of the book characterizes only a part of what is really a mixed-genre work.

Some autobiographies were published alternatively as "novel" or as "memoir." Jerre Mangione's *Mount Allegro* (1943) is representative. Although *Mount Allegro* is narrated in the first-person singular, the first publisher persuaded the author late in the writing stage to change the narrator's name to "Gerlando Amoroso" and identified the book as "fiction." The first edition, however, made the best-seller lists both in fiction and in nonfiction. The last authorized reprint in Mangione's lifetime received the subtitle "A Memoir of Italian American Life." Mike Gold's *Jews Without Money* (1930) is written in the first-person singular, reads like a memoir, and was billed as an autobiography when Liveright first published it in 1930, but was labeled a novel when it was reissued by Sun Dial Press in 1946; it is now often viewed and discussed as autobiographical fiction.

In ethnic prose literature of the first half of the twentieth century, ethnic personae and novelistic inventions were close to each other, since even the most "authentic" autobiographies published in English had to imply certain American audience expectations and since even the most inauthentic ones could contain much intuitively truthful or well-researched social information. Whether true or made up, ethnic autobiographies often implied the questionnaire that was behind Holt's *Life Stories* and constituted answers to what Henry James called "the great 'ethnic' question" that loomed large in the period from 1910 to 1950.[28]

4

Ethnic Themes, Modern Themes

Ethnic literature of the first half of the twentieth century developed a repertoire of ethnic themes. In addition to class mobility and assimilation, generational tensions appear often (at times in ethnic trilogies), as does the conflict between arranged marriage and romantic love. Rifts between children and parents are prominent, and the often complex mother-son and father-daughter relations receive particular emphasis. Encounters with ethnic hatred or hypocrisy are frequently represented, as are friendly and amorous relations across ethnic boundaries. The attenuation of older religious beliefs and ethical standards finds manifold expression in these works. Since a central persona is often correlated to the figure of the aspiring author, difficult negotiations between the world of work and the realm of artistic creation are common. Education tends to be central, both as a school setting and as a possible symbolic area of resolution of the various tensions. Protagonists tend to be relatively young so that the general process of socialization can be described in the context of cultural conflicts and the pressures of American assimilation. Getting lost in a foreign-language cityscape or feeling lost in the vast-seeming countryside are common experiences. The tensions of poor ethnic families in working-class polyethnic neighborhoods in an often mythic-seeming America are omnipresent and at times decisive for the plot. Shame and pride may alternate in characters' responses to their ethnicity. There are scenes in which the contrast between the ethnic group and America is dramatized and others in which it is bridged. Ethnic foodways are mentioned favorably, at times with the appropriate non-English name, and sometimes the details that are given amount to a recipe. The Americanness of a given moment may be underlined by the presence of the flag, a song, or another national symbol, like the Statue of Liberty; ethnic protagonists may recognize their own Americanness when they travel abroad, and especially to a place of symbolic significance for their ethnic identity: in the case of immigrants, when they return for a visit to their country of origin. A sense of double consciousness pervades the literature and often finds its expression in the simultaneous presence of general American and ethnic symbols, of two intertwined flags, for example, or in the descriptions of two settings in terms of each other. In short, ethnic literature offers many details, large and small, that have been of interest to sociologists, anthropologists, and ethnic historians.

When it is not read for its ethnic themes, however, ethnic literature of the first half of the twentieth century shows a remarkable concern for the American world of modernity. In part, this tendency reveals itself in fleeting instances when the ethnic group in question is associated with an older, premodern, or "medieval" ethos. Mary Antin described immigration as if it were time traveling and focused on the paradox that her life metaphorically spanned centuries: "My age alone, my true age, would be reason enough for my writing. I began life in the Middle Ages, as I shall prove, and here I am still, your contemporary in the twentieth century, thrilling with your latest thought."[1] African-American intellectuals, too, used the distinction between the middle ages and the modern period to describe the history of the race. Alain Locke wrote in the introduction to his landmark anthology *The New Negro* (1925) that each wave of migration is "in the Negro's case a deliberate flight not only from countryside to city, but from medieval America to modern."[2] Since America is the proverbial "country without middle ages," such rhetorical (and heavily ideological) strategies put urban America into sharp relief as the embodiment of modern society against the presumably community- and tradition-oriented ethnic group, especially prior to migration. And the term "middle ages" serves as a convenient unifier of the heterogeneous premodern pasts that are assimilated to a single notion of progress. Moreover, this imaginative belief in a single, Anglo-American notion of progress as the embodiment of the "modern" had the effect of giving an appearance of unity to dramatically divergent experiences of modernization: those forms of modernization that came from within American culture and transformed it tended to replace rather than transform existing cultural features in minority and ethnic groups. Yet the pervasive concern with modernity goes far beyond this form of metaphorical postmedievalism, as the reader finds in American ethnic literature images of the details of modernity, from skyscrapers to automobiles and airplanes, and from the machinery of the workplace to fast food and the many features of modern leisure culture.

Mary Antin has a keen eye for such New-World features as speaking tube, soda fountain, cold lemonade, hot peanuts, and pink popcorn as well as chewing candy. Leon Kobrin stages an encounter of strangers at the automat in New York City. Jean Toomer notes cardboard advertisements for Chesterfield cigarettes and Chero-Cola. Zora Neale Hurston (in her "Story in Harlem Slang," 1942) incorporates the soft-drink bottle into urban banter: "But baby! [. . .] Dat shape you got on you! I bet the Coca Cola Company is paying you good money for the patent!"[3] Henry Roth includes such details as the "sword with the big middle on Mecca cigarettes."[4] Anzia Yezierska mentions ketchup stains and "ready-made" clothing (in *Salome of the Tenements*). In *Home to Harlem*, Claude McKay comments on the novelty of hip pockets in his character Jake's suit, and James T. Farrell calls attention to electric malted-milk shakers. Richard Wright's Bigger Thomas sees airplanes flying over Chicago. Popular songs are in the background of Carl Van Vechten's *Nigger Heaven* (1926), and the "Indian Love Call" can be heard on a phonograph in Pietro di Donato's *Christ in Concrete* (1939). In Daniel Fuchs's *Homage to Blenholt* (1936), the character Ruth dozes off at a manicurist's—an event which is stylistically marked by a one-page catalog of popular and commercial culture items ranging from Bing Crosby and Myrna Loy to Hindu brown stockings and an "E.Z. Hair Removing Glove." In Willard Motley's *Knock on Any Door* (1947) the Italian-American Nick Romano looks at a sign in a plate-glass window that reads, in mirrored reverse, "CHILI 10¢" as he leans against a gum machine. And everybody goes to the movies, listens to the radio (some protagonists build crystal radio sets), notices newspaper headlines, leafs through magazines, and takes electric streetcars and subways.

In these aspects ethnic literature participates in general American features. Henry James and Henry Adams may have been the first to introduce brand names to American literature when they wrote of a "Remington" (James's typewriter) or a "Kodak" (Adams's camera); and Hemingway expanded the horizons of American Prohibition-era readers when he gave brand names from Pernod and Cinzano to Veuve Cliquot a firm presence in *The Sun Also Rises* (1926). Salesmen who peddle modern gadgets are ubiquitous in American prose, from Mark Twain's *A Connecticut Yankee in King Arthur's Court* (1889) to Eudora Welty's "Death of a Traveling Salesman" (1936). Mark Twain, Gertrude Stein, John Dos Passos, and Richard Wright were fascinated by newspaper headlines and incorporated them into their writing. Gertrude Atherton mentions nail polish as a device to camouflage supposed "tell-tale" signs of mixed-race origins on the fingernails of "suspicious brunettes." Other writers offered whole inventories of modernity: F. Scott Fitzgerald's *The Great Gatsby* (1925) included the *Saturday Evening Post,* the car repair shop, and the gigantic billboard; John Dos Passos's *U.S.A.* (1938) imitated the forms of camera eye, newspaper clipping, and newsreel.

There are some subtle differences: ethnic literature, because of its more pervasive working-class affinities and urban locales, was more likely to show encounters with public transportation than with the beauty of the most fanciful automobiles, with technology in the world of labor, typified by concrete mixing in di Donato's book, rather than in the realm of conspicuous consumption. At times, ethnic authors also were inclined to dramatize the features of modernity against the background of a premodern community that still seemed within reach. It is indubitable that the themes of modernity are pervasive in American ethnic literature from 1910 to 1950; it is quite possible that ethnic literature was even more extensively engaged with features of modernity than were many mainstream writers. In some cases, the ethnic writers who were connected with modern means of publication reached such a wide or intense dissemination as to elicit envy from more traditionally positioned authors. Thus Theodore Roosevelt yearned for Edward Bok's ability to reach millions of Americans who would read *The Ladies' Home Journal* leisurely in their private sphere. Roosevelt wrote Bok: "My messages are printed in the newspapers and read hurriedly, mostly by men in trolleys or rail-road cars."[5]

Being thematically modern could, but did not necessarily, mean being formally modernist. In a social setting in which incongruity resulting from the incompatibility of various pasts may have been the most widely shared cultural feature, there was perhaps no alternative to modernity. Migration and accelerated culture contacts helped to produce "marginal men," a term the Chicago sociologist Robert E. Park derived from Georg

Simmel's concept of the "stranger" who is simultaneously inside and outside of a community; and the artists among them may have wished to translate the experience of modernity into the aesthetic experiments of modernism. In other words, their marginal location in a world of modernity may have pushed some writers who were immigrants and migrants toward modernism. The "translated" quality of some of their expressions makes them resemble avant-garde prose, as in the story of the Japanese man-servant in Holt's *Life Stories:* "The way to open the door, salute the guest, language to be used according to the rank of the guests and how to handle the name card. Characteristic simplicity of democracy could not be seen in this household" (164). Or one may think of Genya Schearl's expression "it grows late" in Henry Roth's *Call It Sleep,* or of the magical word *girarihir* that, Jerre Mangione writes in *Mount Allegro,* Italian immigrants learned even before they landed in America, and that turns out to mean, "Get out of here." Such cases of a defamiliarization of the English language seem to straddle a borderline between naturalistic verisimilitude and modernist prose.

Yet the language of modernity only occasionally overlaps with that of modernism; no matter how much some modernists may have invoked modernity, there was no inescapable linkage of modernity and modernism. The ways in which individual writers reacted to the modern world of cities and technology varied significantly. It is useful to remember the distinction between modernity (embodied by the processes of secularization on the one hand, and of urbanization and industrialization on the other) and modernism (the formally experimental ways in which many writers, composers, and artists chose to express themselves in the twentieth century). After all, a given writer's views of modernity could be at variance with his or her attitudes toward modernism. Thus four basic literary types emerged:

a. Some writers were critical of modernity and used traditional, premodern (nonmodernist, or antimodernist) literary forms in order to voice their criticism. This was the case for some genteel or nostalgic writing, at times articulated in the name of a mythic homogeneous rural or small-town past. Some *Saturday Evening Post* writing and the Norman Rockwell covers illustrate this orientation, but it was a mode that was relatively rare in ethnic literature.

b. Other authors expressed the themes of modernity yet refrained from employing modernist forms. This was a common mode in ethnic literature (Bok, Yezierska) that described migration, immigration, ethnicity, and modernity in premodernist prose and plotlines.
c. Writers could also be deeply critical of modernity, and prefer, for example, traditional religious beliefs, but express themselves in a modernist fashion. Much literature commonly discussed under the modernist label falls into this category of experimentally expressed critiques of (or laments about) technological modernity. T. S. Eliot is a prime example.
d. Finally, some writing was both promodern and modernist. This was the case for many ethnic and minority writers, especially those from groups who look back to pasts that offer too little invitation for sustained nostalgia (e.g., slavery, persecution, or severe class oppression).

Of course, many writers voiced ambivalence about the mixed blessings of modernity and some were open to at least occasional moments of nostalgia, including nostalgia for pasts that never existed. Furthermore, one cannot always distinguish easily between a writer's fascination with, and contempt for, modernity. Some writers believed, for example, that the movement toward modernity was inevitable, preferable to any alternative, yet ultimately tragic.

What this obviously simplified fourfold distinction helps to visualize, however, is that modernity may have been more popular than nostalgia in ethnic writing. Though some outstanding ethnic works did emerge in the period that were part of the modernist movement, the general trend of American ethnic literature may have been toward modernity without modernism. What is often associated with American "high modernism" may have been a particular Anglo-American blend of opposition to modernity expressed in aesthetically modernist forms, whereas African-American, immigrant, and other ethnic writers may have been less frequently inclined to endorse the modernist strategy of opposing modernity. From a vantage point of classic high modernism, this form of modernism, especially its populist side (the tradition that is audible in modernity-oriented modernist writers) seems lacking in "detachment," hence appears to be "not really" modernist.

5

Mary Antin: Progressive Optimism against Odds

In a short sketch called "First Aid to the Alien" and published in *Outlook* in 1912, Mary Antin describes a trolley-car encounter between an American botanist and the little Italian immigrant boy Tomaso Verticelli. Upset by the mess that Italian children have made in the car, and by the helplessness of the conductor who cannot get through to the immigrants because they do not understand a word he is saying, the botanist sternly lectures the little boy, "*No—rubbish—on—the—floor,*" adding, "That's not *American.*" The Italian boy and his sister seem to understand, and, "like a pair of brown monkeys," they clean the car thoroughly. Later, the boy's teacher discovers that "Thomas" Verticelli strangely believes that the Star-Spangled Banner stands for "America! *No rubbish on the floor!*"[1]

This streetcar encounter resembles that of Stein's "Gentle Lena" more than that of the *Independent*'s southern colored woman, for it seems to show an act of kindness, of "first aid," among strangers on an electric car. Yet Antin's light and vaguely humorous vignette also represents the issue of "Americanization" as a problem of cleanliness, implies that it was foreign-tongued immigrants who made America dirty, and suggests that the problem could be resolved by education, and especially by teaching the English language and American patriotism. The story literally shows "dirty foreigners" (as xenophobic propaganda would vilify immigrants) but then proceeds to persuade the reader that a goodhearted, scholarly Yankee father figure can get the right message across, even to "monkey"-like little aliens. In other words, Antin engaged the negative stereotype, and even accepted some validity in it, in order to transform it. The strategy of going into the stereotype in order to overcome it was characteristic of much of Antin's writing, including her autobiography *The Promised Land* (1912), probably the most outstanding American immigrant autobiography of the twentieth century.[2]

Antin, the daughter of Israel and Esther Weltman Antin, was born in Polotzk in Czarist Russia (now Belarus) on June 13, 1881. Her father emigrated to the United States in 1891, and three years later the mother followed with the four children, arriving in Boston on the *Polynesia* on May 8, 1894. The Antin family lived in generally poor circumstances in the Boston area, where Mary and the younger siblings began public school in Chelsea, whereas her sister "Fetchke/Frieda," only a year older than Mary, had to work as a seamstress. Though Antin's native language was Yiddish, and she came to Boston at age thirteen without knowing a word of English, she became an excellent writer in the English language. As she put it memorably, "I learned at least to think in English without an accent" (282).

Antin was keenly interested in modernity and developed an elaborate contrast between the "medieval" Old World and modern America. Yet her writing clearly was not modernist. She directly attempted to address the "ethnic question" that hung in the air in the period. And she gave much room not only to her social self, but also to some of her inner motives and feelings.

There is no doubt that Antin was deeply aware of the growing hostility to immigration in the United States, for she campaigned in lectures and in much of her published writing against the immigration restrictions that were legislated in 1917, 1921, and 1924. Yet she was among ethnic writers who published autobiographic writing that not only answered the ethnic questionnaire (so familiar from Hamilton Holt's *Life Stories*) but also offered glimpses of a subtle self-revelation that had much power independent of the social context of the immigration debate.

Antin's autobiographic writing followed a trajectory that made her wonderfully representative of the times. Her writing career started with a personal letter in Yiddish about her emigration experience that she sent to an uncle in 1894. She later translated this account into English (with some dramatic changes) and published it, in a circle of philanthropists and Jewish intellectuals, under the title *From Plotzk to Boston* (1899), the printer misspelling the name of her home town Polotzk. The little book carried a glowing introduction by Israel Zangwill, whose celebrated immigrant melodrama *The Melting-Pot* (1908) helped to popularize the term that would soon be commonly used to describe American ethnic assimilation. The essayist Josephine Lazarus—the sister of Statue of Liberty poet Emma Lazarus—reviewed the volume, and Antin became known as a child prodigy, all the more so since it was generally believed that she was two years younger than her actual age. Antin also benefited from the South End Settlement House of Edward Everett Hale—who was famous for such literary works as "The Man Without a Country" (1863)—and she described her own experiences with allusions to Hale's novella, as when she states that in Russia Jews had been "a people without a country" (178). She alludes to the bible, to Augustine's *Confessions*, *Robinson Crusoe* (which she read in translation while she was still in Russia), Coleridge's Ancient Mariner, Emerson's essays, Sewell's *Black Beauty*, Sue's *Wandering Jew*, and the Aladdin of the *Arabian Nights*, Robert Louis Stevenson, George Eliot, Mark Twain, Tennyson, Longfellow, and Whittier. She also mentions popular works ranging from Russian and Yiddish periodical romances to Jacob Abbott's *Rollo* series (which started in 1839) and George Madden Martin's *Emmy Lou: Her Book & Heart* (1902). In short, her literary canon was extensive, and it was also exclusively premodernist. For a Russian immigrant, it was also a remarkably western list; one notices the absence of those great Russian writers whom Claude McKay saw as embodiments of the modern spirit: Gogol, Dostoyevsky, Tolstoy, Chekhov, and Turgenyev.

At age thirty she carried out the project of a full-length literary autobiography, some chapters of which appeared first in Ellery Sedgwick's prestigious *Atlantic Monthly*. In April, 1912, the leading publishing house in Boston, Houghton Mifflin Company, printed the nicely designed book, illustrated with eighteen photographs, and with a golden Statue of Liberty in outline engraved on the front cover, its torch on the spine. The dust jacket, also decorated with a Statue of Liberty, carried the subtitle "The Autobiography of a Russian Immigrant" which appeared nowhere else in the book.

In its twenty chapters, *The Promised Land* gives a vivid account of the author's life in Russia and America, of her childhood, her emigration to Boston, and her Americanization in the public schools. She comes across as a precocious, intellectually probing Jewish child and a happy and observant American adolescent and adult. She had to face much adversity: as a girl in Polotzk, she was excluded from the world of Jewish learning;

and because of her father's occupational failings, she lived under truly poor circumstances in and around Boston. However, as a teacher's pet, she thrived in American school, and the autobiography sounds a note of promise. She pioneers in articulating what became known as "the American dream" ("'America' became my dream," she writes [114], reacting to her father's America letter), embraces America as "my country" (thus rewriting Hale), and ultimately comes to consider herself the "heir of the ages," a biblical phrasing that had been used by Tennyson, John Fiske, and Henry James.

> America is the youngest of the nations, and inherits all that went before in history. And I am the youngest of America's children, and into my hands is given all her priceless heritage, to the last white star espied through the telescope, to the last great thought of the philosopher. Mine is the whole majestic past, and mine is the shining future. (286)

This is the upbeat end of the narrative, followed in the manuscript by a bold "FINIS." Antin's book was published three years after Gertrude Stein had so heartlessly undermined the literary convention of endings. *The Promised Land* reaches such an emphatic crescendo that the end was brought out on a 78 r.p.m. record, read by an agitated male voice. This climactic ending was not only explicitly premodern (in the sense that it adhered to the very conventions Stein sought to undermine), but it also appealed to the general reader and was used as social evidence in books like William P. Shriver's *Immigrant Forces: Factors in the New Democracy* (1913).

In her approach to the frail magic of memory, Antin is representative of the importance of the act of remembering in immigrant literature. *The Promised Land* is the self-conscious, and self-consciously literary, attempt to give aesthetic shape, in remarkably subtle language, to what remain recognizable as fragile memories, wrested from the threatening gray blank of oblivion and cold facts. Memories may fail to return when she invokes them, as the excellent American cherries she eats in a concentrated effort to bring back the taste of Russia cannot evoke in her the fragrant sweet remembrance of things past. She recognizes that this is not just a matter of the contrast between the two countries of her life: "And if I should return to Polotzk, and buy me a measure of cherries at a market stall, and pay for it with a Russian groschen, would the market woman be generous enough to throw in that haunting flavor? I fear I should find that the old species of cherry is extinct in Polotzk." On the other hand, memories may suddenly erupt, as when eating "ripe, red, American strawberries" she is shocked to experience, in breathless amazement, the "very flavor and aroma of some strawberries" she ate twenty years earlier (75).

Antin started her autobiography as she looked back to half a life spent in the Old World and half in the New. "I was born, I have lived, and I have been made over. Is it not time to write my life's story?" she asks at the opening, and it is at this point that she considers herself "absolutely other than the person whose story I have to tell" (1). From the manuscript stage on, her autobiography was always more or less evenly divided between a Russian and an American half.

As a good stylist, Antin supplements her description of the immigration experience by sounding out the vocabulary commonly used to explain it. She writes that she was "transplanted to the new soil" at a most impressionable age: "All the processes of uprooting, transportation, replanting, acclimatization, and development took place in my own soul" (3). And she applied the language of the biblical Exodus to the secular migration from Russia to America, with such chapter headings as "The Tree of Knowledge," "Manna," and "The Burning Bush."

Antin made many fresh and some startling observations. She captures the sense of endlessness that the Russian railroad tracks in Polotzk conveyed to her as a child—a technologically modern feature present in her "mediæval" childhood (36). Later, the view of the "dim tangle of the railroad tracks below" South Boston Bridge gives Antin a sense of the difficulty of finding her own "proper track" (233–234). She is also fascinated by Boston streetcars, the "constant clang and whirr of electric cars" (226), and she plays the dangerous children's game of cutting "across the tracks in front of an oncoming car" (209). "[I]t was great fun to see the motorman's angry face turn scared, when he thought I was going to be shaved this time sure" (209). She uses images of modernity to account for her own situation, and that of immigrants in general. "We are the strands of the cable that binds the Old World to the New," she writes (2). She comments hauntingly on the fears of death the emigrants experienced when they underwent compulsory disinfection in Germany, on their way from Russia to America.

> [O]ur things were taken away, our friends separated from us; a man came to inspect us, as if to ascertain our full value; strange-looking people driving us about like dumb animals, helpless and unresisting; children we could not see crying in a way that suggested terrible things; ourselves driven into a little room where a great kettle was boiling on a little stove; our clothes taken off, our bodies rubbed with a slippery substance that might be any bad thing; a shower of warm water let down on us without warning; again driven to another little room where we sit, wrapped in woollen blankets till large, coarse bags are brought in, their contents turned out, and we see only a cloud of steam, and hear the women's orders to dress ourselves,—"Quick! Quick!"—or else we'll miss—something we cannot hear. We are forced to pick out our clothes from among all the others, with the steam blinding us; we choke, cough, entreat the women to give us time; they persist, "Quick! Quick!—or you'll miss the train!" Oh, so we really won't be murdered! They are only making us ready for the continuing of our journey, cleaning us of all suspicion of dangerous sickness. Thank God! (138)

(This passage was adapted from the Yiddish letter she wrote to her uncle at age thirteen and that was freely translated and first published in *From Plotzk to Boston* in 1899, where Antin continued that they were "assured by the word 'train.'"[3] This sample attests to her early gift as a writer.)

In *The Promised Land* Antin distinguishes the horrifying crowd description of the Russian pogrom—"They attacked them with knives and clubs and scythes and axes, killed them or tortured them, and burned their houses"—from the elating and freeing crowd experience among the milling pedestrians in Chelsea: "A million threads of life and love and sorrow was the common street; and whether we would or not, we entangled ourselves in a common maze" (205).

Again and again, Antin is drawn to explain the vocabulary of her Old World past and of Jewishness, and a linguistic glossary is appended to *The Promised Land*. This is an exceptionally detailed instance of a widespread strategy in ethnic writing. Such a glossary cannot be a systematic instrument; yet it establishes Antin as the mediator who gives to the English-speaking non-Jewish reader (for whom it was prepared and who was imagined by Antin to be ignorant of and perhaps even somewhat hostile to Jews) a minimal ethnic vocabulary. That this is not done value-free is apparent when one reads, for example, under "*Hasid*, pl. *Hasidim*": "A numerous sect of Jews distinguished for their enthusiasm in religious observance, a fanatical worship of their rabbis and many superstitious practices" (290).

One purpose of *The Promised Land* was to offset a growing sense of American nativist hostility to immigration by presenting a young woman's consciousness that successfully underwent the transformation from foreign immigrant to American citizen. Antin at times addresses the imagined Gentile reader as "my American friend" and tries to convince him or her of her point: "What if the ragpicker's daughters are hastening over the ocean to teach your children in the public schools?" (140). (These direct addresses to the reader are in the old vein of Harriet Beecher Stowe, not in the Steinian fashion.)

Antin's American patriotism gives poor Jewish immigrants a special place and an entitlement. In America, a senator and an obscure child from the slums may "seal a democratic friendship based on the love of a common flag" (269). Shouts like "Three cheers for the Red, White, and Blue!" (181, 204) are justified in a country in which a Jewish immigrant school girl can recite poems addressed to Washington, as Antin famously did. Interestingly, while this poem establishes Antin's Americanization, she also states that "a special note" ran through her patriotic Washington poem that "only Israel Rubinstein and Beckie Aronovitch," her Jewish classmates, "could have fully understood" (183). Her homemaking myth is that Jewish immigrants have a special understanding; paradoxically, that is what makes them ideal Americans.

Antin cheers the Red, White, and Blue at another, more troubling occasion when she praises the American system of justice for punishing a "great, hulky colored boy, who was the torment of the neighborhood" and had treated her "roughly." The court hearing seemed completely fair to her. "The evil-doer was actually punished, and not the victim, as might very easily happen in a similar case in Russia. 'Liberty and justice for all.' Three cheers for the Red, White, and Blue!" (203–204). It is remarkable that Antin is not able here to imagine any analogies between the roles of Jews in the Pale and of blacks in turn-of-the-century America.

What interests Antin foremost is the psychological consequence of the social experience of immigration on her as a child and as an adult. She embarks upon the course of becoming an American, but she does not suppress how difficult the shift in immigrant orientation can be. Like many other immigrants, Antin movingly evokes the specific tastes of her homeland: she recognizes that it takes history to make a Polotzk cheesecake, and concedes that the fragrance of childhood cherries may be lost even in the Russia of the author's later years. Thus it is all the more remarkable that even though her faith in America is expressed in such metaphors as "manna," America hardly seems appetizing. In Boston, the family may eat "without any cooking, from little tin cans that had printing all over them" (146). By far the most detailed American eating scene Antin describes is also a haunting ethnic loyalty test. When her Chelsea schoolteacher Miss Mary S. Dillingham invites her to tea, Antin realizes that the strange meat served to her was "ham—forbidden food." She is afraid, then angry at her weakness:

> I to be afraid of a pink piece of pig's flesh, who had defied at least two religions in defence of free thought! And I began to reduce my ham to indivisible atoms, determined to eat more of it than anybody else at the table.
>
> Alas! I learned that to eat in defence of principles was not so easy as to talk. I ate, but only a newly abnegated Jew can understand with what squirming, what protesting of the inner man, what exquisite abhorrence of myself. (196)

Taking "possession" (as she repeatedly puts it) of the New World was also like swallowing down undesirable food, in defense of principles but over the protests of her "inner man," her conscience that accuses her of ethnic treason. What is all the more disturbing about this scene is that this was Antin's "first entrance into a genuine American household" (196) and that her host was the well-intentioned teacher who brought about Antin's first publication of a school composition and who encouraged her to translate her emigration letter into English. Is the stilling of her "hunger" for reading and writing, of which she repeatedly speaks, in any way connected with this painful, traumatic scene of kin betrayal and self-destruction? And does her experience not dramatize the anxiety of many ethnic intellectuals that, in giving up religiously-based maxims of their childhood, they might not be joining, on an equal footing, an international group of modern, cosmopolitan freethinkers but only ingratiating themselves to the host society's sets of superstitions based on another, an alien religion that merely passes itself off as more "modern"?

Antin is extremely self-conscious of the autobiographic project and articulates, in a first-person narrative, the lure of other identity (and pronoun) options in order to examine her pervasive sense of doubleness: "I could speak in the third person and not feel that I was masquerading. I can analyze my subject; I can reveal everything; for *she,* and not *I,* is my real heroine" (1). The word "heroine" suggests the conscious use of novelistic strategies. Of all the American immigrant narratives in which pronoun confusion abounds, Antin's may be the most self-conscious. Antin even proposed to her editor Ellery Sedgwick that she would use her own (maiden) name only on the title page, but a "different name—Esther Altmann, as I have it—in the text."[4] ("Esther Altmann" would have been the symmetrical opposite of Henry James's "Christopher Newman," for Esther was not only Antin's mother's first name, but also an allusion to the biblical figure of the queen who saved the Jews in Persia, and the surname literally means "old man" and is evocative of old-world origins, but also close to Antin's mother's maiden name Weltman.)

Antin's interactions with the Boston editor are telling, for Sedgwick published such genteel little pieces as Estelle M. Hart's "Trolley-Car Ornithology," *Atlantic Monthly* (1908), which encouraged tramway riders to watch birds on ordinary routes since "more of their habits can be noted from a rushing trolley-car than one would at first thought deem possible."[5] But he also ran Randolph Bourne's essay "Trans-National America" (1916), with the central tenet of which he strongly disagreed; in a letter Sedgwick criticized Bourne for sounding "as though the last immigrant should have as great an effect upon the determination of our history as the first band of Englishmen."[6] Tellingly, Sedgwick seriously questioned the wisdom of Randolph Bourne's vision of a transnational America, and simply turned down Gertrude Stein's submissions, but he was very hospitable to Mary Antin—who in their correspondence teasingly asked the Boston Brahmin editor to verify the spelling of some Yiddish words for her.

The book's stylistic range is impressive, from lyrical-mystical to historical-descriptive, from analytical to evocative, from understated to emphatic passages, and from somber notes to the humor of sudden punch lines; it is not surprising that it became a big success. Reviews were often enthusiastic, and the book's welcoming reception in public libraries and educational institutions was especially remarkable: Sedgwick had already noticed the interest of librarians who are "in contact with a large number of foreign-born" when the selection "My Country" was published in the *Atlantic Monthly,* but in the summer of 1912 the *New York Sun* reported "the name of the books most called-for at the various libraries; and Mary Antin's name 'led all the rest.'"[7] *The Promised*

Land was also published in special educational editions with teacher's manuals and student questions, and it was used as public-school civics-class text as late as 1949. It has been taken, with Abraham Cahan's fiction, as the beginning of Jewish literature in America. The editors of the *Outlook* hardly overstated the case when they observed: "Few recent American books have made as strong an impression on the reading public as 'The Promised Land'"[8]; and the publisher also ran blurbs by Louis D. Brandeis and Rabbi Stephen S. Wise. Antin's success undoubtedly inspired the writing of autobiographies by other immigrants to the United States.

It goes without saying that there were also negative voices. The same Mike Gold who accused Gertrude Stein of "literary idiocy" attacked Antin, with similar restraint, for explaining "away all the horror and injustice man has established." Gold calls Antin a "bright slum parvenu who wrote that exuberant book of gratitude." As if she had not written about slums and tenements, Gold addresses and admonishes her directly: "See, Mary, how the . . . roaches and bedbugs venture from our moldy walls." He concludes: "America's slums could never dim the faith of Mary Antin in the spirit of '76, for she and her type have climbed up into a place in the bourgeois sun, and they are grateful—so grateful for their deliverance! Ah, the good God; ah, the Promised Land!"[9] Published in the radical, low-circulation *Liberator*, and six years after the publication of *The Promised Land*, Gold's comment did little to stem the book's success.

Newspapers and periodicals praised Antin's patriotism and compared her with Benjamin Franklin, Jacob Riis, Carl Schurz, Booker T. Washington, W. E. B. Du Bois, and James Weldon Johnson. Reviewers accentuated both the individual and the ethnic aspects of the autobiography, viewing Antin as an "extreme individualist" and the book as "a treatise on sociology, of which education is the dominant feature."[10] With the success of her autobiography, Antin's career seemed made. Yet success was not to be her ultimate destiny.

Under the management of the Boston agency "The Players," she embarked upon a lucrative career as a public lecturer speaking on behalf of Progressive causes and in favor of immigrants. She also showed a rather moderate feminist side (more moderate at least than Roosevelt thought), claiming her right as "woman" and as "immigrant" to speak as a "citizen." She said before the election of 1912: "I am not a suffragist, but I wish I had a vote just this once." Her wish for America to be "the leading nation of this age in respect to justice and humanity" made her want to "send a Progressive President to the White House." This would also be good for immigrants. "I call the attention of all naturalized citizens to the fact that the Progressive party is the only one that has any idea of what is due to the immigrant," she concluded, thus making a special appeal to the immigrant vote.[11]

She traveled extensively and lectured on such topics as "The Responsibility of American Citizenship," "The Civic Education of the Immigrant," "The Public School as a Test of American Faith," "Jewish Life in the Pale: A Lesson for Americans," or "The Zionist Movement." She contributed a series of essays to *American Magazine* that then became her last book, *They Who Knock at Our Gates: A Complete Gospel of Immigration,* published in 1914, again by Houghton Mifflin Company, Mary Antin's Progressive plea for the immigrant and her impassioned brief against immigration restriction.

The book was illustrated by Joseph Stella, the Italian immigrant whose work had already taken a modernist turn toward his famous Brooklyn Bridge images and become popular in the wake of the Armory Show; yet the portraits used here by Antin were of his earlier, realistic stage, and some had previously accompanied such write-ups of immigrants as "A Mixing Bowl for Nations" by Ernest Poole (one of the ghostwriters for the *Life Stories*) in *Everybody's Magazine* (1910). Joseph Stella had also illustrated Poole's novel *The Voice of the Street* (1906) and produced the perfect visual equivalent to Holt's *Life Stories* when he published in the *Outlook* of 1905 a collection of images called "Americans in the Rough: Character Studies at Ellis Island." Stella's images enhanced the "typical" reading of specimen of various ethnic groups in the United States, and their titles—such as "A Russian Jew" or "Pittsburgh Types"; they could vary from one use of an image to another—asked the viewer to think of the specific person who was represented in terms of larger, often ethnic, collective abstractions. For Stella, an aesthetic turning point came in 1913 during a bus ride to Coney Island when he was struck by the amusement park's "dazzling array of lights" and decided to abandon his earlier realist style for a "new kind of art" in order to be able to capture the "brilliance and the dynamic energy of modern life so evident in America."[12] And he focused on subjects like the New York skyscrapers, Brooklyn Bridge, and on such trite settings of modernity as gas tanks (that would also be threateningly present in *Call It Sleep* when David accompanies his father on the milk delivery route). At this time, then,

Stella was widely identified with the modern movement, yet Antin chose his earlier, realistic charcoals of immigrant types as illustrations for *They Who Knock*.

What Antin had done on an individual level in *The Promised Land*, she now extended to a full social view of America as a country in which Jewish immigrants can rightly invoke Pilgrims and Revolutionary heroes as "our Fathers." "The notion of the dignity of man, which is the foundation of the gospel of democracy, is derived from Hebrew sources, as the Psalm-singing founders of New England would be the first to acknowledge," she writes. And: "many of the Russian refugees of to-day are a little ahead of the Mayflower troop, because they have in their own lifetime sustained the double ordeal of fight and flight, with all their attendant risks and shocks."[13]

Like her autobiography, *They Who Knock* featured the Statue of Liberty on the cover. For Antin was a pioneer in supporting Emma Lazarus's reading of the Statue as a symbol of welcome to immigrants. Antin also offered a mild correction to the ambiguous phrase "wretched refuse" from Lazarus's poem "The New Colossus" that was affixed to the Statue in 1903 but became increasingly identified with the Statue only after immigration was stopped in 1924. Antin found "convincing proof that what we get in the steerage is not the refuse but the sinew and bone of all the nations," a statement that was particularly emphasized by Joseph Stella's heroic-realist immigrant portrait that served as the book's frontispiece: "THE SINEW AND BONE OF ALL THE NATIONS." What Antin did for the Statue of Liberty, she boldly extended to core symbols of the American nation: "The ghost of the Mayflower pilots every immigrant ship, and Ellis Island is another name for Plymouth Rock," she wrote, imagining the United States as a cosmopolitan model nation in which no background should convey any particular privilege.[14]

Though Mike Gold had criticized Mary Antin rather sharply, his book *Jews Without Money* (1930) not only contained a juvenile Washington poem resembling Antin's but also elaborated the analogy Antin made between modern mass immigration and the Pilgrims' arrival. In a chapter that starts with the young narrator's discovery that some new immigrant family is sleeping in his bed, "in their foreign baggy underwear" and smelling "of Ellis Island disinfectant, a stink that sickened me like castor oil," Gold goes on with the pronouncement that "every tenement home was a Plymouth Rock like ours."[15] Louis Adamic, who in 1917 arrived in the United States from Austrian Slovenia at age seventeen, was to develop the rhetorical fusion of Plymouth Rock and Ellis Island further in the 1930s and 1940s; at the time Antin was writing, this was still a very radical proposition. Nobody could have foreseen that it would one day become the rationale for the Ellis Island Museum. After all, in 1956 the Eisenhower administration was ready, two years after the immigration center had closed, to put up Ellis Island for sale and private development.

Antin used the title *They Who Knock at Our Gates* and started a representative sentence with the phrasing, "If we took our mission seriously,—as seriously, say, as the Jews take theirs..."[16] Antin's "we" obviously refers to non-Jewish Americans. As has already become apparent, this confusion of pronouns was common in ethnic autobiography and literature: the Jewish immigrant Edward Steiner wrote similarly in *From Alien to Citizen* (1914), "whether or not we threw the immigrant to the dogs did not matter, so long as he was eaten up and his bones gnawed free of anything foreign."[17] In Antin's case the pronoun switching had the effect that she was not pleading "we, who knock at your gates," but, having become an American, was assuming "the American point of view." Yet at the same time she stylized immigrants as more protypically "American" than "native born citizens" who were bent on restricting immigration and had lost the sense of Pilgrim and Revolutionary beginnings. Antin thus offered more than merely a personal or Jewish-American homemaking myth: hers was a homemaking myth writ large that included all immigrants to the United States.

6

Who Is "American"?

What Mary Antin argued in her autobiography and her lectures constituted in the eyes of some critics an erosion of the word "American." As that word was increasingly claimed, or "usurped," by "aliens," alternative terms were launched such as "100% Americans," "native Americans," "only Americans," "real Americans," or "American-Americans." Edward Bok asked in his second autobiography, *Twice Thirty: Some Short and Simple Annals of the Road* (1925): "How many of us, born here or elsewhere, could qualify as a 'hundred per cent American?' Scarcely one, because, in truth, there is no such American."[1] Yet both Brander Matthews and Nicholas Roosevelt resorted to the term "American-Americans" when they critically reviewed Horace Kallen's 1924 book of essays *Culture and Democracy in the United States,* the book in which Kallen introduced to print the term "cultural pluralism," Matthews under the worried headline, "Making America a Racial Crazy-Quilt." The negatively charged image of the quilt which also appeared in satirical cartoons of the cubists at the Armory Show had yet to be reimagined as a positive symbol of America's happily diverse folk heritage.

Antin's own story of Americanization served as a litmus test for the meaning of the word "American." The New Englander Barrett Wendell, who was among the first professors of English to teach American literature at Harvard University, wrote in a letter of 1917 that Antin "has developed an irritating habit of describing herself and her people as Americans, in distinction from such folks as [Wendell's wife] Edith and me, who have been here for three hundred years."[2] For Wendell—whose conceit of epic longevity was more sedentary and New World-based than Antin's metaphorical medievalism—being "American" specifically meant *not* being "Hebrew" or "Ethiopian." Yet Wendell, like Mary Antin, also identified the original Puritan settlers and Old Testament Jews. Perhaps he believed even in an actual kinship, although he found it impossible to include twentieth-century Jewish immigrants in the "American" category.

Wendell articulated his opinion of Antin in a personal letter to an English friend. Yet the provocation embodied by Antin's stance also led to a more public debate about the nature of "America" and the question of just *who* was entitled to call it "our country" or to view Pilgrims and Revolutionaries as ancestors. Whereas some native-born liberals praised Antin for her "admiration" of America, and some immigrant readers found her "gratitude" toward her new country disloyal to her origins, the conservative journalist Agnes Repplier was among those Americans who were troubled by Antin's presumptuousness in calling the Pilgrim fathers "our forefathers" as well as by her critical attitude. "[W]hy should the recipient of so much attention be the one to scold us harshly, to rail at conditions she imperfectly understands, to reproach us for . . . our slackness in duty, our failure to observe the precepts and fulfill the intentions of those pioneers whom she kindly, but confusedly, calls '*our* forefathers.'" Repplier, who failed to see any parallels between Plymouth Rock and Ellis Island, expressed her wartime fear that, for example, German-Americans would now fight the battle of Germany in the American ballot by supporting neutralist peace candidates, and argued pointedly that no other nation cherishes the melting-pot illusion, for "An Englishman knows that a Russian Jew cannot in five years, or in twenty-five years, become English."[3]

It must have been particularly troubling for Antin to find Repplier's sentiment on the pages of "her" *Atlantic Monthly,* edited by "her" editor Ellery Sedgwick, a man with whom she corresponded as late as 1937. Repplier seemed to resent Antin, and she even invoked the Jewish immigrant philosopher Horace Kallen in order to support her dislike of "Mrs. Amadeus Grabau," alluding publicly to the fact that Antin had married an "American" (a Christian, with a foreign-sounding surname). Kallen, who had been one of Wendell's and James's students at Harvard, was described by William James as "a Russian Jew by birth, very intense in character, very able and with high potentialities of all round cultivation, an enthusiastic and aggressive 'pragmatist,' an active political worker, a *decidedly* original mind, neurotic disposition."[4] In his critical essay, "Democracy Versus the Melting-Pot," published in the *Nation* in 1915, Kallen, who was also one of Antin's correspondents and friends, partly adopted Antin's argument and compared Polish immigrants with the Pilgrims when he wrote: "the urge that carries [the Poles] in such numbers to America is not so unlike that which carried the pilgrim fathers"; yet he also criticized Antin for being "intermarried, 'assimilated' even in religion, and more excessively, self-consciously flatteringly American than the Americans."[5] Still, it was assimilation, full American identity, even if claimed unilaterally by declaration of will rather than by American birth or by easy acceptance from old-stock Americans, that entitled Antin to criticize her adopted "promised land"—or to praise it for qualities the United States would still have to acquire by fully including people like her. It was as if Antin was saying, Yes! in thunder.

The radical Columbia intellectual and culture critic Randolph Bourne was acutely aware of the political implications of the Brahmins' critical reactions to Mary Antin's claims. Bourne was depicted vividly in "Newsreel 22" of John Dos Passos's *Nineteen Nineteen* (1932); and the ever-critical Mike Gold praised Bourne for examining "all the political and economic facts . . . when he discussed literature."[6] The term "Brahmin" had been coined in Oliver Wendell Holmes's novel *Elsie Venner* (1859) where it referred to a collegiate "race of scholars" different from the common country boy. Among American intellectuals who embraced the term were not only old-stock descendants but also upwardly mobile young men, some of whom had married into old families. Such intellectuals also adopted and increasingly stressed the symbols of the *Mayflower* and Plymouth Rock as mythic points of origin. Bourne understood that this invented Brahmin identity served as a tool for excluding immigrants. "We have had to watch," Bourne wrote in his famous programmatic essay of 1916, "Trans-National America," "hard-hearted old Brahmins virtuously indignant at the spectacle of the immigrant refusing to be melted, while they jeer at patriots like Mary Antin who write about 'our forefathers.'" Against that position Bourne argued memorably: "We are all foreign-born or the descendants of foreign-born, and if distinctions are to be made between us they should rightly be on some other grounds than indigenousness."[7] For Ellery Sedgwick who criticized Bourne in letters, the United States "was created by English instinct and dedicated to the Anglo-Saxon ideal," and Bourne's essay was thus simply a "radical and unpatriotic paper"—though he did publish it in the *Atlantic Monthly*.⁸

In the course of Bourne's essay he entered a dialogue with Antin, who had let an American teacher tell the immigrant protagonist David Rudinsky in her story "The Lie" (published in the *Atlantic Monthly* in 1913): "Every ship that brings your people from Russia and other countries where they are ill-treated is a *Mayflower*."⁹ Bourne set a different accent:

> Mary Antin is right when she looks upon our foreign-born as the people who missed the Mayflower and came over on the first boat they could find. But she forgets that when they did come it was not upon other Mayflowers, but upon a "Maiblume," a "Fleur du mai," a "Fior di Maggio," a "Majblomst."¹⁰

While implying in this example that various ethnic histories could be understood simply as "translations" of an original *Mayflower* voyage, Bourne did perceive the tremendous cultural opportunity of creating a cosmopolitan civilization that thrives upon the linguistic and cultural richness that ethnic variety brings to a country in which each citizen could also remain connected with another language and another culture. Bourne opposed the English orientation in American culture that Antin had come to love and the requirement that all non-English newcomers shed their cultural, religious, or linguistic pasts, yet he did not think that immigrants would or could remain fixed to their pasts. Instead Bourne advocated the new ideal of "dual citizenship" both for immigrants who came to the United States (104), and for the increasing number of internationally oriented individuals who, like American expatriates in France, were born in one country but went on to live in another. In Bourne's hands the contemplation of Americanness in the face of ethnic diversity led to a reconsideration of the nationalist premises of citizenship.

Yet Bourne's pluralism also alienated radical young intellectuals like him from working people—except insofar as they belonged to distinct ethnic groups. Nowhere is Bourne's blind spot more apparent than in his disdain for assimilation. He writes: "It is not the Jew who sticks proudly to the faith of his fathers and boasts of that venerable culture of his who is dangerous to America, but the Jew who has lost the Jewish fire and become a mere elementary, grasping animal" (99).

It must have been hard for Antin to find that a friend could be so insensitive toward the position she had presented. She had written in *The

Promised Land, with the noted nod to Edward Everett Hale, that in Russia Jews had been "a people without a country," making the great love of "a little Jewish girl from Polotzk" for "her new country" all the more understandable and genuine (178–179). It is telling that Bourne echoed Antin's adaptation of Hale's phrase when he deplored the assimilated "men and women without a spiritual country, cultural outlaws without taste, without standards but those of the mob" (99)—all of this in the context of a passage that reserves animal imagery for the assimilated and employs the nativist term "hordes" to describe them. Bourne's transnationalism preferred stable ethnic identities based on fixed national origins, a dilemma of many pluralist models of American culture from the 1920s to the age of multiculturalism. Antin's advocacy of assimilation was thus controversial to the hostile Repplier on the restrictionist right as well as to the friendly Bourne on the pluralist left. Neither political camp provided much room for an assimilated immigrant who claimed an American identity and the full rights of a citizen.

What it would mean to an immigrant child to sing "Land where my fathers died," or "our fodders" in *Call It Sleep,* was a question both Antin and Henry Roth asked. Can the "founding fathers" be the symbolic "fathers" of children whose real fathers are visible reminders of their own foreignness, who retain exotic accents, fail to conform to American codes, live in the worst neighborhoods, and may ardently believe in America as something to which they can never belong though their children or children's children might? This question, that nativism as well as cultural pluralism of the 1920s came to resolve more and more negatively, was boldly and unequivocally answered with a "yes" by Mary Antin, whose autobiography constituted not only a success story but also a provocation. The patriotism of much of her writing was connected with an egalitarian hope, especially for an integrative, open-door policy toward new immigrants. Yet it was a hope that was to be dashed. The big public and private crisis for Antin came with World War I. It was, in fact the context of the War in which Repplier, Kallen, and Bourne had argued with Antin.

The Promised Land implies that Antin graduated from Boston Latin School and went on to Radcliffe College. The facts of life were somewhat grimmer: she never finished high school or became a regular college student anywhere. And her life took a sharp downturn that was marked by the caesura of World War I. At the time when she wrote *The Promised*

Land, Antin was living in New York and was married, against her father's wishes, to Amadeus William Grabau, a (non-Jewish) German-American science professor at Columbia, who is never mentioned in *The Promised Land,* yet who is implicitly addressed throughout. Some of Antin's cosmically mystical language also appears to echo or foreshadow such Grabau works as "Paleontology and Ontogeny" (1910) or *The Rhythm of the Ages: Earth History in the Light of the Pulsation and Polar Control Theories* (1940). The language of the study of nature permeates the book from the way in which Antin traces her genealogical origins on a paleontological time frame to the inspiration she gets in the "stupendous panorama which is painted in the literature of Darwinism" and in the "book of cosmogony" to learn about what she calls the "promised land of evolution."[11]

In New York City and Scarsdale, Antin and Grabau led a rich social life during the few golden years in her literary and public life that had started with the publication in the *Atlantic Monthly* of the magnificent short story "Malinke's Atonement" (1911), worthy of comparison with Sholem Aleichem's tales. Antin corresponded with Theodore Roosevelt, Horace Kallen, and the literary critic Van Wyck Brooks, entertained such diverse figures as Randolph Bourne, Rabbi Abraham Cronbach, also a correspondent who later published a warm memoir of Antin, and, her profession unknown to Antin, the prostitute Maimie Pinzer, who wrote a mean-spirited account of her visit to Antin's house in a letter to Fanny Howe. The Grabaus' circle included writers, artists, scientists, rabbis, and ministers, Christians and Zionists. Though both Antin and Grabau were very busy professionally, their relationship, a Gentile-Christian intermarriage of a native American Lutheran of German ancestry and a naturalized American freethinker of East European Jewish origins, seems to have been very harmonious. Antin referred to her husband, who was eleven years her senior, as her "counselor and guardian."[12]

The War ended that. Antin remembered a decade later that World War I turned her husband "into a dreadful hostile stranger who terrorized the household and scandalized the community (no, I am not exaggerating; these are matters of history)" and that as a consequence, she suffered a nervous breakdown.[13] The native-born Grabau, who also experienced serious setbacks in health, argued for an American neutralist position in the War, which was considered pro-German and simply untenable for a German-American in the propagandistically heated war climate of 1917

America, lost his position at Columbia, accepted the invitation to become director of research for the China Geological Survey, moved to Peking, and ended up spending the rest of his life as an active and prolific scientist in China. The foreign-born American patriot Antin firmly supported the Allied cause. Their daughter later remembered that the War was fought right in their home. Antin felt that an *Atlantic Monthly* article on "Wives of German-Americans" portrayed the general situation so accurately that it might well have been written with her case specifically in mind. The marriage broke up. At the same time, her father died, the Scarsdale house was sold at a great loss, and she was left destitute after being released from psychiatric care. She spent many years at Gould Farm in the Berkshires, was connected at some points with Zionism but also became deeply interested in Christian universalism, the Indian mystic Meher Baba, and Rudolf Steiner's anthroposophy. She had become estranged from her political positions and felt, after the victory of the immigration restrictionists, that *They Who Knock* had become so dated that she wanted Houghton Mifflin to stop selling the book she now contemptuously called "The Knockers."

Antin's disillusionment was stark. In 1895 her dream of seeing the patriotic poetry she wrote on Washington's birthday published in the Boston *Herald* was fulfilled. In *The Promised Land* Antin wrote up this experience with enthusiasm and mentioned that she dreamed of finding her name "Antin, Mary" in an encyclopedic dictionary, not far from "Alcott, Louisa M." In 1926, however, when she was asked by the publicity department of Houghton Mifflin to contribute something for a portrait gallery of contemporary New Englanders for the Boston *Herald*, she sarcastically commented that it would "soon be time for them to reheat the patriotic hash from *The Promised Land* which they have served up at shortish intervals, about Washington's Birthday, ever since Houghton Mifflin have been paying me royalties."[14] She called her bitter self-assessment a "nice obituary," and she published only two more pieces—one of them, an account of a mystical vision—in the remaining twenty-three years of her life.

7

American Languages

H. L. Mencken was always a provocative essayist, ready to surprise his readers with unpredictable attacks or new directions of cultural inquiry. Ethnic works from Louis Adamic's *Laughing in the Jungle* (1931) to Richard Wright's *Black Boy* (1945) and authors from Claude McKay to John Fante attested to the freeing influence of Mencken's essays. Among the many topics he pursued, Mencken's deepest interest was in language as it was actually spoken in the United States. He observed the linguistic enrichment that came with features of modernity such as the streetcar: "Trolley crews, in the days of their glory, had their jargon, too," he wrote in 1948, "e.g., *boat* for a trolley-car, *horse* for a motorman, *poor-box* for a fare-box, *stick* for a trolley-pole and *Sunday* for any day of light traffic."[1] Drawing on the "Lexicon of Trade Jargon," a Federal Writers' Project manuscript, he also noted that the trolley-car "gave us the expression *to slip one's trolley.*"[2]

Mencken was fascinated by the linguistic consequences of America's multiethnic makeup, and undertook a still unparalleled effort to examine the many ethnic and non-English tributaries to the "American Language." It is telling that Zora Neale Hurston's "Story in Harlem Slang," published in Mencken's *American Mercury,* was accompanied by a glossary of the slang she employed, including "Ofay" for white person, apparently still in need of annotation in 1942.[3] Mencken was interested in all semantic and grammatical features that made American different from British English, and he called attention to many aspects of multilingualism that were present in America. One of Mencken's specific interests was in mixed languages that combined English and non-English elements. In *The American Language* (1919) he recorded features of what he referred to as "Finglish," "American-Greek," "Negro-French," and twenty-five other "non-English dialects in American."

Consciously or unconsciously, many ethnic writers used features of the mixed languages known as Spanglish, FrAnglais, Germerican, or Portinglês and supplied Mencken with materials. At Mencken's suggestion, Louis Adamic contributed an essay on "The Yugoslav Speech in America" to the *American Mercury* (1927), in which he described an imaginary American-Yugoslav housewife who "orders the wailing *bebi* to *šerap* (shut up), and tells two of her other children to cease their *fajtanje* (fighting) and *garjep* (hurry up) to the *rejrod jards* (railroad yards) with the biggest *bosket* in the house and see if they can't pick up some *kol* (coal)."[4] Jerre Mangione also explicitly responded to Mencken's work on ethnic languages. In his *Mount Allegro* (1943)—the very title of which combines an English and an Italian word—he pointed out that if his relatives believed that, after many years in America, they were "still speaking the same dialect they brought with them from Sicily, they were mistaken," for, influenced by "hearing American, Yiddish, Polish, and Italian dialects other than their own, their language gathered words which no one in Sicily could possibly understand." Citing such examples as *storo* for store, *ponte* for pound, *barra* for bar, or *giobba* for job, he agrees that "Mr. Mencken's collection of Italian-American words is a good indication of what happened" to his relatives' vocabulary. And he adds *baccauso,* the word that Mangione used in Sicily to the bafflement of his Sicilian relatives, until the reader realizes that it must be an adaptation of "backhouse" and mean "toilet."[5] Both *Mount Allegro* and *Jews Without Money* mention the immigrant use of the pat phrase, "get out of here," rendered as *girarahir* (in Mangione, already cited) or *gerarahere* (by Mike Gold). Such terms were part of an American lingua franca. Among Konrad Bercovici's many accounts of what was yet to be called multicultural America is the following in *Manhattan Side-Show* (1931): "Bearded Jews, tailors from Russia, Italians, Syrians in their red fezes, Turkish women just out of harems, Greeks and Levantines, worked side by side, day and night, to make our coats and pants. They created their own language: Mercer Street English."[6]

Code-switching and mixed languages are prevalent in American ethnic literature, whether such literature was originally written or published in English or in one of the many other languages that have been used in the United States. For American literature was also written in Yiddish (as was the letter that became Mary Antin's *From Plotzk to Boston*), Polish, Swedish, Welsh, Norwegian, Portuguese, Spanish, Chinese, or German—the list goes on and on—and this little-known non-English literature of the United States offers fascinating insights into American ethnic diversity in some formally accomplished and many thematically provocative works. The propaganda against foreign languages in the course of World War I marked only an interruption in a long tradition of non-English-language literary production in what is now the United States that started with recorded works in Native American and all colonial languages and continued with literature in scores of immigrant tongues. The propaganda may have been at least effective in removing the long multilingual history in all genres of American literature from scholarly attention in the second half of the twentieth century. Yet one only has to recall that the first African-American short story ("Le Mulâtre" by Victor Séjour, 1837) and anthology (*Les Cenelles*, 1845) were both published in French; that an Arabic slave narrative from North Carolina, written by Omar Ibn Said in 1831, predates Frederick Douglass's by fourteen years; that the first American novel depicting a lesbian love scene was published in German (*Die Geheimnisse von New-Orleans*, 1854–1855), or that Eusebio Chacón published Spanish-language novellas in New Mexico in 1892, in order to have a first understanding of what is omitted when "American literature" is defined as literature in English only. There was even a "Streetcar Song, Gay '90's," written by Kurt M. Stein in the humorously mixed idiom of Germerican, which appeared in 1925 in Stein's collection *Die schönste Lengevitch;* the title poem confronts a German-American with a newcomer whose question "Par-dong, Sir, holds ze tramway here?"[7] the old settler needs to have translated before answering it in the same mixed fashion of "die schönste lengevitch."

Despite the linguistic xenophobia (glottophobia?) generated by World War I (when not only German *sauerkraut* officially turned into "liberty cabbage" but when also Spanish, Yiddish, Scandinavian languages, and most any foreign tongue were under siege), literary publication continued, and even increased in some languages. Some examplars of this literature received a new national recognition from the 1920s to the mid-century. One only has to think of Ole Rølvaag (writing in Norwegian), Vladimir Nabokov (writing in Russian and English), Sholem

Asch (writing in Yiddish and English), or Isaac Bashevis Singer (writing in Yiddish) in order to see the centrality of non-English-language works to American fiction from 1910 to 1950. *The Multilingual Anthology of American Literature* (2000) has made some texts available bilingually.[8] For each known author, however, there are dozens of unknown ones, and many works have not yet been identified, let alone been translated into English. There are, for example, the Japanese-language works by Kyuin Okina ("Boss," 1915) and Saburo Kato ("Mr. Yama and the China Incident," 1938), still unrecognized in the United States and little known in Japan. German-language writing was perhaps the hardest hit by World War I. Yet even though no new high point comparable to Reinhold Solger's remarkable social novel *Anton in Amerika* (1862) has been identified in the modern period, German-language writing did continue after World War I. The rise of fascism also brought a lively German-language exile literature and culture to the United States in the 1930s and 1940s; it included writers Bertolt Brecht, Lion Feuchtwanger, and Thomas Mann, modernist artists like George Grosz, and composers like Arnold Schönberg. It is telling that in 1942 the philosopher Theodor W. Adorno published his American dreams (literally, transcripts of his dream life in New York and California) in the German-language New York newspaper *Aufbau*.

Even American authors known for their English-language writings may hold surprises when their non-English oeuvre is examined: thus the Chinese-American Lin Yutang, whose best-selling English-language China book *My Country and My People* (1935) established his fame that increased with his novel *Chinatown Family* (1948), continued to write in Chinese, and there he sounded a more radical note than he did in English. While bibliographies and historical scholarship for the earlier periods are often available, at the end of the twentieth century no one knew just how many short stories, novels, and autobiographies were published in the United States in the twentieth century in languages apart from English, though it is safe to assert that there must be thousands of them, for which the following handful can merely serve as an unrepresentative sampling.

As part of a wave of Welsh-language publishing in Utica, New York, Dafydd Rhys Williams wrote the story collection *Llyfr y Dyn Pren ac Eraill* (The Book of the Wooden Man and Others, 1909). The book, which draws on such traditions as the Welsh folk tale and the ancient heroic narrative, includes stories against drinking, smoking, and assimilation. Among the prolific authors who published prose in Yiddish in the United States was Leon Kobrin whose collected American short stories (published in Yiddish in 1910) added up to more than 900 pages. Often told in the first-person singular, his tales and sketches portray immigrants in their new environments, or focus on chance encounters of strangers in New York. In "Di shprakh fun elnt" (The language of misery, translated by Max Rosenfeld under the title "A Common Language"), the greenhorn narrator gets a job as a night watchman and finds out that the burglars he has beaten to a retreat one night turn out to be a middle-aged Italian immigrant and his small daughter. The narrator feels a strong bond of sympathy toward these poor criminals, even though they have no language in common: "We talked in sign language, with our hands, with gestures. But we understood each other." He lets them free and even gives them kindling wood, but loses his job for this act of kindness. Later his "Italian friend" offers him a banana in return. The solidarity that connects the poor and separates them from the world of hypocritical employers bridges national and linguistic boundaries in Leon Kobrin's tale.[9]

Ole Amundsen Buslett's Norwegian-language tale "Veien til *Golden Gate*" (The Road to the Golden Gate, 1915) depicts the allegorical road, an immigrant's *Pilgrim's Progress* of sorts, from Norway to America's Golden Gate and warns its readers against going too fast on the road of Americanization which may lead to a "Yankee Slough" (Buslett's version of the Slough of Despond) in which all would become alike and ultimately go under and drown. Only those Norwegians who retain their sense of origin and their know-how are able to build safe roads across that slough of Americanization. Yet the tale does not advocate remigration and dismisses the road back to the old country as "the road of nostalgia." The story ends when Rosalita declares her love for Haakon. They will form a couple that has just the right degree of ethnic loyalty, sharing neither Rosalita's father's shallow Americanism nor Haakon's mother's static old-world outlook.

Dorthea Dahl's "Kopper-kjelen" (The Copper Kettle) was published in the Chicago Norwegian-language literary journal *Norden* (1930). Born in Norway, Dorthea Dahl came to South Dakota with her parents at age two, and lived in Moscow, Idaho, for most of her life. Her story focuses on a Norwegian immigrant couple, Trond Jevnaker (the center of consciousness in this third-person narrative) and his wife Gjertrud. Gjertrud is assimilated; she has come to America before her husband, whom she asks to Anglicize her name as "Gørti"—which he refuses indignantly. Dahl's Gjertrud is the typical "language traitor" who rushes into (incomplete) Americanization and is embarrassed by her husband's adherence to old-country ways, symbolized here by an old kettle: it belonged to Trond's grandfather in Norway, but Gjertrud is planning to discard it—when an American lady sees the kettle and expresses her wish to buy it as an antique. Neither Trond nor Gjertrud knows what she means by "æntik," but Gjertrud wants to sell the kettle. Surprisingly, Trond takes command at this point and decides to give the kettle to the American lady as a present. This changes Gjertrud's relationship to Trond, and she now defers to him and promises to abandon her plan for an American "skrinportsen" (screen porch). The eyes of the American native had seen the value of the Norwegian heirloom that the too-speedily assimilated immigrant woman had regarded only as a source of embarrassment.

The Portuguese-language short story "Gente da Terceira Classe" (Steerage, 1938) is representative of José Rodrigues Miguéis's oeuvre. Born in Lisbon in 1901, Miguéis died in Manhattan in 1980, having spent the last forty-three years of his life in political exile in New York City. University-trained and a Portuguese translator of F. Scott Fitzgerald, Erskine Caldwell, and Carson McCullers, he wrote numerous short stories in America. "Steerage," cast in the manner of a log, is set on an ocean liner returning from South America to Portugal. Among the third-class passengers of the title are returning emigrants whose hopes have been dashed, as well as new and hopeful emigrants, "Poles, Portuguese, some lower-class Englishmen (Irish surely), an incommunicative German couple, a large Syrian clan returning from the north of Brazil with jaundiced children, and others of the same breed." The misanthropic narrator mulls over the signs of class and ethnic discrimination, *"For Spanish and Portuguese people only,"* and wonders at the end whether the voyage has created a bond of sympathy among these heterogeneous and largely unsympathetically portrayed passengers.[10]

At first glance, there seems to be in such works only the shared condition of not having been written in English. Yet there are certain features they have in common. Thematically, many tales could be classified as allegorical love-and-assimilation stories. Others stress the possibility of empathy across ethnic and linguistic boundaries, while still others express critique of Anglo-America freely in the non-English tongue. Formally, such works inscribe an English linguistic presence in the texts in a way that works in English—in which English has to serve as the medium of communication—cannot adequately replicate. Dahl spices up his Norwegian with "Hadjudusør" (how do you do, sir), "spærrummet" (spare room), "nervøsbreikdaun," and some complete sentences in English in order to suggest the different speed of assimilation that separates Trond and Gjertrud. Miguéis includes many English words, entire sentences in English and French (suggesting also the importance of "third" languages in such mixed-language locations), and such "Portinglês" (or Luso-American) terms as "cracas" (crackers), "dolas" (dollars), "bossa" (boss), or "racatias" (racketeers).

Even the most obscure non-English-language works shed light on the inward dimensions of America's multicultural past and on linguistic aspects of assimilation; they also offer a multidimensional view of American group relations in the first half of the twentieth century. The founder of modern American immigration history, Marcus Lee Hansen, was right when he wrote in the essay "Immigration and American Culture" (1940): "The student of the future who is willing to conceive of American literature in more than a parochial sense must be the master of at least ten or a dozen languages."[11]

8

"All the past we leave behind"? Ole E. Rølvaag and the Immigrant Trilogy

One of the great and widely recognized works of modern American ethnic literature in a language apart from English was a trilogy originally written in Norwegian by O. E. Rølvaag. It consists of *Giants in the Earth* (1927), *Peder Victorious* (1929), and *Their Fathers' God* (1931).[1] Rølvaag's work marked a high point of American literature, but also the beginning of the end of Norwegian-language writing in the United States, a rich body of works that includes not only Ole Amundsen Buslett and Dorthea Dahl, but a long line of novelistic precursors. Singularly noteworthy among them is the beautifully melancholy (and social-reformist) novel *En saloonkeepers datter* (A Saloonkeeper's Daughter, 1887) by the Norwegian-born author Drude Krog Janson. The heroine of the novel's title is the memorable character Astrid Holm, the daughter of a stern bourgeois businessman and a melancholy actress, who, after her mother's death and the failure of her father's business, follows him (with her much younger brothers) from Norway to Minnesota—where none of the Old World maxims seems to apply any more and where her new identity is simply that of *A Saloonkeeper's Daughter*. The central part of the novel shows the heroine's attempt to find her own way through different suitors, and ultimately, as an ordained minister and close friend of a woman doctor. Janson's novel contains some familiar themes of American-immigrant fiction: the differences between the Old World and the New, generational conflict between immigrant parents and children, the difficulties of courtship by "American" suitors. Yet the novel also has a specifically Scandinavian aura in its pervasive allusions to the ogres of Norse mythology and its evocation, in Astrid's love for the stage, of a particularly Norwegian ideal of serious dramatic art, embodied by Henrik Ibsen and Bjørnstjerne Bjørnson. Published both in Copenhagen and in Minneapolis, the novel calls attention to its transnational character in its original title, *En saloonkeepers datter,* which sandwiches an English term between two Norwegian words.[2]

Also worth mentioning is the Norwegian-American novelist and journalist Waldemar Ager who publicly criticized the "melting pot" concept of assimilation as a metaphor of destruction whose function was "to denationalize those who are not of English descent," as he wrote in 1916.[3] In Ager's novel *Paa veien til smeltepotten* (On the Way to the Melting Pot, 1917; transl. 1995), the antihero Lars Olson embodies the destructive lure of the American melting pot that brings him outward success but destroys him spiritually.

Johannes B. Wist published an immigrant trilogy consisting of *Nykommerbilleder* (Immigrant Scenes, 1920), *Hjemmet paa prærien* (The Home on the Prairie, 1921), and *Jonasville* (Jonasville, 1922), in which he pokes fun at the shallow Americanization of the Norwegian immigrant Salomonsen who has changed his name to Mr. Salmon and whose examples of code-switching make him another ridiculous language traitor: "Amerika er en demokratisk *kontry, ju 'no!* . . . Jeg har *getta saa jused te'* aa *speak English,* at jeg *forgetter* mig *right 'long,* naar jeg *juser* norsk." (In Orm Øverland translation: "America is a democratic country, you know! . . . I have gotten so used to speaking English that I forget myself right along when I use Norwegian.")[4] How could a balance be struck between ethnic and linguistic heritage and the promise of American life?

O. E. Rølvaag answered this question, and like Ager, he polemicized against too rapid a process of Americanization and against the melting pot in essays collected in *Omkring fædrearven* (Concerning Our Heritage, 1922). Rølvaag was born in a little Norwegian fishing village near the Arctic circle, on the island of Dønna in 1876 and emigrated to the United States in 1896. After some years of farm labor, he worked his way through college, graduating from St. Olaf's College in Minnesota at age twenty-eight, and then studying for a year at Oslo. Later he started teaching at St. Olaf's College where he became an active professor of Norwegian with a special interest in immigrant history. He published numerous books, among them the novel *Amerika-Breve* (Letters from America, 1912), based on immigrant letters and published under a pseudonym, and the novel *To tullinger* (1920), significantly revised and altered in its English version under the title *Pure Gold* (1930). Until his death in 1931, he published his literary works in Norwegian. As long as he wrote for a Norwegian-American audience only, there was little interest in him in Anglo-America. However, when his books started to appear in Oslo and received recognition in Norway, things began to change. And it is in this context that his trilogy (or Norwegian tetralogy) emerged.

Giants in the Earth, the first and most famous of the three novels (in the work's English version), follows the lives of Norwegian farmers who in 1873 establish a lonely settlement in Spring Creek in the Dakota Territory. At the center of a small number of families are the Holms. Per Holm, known as Per Hansa, is an active pioneer who faces all kinds of obstacles in establishing the settlement, ranging from winter storms to a plague of locusts. His wife Beret suffers from the isolation in the prairie, is given to bouts of melancholy, and almost loses her sanity. They have two sons, Ole and Store-Hans, and a daughter And-Ongen. Beret almost dies giving birth to their third son, Peder Victorious. Peder is born on Christmas Eve, and, like David Copperfield, he is born with a "helmet"—a caul or veil—often taken as a sign of second sight in Norwegian folklore, for example, as well as in Du Bois's *Souls of Black Folk* (1903). Beret turns toward stricter observance of Lutheran religion under the guidance of a visiting minister. When Per goes out one bitter-cold winter day to fetch a minister to visit a seriously ill neighbor, Per dies in a snowstorm; the novel ends in the spring afterward when his frozen body is found seated on a haystack, his eyes set toward the west.

The sequel, *Peder Victorious,* is set as Peder goes to an American, and then a Norwegian school, but his Americanization and alienation from his mother are unstoppable. After the marriages of the two older sons, who always helped the widowed mother in the farm work, Beret is lonelier and more fanatically religious than ever; Peder becomes the second-generation rebel against the mother's conservatism. He first associates with the daughters of religious dissenters, then falls in love with the Irish-American Catholic Susie Doheny, the sister of an old schoolfriend of his. Surprisingly, Beret consents to the marriage at the end of the book.

The concluding volume, *Their Fathers' God,* continues with Peder and Susie's wedding in 1894. Despite the intergenerational religious, linguistic, and cultural differences, the young couple lives on Beret's farm. Conflicts increase when Susie gives birth to a boy, Petie, and three different ideas of how to raise the child collide. In Susie's absence, Beret arranges a secret Lutheran baptism for Petie; Susie has him christened secretly as a Catholic. Meanwhile freethinking Peder is indifferent to religion and embarks on a political career, during which the bitter political opposition between Irish and Norwegian immigrants becomes apparent. Peder ends an affair with Nikoline Johanson, a young Norwegian immigrant who then returns to Norway, and he goes back to Susie when his mother falls ill. On her deathbed, Beret confesses the child's secret baptism. Susie almost dies from a miscarriage, but survives thanks to Peder's care. Yet during Peder's political election campaign, his character is publicly maligned by his Irish-American opponent with details from his private life, including Petie's secret Catholic baptism, that Peder believes must have come from Susie. Angrily he destroys the Catholic symbols in front of her eyes: he stomps on the white porcelain figure of the crucifix, on the vessel with holy water, and on the beads of the rosary that he first takes apart. Susie is horrified and swoons; the next day she leaves Peder, taking little Petie along with her. If the novel progresses from the faith of the immigrant generation to a secularization of their children, then that process is complicated and disrupted by the different and mutually exclusive meanings of the "fathers' god" for the third and doubly baptized generation. The novel ends with the breakup of the interethnic and interreligious marriage and Susie's return to her father.

Rølvaag's trilogy is a remarkable work. It is a contribution to the classic historical novel, for its beginning is set approximately fifty years before the first volume was written. The three novels trace the historical outline from immigrant settlement to second-generation assimilation to the arrival of a third, American generation, and the books richly represent the themes of language loyalty and loss and of intergenerational tension. Rølvaag is interested in the pressures that migration exerts on language, audible in some inevitable Anglicisms; on religion, either succumbing to sectarian intensification in the case of Beret or to secularization in Peder; on the changing code of values, including ethnic embarrassment or the wish to possess things; and on interethnic relations, especially with Indians and with Irish neighbors. In *Giants in the Earth*, Rølvaag devotes much space to inward feelings and to landscape description—or better, lyrical evocation—so that a sharp portrait emerges of the loneliness of the Norwegian settlers in the challenging environment of the Dakota prairies.

> A grey waste . . . an empty silence . . . a boundless cold. Snow fell; snow flew; a universe of nothing but dead whiteness. Blizzards from out of the northwest raged, swooped down and stirred up a greyish-white fury, impenetrable to human eyes. (249)

In the first volume, Beret's changing states of mind are especially well-portrayed. In Beret's mind, the immigrant family chest, inscribed "Anno 16—" becomes associated with a coffin; later the Lutheran minister uses it as an altar, thus literally transforming and sacralizing an object that accompanied the modern secular process of emigration. The small pieces of wood that mark the confines of the Hansas' territory and that Per moves, so as to own more land, also give rise to Beret's fear, mythically justified in America, that she lives on stolen land. Subtle details add further life to the story. The sod house is vividly represented. The rhetoric of "Promised Land" is developed fully in the course of the novel. English appears as a *lingua franca* for communication between the Norwegian settlers and the Indians, one of whom Per Hansa daringly treats and cures of an infested wound. And the arrival of the railroad is a sinister symbol of nineteenth-century modernity: "The monster crawled along with a terrible speed; but when it came near, it did not crawl at all; it rushed forward in tortuous windings, with an awful roar, while black, curling smoke streaked out behind it in the air" (398). These and many other details that are often presented rather understatedly come into focus through the different lenses in which they acquire meaning for the settlers. In the sequels to the novel, Rølvaag pursues the question of what can hold diverse Americans together by focusing on a Norwegian-Irish, Lutheran-Catholic intermarriage in the second generation, and how American political campaigns reflect and shape ethnicity. *Peder Victorious* presents different and at times incompatible points of view through the metaphor of living in different rooms. In one of them, Peder "lived everything in English" (1), yet a teacher has to tell his mother that Peder "must by all means get rid of that accent!" (138).

As did many other ethnic works—from Willa Cather's *O Pioneers* (1913) to Maxine Hong Kingston in *Tripmaster Monkey* (1987)—Rølvaag explicitly invokes and adapts Walt Whitman's poetry. At a moment when Peder is on horseback in a state of exultation, the lines from "Pioneers! O Pioneers!" that he copied from the blackboard at school become intertwined with the narrative: "Sitting thus high, he could speed away on the wings of the wind. 'Fresh and strong the world we seize'—

heigh, ho! heigh, ho! . . ." (167–168). "He would surely read this poem to Mother! Lashing his horse he raced away to the rhythm of the verse: *Fresh and strong the world we seize*" (173). The Whitmanian hope of "All the past we leave behind" is a hope that Peder's mother cannot share, of course, and the text she lives in is that of the Bible, interspersed in Gothic typefont in the second novel. It is another sign of Rølvaag's imaginative powers that, as he is becoming more frank in representing sexual matters, he draws on the language of the *Song of Songs* (not set in Gothic font). In the third volume, Rølvaag gives room to an elaborate polemic against assimilation, when Reverend Kaldahl challenges Peder's claiming of an American identity: "If we're to accomplish anything worth while," he says, "we must do it as Norwegians." He holds up the example of Jews who made their great contributions to civilization and asks rhetorically: "Did they make their contribution by selling their birthright and turning into Germans, Russians, and Poles? Or did they achieve greatly because they stubbornly refused to be dejewed?" (209). By contrast, the American melting pot would only produce "a dull, smug complacency" (210).

The trilogy has an unmistakable sound to it. Rølvaag employs a lyrical realism which he sets forth with a unique style. Where there are touches of modernism, they are more in the vein of Whitman, or of Carl Sandburg, who wrote a rave review of *Giants in the Earth,* than of T. S. Eliot or Joyce. Other sources of inspiration come from the historical novel tradition of Scott, Cooper, and Bulwer-Lytton, from Rølvaag's systematic study of the modern Norwegians—Ibsen, Bjørnstjerne Bjørnson, Knut Hamsun—and from a famous nineteenth-century collection of Norwegian folktales.

With effective flow and pacing the sentences move easily from third-person description to direct and indirect discourse; the pervasive use of ellipses (". . ."), suggestive of elisions in the narrative, intensifies the effect of the writing. For example, Per Hansa

> asked Beret and Hans Olsa to help pick the best building place; his words, though few and soberly spoken, had in them an unmistakable ring of determination. . . . This vast stretch of beautiful land was to be his—yes, *his*—and no ghost of a dead Indian would drive him away! . . . His heart began to expand with a mighty exaltation. An emotion he had never felt before filled him and made him walk erect. . . . "Good God!" he panted. "This kingdom is going to be *mine!*" (36)

One is amazed at such qualities in what is, after all, a work "translated from the Norwegian."

In his modest introduction to the first American edition, Rølvaag expressed his gratitude to Lincoln Colcord, without whose "constant encouragement" and "inimitable willingness to help" *Giants of the Earth* never would have "seen the light of day in an English translation" (ix–x). And he noted the difficulty of rendering the characters' untranslatable Norwegian dialect in English. For his part Colcord, a professional writer who during World War I had brought out a volume of poetry entitled *Visions of War* and was best known in the 1920s for volumes of stories of the sea, raised the question of how Rølvaag's novel should be classified, "so European in art and atmosphere, so distinctly American in everything it deals with" (xi).

The translation of *Giants in the Earth,* a leading Rølvaag critic tells us, was really a complex process, in the course of which Colcord alone would work through student-and-amateur-produced draft translations before meeting with Rølvaag to decide together on the final version.⁵ In those sessions the original text was apparently significantly expanded, in part made more poetic, by the addition of descriptive adjectives, adverbs, and whole phrases. The cited passage about Per Hansa's vision of the kingdom on the prairie, for example, was, in its entirety, added to the English "translation" only; an equivalent passage is not to be found in the earlier Norwegian "original" text of *I de dage.* Apart from such expansions and from the introduction of American colloquialisms, Rølvaag's English version differs in its absence of the subtle effect of having more and more Anglicisms in the characters' Norwegian as the trilogy progresses, an untranslatable feature. Rølvaag worked with other translators for the second and third volumes, but he adhered to the method of "double action" for the translation that he had worked out with Colcord. One might speak, in this case, of two authorized versions of the same work.

This is not an uncommon phenomenon in those instances of American ethnic literature in which an author tells the same story twice in different languages—as did Luigi Ventura in the French and English versions of *Peppino* (1885, 1886), Abraham Cahan in the English and Yiddish versions of *Yekl* (1896), and Mary Antin in the transformation of the 1894 Yiddish letter to her uncle into *From Plotzk to Boston* (1899).

The aesthetic accomplishment of Ole E. Rølvaag's *Giants in the Earth,*

Peder Victorious, and *Their Fathers' God,* as well as of his larger oeuvre, makes one wonder how many other masterpieces will yet emerge in the now dusty shelves of non-English-language literature of the United States. As Lincoln Colcord wrote in his introduction, "It has not yet been determined, even, what America is, or whether she herself is strictly American" (xxi). And three-quarters of a century later, one can only agree with Colcord's conclusion that some of this literature should be "translated into English, to enrich our literature by a pure stream flowing out of the American environment—a stream which, for the general public, lies frozen in the ice of a foreign tongue" (xxii).

If Mary Antin set the standard for immigrant autobiography, then Rølvaag—whose *Giants in the Earth* also was a popular success and a 1927 Book of the Month Club selection—provided the most compelling model for the American immigrant saga, fiction that spans generations and that often found expression in the form of a trilogy. Among the other ethnic trilogies published in the period were John Cournos's *The Mask, The Wall,* and *Babel* (the third volume appearing in 1922, about a Russian Jewish immigrant coming of age in America), James T. Farrell's Irish-American *Studs Lonigan* trilogy (completed in 1935), Danish-born Sophus Keith Winther's *Take All to Nebraska* (1936), *Mortgage Your Heart* (1937), and *This Passion Never Dies* (1938), and Daniel Fuchs's Jewish *Williamsburg Trilogy* (completed in 1937).

Published after the watershed of World War I and after the deep divide marked by the end of immigration in 1924, Rølvaag's work viewed immigration and assimilation in far more somber terms than did Antin's *Promised Land.* This may be due, in part, to the original use of a medium other than English. However, Rølvaag also represented the historical shift that Horace Kallen had seen coming when he wrote his critique of Mary Antin and Edward Bok: "*The Americanization of Edward Bok* . . . may indeed be regarded as the climax of the wave of gratulatory exhibition which Mary Antin's *Promised Land* began. Now there are signs that the ebb is at hand, and the doctrinal pattern of autobiography for the Americanized is likely to be more analytical, discriminative, and sad."[6] Kallen was thinking of Ludwig Lewisohn and Samuel Ornitz. James T. Farrell, who was part of the "new" literature, written after World War I and conscious of the watershed that the war years came to mark, vividly described in similar terms what he perceived as the progress of ethnic literature as it emancipated itself from the local-color formula:

> In early years, there was the literature of the American immigrant, of first-generation groups, written in an unreal and patronizing vein. The melting pot was a typical literary theme. The treatment in such works was without vitality, conventional, intended to be humorous. The stories contained little truth and were written from the outside. [...] It was a literature of the Cohens and the Kellys, of Abie's Irish Roses, Uncle Remus, a literature of the upper classes and of good old Star-Spangled Banner patronage.[7]

Writing starting with Abraham Cahan's *Rise of David Levinsky* (1917) and continuing with Rølvaag's trilogy bore out such observations more broadly. The new, "sad," and reflexive attitude was not only present in Rølvaag but also in the later writing by Antin herself for whose career World War I was so traumatic an event. And it characterized the best ethnic literature at the peak of modernism, from Jean Toomer to Henry Roth.

9

Modernism, Ethnic Labeling, and the Quest for Wholeness: Jean Toomer's New American Race

"Seventh Street," set in post-World War I Washington D.C., opens and closes with the same short poem:

> Money burns the pocket, pocket hurts,
> Bootleggers in silken shirts,
> Ballooned, zooming Cadillacs,
> Whizzing, whizzing down the street-car tracks.

The page that is framed by this poem of urban modernity is both lyrical invocation and apostrophe of the black migrants who form a "wedge" of jazz songs and life driven into "the white and whitewashed wood of Washington." "Seventh Street" is part modernist prose poem that expresses the rhythms and noise of the city of Prohibition, and part meditation on the meaning of migration. At its center is the repeated question, "Who set you flowing? Flowing down the smooth asphalt of Seventh Street, in shanties, brick office buildings, theaters, drug stores, restaurants, and cabarets?"[1]

"Seventh Street" opens the second part of Jean Toomer's *Cane* (1923), an experimental book that marks the full arrival and a high point of achievement of American ethnic modernism. Published by the prestigious house of Boni and Liveright in 1923, still before Ernest Hemingway's and William Faulkner's first important books were to appear, *Cane* was a powerful contribution to the specific stream of modernism that included Stein's *Three Lives,* James Joyce's *Dubliners,* and Sherwood Anderson's *Winesburg, Ohio,* though Toomer also was inspired by modern poetry (Hart Crane's poem *The Bridge*), Eugene O'Neill's plays, Waldo Frank's manifesto *Our America,* Georgia O'Keeffe's paintings, and Alfred

Stieglitz's photographs. An avid reader, Toomer was drawn to Shaw, Ibsen, Dostoyevsky, Tolstoy, Baudelaire, Flaubert, and Melville. *Cane* is on our side of the transformation toward aesthetic modernism, psychological scrutiny, bohemian self-searching, increasing ethnic expression, and engagement with new ideologies, a transformation that was initiated at the beginning of the century and accelerated by the experience of World War I.[2]

Toomer took up, but never completed, studies in history, anthropology, agriculture, and physical training; he was early on attracted to atheism and socialism, and later to the mystical and introspective Gurdjieff movement, to the Quakers, and to an Indian guru. He spent important years in such artists' colonies as Greenwich Village, Carmel (California), Mabel Dodge Luhan's Taos (New Mexico), and participated in an early experiment in group psychology in Portage (Wisconsin) that neighbors suspected was a free-love movement. He published poems, plays, and prose pieces on the pages of such small, experimental, and often radical literary magazines as *Broom, Dial, Liberator,* and *Modern Review.* Toomer was a star contributor to Alain Locke's anthology *The New Negro* (1925), and Winold Reiss painted his portrait, as he portrayed many other Harlem Renaissance intellectuals. Toomer submitted a play to O'Neill's Provincetown Playhouse and wrote a rave notice on O'Neill's "The Emperor Jones," was friends with Sherwood Anderson and Hart Crane, and was intimate with Georgia O'Keeffe; his second wife Marjorie Content had previously been married to Harold Loeb, the editor of *Broom* who had published Stein's "As Fine as Melanctha" and was caricatured as Robert Cohn in Hemingway's *The Sun Also Rises* (1926). Both Toomer and Stein contributed an homage to Stieglitz in a volume published in 1934.

Toomer's outlook had a strong visionary component. One April evening in 1926 Toomer had a mystical conversion experience at a prime site of modernity, the platform of the 66th-Street L stop in Manhattan, where he was waiting idly, not hurrying to get home, when he felt "a mysterious working in [his] depths," as if he were "being taken apart" and sensed a soft light unfolding behind him and in his body: "This was no extension of my personal self, no expansion of my ordinary awareness. I awoke to a dimensionally higher consciousness. Another being, a radically different being, became present and manifesting." The apt metaphor he used to describe this experience was "transport": "Precisely *I* was being transported from exile into Being. Transport is the exact term. So is transcendence. . . . Liberation is the exact term. I was freed from my ego-prison." He felt as if he were towering above the platform now and saw the "dark earth . . . far down."³ And he realized that the earth-beings sitting on the train could only see his body and not his Being—which made him wonder whether their true selves were also hidden to *him*, since he could only see their bodies. It was this experience of "discovering the Life behind labels" (41) that confirmed him in his turn toward Gurdjieff's "Harmonious Development of Man" (but also distanced him from his focus on literary efforts).

Toomer was deeply and existentially concerned about American ethnic issues, and his writing, most excellently embodied by *Cane*, represents an attempt to answer his close friend Waldo Frank's demand that American writers "study the cultures of the German, the Latin, the Celt, the Slav, the Anglo-Saxon and the African . . . and their disappearance as integral worlds."[4] Frank and Toomer spent some time together in Spartanburg (South Carolina); inspired by this trip, Frank contributed to the little magazine *Secession* "Hope," an odd short story of a nameless white man who makes love to a nameless black woman, and published an experimental and lurid novel of perverted interracial lust and violence, *Holiday* (1923).

Toomer had previously worked as acting principal in a black school in Sparta (Georgia) for two months—the Washingtonian's first extended stay in the rural South—during which time the idea for *Cane* germinated. He read the town newspaper, the *Sparta Ishmaelite,* and lived in a former slave cabin. *Cane* was published in 1923, a year that marked the sixtieth anniversary of the end of slavery as well as the tenth anniversary of the Armory Show. It is the most important American book to contemplate the legacy of African slavery in a thoroughly modernist idiom.

What struck Toomer about the rural South was that "the trend was toward the small town and then toward the city—and industry and commerce and machines. The folk-spirit was walking in to die on the modern desert. That spirit was so beautiful. Its death was so tragic. Just this seemed the sum of life to me. And this was the feeling I put into *Cane*. *Cane* was a swan-song. It was a song of an end."[5] *Cane* is a meditation on what Toomer felt was the disappearing African culture in the modern desert of the American continent.

It is also an ambivalent book that describes modernity both with exuberance and with melancholy. Against the background of the mass movement from soil to pavement, *Cane* reflects on the country without idyllic nostalgia and on the city without teleological hope. Both are historically changing worlds of failed human understanding and of at times comic and at other times horrifyingly brutal encounters. The reader is drawn into a magical and mysterious world of pine needles and clay, of autumn leaves and dusk, of spiritual striving and human failing, of love and violence, but is also exposed to the exciting movement from country roads to city streets and from natural to industrial sounds.

Toomer achieves his effects by a carefully orchestrated system of verbal repetition and musical progression in a book whose very form resists classification by genre. It is sui generis, as it fuses poetry, prose, and drama (in "Bona and Paul" and "Kabnis"), and its form attempts to find a literary equivalent for the dislocations wrought by modernity. Can the lost soul of a fertile peasant past be recuperated in the elusively modernist form of a book that artistically, even artificially, reconstitutes life-asserting wholeness by resisting easy generalizations and a priori assumptions? *Cane* attempts to do just that—even though Toomer articulated his keen awareness that there is no possibility for modern Americans to be going back to a shared past.

> "Back to nature," even if desirable, was no longer possible, because industry had taken nature unto itself. Even if he wanted to, a city person could not become a soil person by changing his locale and living on a farm in the woods.
> So then, whether we wished to or not, we *had to go on*.[6]

Toomer's answer to the problem could not lie in a nostalgic wish for a return to traditional country values, for "those who sought to cure themselves by a return to more primitive conditions were either romantics or escapists." No, going on, and going on to create, searching for aesthetic wholeness and a new vision in a fragmented modern world, those were the only viable answers. The contemplation of modernity impelled Toomer to move forward the project of modernism.

Cane makes its readers self-conscious in order to let them yearn for a fresher and fuller look at the world. This effort is captured in the book's repeated allusions to St. Paul's first letter to the Corinthians: "For now we see through a glass darkly; but then face to face; now I know in part; but then shall I know even as I am known"—a passage that Ralph Waldo Emerson and Nathaniel Hawthorne had also cherished, that Henry Roth and Ralph Ellison were to draw on later, and that Isaac Rosenfeld's

Passage from Home (1946) used as general motto. Toomer also searched for a more cosmic understanding of the wholeness of a polyvocal America as it was once sung by Walt Whitman and now proclaimed by Waldo Frank. Like many earlier visionaries, Toomer espoused the fragmentary as the necessary part of larger totalities.

The interrelatedness of fragmentation and quest for wholeness structures *Cane*. The book is divided into three parts that are marked by figures that resemble parentheses: (,), and ( ). "Between each of the three sections, a curve. These, to vaguely indicate the design," Toomer wrote to Frank.[7] The two segments realign and aim for a circle without fully achieving its closure in the third part.

Part one is set in Georgia, the rural South. It is mostly focused on women, starting with Karintha, whose very name is reminiscent of Gertrude Stein's "Melanctha." "Karintha" originally appeared in the context of the drama *Natalie Mann* (1922) in which Toomer's mouthpiece Nathan Merilh reads the story as an artist's valid response to modern Marxist and nationalist interrogators.[8] Men bring Karintha money, and her imagistic constitution is that of a woman whose running is a "whir" and whose "skin is like dusk when the sun goes down"—a leitmotif of the story in the repetition of which Toomer visibly blurs the line between poetry and prose: it appears typeset as a prose sentence and as a poem (1, 3, 5).

The poems and the portraits of rural women that follow intensify the reader's sense of hearing Toomer's "swan song," of experiencing fragments of a passing rural world in which natural images (especially those of sunsets and autumn) and religious sentiments, increasingly give way to such intrusions of modernity as railroad tracks and factory door—and to scenes of violence. Becky, introduced as "the white woman who had two Negro sons," lives on a "ground islandized between the road and railroad track" (9). Fern is presented as if narrator and reader were seeing her from a segregated train thundering by:

> I ask you, friend, (it makes no difference if you sit in the Pullman or the Jim Crow as the train crosses her road), what thoughts would come to you [. . .], had you seen her in a quick flash, keen and intuitively, as she sat there on her porch when your train thundered by? (29)

Toomer's enigmatic questions to the reader seem located somewhere between Stowe's and Stein's. They too may ultimately be unanswerable, but they suggest a lyrical feeling altogether different from Stein's cold interrogations.

Esther, who has come to sexual maturity, walks into a jeering crowd like a somnambulist, and the story ends as if it were a Franz Kafka tale: "She steps out. There is no air, no street, and the town has completely disappeared" (48). The undercurrent of violence erupts at the end of the first section as the factory town mob lynches Louisa's black lover Tom Burwell whose steel blade had slashed across his white rival Bob Stone's throat. The beautifully restrained prose contrasts sharply with Tom's violent death that it represents: "The mob yelled. The mob was silent. Now Tom could be seen within the flames. Only his head, erect, lean, like a blackened stone. Stench of burning flesh soaked the air. Tom's eyes popped. His head settled downward. The mob yelled" (66–67).

In part two *Cane* takes us to cities, especially Washington and Chicago in the age of mass migration and urbanization. As in "Seventh Street," this world has a new and fast-paced rhythm, characterized by postwar disillusionment, by a proliferating entertainment industry, and by the syncopation of jazz that Toomer incorporates into his prose in order to render a life that is "jagged, strident, modern." The surrealistic Rhobert who wears his house like a diver's helmet is an urban counterpart to Becky, as the narration again repeats prose sentences as poems. The image of the man who sinks is connected with the World War I experience, which violently reduced God to "a Red Cross man with a dredge and a respiration-pump" and makes the singing of the traditional spiritual "Deep River" seem out of place in a secularizing world (74). The self-conscious narrator of "Avey" resembles that of "Fern." Again, the wish for a performance of the spiritual "Deep River," this time by the Howard University Glee Club (86), marks the contrast to rural religion, a contrast that shapes also the vignette of the young woman on the street in "Calling Jesus." "Theater" continues the jazz theme, and Toomer adopts some blues lines here: "Arms of the girls, and their limbs, which . . jazz, jazz . . by lifting up their tight street skirts they set free, jab the air and clog the floor in rhythm to the music. (Lift your skirts, Baby, and talk t papa!)" (92). In "Box Seat," Dan Moore reflects on a man who saw the first Oldsmobile but was born a slave: "He saw Grant and Lincoln. He saw Walt—old man, did, you see Walt Whitman?" (125). The new urban world is not even one lifetime removed from Civil War and slavery; this recent history also casts its shadow over the failed interracial romance between Bona and Paul in the story that ends the second part and corresponds most directly to "Blood-Burning Moon": just as Bob Stone wanted Louisa because she was black and "went in as a master should and took her. Direct, honest, bold," so Bona in the new world of a Chicago gymnasium and the nightclub Crimson Gardens is attracted to Paul *because* she suspects he is black: "That's why I love—" (135). Bona's (and Toomer's) lyrical labels "harvest moon" and "autumn leaf" cannot displace the racial slur "nigger"—that is, for Bona, however, a source of attraction. The weight of such historical racial categories (the phrase "a priori" recurs) impinges upon the consciousness of the youths: "Bona is one window. One window, Paul" (137). Rølvaag's *Peder Victorious* shared with *Cane* this association of different identities with divided interiors. This may be an ironic affinity, since Toomer's narrator also contrasts the racially ambiguous Paul ("What is he, a Spaniard, an Indian, an Italian, a Mexican, a Hindu, or a Japanese?" [145]) with his friend Art, who is described as "this pale purple facsimile of a red-blooded Norwegian friend of his" (141).

The representation of the nightclub Crimson Gardens gives Toomer an opportunity to find verbal equivalents for the musical experience in strong-sounding sentences with striking images (and stylish two-point ellipses) that amount to a prose poem.

> Crimson Gardens. Hurrah! So one feels. The bare-back rider balances agilely on the applause which is the tail of her song. Orchestral instruments warm up for jazz. The flute is a cat that ripples its fur against the deep-purring saxophone. The drum throws sticks. The cat jumps on the piano keyboard. Hi diddle, hi diddle, the cat and the fiddle. Crimson Gardens .. hurrah! .. jumps over the moon. (149)

The stride piano merges with Joyce's technique of playing with familiar nursery rhymes, and puns and conceits intensify the progression from "rider" to "tail" and from a furry sound to the literal presence of a cat on the piano, to the cat and the fiddle from the nursery rhyme. This modernist blending was inspirational to young Langston Hughes when he wrote the poem "The Cat and the Saxophone (2 A.M.)." Toomer's pervasive interest in jazz was related to his hope for an aesthetic fusion brought about by new forms of artistic expression. This put him at odds with contemporary conservatives who deplored the growth of jazz as well as with some political radicals who believed, as did the Marxist Mike Gold in the *New Masses*, that the emerging African-American literary voice should have no room for "saxophone clowning" but aspire to "Beethoven's majesty and Wagner's might."[9]

In part three, "Kabnis," the artist himself is a character *seen* rather than being merely an observing subject. Like Toomer, Kabnis is a secular urban intellectual who goes to rural Georgia to teach. Partly inspired by Joyce's *Portrait of the Artist as a Young Man*, "Kabnis"—written as a play—shows the development of a tortured mind through encounters with nursery rhymes, religion, and the various role models such as a teacher, preacher, cartwright, radical, and visionary. Kabnis must face many issues in society, history, and in himself, but the core of what he must come to terms with is a legacy of violence. The ending of "Kabnis" is like a rebirth, and the book ends as a birthsong with a sunrise.

The three parts of *Cane* confront the divisions of South and North, women and men, and black and white, while the structure of the book tends to bridge such divisions and strive toward unity. The fact that words, phrases, and shorter and longer sentences are repeated throughout the book gives the reader a sense of acoustic and visual familiarity, a phenomenon reminiscent of *Three Lives*. For example, *Cane* is a book of repeated "thuds," harsh knocking sounds that syncopate the reading from "Becky" to the end of "Kabnis." In "Blood-Burning Moon" the "thud" is the sound of Bob's lynched body falling and of the mob's yell, giving a menacingly violent undercurrent of meaning to such later thuds as those in the gymnasium of "Bona and Paul." The book is woven of recurring sounds and images in such words as sawmill, pine, cotton, dixie pike, street, smoke, wedge, window, moon, cloud, purple, cradle, sin, and, of course, cane. Toomer shared Gertrude Stein's love for –*ing* forms, and "Seventh Street" alone offers the examples "zooming," "whizzing," "thrusting," "pouring," "flowing," "eddying," and "swirling." These examples suggest also how sensuous Toomer's sense of language is and how little he shares Stein's thrust toward abstraction. *Cane* is a book full of sunset and dusk imagery that is virtually omnipresent in the poems and the prose, thus calling particular attention to the very emphatic sunrise at the end.

"Fern" opens with a simple sentence in which "face" is the grammatical subject: "Face flowed into her eyes" (24). The image is strong, the precise meaning elusive. Such a phrasing is reminiscent of Ezra Pound's "In a Station of the Metro." Toomer may, in fact, be consciously following F. S. Flint's and Ezra Pound's 1913 imagist maxims which exhorted poets to arrive at an image which presents an intellectual and emotional complex in an instant of time.[10] The "oracular" strangeness in Toomer's images comes out of this poetic tradition.

He writes (about Louisa): "Her skin was the color of oak leaves on young trees in fall" (51).[11] The strongly visual image makes the reader see things freshly, yet it would be difficult to associate one very specific color with the description. Perhaps, for Toomer, an oak was not an oak was not an oak? It is no coincidence that for Toomer lyricism also functions as an avoidance of a label; after all, he chose to publish under the enigmatically androgynous first name "Jean" (rather than his correct baptismal first names "Nathan Eugene"). Toomer shared with the imagists a disdain for labels and abstractions and a desire to let fresh metaphors take their place. It is no coincidence that Toomer does not call Karintha a "prostitute" (though reviewers like W. E. B. Du Bois did); the narrator only says that men bring her their money. Yet Toomer brings to this program a wish that goes beyond the aesthetic.

Louisa's skin color is particularly an alternative to a racial label, a needling engagement with a reader's desire to know whether a character is black or white. Toomer's response is, "Her skin was the color of oak leaves on young trees in fall." Toomer's aesthetic modernism was thus connected to an attack on false perceptions, prejudices, a priori assumptions, and stereotypes. "Damn labels if they enslave human beings—above race and nationality there is mankind," he writes in one of his aphorisms. If America was fragmented, black and white, male and female, southern and northern, rural and urban, Toomer saw his own mission, by contrast, in providing a literary ground for spiritual unity. His method of subverting ethnic stereotypes was different from Stein's "negro sunshine" approach.

Toomer was not alone in the belief that modernist forms helped to complicate facile notions about social life. Georgia O'Keeffe, for example, had painted *Birch and Pine Trees—Pink* (1925), as a modern version of a "surrogate portrait" of her friend Jean Toomer, to whom she wrote, "there is a painting I made from something of you the first time you were here." This was, of course, also a way of deflecting from portraits as realistic representations (including typifying ones) to portraits as purely *formal* expression. Toomer told O'Keeffe in a letter that there was an analogy between his "Bona and Paul" and Stieglitz's cloud photographs, the "Equivalents," though most people would probably not be able to see either:

When I say "white", they see a certain white man, when I say "black", they see a certain Negro. Just as they miss Stieglitz's intentions, achievements! Because they see "clouds."[12]

Toomer had a modern, analytical understanding of the mechanisms of racial differentiation. In his essay "Race Problems and Modern Society" (1929), he wrote that "the new Negro is much more Negro and much less American than was the old Negro of fifty years ago." The greater similarity of professional types "makes the drawing of distinction supposedly based on skin color or blood composition appear more and more ridiculous." Paradoxically, however, these "lines are being drawn with more force between the colored and white groups."[13] This was certainly the case, as segregationist laws proliferated; for example, the Virginia legislature passed the *Act to Preserve Racial Purity* in 1924, defining as white only a person "who has no trace whatsoever of any blood other than Caucasian."[14]

Against this trend, Toomer kept stressing the unity of what was being separated, and, as Charles W. Chesnutt had done before him in the prophetic essay "The Future American" (1900), Toomer imagined the term "American" in a utopian fashion. In the essay, "The Americans," he viewed America ethnically as the place "where mankind, long dismembered into separate usually repellant groupings, long scattered over the face of the earth, is being re-assembled into one whole and undivided human race." However, to arrive at this goal of an inclusive "America," one had to first break "the suggestion of hypnotic labels and false beliefs." And here he became a prophetic visionary who proclaimed that "these labels and beliefs will die":

> And the sight of people will be freed from them, and the people will become less blind and they will use their sight and see.[15]

Toomer likened the blending of races and bloods into something new to the formation of water out of hydrogen and oxygen, but then amended his comparison, "for the blood of all the races is *human* blood. There are no differences between the blood of a Caucasian and the blood of a Negro as there are between hydrogen and oxygen. In the mixing and blending of so-called races there are mixtures and blending of the same stuff." Stressing in 1929—in a very modern way—the sociological (not biological) nature of racial distinctions he concluded:

There is only one pure race—and this is the *human* race. We all belong to it—and this is the most and the least that can be said of any of us with accuracy. For the rest, it is mere talk, mere labeling, merely a manner of speaking, merely a sociological, not a biological, thing.[16]

In his collection of aphorisms, *Essentials* (1931), he drew the consequences from such reflections and wrote about himself: "I am of no particular race. I am of the human race, a man at large in the human world, preparing a new race."[17] Toomer would express similar sentiments in his Whitman-inspired poem "Blue Meridian" (1936) and in autobiographical prose writings in which he tended to see not only his utopian "America" but also the first-person singular "I" as potentially all-inclusive. He polemicized in "On Being an American" against those who "put value upon, their hearsay descents, their groupistic affiliations" and are not "aware of being *Americans*."[18] And he suggested to the editor of *Prairie* magazine: "It is stupid to call me anything other than an American."[19]

Nathan Eugene Pinchback Toomer was born into a family with a long-standing tradition of racial ambiguity on both sides. He described his own ethnic background as consisting of "seven blood mixtures: French, Dutch, Welsh, Negro, German, Jewish, and Indian. Because of these, my position in America has been a curious one. I have lived equally amid the two race groups. Now white, now colored." Though the experience preceding the writing of *Cane* pulled him "deeper and deeper into the Negro group," he concluded on his familiar note: "From my own point of view I am naturally and inevitably an American."[20] "American" as an ideal self-description meant for Toomer an identification for people of all backgrounds who can acknowledge their shared and mixed characteristics—against the more common silent usurpation of the term "American" to stand for "white American."

When in March of 1931 (after the group psychology experiment at Portage, Wisconsin), Toomer married Margery Latimer, the author of the interracial short story "Confession" (1929), and a descendant of Anne Bradstreet, he proclaimed the arrival of "A New Race in America":

It is neither white nor black nor in-between. It is the American race, differing as much from white and black as white and black differ from each other. . . . My marriage to Margery Latimer is the marriage of two Americans.[21]

By contrast, the *World Telegram* headline read "NEGRO WHO WED WHITE NOVELIST SEES NEW RACE." Toomer's vision of a world beyond ethnic labeling was not shared by popular journalism at a time when interracial marriage was prohibited in a solid majority of the United States.[22] Toomer would not only deplore such sensationalist and hostile labeling; upon the completion of *Cane* he also came to reject the label "Negro writer." He did not wish to be included in anthologies such as Nancy Cunard's *Negro* and was apprehensive of friendly writers who, like Sherwood Anderson, saw him too exclusively as, and thus limited him to, "Negro."[23] On the other hand, he was critical of attempts to understand America ethnically without including the Negro: "No picture of a southern person is complete without its bit of Negro-determined psychology," he wrote about Frank's own failure to include the Negro more fully in *Our America*.[24]

In one of his later manuscripts (written between 1937 and 1946), Toomer describes another mystical experience of oneness in modern Manhattan that shows his continuing quest for human unity among "beings called bums" and others called "street walkers, and business men, Americans, foreigners, Jews, Christians, blacks, whites."

> I rode a street car up Broadway. Beings were packed close around me. I could smell their body-odors, hear their bodies breathing.[25]

The Whitman-inspired experience of being close to these heterogeneous human bodies in a streetcar gave Toomer a sudden sense of a divine presence. Whether he aimed for this goal through the poetics of *Cane*, through the experiment of some of his later "sound poems" ("Mon sa me el kirimoor, /Ve dice kor, korrand ve deer"),[26] or through his various spiritual undertakings, the quest for a divinely inspired human oneness remained.

Toomer conceived of his art and striving as a spiritual analogy to a much-needed "racial intermingling."[27] He thought that *Cane* was only the beginning of a long road. Though, indeed, many projects and fragments, long manuscripts, a few literary works, and published essays and aphorisms followed, no second Toomer book equal to the brilliance of *Cane* ever appeared.

10

Freud, Marx, Hard-Boiled

In the course of the interwar period ethnic literature proliferated, turned to new themes, and developed a new tone. Among many other influences, Freud, Marx, and Hemingway made their presence felt in some of the new writing. Freudian issues were brought to the fore, for example, by the German Jewish immigrant and critic Ludwig Lewisohn whose marriage-as-hell novel *The Case of Mr. Crump* (1926) was termed "an incomparable masterpiece" by none lesser than Freud himself; and in his introduction Thomas Mann places Lewisohn—who also published the autobiographies *Up Stream* (1922) and *The Island Within* (1928)—"in the forefront of modern epic narrative" and praises him for his "manly style," his "dry and desperate humor," and his characterization: "even the woman, Anne Crump, remains human in all her repulsiveness," Mann comments.[1]

Lewisohn's little-known novel *The Vehement Flame: The Story of Stephen Escott* (1930, 1948) was a particularly noteworthy attempt to represent the theme of repressed sexuality in the interaction among Jews and Gentiles in New York at the turn of the century. The narrator is the middle-class Christian New Englander Stephen Escott (who is symbolically positioned between his Jewish immigrant hometown friend David Sampson and the upper-class Oliver Adams Clayton). Stephen and David work as law partners in Manhattan, specializing in domestic dispute cases; Oliver is a genteel publisher who is shocked by modernist literature. Their differing attitudes toward sexuality, class-based expectations of life's rewards, and art come to a head in a traumatic murder trial of the Freud-savvy, avant-garde Greenwich Village poet Paul Glover, who publishes in *The Little Review* and *Poetry*, embodies the modern defiance of aesthetic and sexual conventions, yet kills Jasper Harris for having an affair with Paul's wife Janet. Though David defends Paul well enough to secure a mistrial, Paul joins "some army" and gets killed "on an obscure and alien field."[2] David, who still remembers the Jewish village in Poland where he was born and who vividly recalls the emigration experience—"the dreadful herding in freight-cars of immigrant families to Hamburg and the more dreadful steerage" (15)—resigns from the law firm and prophesies with a sad smile that "Western mankind has an evil conscience and there are people in all countries who need a scape-goat for their sins. The scape-goat, as always, are the Jews" (240).

Indeed, the public outrage at the outcome of the trial leads to David's disbarring. Yet David is strangely calm about the anti-Semitically inflected reactions even by his former friend Oliver Clayton; the novel ends as Stephen Escott takes a Sabbath dinner at the Sampsons' house and Ruth Sampson toasts "to a time when things will not be so unevenly divided, when all people will have love enough and justice enough to make life bearable" (243).

As a student, Stephen represses his erotic reveries and reacts hypocritically to David's admonition that what he needs "is a little honest dissipation" (19). His marriage to the Midwesterner Dorothy Johnson is the logical consequence of this attitude, for Stephen's wife is extremely repressed, upwardly mobile (she worships Oliver Clayton) and—as it turns out in her sharply negative reaction to the Sampsons—also anti-Semitic. Dorothy feels threatened by the Sampsons, both sexually and socially, and defensively says that they are "vulgar," adding revealingly: "I suppose it's because they are Jews" (74–75). Stereotyping, a pervasive issue in ethnic writing, is here examined psychologically.

Stephen is unhappy that he cannot get real affection from Dorothy, but her negative reaction to David Sampson (who has become Stephen's law partner) only heightens Stephen's attraction to him. He confesses to the reader that he "might not have clung so assiduously to David's friendship had Dorothy been indifferent to it and to him" (55). Dorothy's opposition makes Stephen aware that he has to hold on to and do what she dislikes in order to preserve his "individuality." Dorothy becomes sickly and ultimately dies.

When Stephen starts a relationship with the sexually free "new woman" Beatrice Loth, a female Don Juan figure and Hemingwayesque libertine, he soon finds out that Beatrice is merely the obverse of Dorothy—the vehement flame that one repressed the other expresses more or less exclusively, like a maenad. Stephen realizes in France that Beatrice is ever-afraid of boredom, has no real tenderness, and has merely "driven love back within its physiological limits" (128). Beatrice was "as much as Dorothy a victim of Puritanism. Only she was rich and free and belonged to the feminist generation" (126). When Dorothy says that "sentimental intimacy" makes her sick and adds, "You don't expect me to baby talk to you, I hope," Stephen asks her whether there isn't "a happy medium between baby talk and being hard boiled." (127). (Lewisohn here employed the term that was coming in vogue in the 1920s and 1930s and that will concern us later.)

Such a happy medium, the novel suggests, is actually achieved by "quite a number" of Jewish marriages that are as good and sound as the Sampsons', and this is, David explains, due to the fact that Jewish women "have learned humility, which is a very different thing from a lack of self-esteem. I mean humility in the face of life" (188). In the novel, only David and Ruth Sampson have a sexually fulfilled union, and the dissatisfaction and sexual frustration of the others serve as a partial explanation of their anti-Semitism. The Sampsons are not only free from Clayton's overt bigotry or Stephen's own earlier hypocrisy; David Sampson also has a benignly condescending understanding of Paul Glover's modernism, with its "libertarian theories" and "revolutionary ardors," for he has "heard them years ago expressed in Russian and Yiddish at the old Café Monopole on Second Avenue" (102).

This is made clear by an encounter of Paul with Berl Fligelmann, the ultimate embodiment of the old-world modernist spirit who responds to Paul's wish for the "liberation of people through the world" by spreading out "his hands in his old, strangely birdlike fashion" and proclaiming: "How younk! How younk! Dese t'ings come late to America. Ve hav finished wit dem. Do you know de 'Faust' from Goethe? 'In de beginnink vass de *deet!*'" (102–103). From the point of the ancient-seeming Fligelmann, Paul's deed is nothing but the absurd reenactment of Faust's attempt to rewrite the beginning of the gospel of St. John. "Ach, these modern women" (188), David moans. The flame of sexuality and American modernism may destroy Paul, reveal Oliver's hypocrisy, and force Stephen to rethink his life, but it is nothing but an old story for Jewish figures like Fligelmann or Sampson. In view of this assessment of modernism, Lewisohn's choice of a realistic psychological narrative seems programmatic. In Jewish wisdom about human strivings and artistic stirrings—however comically accented its articulation may be at times—Lewisohn seems to see a safeguard against American Puritanism and its modern inversion, embodied by the new woman: "David Sampson and his family were sustained in the meaningless welter of modern life by a tradition, a sense of continuity and the conviction of belonging to a community that stretched across the ages and annihilated space" (243). However, the possibility that Jews will get scapegoated for their very wisdom is also very real in a novel that is quite unusual in ethnic fiction, though it has been dismissed as too much of a roman à thèse.

Whether or not Freud was explicitly invoked, sexual frankness in ethnic writing increased in the 1930s. Richard Wright wrote (but excised for Book of the Month Club considerations) a scene from *Native Son* (1940) in which Bigger Thomas and his friends masturbated in a movie theater. Of all ethnic writers in the period, Henry Miller, third-generation German-American, was probably the most sexually explicit author, so much so that much of his work, most famously his trilogy *Tropic of Cancer* (1934), *Black Spring* (1936), and *Tropic of Capricorn* (1939), remained inaccessible in the United States until the early 1960s. In addition to extending misogyny to greater physiological details than did most of his competitors, Miller, whose Brooklyn birth certificate was in the German language, also wrote an ethno-autobiographic narrative, "The Tailor Shop," and included it in the center of the middle volume of his trilogy. It continued not only Miller's sexual story but also gave ample room to reminiscences about working in his father's shop during World War I and about German-American festivities, ascribing to this milieu the first inklings of his artistic development.

In *The Story of American Literature* (1939) Ludwig Lewisohn developed in depth a Freudian view of American literary history, in which immigrant, ethnic, and minority writers are in the modern phalanx in combating Anglo-American repression, neo-Puritanism, and hypocrisy. Lewisohn saw the legacy of Puritanism in the modern "American folk-beliefs that men are either total abstainers or drunkards, either monkish or libertine, either hustlers or idlers, either political and economic conformers or enemies of all social order" (1). World War I brought the Anglo-Americans into sharp confrontation with "the later immigrant strains: the German, the Jewish, the Latin and the Slav." The war years also heightened the "sexual ambivalence toward the Negro" in the whole country. Yet despite powerful neo-Puritan repression, the modern writers—not only the ethnics among them, but also "men and women of undivided American and Puritan descent"—set out to "destroy and transform Puritanism." The result was the "treatment of the sexual life in the books of Farrell and Caldwell" as well as similar themes in "the fictions of John O'Hara and James M. Cain and Bessie Breuer and the overrated John Steinbeck." The new literature's excessive, hardly ironic, and unveiled preoccupation "with the body as love-object and with the immediate sexual act" shows that "contemporary America has set a new standard of frankness—mild word enough!—in the treatment of man's sexual life." Lewisohn, who pioneered in Freudian criticism of American literature, deplored this tendency, for it sought "not only ecstasy but anodyne, not so much life as a kind of death" (604). He was no more enthusiastic about the bulk of social protest fiction, though he did think of James T. Farrell's *Studs Lonigan* trilogy as "one of the most massive and impressive literary achievements" of the 1930s (600).

Marxian themes of class struggle and dismal social conditions in city and country took center stage in the genre of proletarian fiction to which ethnic writers contributed with growing intensity during the Great Depression. Apart from Farrell, there were Edward Dahlberg, Pietro di Donato, Richard Wright, and, perhaps most notably, Mike Gold, who also propagated proletarian realism in book reviews and theoretical essays and who ended his autobiographically inspired *Jews Without Money* (1930) with a Communist soap-box orator who effectively merges the immigrant/ethnic with the proletarian tendency in literature:

> A man on an East Side soap-box, one night, proclaimed that out of the despair, melancholy and helpless rage of millions, a world movement had been born to abolish poverty.
> I listened to him.
> O workers' Revolution, you brought hope to me, a lonely suicidal boy. You are the true Messiah. You will destroy the East Side when you come, and build there a garden for the human spirit.
> O Revolution, that forced me to think, to struggle and to live.
> O great Beginning!
> THE END[3]

This may have been an abruptly propagandistic ending to a book which presents some classic immigrant themes such as greenhorns and Americanization, interethnic encounters, name changes, the problem of ethnic slurs ("Christ-killer!" [134]), the protective immigrant mother, and the father's remarkable love for the Yiddish theater. Gold engages with common ethnic stereotypes: "Jews are as individualized," he writes very directly, "as are Chinese or Anglo-Saxons. There are no racial types. My father, for instance, was like a certain kind of Irishman more than the stenciled stage Jew" (55). As in the case of Mary Antin's *The Promised Land,* the reader is imagined to be non-Jewish and is provided with numerous explanations (though not a glossary) of Jewish customs: "The Jewish holidays were fascinating to children. It was like having a dozen Christmases during the year" (132).

Jews Without Money also represents many facets of modernity: Gold interestingly writes of the "newsreel of memory" (57) in evoking the past, he describes the death of a playmate who is run over by a horse car, and he gives an account of a Sunday outing to the Bronx Park on an elevated train:

> [T]he train was worse than a cattle car. It was crowded with people to the point of nausea. Excited screaming mothers, fathers sagging under enormous lunch baskets, children yelling, puking and running under every one's legs, an old graybeard fighting with the conductor, a gang of tough Irish kids in baseball suits who persisted in swinging from the straps—sweating bodies and exasperated nerves—grinding lurching train, sudden stops when a hundred bodies battered into each other, bedlam of legs and arms, sneezing, spitting, cursing, sighing—a super-tenement on wheels. (106)

Well before the ending of the book, then, the focus on the injuries of class is unmistakable, as Gold writes about the many horrors of urban life among the poor: the lack of privacy in overcrowded, filthy, and infested tenements; badly paying jobs and unemployment; gangsters, crime, and violence; as well as pimps, prostitution, and syphilis.

Granville Hicks's *The Great Tradition: An Interpretation of American Literature since the Civil War* (1933) ends with "Direction," a forward-looking, hopeful chapter which predicts the broadening of the Marxist tendencies in American literature and mentions such novels as Albert Halper's *The Foundry* (1934, focusing on everyday working-class life), Isidor Schneider's autobiographical *From the Kingdom of Necessity* (1935), and Nathan Asch's experimental *Pay Day* (1930), a remarkable novel set on a single night that happens to be the date of Sacco and Vanzetti's execution.

Nathan Asch was the son of the Polish immigrant Sholem Asch, a versatile Yiddish writer in many genres who was to achieve his highest American fame for his multiethnic New York novel *East River* (1946). Nathan Asch had caught Hemingway's attention when he submitted a short story to the *transatlantic review* that Hemingway was eager to help revise and usher into print. *Pay Day,* a Joyce-inspired novel dedicated to Sholem Asch, follows the clerk Jim Cowan through such sections as "The Subway," "The L," "The Street," "The Movie," and "The Speakeasy." Public transportation provides occasions for melting-pot encounters ("There were two wops talking in Italian, every now and then saying 'All right' in English")[4] and for sexual fantasies ("A desire came over him to reach down and touch those breasts, fondle them; his hand even relaxed its grip on the strap, but quickly he controlled himself, tightened his hold, and still he looked" [18]). The section entitled "The Movie" is a montage experiment of simple prose sentences strongly evocative of images—a long, avant-garde prose poem rather than a novel chapter. In the background of the novel are newspaper headlines about the Sacco and Vanzetti case, and only the last section, "Home Again," intertwines the two stories, as Jim says at dawn, "Oh, my God. They're dead" (265). Nathan Asch's Bloomsday was August 23, 1927.

Hicks saw in revolutionary novelists who "come from very different backgrounds," are experts on social conditions and strikes, strive for a new sensibility, and find themselves attracted to Communism, the confirmation of Marx and Engels's prophecy that honest and clear-sighted intellectuals from all classes would join the anticapitalist ranks. "And participation in the common struggle against the exploiters brings these very different persons closer and closer together, so that there is a fundamental unity side by side with a rich diversity."[5] Interestingly, Henry Adams, who was seen as a hero in Lewisohn's Freudian view, also is praised by Hicks for his Marxian understanding of social relations.

Perhaps the most remarkable development in the literature after the mid-1920s was a changing tone in prose writing. Gertrude Stein remained the large super-ego figure hovering over modern American prose writers, so that even her detractor Gold used fourteen *-ing* forms in his brief description of the Third Avenue L (just quoted, see page 118). Yet many readers could not warm up to Stein as a model, even though they may have been mesmerized and occasionally influenced by her. The truth is that no matter how much they invoked Stein, many writers did not actually like her cold style.

Young writers were therefore also looking for different established, yet modern-sounding models. One option was F. Scott Fitzgerald, who was a model for José Rodrigues Miguéis's lusophone writings, after Miguéis had translated Fitzgerald into Portuguese. Yet Fitzgerald's obsession with unrequited love for the very rich remained an idiosyncrasy—though his most famous hero's upwardly mobile name change from Gatz to Gatsby and his made-up past would also have held an obvious appeal to immigrant and ethnic writers concerned with assimilation and racial "passing." Sherwood Anderson's humanity and impressive sharpness of perception was marred by more than occasional flashes of naïveté and pettiness. John Dos Passos was intriguing in his remarkable and unparalleled openness to modernity, yet he also frightened writers by the sprawling endlessness of his enterprise, so that it seemed at times more interesting to talk about him than to read him page by page, or sentence by sentence—let alone to follow his work as a model.

In retrospect, William Faulkner would appear to be the most likely candidate for a position of central importance to modern immigrant and ethnic writers. Yet, as has already been suggested, Faulkner was still understood as an unnecessarily difficult regionalist writer. Faulkner's career started in the opposite manner from the way in which Henry Roth's came to a halt. If the immigrant Roth could not imagine what the meaning of the Civil War could be for American culture, then the native-born Faulkner knew only too well—though the sources of his knowledge came from the defeated side. Faulkner did valiantly start out, in good Lost Generation fashion, to write *Soldier's Pay* (1926), a novel about a veteran returning from World War I. Faulkner even stylized himself as a World War I war hero and made up tales of his supposed experiences as a fighting pilot who had received a war wound and needed to drink much bourbon because of the pain (tall tales in which Sherwood Anderson seriously believed and which he foolishly wrote up and published). But Faulkner's significant past was symbolized not by World War I but by the Civil War. Faulkner's major works reach back to the memory of the Old South, and it is telling that his chronology informs readers that his protagonist Quentin Compson commits suicide in 1910—well before World War I.

Like many ethnic writers, Faulkner represented a very specific past, marginalized and "ethnicized" by the dominant Yankee culture, a problematic and often traumatic past that was examined at times against the implied or explicit voice of questions from the outside ("Why do you hate the South?"). In *Light in August* (1932), *Absalom, Absalom!* (1936), and *Go Down, Moses* (1942), Faulkner explored the tragic web of race relations within the Southern family, making him particularly relevant to all writers concerned with issues of ethnicity, race, interracialism, and multigenerational families. Like many modernists, Faulkner tried his hand at imitating T. S. Eliot and, as has already been seen, wrote many a Steinian sentence. Developing his own style, he arrived at experiments in time shifts and different points of view that set a new standard for modernist authors after World War II (Ann Petry's *The Narrows,* James Baldwin's *Go Tell It on the Mountain,* Ross Lockridge's *Raintree County,* and Ralph Ellison's *Invisible Man* come to mind). Faulkner came to be the most revered American writer for the Latin-American magical realists like Gabriel García Márquez and for Europeans like Günter Grass. Toni Morrison, whose relation with Faulkner is complex, wrote her 1955 M.A. thesis at Cornell University on "Virginia Woolf's and William Faulkner's Treatment of the Alienated."

Faulkner's haunting themes and his meditations on fragments of the past found their perfect equivalent in experimental sentences, as in the use of fragments rendering Quentin Compson's state of mind in *The Sound and the Fury* (1929):

> If that was the three quarters, not over ten minutes now. One car had just left, and people were already waiting for the next one. I asked, but he didn't know whether another one would leave before noon or not because you'd think that interurbans. So the first one was another trolley. I got on. You can feel noon. I wonder if even miners in the bowels of the earth. That's why whistles: because people that sweat, and if just far enough from sweat you won't hear whistles and in eight minutes you should be that far from sweat in Boston. [. . .]
>
> I could hear my watch whenever the car stopped, but not often they were already eating *Who would play a* Eating the business of eating inside of you space too space and time confused Stomach saying noon brain saying eat o'clock All right I wonder what time it is what of it. People were getting out. The trolley didn't stop so often now, emptied by eating.[6]

It would be hard to find a modernist match to Faulkner's stream-of-consciousness trolley. Jean-Paul Sartre wrote that "for young writers in France, Faulkner is a god."[7] Yet this was in 1945; and in the United States of the 1930s and early 1940s Faulkner's many accomplishments did not yet give him a position of centrality, for he still seemed intractable and forbidding.

As late as 1956 Ernest Hemingway bluntly expressed what was undoubtedly a more widespread American opinion about Faulkner. "Faulkner gives me the creeps," Hemingway wrote in a letter and continued: "Never trust a man with a Southern accent." He went on to expand on his prejudice against Southerners: "They could talk reasonable English as we talk it if they were not phony."[8] Elsewhere Hemingway also referred to Faulkner simply as "a no good son of a bitch."[9]

Hemingway's reaction might have been colored by the fact that the versatile Faulkner had parodied Hemingway's style in (the idiot) Benjy's section in *The Sound and the Fury,* a book in which Faulkner writes in many different stylistic registers. Benjy has a most radically limited point of view in which only external perception matters, since the center of consciousness lacks the power of synthesis. Benjy describes his first drunken experience:

> The ground kept sloping up and the cows ran up the hill. [. . .] Quentin held my arm and we went toward the barn. Then the barn wasn't there and we had to wait until it came back. I didn't see it come back. It came behind us and Quentin set me down in the trough where the cows ate. I held on to it. It was going away too, and I held to it. The cows ran down the hill again, across the door. (892–893)

This flat, noninterpretive accounting of sensations in a clear, childlike vocabulary which forces the reader to supply an interpretation sounds very much like a parody of Hemingway's voice. Here is Jake Barnes experiencing drunkenness in *The Sun Also Rises:*

> I went out the door and into my own room and lay on the bed. The bed went sailing off and I sat up in bed and looked at the wall to make it stop. [. . .]
> I got up and went to the balcony and looked out at the dancing in the square. The world was not wheeling any more.[10]

Faulkner also parodied himself, using the pen name "Ernest V. Trueblood," and Wyndham Lewis thought that both Faulkner and Hemingway were "men without art." Faulkner was certainly not alone in imitating and perhaps parodying Hemingway. In fact, the writer who did become identified with modern American literature and who was the most imitated and parodied author in the interwar period was Ernest Hemingway.

Hemingway himself had started imitating Sherwood Anderson and, especially, Stein, but he seemed to have written Anderson out of his system with the parody *The Torrents of Spring* (1926), a book in which Hemingway also took on Stein in a section entitled "The Making and Marring of Americans." "A bitch is a bitch is a bitch," Hemingway also penned in caps arranged in a circle on the front page of the copy of his *Death in the Afternoon* (1932) that he gave to Stein. Yet no matter how much he distanced himself from her at times, Hemingway continued to use some of Stein's idiosyncrasies (repetitions, simple adjectives, an objective and detached stance) and achieved the widest national and international audience appeal of any serious American author in the first half of the century. He shared Stein's emphasis on the sentence as the most important element of modern prose; and he wrote in *A Moveable Feast:* "I would stand out and look over the roofs of Paris and think, 'Do not worry. You have always written before and you will write now. All you have to do is write one true sentence. Write the truest sentence that you know.'"[11] Hemingway self-consciously thought of single sentences as possibly the truest legacy of a writer and said: "Some writers are only born to help another writer to write one sentence."[12]

What happened to Stein's sentences in Hemingway's hands? Among Hemingway's representative sentences is the following (from *The Sun Also Rises*) in which the detached observer adds an aspect of masculine-coded violence: "He was a good trout, and I banged his head against the timber so that he quivered out straight, and then slipped him into my bag" (119). In an example of a ride on a bus (in *Paris 1922*) the narrator plays the insider to Paris life: "I have stood on the crowded back platform of a seven o'clock Batignolles bus and lurched along the wet lamp lit street while men going home to supper never looked up from their newspapers as we passed Notre Dame grey and dripping in the rain."[13] In *The Sun Also Rises* there is an abundance of such Paris scenes, for example:

> In the morning I walked down the Boulevard to the Rue Soufflot for coffee and brioche. It was a fine morning. The horse-chestnut trees in the Luxembourg gardens were in bloom. There was the pleasant

early-morning feeling of a hot day. I read the papers with the coffee and then smoked a cigarette. [. . .] The Boulevard was busy with trams and people going to work. I got on an S bus and rode down to the Madeleine, standing on the back platform. (35)

Lady Brett Ashley articulates an ethos of secularized modernity when she announces that "it makes one feel rather good deciding not to be a bitch," adding: "It's sort of what we have instead of God" (245). A battlefield description in *A Farewell to Arms* (1929) shows Hemingway's readiness to face the loss of meaning in wars: "the sacrifices were like the stockyards at Chicago, if nothing was done with the meat except to bury it."[14]

Carl Van Doren, assessing Hemingway's power in 1940, writes: "If Hemingway had learned about style and cadence from Gertrude Stein, he had none of her obscurity and he used none of her materials. . . . He had a terse, cold magic in his story-telling that made Scott Fitzgerald seem flimsy in comparison, Dos Passos loose-gaited."[15] Hemingway "took"—for his highly stylized yet surprisingly "natural"-seeming prose gave readers a full experience of taking part in modernism while still getting some traditional characterization, story lines, and sentiments (all the more so if these aspects were withheld or suppressed on the page). His was a modernism that was both "easy," never as difficult for the reader as was Stein's, and "tough," as he demonstratively embodied the particularly "masculine" flavor of the term "hard-boiled." Mark Twain had used the word once in the 1883 speech "General Grant's Grammar," when he defended Grant's, perhaps ungrammatical, phrase "I propose to fight it out on this line if it takes all summer" because "it did certainly wake up this nation as a hundred million tons of A No. 1, fourth-proof, hard-boiled, hide-bound grammar from another mouth could not have done." Yet the word "hard-boiled" (in reference to an attitude or to prose writing rather than to eggs) was coming into wider circulation only in the 1920s. Hemingway's Jake Barnes, for example, employs it to name a pose; feeling "like hell again," he declares at the end of chapter four of *The Sun Also Rises*: "It is awfully easy to be hard-boiled about everything in the daytime, but at night it is another thing" (34). In the draft manuscript of the novel, the narrator still felt "like crying again," and the chapter ended without any comment on being hard-boiled.[16] The *Nation* ran Allen Tate's review of *The Sun Also Rises* under the heading "Hard-Boiled." In the same year 1926 the *Ladies' Home Journal* wrote that "the hard-boiled cynic has a shell" that satire "can never penetrate." Even the archconservative literary critic Stuart Sherman used the term "hard-boiled" when he argued in *The Main Stream* (1927) that it was impossible to take Ring Lardner's "hard-boiled Americans" seriously. Sherman's own meandering style serves as a perfect counterpoint to hard-boiled prose when, in support of the term "main stream" to which his book helped give currency, he imagines the ideal literary critic as a man who

> conceives of literature perhaps as a river, himself as a scout seeking for the main channel of intellectual and emotional activity in his own tract of time, recurring constantly to the point where the full rush of living waters comes in from the past, and eagerly searching for the point where the flood breaks out of the backwater and through the dams, and streams away into the future.[17]

Lewisohn, as we saw, used "hard boiled" as the opposite excess to "baby talk."

Overtly antisentimental, Hemingway's detached, stoic, and wisecracking narrators and characters manage to feed sentimental reader expectations at the same time. Hemingway may have been the most successful compromise modernist, parallel to Edward Hopper in painting or George Gershwin in music. When *Scribner's* published Hemingway's short story "The Killers" in 1927, Hopper wrote the editors that he found it "refreshing" to read such an "honest piece of work in an American magazine, after wading through the vast sea of sugar coated mush that makes up most of our fiction."[18]

Hemingway produced the first full version of American modernism for the millions that made the subculture of artists, existentialists, and bohemians in avant-garde cliques generally available as an object of popular identification. He appealed to artists, to middlebrow readers, and to a wide general audience who became vicarious aficionados and insiders en masse. Hemingway's penchant for parataxis may have helped in this process, for as the literary critic Joseph Warren Beach observed in 1941, Hemingway worked "to reduce all ideas to a single order of relationship, the conjunctive coordinate relationship, in which no one item is subordinated to any other."[19] Here is an example from "The Snows of Kilimanjaro" (1936): "It was evening now and he had been asleep. The sun was gone behind the hill and there was a shadow all across the plain and the small animals were feeding close to camp."[20] Hemingway's love for parataxis, Beach noted, may have run against the attempts of English teachers to inspire their students to express "their ideas in the proper order of subordination." Hemingway wanted storytelling "to flow and not be lost in eddies of logic"—which is why he relied on what Beach called "the great leveling democracy of the *and*."[21]

Hemingway was also a master of deadpan dialogues:

> "This is a good place," he said.
> "There's a lot of liquor," I agreed.[22]

The response was the result of revision, for the manuscript still read: " 'It's a nice place,' I agreed." Or, most famously:

> "Oh, Jake . . . we could have had such a damned good time together."
> "Yes. . . . Isn't it pretty to think so?"[23]

This quick and memorable repartee was also refined in the revision process from the original manuscript's "It's nice as hell to think so."

These dialogues in simple, vigorous words suggest nothing so much as a fatalist ethos that comes across more persuasively because it is understated. Hemingway's art follows what he called the "principle of the iceberg," for "there is seven-eighths of it underwater for every part that shows."[24] A feeling of modern hopelessness, symbolized by Jake's war wound, combines with a Quixotic element of chivalry in a bad time, a quest for a "Roncevaux" that may have become more elusive after World War I than it ever was.

The stylized vernacular absorbed everyday language, including advertisements and ubiquitous brand names. While many writers incorporated the names that attached themselves to articles of consumption, Hemingway extracted near-transcendental meaning from them. For example, when the German artist Kandisky describes to the narrator in *Green Hills of Africa* (1935) the pleasure of having a thirteen-year-old daughter, he says that her participation in the family conversations is "the Heinz ketchup on the daily food."[25]

Hemingway's tone struck the right chord for the time. His ethos of finding oneself in a strange world in which the codes one believes in no longer seem to apply spoke to immigrant and minority writers and readers. Themes of suddenly erupting violence and of complex initiation were compatible with the experience of ethnoracial hostility and of socialization into, or exclusion from, American codes of conduct. Hemingway's style was equally resonant with lives lived in translation, and his repetition of simple words like "nice," "fine," and "pretty" resembled the immigrants' famous "all right" or the understated terms derived from black slang ("cool"). In a passage Delmore Schwartz highlighted from the short story "The Gambler, the Nun and the Radio" (1933; first titled "Give Us a Prescription, Doctor") an American detective asks a mortally wounded Mexican gambler to tell him who shot him:

> "Listen," the detective said, "this isn't Chicago. You're not a gangster. You don't have to act like a moving picture. It's all right to tell who shot you. That's all right to do."

Yet an American writer goes right on to "translate" the detective for the Mexican:

> "Listen, amigo [. . .] The policeman says that we are not in Chicago but in Hailey, Montana. You are not a bandit and this has nothing to do with the cinema."
> "I believe him," said Cayetano softly. *"Ya lo creo."*
> "One can, with honor, denounce one's assailant. Everyone does it here, he says."[26]

Hemingway's deceptive simplicity of language was not only attractive to writers who had come from backgrounds in which English did not have a multigenerational presence or was not the writer's family or first language, but Hemingway's style also suggested the presence of translation or created the illusion of being a literal translation from another tongue. Perhaps this is one reason for Hemingway's tremendous international success also. Here is an example from *For Whom the Bell Tolls* (1940): "Thou wert plenty of horse." As Harry Levin noted in 1951, Hemingway was translating *"Eras mucho caballo"* literally.[27] Levin marveled that, "having cut down his English vocabulary," Hemingway "should augment it by continual importation from other languages." These imported words often are placed right next to the English equivalent, as in *The Sun Also Rises*, when Jake asks Bill and Robert what they are drinking: "'Sherry,' Cohn said. 'Jerez,' I said to the waiter" (153).[28] And as if he wished to make the reader more self-conscious about the back-and-forth process of translation, Hemingway makes his characters use the very word "translate" in the sense of "carry": In a religious procession in Pamplona, Jake narrates that "San Fermin was translated from one church to another" (155); and a few pages later, Bill says, "Let's translate Brett to the hotel" (159).

11

Hemingway Spoken Here

Delmore Schwartz argued in 1955 that Ernest Hemingway's style was neither primitive nor proletarian:

> Its devices include eloquent reticence, intensely emotional understatement, and above all the simplified speech which an American uses to a European ignorant of English. . . .
>
> Hemingway's style is a poetic heightening of various forms of modern colloquial speech—among them, the idiom of the hardboiled reporter, the foreign correspondent, and the sportswriter. It is masculine speech. Its reticence, understatement, and toughness derive from the American masculine ideal, which has a long history going back to the pioneer on the frontier and including the strong silent man of the Hollywood Western. The intense sensitivity to the way in which a European speaks broken English, echoing his own language's idioms, may also derive from the speech of the immigrants as well, perhaps, as from the special relationship of America to Europe which the fiction of Henry James first portrayed fully.[1]

Schwartz's linking of Hemingway's "Americanness," employment of the international theme, and possible reliance on immigrant speech was perceptive. "Hemingway spoken here" might well have been the motto of much prose writing of the 1930s, and American ethnic writers gave ample testimony to their indebtedness.

Meyer Levin, a Jewish novelist from Chicago who wrote the trilogy-length novel *The Old Bunch* (1937) and was later instrumental in publishing Anne Frank's *Diary of a Young Girl* (1952) in English translation, started his career with two Hemingwayesque novels. *Reporter* (1929), a city desk book, and *Frankie and Johnnie* (1930), the story of a failed romance with such sentences as: "All the time Johnnie was thinking these things Frankie wasn't riding home on the L at all. All that time, Frankie was riding home on the bus."[2]

In his autobiography *A Long Way From Home* (1937) Claude McKay confessed to "a vast admiration" for Hemingway and reported that left, liberal, as well as some conservative writers he met in France "all mentioned Hemingway with admiration." "Many of them felt that they could never go on writing as before after Hemingway." McKay also thought that it was not Hemingway's fault if in the 1930s he came to be "mainly admired by a hard-boiled and unsophisticated public." Yet at the same time McKay felt that Hemingway had achieved a quality "distinctly and definitely American" (and "altogether un-European") in illuminating "the hard-boiled contempt for and disgust with sissyness expressed among all classes of Americans"—a "conventionalized rough attitude." And further: "Mr. Hemingway has taken this characteristic of American life from the streets, the barrooms, the ringsides and lifted it into the realm of literature. In accomplishing this he did revolutionary work with four-letter Anglo-Saxon words." With all this praise McKay also found it worth mentioning that his own "loose manner and subjective feeling" had little in common with Hemingway's "objective and carefully stylized form" and that his own novel *Home to Harlem* (whose protagonist happens to be a proto-existentialist World War I veteran named Jake) followed the "clearly consistent emotionalist realist thread" that McKay had established before Hemingway started publishing.[3]

James T. Farrell's 1943 essay on Hemingway's *The Sun Also Rises* mentions the imitations it generated, not only among younger authors but also in real life: "Boys and girls on campus after campus began to talk like Hemingway characters." There is thinness in his imagination, Farrell observes: his Europe is a tourist's Europe and most of his characters have only a meager past, do not really think, and feel quite alike in the stoic acceptance of the ills of life. Yet in *The Sun Also Rises,* which "remains one of the very best American novels of the Twenties," "he has saved himself from the crudities of simple behaviorism because of his gift of suggestiveness and his developed skill of understatement."[4]

Ludwig Lewisohn thought that before *A Farewell to Arms* Hemingway had been "merely the most gifted of the new 'hard-boiled' writers, that is to say, of those impelled to depict life in order to express their disgust for it and hence their own spiritual despair." But with a novel of such excellence Hemingway had transcended "the moral nihilism of the school he had himself helped to form." Lewisohn admired one of the novel's culminating moments and singled out a sentence, "with its classically curbed rage and pity" about the interrogation by the battle police: "The questioners had that beautiful detachment and devotion to stern justice of men dealing in death without being in any danger of it."[5]

Alfred Kazin noted in *On Native Grounds* (1942) that Hemingway's example

> as a stylist and craftsman [. . .] was magnetic on younger men who came after him; as the progenitor of the new and distinctively American cult of violence, he stands out as the greatest single influence on the hard-boiled novel of the thirties, and certainly affected the social and left-wing fiction of the period more than some of its writers could easily admit. [. . .] Hemingway is the bronze god of the whole contemporary literary experience in America.[6]

(Sartre had not yet propagated the other "god.")

Kazin's observation was true even for the extremely qualified Hemingway assessment that the ever-critical Mike Gold offered in 1928. Gold complained that Hemingway only satisfied the daydreams of the "American white-collar slave" with his chief three themes of liquor, sex, and sport, and gave the young "liberal" authors who wrote "advertising copy meekly all day" a fantasy world of an "irresponsible Europe, where everyone talks literature, drinks fine liqueurs, swaggers with a cane, sleeps with beautiful and witty British aristocrats, is well informed in the mysteries of bullfighting, has a mysterious income from home." The gratification of these fantasies explained why Hemingway was "suddenly popular." However, "the revolutionary writers of the future will be grateful to him; they will imitate his style. But they will have different things to say."[7]

One such revolutionary writer was Richard Wright who explained at Columbia University in 1938:

> When I was employed on the Federal Writers Project in Chicago, practically all us young writers were influenced by Ernest Hemingway. We liked the simple, direct way in which he wrote, but a great many of us wanted to write about social problems. The question came up: how could we write about social problems and use a simple style? Hemingway's style is so concentrated on naturalistic detail that there is no room

for social comment. One boy said that one way was to dig deeper into the character and try to get something that will live. I decided to try it.[8]

One of the short stories first published in *Uncle Tom's Children* (1938), "Long Black Song," was the result.

Hemingway did not only inspire the ethnic left to imitate his style. When Farrell pointed out that boys and girls had started to speak like Hemingway characters, he was thinking of colleges as one arena in which Hemingway dissemination was taking place. Another such arena was the increasingly proliferating popular culture of the 1930s and 1940s. A ready example is the genre of pulp fiction, represented for example by a writer like Raymond Chandler whose life shares some features with an immigrant's. Although he was born in Chicago in 1888, his British mother took him to England at age seven when his parents divorced, and he completed a thoroughly English education and began a career in the Admiralty before returning to the United States at age twenty-four. His early writings had a distinctly English style; when, after a checkered career, he returned to writing in the early 1930s, he did so with reflections on the differences between English and American prose, with sketches, and with a Hemingway parody. In his "Notes (very brief, please) on English and American style," Chandler commented sharply on American English. Among the critical points he made were its overworking of catchphrases, the phony sound of its slang, "being invented by writers and palmed off on simple hoodlums and ballplayers," its feeble awareness of "the continuing stream of culture . . . due to a lack of the historical sense and to shoddy education," and its "too great a fondness for the *faux naïf*," that is "the use of a style such as might be spoken by a very limited sort of mind."[9] Here Chandler qualifies his critique: "In the hands of a genius like Hemingway this may be effective, but only by subtly evading the terms of the contract, that is, by an artistic use of the telling detail which the speaker never would have noted. When not used by a genius it is as flat as Rotarian speech."[10]

Chandler clearly aimed for the genius spot; and if as a youth he had imitated Henry James, in 1932 he parodied Hemingway on his way to write his major "hard-boiled" detective novels of the 1930s and 1940s. The exercise was not so subtly called "Beer in the Sergeant Major's Hat (or The Sun Also Sneezes)" and dedicated "with no good reason to the greatest living American novelist—Ernest Hemingway." This is a sample:

> Hank drank the alcohol and water. It had a warm sweetish taste. It was warm as hell. It was warmer than whiskey. It was warmer than that Asti Spumante they had that time in Capozzo when Hank was with the Arditi. They had been carp fishing with landing nets. It had been a good day. After the fourth bottle of Asti Spumante Hank fell into the river and came out with his hair full of carp. Old Peguzzi laughed until his boots rattled on the hard gray rock. And afterward Peguzzi got gonorrhea on the Piave. It was a hell of a war.[11]

Only after such writing exercises did Chandler begin to publish in the pulp magazine *Black Mask* (that H. L. Mencken had helped found) and develop his most famous detective novels *The Big Sleep* (1939), *Farewell, My Lovely* (1940), *The High Window* (1942), and *The Lady in the Lake* (1943). Some of the hard-boiled terms Chandler coined gained wide currency later, for example, Marlowe's novel use of the phrase "I'll take him out" (in the approximate sense of neutralizing or killing one of General Sternwood's blackmailers so that "he'll think a bridge fell on him") in *The Big Sleep*.

In an imaginary interview on "The New American Novelists" (1949), André Gide praised Hammett's dialogues, "in which every character is trying to deceive all the others and in which the truth slowly becomes visible through the haze of deception," as comparable "only with the best in Hemingway."[12] It was through Chandler, Dashiell Hammett, and James M. Cain, and even more so through the Hollywood movies that were made from their novels, that the hard-boiled style became universalized. What took place, especially in the genre of film-noir, might be termed the Hemingwayization of American culture. The effect of the hard-boiled dialogues was further enhanced by the visual aid of film noir movie sets: a critic noted that in Fritz Lang's *Scarlet Street* (1945) the "unpeopled streets, the elongated shadows, the angular buildings that guard empty space like grim sentinels, recall the eerie night-time cityscapes in the paintings of Edward Hopper."[13] This was true for many films of the genre, including Henry Hathaway's *The Dark Corner* (1946), based on a story by ethnic writer Leo Rosten (of Hyman Kaplan fame), with jazzy interludes and a professional, Hopperesque set designed by Paul S. Fox and Thomas Little.

To be sure, Gertrude Stein's style also inspired occasional moments in Hollywood movies. The film *The Awful Truth* (1937), for example, directed by Leo McCarey, and with a screenplay by Viña Delmar based on a 1922 play by Arthur Richman, lets the nearly-divorced Mr. and Mrs. Warriner (played by Cary Grant and Irene Dunne) find their way back into their marital bed literally at the last minute before a divorce decree takes effect. This reconciliation is accompanied by what sounds like a pure Steinian dialogue:

> *Lucy*: It's funny that everything is the way it is on account of the way you feel.
> *Jerry*: Huh?
> *Lucy*: Well, I mean, if you didn't feel the way you do, things wouldn't be the way they are, would they? I mean, things could be the same if things were different.
> *Jerry*: But—eh—things are the way you made them.
> *Lucy*: Oh no! No, things are the way you think I made them. I didn't make them that way at all. Things are just the same as they always were. Only you are the same as you were, too, so I guess things will never be the same again.

And a little later:

> *Lucy*: You are all confused, aren't you?
> *Jerry*: Uh-uh. Aren't you?
> *Lucy*: No.
> *Jerry*: But you should be because you are wrong about things being different because they are not the same. Things are different, except in a different way. You're still the same, only I've been a fool, but I'm not now.
> *Lucy*: Ah!
> *Jerry*: So long as I am different, don't you think that, well maybe things, could be the same again, only a little different, huh?
> *Lucy*: You mean that, Jerry? Are you sure?

This wonderful insertion of a Steinian moment into an otherwise more conventionally scripted screwball comedy of remarriage sent a critic to double-check Plato's *Parmenides* as a possible source.[14] Still, *The Awful Truth* may have been an exception. More pervasive were the prolific contributions to the film-noir cult of the 1930s and 1940s. They created the illusion that a stylistic convention derived from Hemingway was actually a lived idiom that was spoken by America's existentialist detectives and gangsters.

In Billy Wilder's *Double Indemnity* (1944), adapted for the screen by Wilder together with Raymond Chandler from James M. Cain's novella "Three of a Kind" (*Liberty Magazine*, 1936), the insurance agent Walter Neff admits: "Yes, I killed him. I killed him for money and for a woman. I didn't get the money and I didn't get the woman. Pretty, isn't it?"[15] What makes this confession all the more intriguing is that Neff makes it in the form of a dictated office memorandum: even that typically tame genre could take on the irresistible, tough-talking, hard-boiled, and Hemingwayesque tone of film noir. In Howard Hawks's *The Big Sleep* (1946), based on the 1939 Chandler novel and adapted (in part) by William Faulkner, we hear the following dialogue:

> *Sternwood*: How do you like your brandy, sir?
> *Marlowe*: In a glass.[16]

As in the case of Hemingway, revision strengthened the wisecracking repartee, for in Chandler's novel Marlowe had still answered "Anyway at all."

In his essay on "The Language of Hollywood" (1944) Farrell disagrees with Horace Kallen's more optimistic view of mass culture and looks at Hollywood as a "counterfeit culture" in which "common speech" may create the illusion of a democratic emphasis but actually only serves "to glorify the status quo." He observes that much "literary talent of America is now diverted to Hollywood and radio writing" and mentions the "penetrating influence of Hollywood on the novel" that can be seen in "the stimulation it has given to a kind of hard-boiled realism that imitates all the manners of serious writing but contains none of the inner meaning, the inner protest against evils, the revelation of the social mechanisms and social structures found in serious realism."[17] He cites as examples *The Postman Always Rings Twice* and *Double Indemnity*.

James Agee examined twice the relationship of the movies to the spirit of hard-boiled prose. Agee commented on the 1946 movie version of Hemingway's *The Killers* that "Hemingway's talk, which on the page used to seem so nearly magical and is still so very good, sounds, on the screen, as cooked-up and formal as an eclogue." Yet, writing about the movie version of Chandler's *Farewell, My Lovely* on December 16, 1944, Agee found that this film preserved both the faults and virtues of the book, and he came up with an excellent formula that describes the intellectual limits of the hard-boiled genre, including some of its ethnic contributors: "poetic talent, arrested-adolescent prurience, and the sort of self-pity which, in rejoicing in all that is hardest-boiled, turns the two former faculties toward melodramatic, pretentiously unpretentious examination of big cities and their inhabitants."[18]

The literary beginnings of James T. Farrell, Pietro di Donato, Meyer Levin, Richard Wright, Ralph Ellison, and even some of Mike Gold's works would have been different had it not been for Hemingway's example. This was not always a matter of the nurture these writers received (as did Nathan Asch, for example), for Hemingway was not famous for being generous to all literary newcomers, as the example of the young William Saroyan shows.

Fresno-born, William Saroyan was the only son of the Armenian immigrants Armenak and Takoohi Saroyan who had come to the United States from Bitlis in eastern Anatolia. Saroyan published a story in *Hairenik* ("Homeland"), an Armenian journal in Boston, and then in Edward J. O'Brien's *Best Short Stories of 1933*. After this first success, other stories followed in Mencken's *American Mercury,* in *Harper's*, in the *Atlantic Monthly,* and in Burnett and Foley's *Story Magazine;* soon Random House published Saroyan's first book collection, *The Daring Young Man on the Flying Trapeze and Other Stories* (1934). Reviews were mixed, though Saroyan was generally read in the context of modernism. The *Christian Century* opined that Saroyan's book "has qualities in common with the 'Nude Descending a Stairway,' but it is much better than 'a rose is a rose is a rose.'"[19] Saroyan had invited such contexts, since he mentioned some modernists by name, for after contemplating the possibility to continue the Tarzan series if Edgar Rice Burroughs were to die, he pronounced: "if I felt inclined, I could write like John Dos Passos or William Faulkner or James Joyce."[20] As he himself observed, however, he did not actually write like any of them; and only in a few instances—such as the experimental short story "Quarter, Half, Three-Quarter, and Whole Notes" (in *Three Times Three,* 1936)—did he write like Stein to whom he had written the adulatory letter already cited.

Another author whom Saroyan occasionally imitated was Hemingway. In the story "Aspirin Is a Member of the N.R.A." (first published in *American Mercury*) Saroyan contemplates the certainty of death and the pervasiveness of human pain, visible on the faces of everybody on the subway. "I looked everywhere for one face that was not the mask of a pained life, but I did not find such a face. It was this that made my study of the subway so fascinating." He reaches the decision that "the subway is death, all of us are riding to death." (The theme of the sad lonely faces in crowded urban subways remained with Saroyan, and in his play *Subway Circus* he permitted some of the subway riders, Thornton Wilder-style, to reveal their thoughts to the audience.) From the recognition that aspirin is an evasion of death, he imagines a future advertisement in the "*Saturday Evening Post,* making a slogan on behalf of death. *Do not be deceived . . . die and see your dreams come true . . . death does not harm the heart . . . it is absolutely harmless . . . doctors everywhere recommend it . . .* and so on." And this is when he nods toward Hemingway: "You hear a lot of sad talk about all the young men who die in the Great War. Well, what about this war? Is it less real because it destroys with less violence, with a ghastlier shock, with a more sustained pain?"[21]

In another story in *The Daring Young Man* Saroyan half-seriously sets up Hemingway as an ideal: "I hope some day to write a great philosophical work on the order of *Death in the Afternoon*, but I am aware that I am not yet ready to undertake such a work. I feel that the cultivation of tennis on a large scale among the peoples of the earth will do much to annihilate racial differences, prejudices, hatred, etc." Worried that some sophisticated readers might think that he is making fun of Hemingway, Saroyan states: "I am not. *Death in the Afternoon* is a pretty sound piece of prose. . . . Even when Hemingway is a fool, he is at least an accurate fool. He tells you what actually takes place and he doesn't allow the speed of an occurrence to make his exposition hasty. That is a lot."[22]

This was too much for the master. In January 1935 Hemingway commented on the book for *Esquire*, a men's magazine founded in the fall of 1933 in which Hemingway regularly contributed letters from Tanganyika, Paris, and Cuba, and in which Dreiser, Farrell, James M. Cain, and Meyer Levin were publishing and Dos Passos's realist watercolors of the port of New York and of a Spanish fiesta appeared. Their contributions were interrupted by ads for whiskey, cigarettes, sharp-looking men's clothing (including not only hats and shirts but also such paraphernalia as cuff links, socks, and even zippers), and enticingly illustrated *Esquire* self-promotion focusing on such forthcoming taboo-breakers as Langston Hughes's story "A Good Job Gone" (a story of interracial romance and intrigue that "no commercial magazine would touch with a ten foot pole"). There were also risqué cartoons, off-color jokes, and somewhat revealing photographs of actresses.

Writing in the context of this men's magazine, Hemingway was not generous when he took to task Saroyan, the ethnic newcomer to the literary scene, whose first *Esquire* story had just been published, who had invoked and attempted to imitate Hemingway in his first book, and in whose writings Edmund Wilson had also noticed some Hemingway traits. Hemingway struck the pose of a drunkard picking a barroom fight with Saroyan "who tells the boys in his stories how he can write like, or better than, other people if he wanted to try." Hemingway lectures the young contender: "Anybody can write like somebody else. But it takes a long time to get to write like yourself and then what they pay off on is having something to say. . . . You've got only one new trick and that is that you're an Armenian." But that was hardly enough, Hemingway said, invoking the example of Michael Arlen, who had disappointed after some early promise. "Now you see us, the people you can write like and better than, have some of us been shot, and some of us been cut, and all of us been married, and we've been around a long time and we've been a lot of places and seen a lot of things that you haven't seen, Mr. Saroyan, and that you won't ever see because the things are over and lots of the places aren't there any more." After more derogatory comments on Saroyan's abilities, Hemingway asks: "Do I make myself clear? Or would you like me to push your puss in. (I'm drunk again now you see. It's a wonderful advantage when you're arguing.)" And on and on the brawling style goes, as Hemingway calls Saroyan to whose name the world may echo "like Roland's horn at Roncevaux," a "poor ignorant bastid." He asks rhetorically whether there is a doctor in the house: "Good. Mr. Saroyan wants him. . . . Mr. Saroyan isn't feeling so good."[23] The champion clearly felt that he had knocked out the lightweight contender and that ethnic credentials were meaningless in the battle for good writing. Saroyan answered this public attack with a restrained personal letter in which he conceded that Hemingway might be "right" that Saroyan was an Armenian but added: "I hope you don't want me to feel bad about [. . .] being who I am because I don't feel any worse about this than any Englishman (for example) feels about what he is, although I suppose neither of us feels any too good about it."[24]

One of the ethnic writers Hemingway publicly supported was Nelson Algren. Upon Algren's collection *The Neon Wilderness* (1947) Hemingway conferred lavish and wisecracking praise: "Mr. Algren, boy are you good—one of the two best authors in America," the blurb read (and the reader just knew who the other one had to be).²⁵ Algren, who had worked on the Illinois Project of the Writers Guide Series, was one of the first major ethnic writers to take up the theme of heroin addiction that the rise of the Mafia during the Prohibition years made possible at such a large scale in twentieth-century America. A typical sentence from *The Man with the Golden Arm* (1949) reads: "The light was fading in his eyes now, they were sinking to his head and the freshness the drug had brought to his cheeks had turned into a dull putty-gray."²⁶ Just before the doomed hero and war veteran Francis Majcanek, known in Polish immigrant Chicago as Frankie Machine, crosses "the last dark wall of all," he still hears the streetcar's scream: "One flight below a Madison Street trolley charged past in a streamlined, cat-howling fury that left him strengthened by an odd excitement" (331). There was such hard-boiled urban cynicism in the novel that Algren represented a new post-Hiroshima drink served in the "Tug & Meal," called "Antek's A-Bomb Special" and "made simply by pouring triple shots instead of doubles." Fittingly, the scene is accompanied by a jukebox playing "one last sad bar of the final song of a world that had known neither A-bombs nor A-Bomb Specials."

> *There's nothing left for me*
> *Of days that used to be* (68)

Algren, who was also famous for a love relationship with Simone de Beauvoir that affected her (and Sartre's) view of the United States, elicited a terse comment from Hemingway in a 1956 letter. "I like young Nelson," Hemingway starts, but continues: "He is a rough boy but has not learned that if you are really bad you do not have to talk out of the side of your mouth nor that it is only with alchemy that you combine poetry and prose." Finally, he gets to the punchline: "if Nelson is as tough a boy inside as he thinks he is how could he have devoted more than one evening to Simone de [Beauvoir] etc.? Riddle me that?"²⁷

In the intervening half-century Hemingway has often been taken to task for thematizing what had become central failings in the age of multiculturalism: misogyny, homoerotically charged male friendship in a generally homophobic climate, lack of sympathy for ethnic outsiders like the Jewish Robert Cohn who is the only one who does not seem to "get" Jake Barnes's ethos in *The Sun Also Rises*. Toni Morrison undoubtedly spoke for many when she lamented in 1991 that Hemingway had "no need, desire, or awareness" of African Americans "either as readers of his work or as people existing anywhere other than in his imaginative (and imaginatively lived) world."[28] Yet no amount of Hemingway-bashing can clear the record of the first half of the century when, more than any other American author, Hemingway not only offered a contagious hard-boiled style that provided native-born Americans and immigrants, mainstream writers and ethnics, with a literary language, but also participated in publicizing his very life as a romance for modern readers, like a romantic poet in the age of modern media. Hemingway's bullfights or Harry's bar ("Sank Roo Donoo"), his midwestern childhood, his life as a *Kansas City Star* reporter, his World War I experience in Italy, his expatriate years as a Paris correspondent starting in 1921, his Republican engagement in the Spanish Civil War, his international fame, and his mysterious suicide—all these aspects coalesce into a biographical myth of the tough-talking yet sensitive (and at times even sweet) man who was also inspiring as the only major modernist who never went to college. After Hemingway, it has become simply futile to ask if there could have been a modern American literature without him. "Isn't it pretty to think so?"

12

Henry Roth: Ethnicity, Modernity, and Modernism

In Henry Roth's novel *Call It Sleep* (1934), the strands of ethnicity, modernity, and modernism come together inseparably, and at a very high point of American literary achievement. This autobiographically-inflected novel is an outstanding example of their fusion into "ethnic modernism." When the eight-year-old Jewish immigrant protagonist David Schearl attempts, in the experimental twenty-first chapter of book four ("The Rail"), to stick a milk ladle into the electric rail of the Eighth Street trolley tracks on New York's Lower East Side, a high modernist verbal explosion accompanies this climactic moment in the novel.

> On Avenue D, a long burst of flame spurted from underground, growled as if the veil of earth were splitting. People were hurrying now, children scooting past them, screeching. On Avenue C, the lights of the trolley-car waned and wavered. The motor-man cursed, feeling the power drain.[1]

Such external descriptions alternate with, and the pervasive *-ing* forms here seem to echo, the sounds of the streetcars: "Klang! Klang! Klang!" (560)—as an avant-garde anticipation of Hugh Martin's and Ralph Blane's cheerier and more popular "Trolley Song" in the film *Meet Me in St. Louis* (1944). A surrealistic melting-pot melange of people's *eyes* observes David's body lying on the tracks.

> Eyes, a myriad of eyes, gay or sunken, rheumy, yellow or clear, slant, blood-shot, hard, boozy or bright swerved from their tasks, their play, from faces, newspapers, dishes, cards, seidels, valves, sewing machines, swerved and converged. (570)

There are familiar echoes of Paul's letter to the Corinthians and of Isaiah's prophetic image of burning coal.

> (As if on hinges, blank enormous mirrors arose, swung slowly upward face to face. Within the facing glass, vast panels deployed, lifted a steady wink of opaque pages until an endless corridor dwindled into night.) (579–580)

> (Coal! And it was brighter than the pith of lightning and milder than pearl,) . . . (And made the darkness dark because the dark had culled its radiance for that jewel. Zwank!) (584)

James Joyce- and T. S. Eliot-inspired, Yiddish-inflected, and multilingually enriched expressions by the bystanders also sustain the fusion of the secular and the sacred in the modern city:

> "Oy! Oy vai! Oy vai! Oy Vai!"
> "Git a cop!"
> "An embillance—go cull-oy!"
> "Don't touch 'im!"
> "Bambino! Madre mia!"
> "Mary. It's just a kid!" (571–572)

While David is shaken by the electric power on the streetcar tracks, all the strands of thinking about modernity seem to coalesce. He views the electric current as if it were a divine power. It is telling that he disregards a rabbi's admonition that "God's light is not between car-tracks" (346).

Call It Sleep has been justly praised as a twentieth-century masterpiece of American literature. Written by a young Communist, it became part of the controversies surrounding proletarian art; yet it includes only a brief moment in which a soapbox orator makes overt social commentary: "Only the laboring poor, only the masses embittered, bewildered, betrayed, in the day when the red cock crows, can free us!" (566). This was not enough for the *New Masses*, where an anonymous reviewer (who sounds very much like Mike Gold) expressed anger at the "sex-phobias" of "this six-year-old Proust" (Gold had also accused Proust of masturbatory modernism). "It is a pity," the reviewer complained, "that so many young writers drawn from the proletariat can make no better use of their working class experience than as material for introspective and febrile novels."[2] This dismissal of *Call It Sleep* provoked Kenneth Burke and Edwin Seaver to come to Roth's defense for his honesty and skill in portraying the "pre-political thinking of childhood."[3]

Call It Sleep was also developed with evident psychoanalytic interest in such concepts as Freud's "family romance," the child's wish to imagine a fantasy ancestry and to regard his real parents as foster parents, a wish intensified here in the immigrant situation.[4] Another famous Freud essay seems to have provided the model for a passage in the novel. In *Beyond the Pleasure Principle* Freud, exploring "repetition" and its connection to the death instinct, gave an account of a lonely child's imaginative method of making himself disappear during absences of his mother, whom he greeted with an enigmatic "Baby o-o-o-o!" upon her return. "He had discovered his reflection in a full-length mirror which did not quite reach the ground, so that by crouching down he could make his mirror-image 'gone.'"[5] In *Call It Sleep*, there is a memorable scene in which David sees his mirror image appear and disappear in shop windows:

> Only his own face met him, a pale oval, and dark, fear-struck, staring eyes, that slid low along the windows of the stores, snapped from glass to glass, mingled with the enemas, ointment-jars, green globes of the drug-store—snapped off—mingled with the baby clothes, button-heaps, underwear of the dry-goods store—snapped off—with the cans of paint, steel tools, frying pans, clothes-lines of the hardware store—snapped off. A variegated pallor, but pallor always, a motley fear, but fear. Or he was not.
> On the windows how I go. Can see and ain't. Can see and ain't. And when I ain't, where? In between them if I stopped, where? Ain't nobody. No place. Stand here then. BE nobody. Always. Nobody'd see. Nobody'd know. Always. Always? No. Carry—yes—carry a looking glass. Teenchy weenchy one, like in pocket-book, Mama's. Yea. Yea. Yea. Stay by house. Be nobody. Can't see. Wait for her. Be nobody and she comes down. Take it! Take looking-glass out, Look! Mama! Mama! Here I am! Mama, I was hiding! Here I am! But if Papa came. Zip, take away! Ain't! Ain't no place! Ow! Crazy! Near! I'm near! Ow! (514–515)

David's vividly rendered experience of losing his self-image is connected to his obsession with death, with "sleep eternal years," and with coffins (85). Yet Henry Roth claimed not to have read Freud at the time of the novel's publication.[6]

Call It Sleep was, as the quoted excerpts suggest, part of the modernist movement as it experimented with stream-of-consciousness technique, with a literary equivalent of cinematic montage, with allusions to Stein,

Eliot, Joyce, Conrad, Yeats, and other moderns and contemporaries. As a young man, Roth helped the New York University Professor Eda Lou Walton edit the volume of modern urban poetry *The City Day* (1929).[7] The novel's many stylistic registers show this exposure, as he incorporates into the book, without apparent effort, such Stein-like phrases as "A bath-tub is a bath-tub" (248), alludes to Eliot's "Jugjugjugjugjugjug" (333), "unreal" city (383), or "heap"—Roth calls it "swirl"—"of broken images" (586) from *The Waste Land,* invokes Joseph Conrad with the phrasing "heart of darkness" (582), or makes a Joycean pun, as in the dialect rendition of "a whore master" as "a hura mezda"—sounding like the Zoroastrian god of light, Ahuramazda (562).[8] And the novel's central biblical image from Isaiah of the power of the seraph's coal that can cleanse dirty lips (which feeds David's wish to seek a vision and to find purification on the trolley tracks) may have been inspired by William Butler Yeats's poem "Vacillation" (1932) where it is connected with the theme of modern art.[9] There are also brief and, on the whole, exceptional moments where the style gestures toward Hemingway: "'And this is the Golden Land.' She spoke in Yiddish" (6). Or: "'No, I don't want it.' He answered in Yiddish" (419).

Authored by an immigrant who had come as a young child from Polish Galicia (then belonging to Austria-Hungary), the book that opens with a prologue at Ellis Island and the Statue of Liberty is also part of "immigrant fiction." Significantly, the prologue is set in 1907, a peak year for immigration, during which more than 1.28 million people came through Ellis Island. The steamer on which the family that is at the center of the novel arrives is named *Peter Stuyvesant,* after the Dutch governor who attempted (in vain) to prohibit the immigration of the "deceitful race" of Jews to New Amsterdam in 1654; the novel may be the very best literary representation of the "second generation" of immigrants to the United States, and the most successful experiment in using immigrant dialect and non-English-language elements as an idiom in an English-language novel. In *Call It Sleep,* the Statue of Liberty is described somewhat differently from the tradition marked by Holt's *Life Stories* or Emma Goldman's autobiography:

> And before them, rising on her high pedestal from the scaling swarmy brilliance of sunlit water to the west, Liberty. The spinning disk of the late afternoon sun slanted behind her, and to those on board who gazed, her features were charred with shadow, her depths exhausted,

her masses ironed to one single plane. Against the luminous sky the rays of her halo were spikes of darkness roweling the air; shadow flattened the torch she bore to a black cross against flawless light—the blackened hilt of a broken sword. Liberty. (10)

This is a modernist defamiliarization of the silhouetted Statue. Franz Kafka's *Amerika* deforms Lady Liberty in a similar fashion: "a sudden burst of sunshine seemed to illumine the *Statue of Liberty* so that he saw it in a new light, although he had sighted it long ago. The arm with the sword rose up as if newly stretched aloft, and round the figure blew the free winds of heaven."[10] Roth's description contains some of the key terms of the novel: brilliant light, the raised broken hilt of a menacing sword, and the cross. Whereas Mary Antin had helped to redefine the official meaning of Liberty to stand for a welcome to immigrants, Roth casts her as the war god Ares or the angel with the flaming sword ready to drive humans out of paradise. And near the end of the novel the Statue of Liberty returns as Roth incorporates a voice who says that "you can go all the way up inside her for twenty-five cents" (565)—as if Lady Liberty were a cheap prostitute.

The prologue, written after the rest of the novel was completed, introduces the central characters, as David Schearl and his mother Genya arrive at Ellis Island and meet David's father Albert. It prepares the reader for a sociological novel about immigrant life that does not follow this opening, though it significantly establishes a crossing, a migration, as the first action of the book. If Roth had not added the prologue, the novel's first sentence would have come closer to the opening of Joyce's *Ulysses:* "Standing before the kitchen sink and regarding the bright brass faucets that gleamed so far away, each with a bead of water at its nose, slowly swelling, falling, David again became aware that this world had been created without thought of him" (15).

Roth represents the Jewish immigrants' Yiddish as *good* English—for Roth a highly stylized and lyrical language—and their English as broken English. This procedure suggests an inner world of richness and lyrical expression, a full range of feelings and words that might remain hidden to an English-only reader were it not for the narrator's mediation. In the "broken English" sections, however, Yiddish words do enter into the text, at times with the humorous effect of a bilingual pun. One example hinges on the double meaning of the word "kockin" as English "cocaine" and Yiddish "to shit," which explains the apparent paradox that in America "kockin" "will clear the mouth of pain" (211). Sometimes Yiddish meanings are rendered in English, at other times they remain on the level of in-jokes; for Roth does not put the reader in the comfortable position of the standard-English speaker who finds amusement in the fully accessible humorous dialect of the kind that Leo Rosten ("Leonard Q. Ross") created with great public resonance for *New Yorker* readers and in *The Education of H*y*m*a*n K*a*p*l*a*n* (1937).

On many occasions, the reader is invited to hear a Yiddish original *through* a strangely poeticized English text in which it is buried but apparently not completely lost in translation. Albert repeatedly asks, "Where's the prayer?" (referring to David who will presumably say Kaddish upon the father's death [91]) and Genya's sister Bertha wonders, "How fares a Jew?" (420). At times, the technique is subtle: "Do you still ask?" (11), "It grows late" (54), or "Nothing fulfills itself with me! It's all doomed!" (176). In other instances, an unfamiliar English phrasing calls attention to itself, as in: "Will you vomit up past shame?," "Go talk to my buttocks!" (519), "All buttocks have only one eye," or "May your brains boil over!" (289). This form of linguistic transposition, in which even vulgar terms may take on a poetic glow, was also tried out by Roth's contemporaries. Alter Brody's "Lowing in the Night" (1927), for example, includes such lines as "Try to joke with such a blister on your tongue," "Who smears salt on a herring?," and "Just a bed pan for you to empty your lust in."[11] (Brody's comic man-woman dialogue also serves as an antidote to Lewisohn's idealization of Jewish marital rapport in *The Vehement Flame*.)

Roth uses, without translation, Hebrew, Aramaic, Slavic, and Italian words and phrases. Here is the Italian/Yiddish exchange between a butcher and a sweeper: "Verstinkeneh Goy!" . . . "Sonnomo bitzah you! I fix" . . . "You vanna push me? . . . I'll zebreak you het." "Vai a fanculo te! . . . Come on! Jew bast!" (328). Roth employs various dialects, and he makes the reader listen to a boy's speech-impediment: "If I blyibm duh ywully ylyod, den he wonthye hilyt me so moyuch, myaytlybe." As the narrator puts it, "In trying to divine Benny's meaning, one could forget all else" (488).

Roth's varied method of representing language difference contributes much to the poetic quality of *Call It Sleep*. It also permitted Roth to insert many literary phrasings that, whether they had their origins in Anglo-American modernist aesthetics, in the world of technological modernity, or in conventional Yiddish speech, seem natural parts of dialogue or narration. It may be hard to determine what, in a given instance, is sociolinguistic reference to a foreign-language original ("the prayer" [281]), what is a mistake ("I'm losted" [126]), and what is specific to an interior monologue in the modern novel ("Tomorrow came" [148]). Is Bertha's (hardly traditional) curse "May a trolley-car crack his bones" (209) a translation from the Yiddish? Is her expression, "A bath-tub is a bath-tub" (248) a common immigrant wish or an echo to Gertrude Stein? When the phrase "suddeh vuddeh" (419) appears, is this merely the dialect deformation of "soda water"—or is it an allusion to Mrs. Porter and her daughter who wash their feet in soda water, from *The Waste Land*? Is there a correct English equivalent of "Boddeh" Street on which David says he lives when he is lost in Brownsville? Bodder, Potter, Poddeh, Bodder, Body, Pother, Powther, Bahday, and Barhdee Street are among the suggestions offered in the book (124–128, 135); yet does such a street exist at all? Are there limits to translation, the novel seems to ask—which is extraordinarily successful in giving the English-language reader the feeling of living in an uneasily translated world.

At times, translation and explanation to linguistic and religious outsiders come close to ethnic treason in the novel, when David "explains" things Jewish to his admired Polish-American and Catholic friend Leo Dugovka whom he considers part of a "rarer, bolder, more carefree world" and who has a "glamour about him" (414):

> When Leo had asked him whether Jews wore amulets on their persons, David had described the "Tzitzos" that some Jewish boys wore under their shirts, and the "Tfilin", the little leather boxes, he had seen men strap around their arms and brows in the synagogue—had described them, hoping that Leo would laugh. He did. And even when Leo had said of the "Mezuzeh", the little metal-covered scroll that all Jews tacked on the door-posts above their thresholds—"Oh! Izzat wotchuh call 'em? Miss oozer? Me ol' lady tore one o' dem off de door w'en we moved in, and I busted it, an' cheez! It wuz all full o' Chinee on liddle terlit paper—all aroun' an' aroun'." David had not been hurt. He had felt a slight qualm of guilt, yes, guilt because he was betraying all the Jews in his house who had Mezuzehs above their doors; but if Leo thought it was funny, then it was funny and it didn't matter. He had even added lamely that the only things Jews wore around their necks were camphor balls against measles, merely to hear the intoxicating sound of Leo's derisive laugh. (414–415)

Interestingly, the narrator provides explanations to a presumed non-Jewish reader even as the danger of explaining religious secrets to outsiders is being invoked. David (and Roth) thus seem to be doing here what Rabbi Judah Leib Lazerow explicitly worried about when he wrote in his sermon *The Staff of Judah*, published in New York in 1921: "I hereby order the translator upon oath not to translate these following statements of mine. . . . I do not want the gentiles to know what is taking place amongst us."[12] One of Lazerow's concerns was the forsaking of the wearing of *zizis*, or fringes on four-cornered garments, in America.

Call It Sleep does not only highlight linguistic divides between established adult languages, but also follows the process of a child's language acquisition. David is twenty-one or twenty-two months old in the Prologue, and the novel focuses on his life from just before his sixth birthday to a little after his eighth. For example, in contemplating the omnivorous nature of non-Jews, David, at age six, thinks of the following:

> Ham. [. . .] And chickens without feathers in boxes, and little bunnies in that store on First Avenue by the elevated. In a wooden cage with lettuce. And rocks, they eat too, on those stands. Rocks all colors. They bust 'em open with a knife and shake out ketchup on the snot inside. Yich! and long, black, skinny snakes. Goyim eat everything. (303)

The context permits us to decode "snot" (a word Joyce had helped to poeticize) in "rocks" as David's personal term for "oyster" (a word withheld by the narrator in order to approximate David's consciousness), just as the "snakes" are recognizable but not identified as "eels."

The oedipally charged child's point of view accounts for the view of the mother "tall as a tower" (15) and representing physical closeness and intimacy by the "faint familiar warmth and odor of her skin and hair" (17). The father is seen in more grotesque or surrealistic but generally menacing close-ups: "The fine veins in his nose stood out like a pink cobweb" (24).

The parents' emigration distances (and alienates) David forever from the world of their origins:

> Filled with a warm, nostalgic mournfulness, he shut his eyes. Fragments of forgotten rivers floated under the lids, dusty roads, fathomless curve of trees, a branch in a window under flawless light. A world somewhere, somewhere else. (23)

This passage makes vivid the second (or the first *American*) generation's difficulty with nostalgia. The village Veljish, David's own place of birth, is available to him only through his mother's narration (called "mother's yarn" in the novel's manuscript) and not through concretely remembered sensual experience. The mother's warm and living body, the goal of David's oedipal yearnings, is also the physical space designating his origins, a space all the more important to David since he does not directly know his geographic place of birth. In the world of objects, David's "warm, nostalgic mournfulness" has only fragments to work with, a hill, or a tree. (It is indicative of Roth's stylistic self-consciousness that the sentence starting with the word "fragments" is itself followed by a sentence fragment.) Even when his mother gently chides him, her reference is to a world that has to remain inaccessible to David: "You're like those large bright flies in Austria that can fly backwards and forwards or hover in the air as though pinned there" (450). Yet there are no dragonflies in David's New York. Much of the past is lost to him, and Roth uses the Joycean technique of incorporating English children's tales ("Goldilocks and the Three Bears") and nursery rhymes to show David's odd cultural situation. The following passage is characteristic of Roth's experimental method of rendering David's chain of associations:

> Hickory, dickory dock. Clock. Never had. But—wheel—what? Once . . . Once I . . . Say again and remember. Hickory, dickory, wickory, chickory. In the coffee. In a white box for eight cents with yellow sides. In a box. Box. Yesterday. God it said and holier than Jew-light with the coal. (447)

His "nostalgia" becomes, paradoxically, *forward*-looking, directed away from concrete and local sensual memory impressions and toward transportable abstractions such as the "flawless light" that he ultimately seeks to find through electricity on the trolley tracks.

Genya and Albert incorporate into their New York home cheap and inauthentic items of nostalgia that turn out to be charged with deeper meaning. This is something that David senses. There is a strange parallelism in the aesthetic representations Albert and Genya choose. For the mother, it is a ten-cent reproduction of a generic country scene that she hangs up and that significantly gives a name to one of the four books of the novel. Can "The Picture" "of a small patch of ground full of tall green stalks, at the foot of which, tiny blue flowers grew" (227) evoke the aura of Veljish to Genya and David?

"I bought it on a pushcart," she informed him with one of her curious, unaccountable sighs. "It reminded me of Austria and my home. Do you know what that is you're looking at?"

"Flowers?" he guessed, shaking his head at the same time.

"That's corn. That's how it grows. It grows out of the earth, you know, the sweet corn in the summer—it isn't made by pushcart pedlars."

"What are those blue flowers under it?"

"In July those little flowers come out. They're pretty, aren't they? You've seen them, yes, you have, fields and fields of them, only you've forgotten, you were so young." (227)

The mother-son dialogue marks the distance of the urban boy not only from the place of his mother's youth but from *any* countryside: He has forgotten the country and cannot even identify corn. David finds himself staring at the picture, searching for hidden meanings behind what was "only a picture of long green corn and blue flowers under it" (250).

And she had said that he had seen it too, real ones, long ago in Europe. But she said he couldn't remember. So maybe he was trying to remember the real ones instead of the picture ones. But how? If—No. Funny. Getting mixed and mixed and—. (250)

The picture constitutes David's opening to and veil over "real" memories. It also elicits Bertha's ironic question, "Are you starting a museum?" (249). Sixty years later, Roth described the impression the art in Eda Lou Walton's apartment made on him: "He had never seen sheer white walls like that before. So simple, plain, with just three pictures on them, reproductions, one of crude golden flowers almost leaping out of the frame. And another of a blue farm wagon. Whose were they?" This raises the question whether even such small fictional details as the picture were merged out of childhood and adulthood materials.

Albert would have preferred a picture of "something alive," for example, a "herd of cattle drinking such as I've seen in the stores. Or a prize bull with a shine to his flanks and the black fire in his eyes" (252). The father ultimately gets something in this genre, a plaque with bull's horns that has a more threatening effect on David:

Before him on a shield-shaped wooden plaque, two magnificent horns curved out and up, pale yellow to the ebony tips. So wide was the span between them, he could almost have stretched his arms out on either side, before he could touch them. Though they lay there inertly, their bases solidly fastened to the dark wood, there pulsed from them still a suggestion of terrific power, a power that even while they lay motionless made the breast ache as though they were ever imminent, ever charging. (404)

David recognizes what he thinks is a cow—not from life but from pictures and from a movie he saw with Aunt Bertha. Genya responds with a laugh, "A cow, but a he-cow!" (404). She explains that "it reminded him of the time when he took care of cattle," and significantly, her eyes wander "to the picture of the corn flowers on the wall" (404). Both parents thus establish an equivalence between the two purchased items. David is affected by the horns and contemplates them:

> Somehow he couldn't quite believe that it was for memory's sake only that his father had bought this trophy. Somehow looking at the horns, guessing the enormous strength of the beast who must have owned them, there seemed to be another reason. He couldn't quite fathom it though. (405)

David's relationship to his parents' city-bought fetishes strengthens his oedipal view of the laughing mother as land, summer, beauty, and fertility, and the scowling father as enormous and unfathomable animal power; yet Roth's fictionalization of David's predicament—the city boy does not recognize corn and cannot tell a cow from a bull—also brings his aesthetic close to Eda Lou Walton's observation that young urban writers are no longer "intimate with the ritual of the seasons" and "have no associations with the names of flowers."[13] Hence they suffer from "rootlessness," a topic Nathan Asch proposed to investigate in a (denied) Guggenheim fellowship application of 1936. They may become interested in "country" as an abstraction, embracing, for example, anthropology as a way of understanding past folkways *in general,* and substitute a lost realm of their own family experience by reading Sir James Frazer's *Golden Bough* (1890) or any of the sources that the footnotes to *The Waste Land* sent them to read, and where they found comprehensive and global accounts of mistletoe, corn-spirit, magical coal, fertility and "Fire King" lightning myths from Galicia to Cambodia. The mythical method (as advocated by T. S. Eliot) permitted artists to unite past and present, letting modernism function as a curious equivalent for twentieth-century nostalgia.

David's aunt Bertha plays the *buffo* part in this drama, providing comic relief. Bertha is hardly uncritical of the New World, yet she prefers the restlessness and the noise of the city to the boredom of the country.

True I work like a horse and I stink like one with my own sweat. But there's life here, isn't there? There's a stir here always. Listen! The street! The cars! High laughter! Ha, good! Veljish was still as a fart in company. Who could endure it? Trees! Fields! Again trees! Who can talk to trees? Here at least I can find other pastimes than sliding down the gable on a roof! (201)

The trees of Bertha's origins are not only dusty, they are boring; and her vulgar metaphor of the idiocy of country life, "still as a fart in company," provides a dramatic alternative view to Genya's picture of Veljish. Bertha wishes to see America as the fulfillment of everything the immigrant could not be in the country of origin. It is fitting that she is thrilled by shopping in New York and comments on the huge underpants she bought that "when I hold them at a distance upside down this way they look like peaks in Austria" (206). For Bertha, purchasing cheap and large-sized underpants seems to take the emotional place of remembering the sublime view of the Carpathian mountains—and by bargain-hunting in the American marketplace she can symbolically take revenge on the Old World class hierarchies: "Twenty cents, and I can wear what only a baroness in Austria could wear" (206).

Bertha and Genya are not only "worlds apart in temperament" (196), but in their combination they also suggest the ambivalence of immigrants toward embracing new environments and yearning for the past. Bertha lacks depth, yet she is the catalyst who makes Genya speak about her past secret. For Genya, corn is associated with the romantic figure of Ludwig, a Christian organist with whom she was in love but who spurned her before she married Albert. When Ludwig gets married, Genya watches the wedding procession, as she confides to Bertha: "I hid in the corn-field nearby. [...] I felt empty as a bell till I looked at the blue cornflowers at my feet. They cheered me. That was the last I saw of him I think" (271). Genya has substituted an image of beauty for an experience of pain and loss; and she repeats the substitution when she buys the picture. This lends meaning to her unaccountable sighs. David, who overhears the conversation, senses a connection though he does not get the full meaning. Genya's corn story becomes part of David's family romance of imagining the "organist" not only as the mother's first lover but also as his real father. Thus David fancies that he is an illegitimate child, a "benkart" (273).

For Albert the specific meaning of cattle is the story of his guilt for his father's death: Although Albert could have saved his father, who was gored by a bull, he did not lift a finger (530). No wonder David notices a speech hesitation, a hitch, whenever Albert says "my father" (148). Albert's sense of persecution would seem to derive from that trauma of the past, and his guilt for his father's death becomes fear of his own son, fear that another "prayer" will continue the drama and become a "butcher."

This heavily charged family drama is accentuated by David's own guilt feelings connected with sexuality and betrayal of family and ethnic group to his non-Jewish peers. In his childish beginnings with sexuality he experiences a fairy-talelike double-bind in "playing bad" with Annie. These "dirty" sexual games draw on family language and would require David to play the "poppa" (64–65). David's quest is for the purification of the "dirt" inherent in the family story, for an escape from the darkness of the cellar and the closet to the world of light.

In his friendship with Leo Dugovka, David feels a "bond of kinship" (407). This cross-ethnic kinship looks all the more glamorous to David since it starts with a rooftop encounter that appeals to his visionary side. David instantly worships the blond and blue-eyed boy who is four years older and not afraid. Leo flies kites, is daring, and, David thinks, "There was no end to Leo's blessings—no father, almost no mother, skates" (411). Skates are associated by the rabbi with non-Jews (508). The children's bond is based on David's weakness and stems from all the charged areas of his young life including family, sex, and faith. It leads David right back into the darkness of the cellar. He reaps the reward of the rosary only for letting Leo "play bad" with David's cousin Esther and witnessing this momentous event while pretending not to care and exploring the "Big-little-big-little-little-little-big-busted" beads of the rosary against the background of gurgles and whines (478).

David's forward-looking nostalgia for "flawless light" is thus also a wish for an escape from his traumas and predicaments. The religious schooling in the *cheder* strengthens his wish for a cleansing transformation of the profane into the sacred that would reenact the power of Isaiah's coal. Reading the sacred text about the seraph's coal that can cleanse dirty lips (305) focuses David's energies onto his attempt to seek a vision, to find purification, and to provoke a crisis that will resolve his generational impasse, address his religious needs, and fuse the fragments of the past with modern technology as a secular substitute for transcendence. David has a vision of hypnotizing brilliance at the edge of the river. Afterward David feels "as though he had seen it in another world, a world that once left could not be recalled. All that he knew about it was that it had been complete and dazzling" (334). The world elsewhere of the parents' past has been transformed into a mysteriously surrealistic and modern vision that can be experienced in the city. It is at this point that the gentile boys Pedey and Weasel—to whom David denies his Jewishness—make him drop a sword-shaped zinc sheet on the live electric wire under the trolley tracks. Fascinated by the terrific light that is unleashed, consuming the mock-Arthurian "sword" with radiance (340), David now embarks on the project of seeking an illuminating experience on the streetcar tracks. He breaks into the *cheder* in order to reread Isaiah and continues to build up associations between his idea of a sacred vision and the world of technology, the rabbi's laughter notwithstanding.

Later David interrupts the recital of the biblical verse, crying that his mother died "Long ago! Long ago!" (498). He calls his mother his aunt and, when asked about his father, says that his father was an organ player in a church in "Eu-Europe" (500), a Christian! Asked "in what land" the mother met the organ player, David, misunderstanding the concrete land for the abstract country, answers: "In where there was—there was c-corn" (501). It is Freud's family romance—but with the difference that the immigrant child was separated early from his father, has no recollection of the meaningful physical world of the parents, and may perhaps develop a more exaggerated drive not toward Freud's exaltation of the actual father, but toward the creation of a homemaking myth, a whole vision that would symbolically fuse David's divided worlds.

Moving toward the climax of the novel, David picks up a milk dipper and breathlessly approaches the trolley tracks with the statement, *"Now I gotta make it come out"* (556), and the "crack" (558) out of which the rebirth is to take place blends technological site, sexual allusion, and reference to the fissure between worlds that David acutely experiences. David miraculously survives his near-electrocution from a shock of 550 volts. His burnt foot (594) reinforces the Oedipus motif; but preliminary intergenerational recognition and family reconciliation also emerge as the result of the crisis of David's injury.

In the last paragraph of the novel Roth uses three times the phrasing that gives the novel its title, and the passage is a masterpiece at sustaining ambiguity: What is the "it" of *Call It Sleep?* Answers have ranged from rebirth and hope to oblivion and nothingness. Roth stated variously that the title referred to "an artistic accession or an assumption into artistry" or to "the end of that kind of creative life"—a contradiction that is analogous to Coriolanus's proclaiming "a world elsewhere" only in haughty reaction to his banishment, so that "accession" also means "end."[14] Coriolanus's phrase to which Roth alludes was applied also to Edward Hopper who was misunderstood as realist because he adhered to the American belief that visionaries need not retreat to a "world elsewhere" but can turn to the experience of their daily lives.

The ending is also the extraordinary realization of "a world elsewhere" that David experiences and that finds its aesthetic equivalent in the world of the arts that Roth hoped to enter with the writing of *Call It Sleep*. David's electric experiment finds its counterpart in Roth's aesthetic experimentation. Roth's method in this chapter is an alternation between external scenes and italicized passages, set as prose poems, that continue David's interior monologue, like cinematic cross-cutting. The bantering vulgarities of the various characters on East 10th Street are juxtaposed ever more rapidly against David, who is about to reach the third rail with his milk dipper.

>   *And his eyes*
> "Runnin' hee! hee! hee! Across the lots hee! hee! jerkin' off."
>   *lifted*
> "An' I picks up a rivet in de tongs an' I sez—"
>   *and there was the last crossing of*
>   *Tenth Street, the last cross-*
> "Heazuh a flowuh fer ye, yeller-belly, shove it up yer ass!"
>   *ing, and beyond, beyond the elevateds,*
> "How many times'll your red cock crow, Pete, befaw y' gives up? T'ree?" (568)

In the manuscript of the novel the cinematic procedure is evident, as Roth wrote the different sections sequentially and indicated with a system of Greek letters where they should be cut and spliced into each other.[15]

If only for a moment David's electric vision of light, power, and modernity makes possible a sense of a "world elsewhere." The ending brings together the central images of the novel. Cellar, picture, coal, and rail, sword, dipper, electricity, transcendent vision, and polyethnic setting, father and mother, parents and child, Old World and New World, vulgarity and the sacred, sexual imagery, cusswords, and metaphysical yearning, Christianity, Judaism, Zoroastrianism, and secularism, revolutionary action and betrayal, fear and triumph, coexist and fuse in one powerful surge of dangerous brightness that lasts for only a moment but holds in suspension all the tensions under which David suffered—as if he were one of Sir James Frazer's "sacred or tabooed persons" who is, according to *The Golden Bough,* "charged just as a Leyden jar," an early device used for storing and discharging static electricity, "is charged with electricity."[16]

Roth had originally planned to use materials of his own life "from ghetto child to Greenwich Village,"[17] yet he ended *Call It Sleep* when David is only eight years old. In later writings, Roth emphasized the importance of Eda Lou Walton with whom he became intimate in the mid-1920s, when he was not yet twenty years old and she was twelve years his senior. Roth recalled Walton's Greenwich Village apartment, where "dust scuffed up from hectic Eighth Street, just above the window."[18] He heard the "clash of crosstown trolley, blast of auto horn, brought into the room along with the normal drone of the city" and remembers "for the nth time, conning T. S. Eliot's 'Waste Land'" while "Eda Lou tittered girlishly in the arms of her young lover," a friend of Roth's. He read *Ulysses* under similar circumstances.

After he became the New York University professor's young love interest, he started writing the manuscript of what became *Call It Sleep*—on NYU blue and pink exam books. In the light of Roth's later writings, the "clash of the crosstown trolley" connected not only to Eliot's imagery ("Trams and dusty trees") but also referred literally to the line that connected the two poles of his life, the Lower East Side and Greenwich Village. The world of the Lower East Side, culminating in the electric shock at the Eighth Street trolley, was thus remembered and re-created at the other end of the Eighth Street crosstown line. It must have seemed like magic that, from both points of view, the "world elsewhere" was only a trolley ride away, linked by rails; there was all the more autobiographic significance to the trolley since Roth's father worked as a motorman on a New York tramway for some time.

It only reinforces the symbolism of the Eighth Street trolley that its tracks led not only from the immigrant ghetto to Greenwich Village, but also went by the Cooper Union (where the radical soapbox orator can be heard), by the first site of the Whitney Museum (where "Eighth Street Rebels" Juliana Force and Gertrude Vanderbilt Whitney exhibited the modernist art that the Metropolitan Museum had refused to accept as a gift), by the Hans Hoffman School for modernist artists, and close by where Mabel Dodge had held her radical bohemian salon at 23 Fifth Avenue. As art critic Clement Greenberg remembered in 1957, Eighth Street was "the center of New York art life." Eighth Street was also a world off limits to Marjorie Content (married first to Harold Loeb and later to Jean Toomer) when she grew up in midtown Manhattan and was not permitted to ever go further south than Fourteenth Street.

Although Roth's novel ends shortly after his protagonist has turned eight, the whole span of Roth's life "from ghetto child to Greenwich Village" may yet be secretly represented in the book. Crossing worlds, the defining experience of the prologue, may also be the central theme for the "detached artist" Roth.

The fusion of ethnicity and modernism was so successful in *Call It Sleep* because both ethnic childhood and artistic modernism were strongly and simultaneously felt by the writer, each reminding him of the other—and thus doubly moving the reader. The novel may present a deep expression of second-generation art by merging East Side and Village origins so fully that a powerful and haunting bilateral descent myth of Jewish immigrant childhood and American modernist initiation emerges. Two worlds are connected in such a way that there was always "a world somewhere, somewhere else," different from and yet similar to the one inhabited *or* fictionalized. This process was also experienced as a deep crisis, a burnout, and a short-circuit (metaphors close to the language of the novel's ending that Roth also applied to his life), and as an intense experience for which such a price had to be paid that—even though Roth began a novel about a Cincinnati-born proletarian in the 1930s and completed and published several autobiographically inspired books near the end of his life—no new work emerged that was comparable to his 1934 masterpiece.

13

Brrrrrrriiiiiiiiiiiiiiiiiiiinng! The Clock, the Salesman, and the Breast

Henry Roth's verbal explosion and his hero's near-execution at the trolley tracks marked a violent escalation from such streetcar scenes as Stein's enactment of sympathy or Antin's memories of daring trolley-track games among immigrant children. As a setting of a vision, Roth's choice of the Eighth Street trolley also resembled Toomer's mystical experience at the 66th Street L station. By contrast, Richard Wright returned to the troubling historical legacy that the means of modern transportation were also prime places of racial segregation and tension, an experience that the southern colored woman's life story had recorded. In the racially bifurcated world that Wright confronted in his life and exposed in his writing, violent explosions were always a possibility. Wright made it his lifelong task to attack segregation, calling attention to its social and psychological consequences, as he often focused on the transformation of fear into violence or rage.

In a section tellingly entitled "Squirrel Cage" that forms part of Wright's first novel, completed in 1937 under the title "Cesspool" and published only in 1963 as *Lawd Today*, a conversation takes place among four young black men who have migrated from the South to the city of Chicago.

"I heard a man say he saw a black guy slash a white streetcar conductor from ear to ear."

"It's bad luck for a black man anywhere."

"There's somebody always after you, making you do things you don't want to do."

"You know, the first time I ever set down beside a white man in a streetcar up North, I was expecting for 'im to get up and shoot me."

157

"Yeah, I remember the first time I set down beside a white woman in a streetcar up North. I was setting there trembling and she didn't even look around."

"You feel funny as hell when you come North from the South."[1]

In *Lawd Today,* Wright's wish clearly is to combine a social message with modernist experimentation, as the novel focuses on a day in the life of Jake Jackson, postal employee in Chicago, a jealous and mean husband who seems happiest with male peers. He roams Chicago, goes to work, is robbed in a nightspot, comes home drunk, and beats up his wife who has a tumor and needs an operation. Unlike Wright's later works, *Lawd Today* presents its characters in rich social detail and in a web of human (or perhaps better, dehumanized) relations.

Wright's employment and mixing of various modernist methods is noteworthy. Following Joyce's *Ulysses,* the apprenticeship novel is set on one single day. Ironically, it is the date of Lincoln's birthday, for Wright's Bloomsday was February 12, 1936. The protagonist is, after Hemingway, another Jake, a monosyllabic tough guy at least in part indebted to the hard-boiled school. The novel does not only invoke Gertrude Stein directly and by name, but also plays around with Steinian techniques. When Jake looks at movie posters for "The Death Hawk," Wright sets the seven posters as blocks of prose, without punctuation or capitalization, and with many *-ing* forms. For example: "a bluehelmeted aviator in a bloodred monoplane darting shooting speeding zooming careening out of a bank of snowwhite clouds in hot pursuit of two green monoplanes" (52). And in a scene in which Jake's friend Bob laughs so contagiously that not only Jake, but also their opponents Al and Slim, just have to laugh along, Wright begins with a physiological account of laughter ("a sharp expulsion of breath coming from the diaphragm") but then uses the occasion to experiment with repetitions of the simple word "laugh": "And they laughed because they had laughed. They paused for breath, and then they laughed at how they had laughed; and because they had laughed at how they had laughed, they laughed and laughed and laughed" (87–88). This passage which aims at finding a formal equivalent to the experience and rhythm of contagious laughing is all the more noteworthy since Wright would refrain from representing mirth, humor, or laughter in most of his later writings. In *Lawd Today,* interior monologues, modernist collages of newspaper headlines ("HITLER CALLS ON WORLD TO SMASH JEWS" [32]), the incorporation of radio programs with fragments from Lincoln's First Inaugural Address (64), diagrams of card games (80, 83, 85), and mottos by Van Wyck Brooks, T. S. Eliot, and Waldo Frank round off the experiment. Rejected by several publishers, for one of whom James T. Farrell was the reader, *Lawd Today* was published only in 1963, after Wright's death; ironically, Granville Hicks's lukewarm review stressed Farrell's influence on the young Wright.

Compared to *Lawd Today*, Wright's most famous novel, *Native Son* (1940), was more mature and accomplished but also seemed less experimental in form. Its dramatic opening signaled the end of an era and the full arrival of a sociologically inspired and realist-inflected left-wing modernism. The "undistinguished American" sweatshop worker Sadie Frowne had been able to live without an alarm clock and maintain the premodern belief that no such clocks could possibly exist because she could not imagine how "the clock would know" how to call you "at the very time you want to get up."[2] Henry Roth's sketch "Impressions of a Plumber" (1925) began with the sentence, "The alarm clock rings with frightened intensity."[3] Wright's own *Lawd Today* and several manuscript versions of *Native Son* had started with the scene of a protagonist slowly waking up (because "somebody was calling," or "a loud knock at the door made him jerk fully awake").[4] By contrast, the published version of *Native Son* (1940) opened very dramatically with the word "*Brrrrrrriiiiiiiiiiiiiiiiiiiinng!*"—an onomatopoeic representation of the ringing of an alarm clock.[5] It is a first line that few readers are likely to forget and that has been regarded as the end of the Harlem Renaissance or the beginning of a Chicago Renaissance. The sound is intelligible to readers around the globe—the novel has been translated into most European languages as well as Japanese, Turkish, Hebrew, Chinese, and other tongues—as it embodies the intrusion of the most familiar instrument of modern time into the natural world of sleepers, a small, capsule version of *the* story of modernization.

The topics of modernity reached Wright and other authors through the writings of the Chicago School of Sociology—works by W. I. Thomas and Robert E. Park (both from small-town backgrounds), Ernest W. Burgess, the immigrant Louis Wirth (whose wife was the welfare supervisor for Wright's aunt), and the African-American Horace Cayton (whom Wright befriended). Burgess, for example, famously argued in a landmark manifesto of 1924, "The Growth of the City: An Introduction to a Research Project," that the "manifestations of modern life which are peculiarly urban—the skyscraper, the subway, the department store, the daily newspaper, and social work—are characteristically American."[6] Wirth's 1940 essay "Urban Society and Civilization" viewed "culture" and "civilization" as two poles of human existence, correlated to folk societies on the one hand and to the rise of cities on the other, for "what we call civilization as distinguished from culture has been cradled in the city."[7] Burgess's and Wirth's approaches went back to Park's work on the "ecological organization" of the city, his research emphasis on "transportation and communication, tramways and telephones, newspapers and advertising, steel construction and elevators—all things, in fact, which tend to bring about at once a greater mobility and a greater concentration of the urban populations."[8] Park's son-in-law Robert Redfield published *Tepoztlán* (1930), an influential study of a Mexican village which theorized about modernity transforming natural into clocked time, traditional, sacred, local, rural, "primitive" life into modern, secular, widely shared, urban, and industrial life; "folk" into people and orally transmitted folklore into mechanically reproduced popular arts; *Gemeinschaft* into *Gesellschaft,* in short, culture into civilization. These were concepts that held an obvious appeal to ethnic writers.[9]

The Mississippi-born Richard Wright, like Hemingway, never went to college, and, unlike any other major American modernist, never even finished high school; but as a poor southern migrant to Chicago he was drawn to, and absorbed, the milieu of the Chicago sociologists. In his preface to St. Clair Drake and Horace Cayton's sociological study *Black Metropolis* (1945), Wright summarized the Chicago sociologists' assessment of modernization: "Holy days became holidays; clocks replaced the sun as a symbolic measurement of time. As the authority of the family waned, the meaning of reality, emotion, experience, action, and God assumed the guise of teasing questions." Wright claimed: "it was not until I stumbled upon science that I discovered some of the meanings of the environment that battered and taunted me.... The huge mountains of fact piled up by the Department of Sociology at the University of Chicago gave me my first concrete vision of the forces that molded the urban Negro's body and soul."[10]

Many writers around the world fictionalized modernization. What made Richard Wright's version of the story of the rupture brought about by modern time particularly powerful was the fact that the beginning of *Native Son* eradicates any sense of a "sacred" folk existence prior to the alarming intrusion of clocked time. In the novel, in which the family has no authority and religion has become meaningless, there is literally no *word* before the sound of the alarm clock; the clock is also the subject of the first sentence after the *"Brrrrrrriiiiiiiiiiiiiiiiiiinng!"*: "An alarm clock clanged in the dark and silent room" (447). After that opening, and for the rest of the book, characters are thrown into, and live and die in, the modern world of the city of Chicago.

Human beings seem to be little but objects of modernization. Their first appearance is consciously reified: they make themselves felt simply as "a woman's voice," "a surly grunt," or "naked feet," as if they were parts rather than a whole (447). The hero's or antihero's name is Bigger Thomas, his last name probably an allusion to Harriet Beecher Stowe's *Uncle Tom's Cabin;* after all, Wright's first published book was entitled *Uncle Tom's Children* (1938). In the famous scene of Bigger's killing of the rat with a kitchen skillet that follows soon (450), the animal image seems like an allegory of the protagonist himself: both are killed in metallic environments. Significantly, the three-part novel, divided into the books entitled "Fear," "Flight," and "Fate," ends as Bigger Thomas, sentenced to death, "heard the ring of steel against steel as a far door clanged shut" (850). Bigger's life in *Native Son* is thus framed by two clangs. He is trapped in a world that here seems to extend only from the clock to the cell door on death row.

Eager to show Bigger's fascist potential, Wright makes him a hero who first commits an accidental homicide of his white employer's daughter Mary Dalton and then atrociously rapes and murders his black girlfriend Bessie Mears; yet Bigger never is capable of confronting his own guilt, an inability which Wright insisted was central to the characterization. Instead, Bigger settles on the unforgettable nonconfession, "what I killed for I *am!*" (849). This is not so much in the hard-boiled manner as it conveys a frighteningly existentialist sensation: "What I killed for must've been good!" (849). In the absence of recognition or access to social meaning, Bigger Thomas had only his murders to define him: "He had murdered and had created a new life for himself" (542). And: "He had committed murder twice and had created a new world for himself" (671). For Wright, this was both an existentialist option of experiencing a perversely creative self-definition in the most negative social image that had been thrust upon him and the frightening possibility that someone like Bigger could become the violent parody of a Christ-like redeemer figure:

"Had he not taken fully upon himself the crime of being black? Had he not done the thing which they dreaded above all others? Then they ought not to stand here and pity him, cry over him; but look at him and go home, contented, feeling that their shame was washed away" (721).

In describing Bigger's brutal actions Wright employs a tough style that creates an urban gothic effect and inhibits an easy identification of the reader with Wright's protagonist, who is both pitiable victim and horrifying perpetrator: "The head hung limply on the newspapers, the curly black hair dragging about in blood. He whacked harder, but the head would not come off" (531–532). Or: "He lifted the brick again and again, until in falling it struck a sodden mass that gave softly but stoutly to each landing blow" (667). It is such sentences that have earned Wright the reputation of being a "naturalist," but *Native Son* has many different levels of style, including such Toomer-like phrasings as "The room was black-dark and silent; the city did not exist" (665–666) and the following, quite remarkable *tour de force* of a single sentence that takes off from the sound of a distant church bell while Bigger is asleep:

> It sounded suddenly directly above his head and when he looked it was not there but went on tolling and with each passing moment he felt an urgent need to run and hide as though the bell were sounding a warning and he stood on a street corner in a red glare of light like that which came from the furnace and he had a big package in his arms so wet and slippery and heavy that he could scarcely hold onto it and he wanted to know what was in the package and he stopped near an alley corner and unwrapped it and the paper fell away and he saw—it was his *own* head—his own head lying with black face and half-closed eyes and lips parted with white teeth showing and hair wet with blood and the red glare grew brighter like light shining down from a red moon and red stars on a hot summer night and he was sweating and breathless from running and the bell clanged so loud that he could hear the iron tongue clapping against the metal sides each time it swung to and fro and he was running over a street paved with black coal and his shoes kicked tiny lumps rattling against tin cans and he knew that very soon he had to find some place to hide but there was no place and in front of him white people were coming to ask about the head from which the newspapers had fallen and which was now slippery with blood in his naked hands and he gave up and stood in the middle of the street in the red darkness and cursed the booming bell and the white people and felt that he did not give a damn what happened to him and when the

people closed in he hurled the bloody head squarely into their faces *dongdongdong.* (598–599)

This is a truly Faulknerian sentence, part of a self-consciously modernist prose experiment employed by Wright in representing a dream sequence. The *dongdongdong* is the "trigger," the sensory stimulus that connects the inner world of Bigger's dream with the outer world of the bell ringing, a common stream-of-consciousness device. And this is not the only instance of Wright's modernism, even though modernist techniques were less prevalent in *Native Son* than they had been in *Lawd Today.*

Wright also alluded to T. S. Eliot's *Waste Land* when he called Chicago an "unreal city."[11] In his manifesto "Blueprint for Negro Writing," Wright invoked Joyce's famous phrasing when he encouraged black writers to "forge in the smithy of our souls the uncreated conscience of our race," a Joyce adaptation later echoed by Ralph Ellison.[12] The ending of his short story "Bright and Morning Star" was a response to the conclusion of Joyce's "The Dead."[13] His experimental novella "The Man Who Lived Underground" (1945) used a collage technique. Wright was fascinated by D. H. Lawrence, and, as we saw, admired Stein and Hemingway.

For Wright, the central question was the one he asked in his preface to *Black Metropolis* (1945): "What would life on Chicago's South Side look like when seen through the eyes of a Freud, a Joyce, a Proust, a Pavlov, a Kierkegaard?" (xxxi). The point was not to choose between realism and modernism, but to use any technique that was likely to shake up readers and direct them toward the serious questions of the times, among which class inequality and racial segregation were prominent.

In order to suggest the psychological consequences of racism, Wright invoked William James, who wrote in the section "The Self" of *The Principles of Psychology:*

> No more fiendish punishment could be devised, were such a thing physically possible, than that one should be turned loose in society and remain absolutely unnoticed by all the members thereof. If no one turned round when we entered, answered when we spoke, or minded what we did, but if every person we met "cut us dead," and acted as if we were non-existent things, a kind of rage and impotent despair would ere long well up in us, from which the cruelest bodily tortures would be a relief; for these would make us feel that, however bad might be our plight, we had not sunk to such a depth as to be unworthy of attention at all.[14]

Wright applied James's observation to African-Americans:

> The American Negro has come as near being the victim of a complete rejection as our society has been able to work out, for the dehumanized image of the Negro which white Americans carry in their minds, the anti-Negro epithets continuously on their lips, exclude the contemporary Negro as truly as though he were kept in a steel prison, and doom even those Negroes who are as yet unborn.[15]

For Wright, it was the condition of social inequality that helped to sustain the belief in racial difference, and he was anything but an essentialist. He wrote in the nonfictional *12 Million Black Voices* (1941):

> The differences between black folk and white folk are not blood or color, and the ties that bind us are deeper than those that separate us. The common road of hope which we all have traveled has brought us into a stronger kinship than any words, laws, or legal claims.
>
> Look at us and know us and you will know yourselves, for *we are you*, looking back at you from the dark mirror of our lives.[16]

Yet inequality distorted and perverted this mirror, as Bigger Thomas's case so brutally illustrates. Riding an eastbound streetcar from Chicago's Forty-seventh Street, Bigger "looked anxiously at the dim reflection of his black face in the sweaty windowpane. Would any of the white faces all about him think that he had killed a rich white girl? No! [. . .] He saw it all very sharply and simply: act like other people thought you ought to act, yet do what you wanted" (549).

Wright took pains to emphasize the human condition in the black experience and wrote in a blurb he prepared for the publicity of his autobiography *Black Boy* (1945): "[To] those whites who recall how, in the early days of this land, their forefathers struggled for freedom, BLACK BOY cannot be a strange story. Neither can it be a strange story to the Jews, the Poles, the Irish, and the Italians who came hopefully to this land from the Old World."[17]

If there was a writer of the 1930s and 1940s who was truly at odds with Wright it was Zora Neale Hurston. The young Wright, who had not yet published a single book, attacked Hurston's most famous novel *Their Eyes Were Watching God* (1937) in the *New Masses* with a then rarely noticed but later frequently invoked diatribe that includes the verdict that "Miss Hurston *voluntarily* continues in her novel the tradition which was forced upon the Negro in the theater, that is, the minstrel technique that makes the 'white folks' laugh," a passage which also helps to explain why Wright grew reluctant to portray humor in his own work.[18] A year later, the Rosenwald and two-time Guggenheim fellowship winner Hurston retaliated when she panned *Uncle Tom's Children* in the widely circulating *Saturday Review:* "Mr. Wright serves notice by his title that he speaks of people in revolt, and his stories are so grim that the Dismal Swamp of race hatred must be where they live. Not one act of understanding and sympathy comes to pass in the entire work. . . . Since the author himself is a Negro, his dialect is a puzzling thing. One wonders how he arrived at it. Certainly he does not write by ear unless he is tonedeaf."[19] The disagreements were profound and they were aired publicly.

Yet like Wright, Hurston saw a need to stress universalism and the inequalities that inhibited the growth of a shared culture. Hurston was a professional anthropologist who received her graduate training from a central figure of twentieth-century anthropology, the Columbia professor Franz Boas, and who worked for Melville Herskovits, wrote for Ruth Benedict, and knew Margaret Mead. Like Wright, she seems to have found her story through an academic discipline: "I needed my Barnard education to help me see my people as they really are."[20] And elaborating upon anthropology as a vehicle for her perception, Hurston wrote that the folklore she was familiar with since childhood was too close to her, so she "had to have the spy-glass of Anthropology to look through at that."[21] What Hurston saw through that spyglass was the resilience and adaptability of common folk. She was more interested in folk culture than in urban civilization and focused on the internal cohesion of black culture rather than on the social interaction of blacks and whites.[22]

As a universalist, Hurston was one of many African-American writers who commented upon the "forced grouping" that takes place in many social as well as intellectual encounters. Using an example set in a means of modern transportation she observed that when a black student couple (Barnard-Yale) goes on a New York uptown subway after a concert and, at 72nd Street Station, two scabby-looking Negroes enter the same car, all other identities of the couple (college students on a date, theatergoers, etc.) get eclipsed by the category "Negro." The white passengers identify the students with the two lowlifes who "woof, bookoo, broadcast, and otherwise [discriminate] from one end of the coach to the other," and are perceived to be "typical." Hurston spelled out the silent comments in the white glances: "Only difference is some Negroes are better dressed" or "you are all colored aren't you?" The students are left with paradoxical thoughts of the kind, "My skinfolks but not my kinfolks."[23] Hurston's point was to expose the strange cultural logic of "forced grouping" that corresponds to a denial of individuality to members of visible minorities. As a writer Hurston therefore tried to resist compulsive representation. "I know," she wrote in chapter intended for her autobiography *Dust Tracks on a Road* (published in 1942, one year after Wright's programmatically titled *12 Million Black Voices*), "that I cannot accept responsibility for thirteen million people. Every tub must sit on its own bottom regardless."[24]

Hurston echoed Boas's environmentalism and universalism when she wrote in her autobiography: "It seemed to me that the human beings I met reacted pretty much the same to the same stimuli. Different idioms, yes. Circumstances and conditions having power to influence, yes. Inherent difference, no."[25] And in "What White Publishers Won't Print" (1950), Hurston emphasized not only the analogies of blacks and Jews in the American imagination but also stressed the significance of *all* minorities for the country: "But for the national welfare, it is urgent to realize that the minorities do think, and think about something other than the race problem. That they are very human and internally, according to natural endowment, are just like everybody else."[26]

Both Wright and Hurston were part of the greater emphasis placed on universalism in the 1940s and 1950s and of which novels that crossed lines of expected racial representation were representative. A perfect genre novel for the universalist postwar moment was the African American Willard Motley's best-selling *Knock on Any Door* (1947), which was also made into a Hollywood movie. Inspired by the hard-boiled crime writers, by James T. Farrell, and by Richard Wright, *Knock on Any Door* focused not on a black man but on the Italian-American criminal Nick Romano and ended with a detailed description of his execution on the electric chair. As did Ann Petry in *Country Place* (1947), William Gardner Smith in *Anger at Innocence* (1950), James Baldwin in *Giovanni's Room* (1956), and Frank Yerby in much of his oeuvre, both Hurston and Wright also published novels without major black characters (books that were once called "raceless novels"), Hurston's *Seraph on the Suwanee* (1948) and Wright's *Savage Holiday* (1954).

Both Hurston and Wright also worked for the Federal Writers' Project in the Works Progress Administration (WPA), Hurston in New York and on "The Florida Negro," and Wright on *New York Panorama* and in Illinois. Other writers who participated in the FWP or had WPA jobs were Nelson Algren, Saul Bellow, Arna Bontemps, Sterling Brown, Jack Conroy, Pietro di Donato, Ralph Ellison, Claude McKay, Henry Roth, Margaret Walker, and Frank Yerby as did social scientists W. Lloyd Warner, Horace Cayton, Allison Davis, and Burleigh B. and Mary Gardner. And Jerre Mangione administered the FWP and later published a history of it.

What Hurston and Wright saw in the theme of modern clocked time also marked their difference. Hurston collected a cheery song poem in which measured time has become part of a courtship story that goes literally "around the clock": "When the clock struck ten I was in the bin, in the bin with Sue,/ in the bin with Sal, in the bin with that pretty Johnson gal/ When the clock struck eleven, I was in heaven, in heaven with Sue,/ in heaven with Sal, in heaven with that pretty Johnson gal."[27] Hurston also included a lively story in her folklore-inspired *Mules and Men* (1935) in which a man takes a turtle on a string as if it were a pocket watch on a chain, and, when asked what time it is, pulls out the turtle and says: "it's quarter past leben and kickin' like hell for twelve."[28] This was an instance of resilient folk survival and even tricksterish folk one-upmanship in response to modernization. In *12 Million Black Voices* Wright imagines another type of dialogue about telling time that grimly connects it to racial domination:

> If a white man stopped a black man on a southern road and asked: "Say, there, boy! It's one o'clock, isn't it?" the black man would answer: "Yessuh."
>
> If the white man asked: "Say, it's not one o'clock, is it, boy?" the black man would answer: "Nawsuh."[29]

In Wright's world, the power of modernity, compounded by racial domination, was simply crushing. For him, segregation was omnipresent; for Hurston it was so marginal that she was the only major black writer to attack the first important Supreme Court decision for integration, *Brown v. Board of Education* in a segregationist white Southern newspaper.[30]

* * *

One way in which the confrontation of the premodern world with modernity was represented in literature was through the figure of a seductive stranger, typically a salesman of sorts, who brings modern commercial leisure culture to remote, traditional settings. For some reason, "tradition" could readily be imagined as a good, but temptable young black woman in a rural or provincial setting who had to brave the salesman's lure. And readers could marvel at the attractiveness of the new that those handsome-seeming modern devils of the trade tried to sell.

Julia Peterkin's tale "The Merry-Go-Round," first published in *Smart Set* (1921), was one such story from the 1920s. The intruder is the white man Carson who brings, as a symbol of leisure culture, a merry-go-round to a black village setting. Soon Jesse Weeks and his girlfriend Meta Parker, Maum Mary's daughter, ride the merry-go-round every night. Maum Mary, who cooks Carson's food, rejects his request to let him sleep in her house, saying firmly, "No white man ain' nebber yet sleep in no bed o'mine, an' I know I ain't gwine sta't wid you."[31] Meta, too, resists the white man's temptation to take some free rides when she brings him her mother's food. When Carson approaches Meta on the merry-go-round while Jesse is buying peanuts, Jesse strikes Carson who takes revenge a day later and shoots Jesse. The whites of the town, mobilized by the village store clerk, and the black policeman escort Carson onto a train; the black townsfolk set fire to the merry-go-round. Carson becomes involved with a tent mission; Jesse, who was crippled by the shot, works as a basket-and-fish-trap maker; Maum Mary and Meta make a living by taking in washing and give part of their income to the preacher. The temptation of secular modernity and leisure culture had been resisted, though it leaves wounds.

Both Hurston and Wright wrote stories following this pattern and intensifying it. In Hurston's "The Gilded Six-Bits," first published in 1933 in Martha Foley and Whit Burnett's *Story Magazine,* the Florida factory worker Joe wants to take his wife Missie May to a new ice-cream parlor operated by a stranger, Mister Otis D. Slemmons from Chicago. Slemmons has the distinction of owning a five-dollar gold piece for a stickpin and a ten-dollar gold coin on his watch chain, and Joe worships him as a black Rockefeller or Ford and is excited after their visit to Slemmons's parlor, though Missie May thinks that the gold would look better on Joe.

One night when Joe comes home early from his shift in the plant, he finds Slemmons in bed with his wife. He beats him, chases him away, and is left with the golden watch chain in his hands, which he now sulkingly uses to remind Missie May of her unfaithfulness. After months of acting sullenly like a "stranger," they finally make love again, but when Missie May afterward finds the gold piece in their bed she wonders if Joe meant it as "payment" for her lovemaking. She also discovers that the coin is merely a gilded half-dollar. Soon Missie May is pregnant, and before long, gives birth to a baby boy who, according to Joe's mother, looks exactly like Joe. The husband feels reconciled, goes to Orlando, and buys the coin's worth of candy kisses for his wife. The couple's life continues as it had before the Slemmons episode.[32]

Wright's four-part story "Long Black Song," first published in *Uncle Tom's Children* (1938), is told from the point of view of Sarah, whom Wright once described as "a very simple Negro woman living in the northern hills of Mississippi."[33] Sarah is waiting for her husband Silas to return, soothes her baby, and thinks of the past—her first love Tom, who was sent almost a year earlier to Europe to fight in World War I, and for whom she still yearns. A white salesman arrives in a car. He demonstrates to Sarah a gilt-edged $50 clock-phonograph, plays a religious recording of a song about judgment day, and makes sexual advances to her. Sarah keeps saying "no" to him, but the salesman succeeds in making love to her. He leaves the clock-phonograph behind and offers it to Sarah, now for the reduced price of $40, promising to return the next morning.

When Silas comes home, his happy mood soon changes when he discovers the graphophone and the white salesman's suspicious traces. Silas explodes, breaks the phonograph, and starts whipping his disloyal wife, who manages to escape with Ruth into the hills. The next morning Sarah observes from the hills the arrival of the salesman's car and the ensuing struggle between Silas, the salesman, and the salesman's associate. Silas shoots one of the two white men as the second one drives off. Silas drags the white man's body into the street and throws Sarah's belongings out of the house. Cursing all white men, he bitterly accepts his fate—certain death. From the hills Sarah sees the arrival of a long line of cars full of white men. Silas shoots some of them until they set fire to the house in which Silas dies without a murmur. Sarah runs away from the scene crying "Naw, Gawd!"[34]

Compared with Peterkin's story from 1921, these two tales of the 1930s suggest that "The Merry-Go-Round" seems not to have been taken to the possible climactic moment of the rural woman's actual unfaithfulness; in Peterkin's tale the modern, seductive, and ruthless aspects of the merry-go-round man are ultimately rejected even by the intruder himself. At the end of the story, the vehicle of leisure-culture seduction is burned and religious authority reasserted. Peterkin thus offered a resolution to the drama that no longer seemed plausible to either Wright or Hurston. Peterkin's Meta is also much more passive than Sarah in Wright's story, let alone Missie May in Hurston's tale. And neither Wright nor Hurston were willing to adopt the patronizing voice of Peterkin's narrator who describes the arrival of the merry-go-round with the sentence: "Every evening when work on the plantations was over the gay music sounded clear in the still air, and the darkies flocked down to the village and rode out all the money they had."[35]

Wright's and Hurston's stories, in pushing further the kind of plot Peterkin had told, let the tradition-oriented female characters yield to the temptation from the snake of the salesmen of leisure, and showed that the glitter of leisure-oriented capitalism is not golden but merely gilded. In both stories, the intrusion is represented not simply as a loss of innocence but as married women's adultery and unfaithfulness to relatively good though jealous husbands—men who furthermore also have achieved some, and yearn for more, access to the world of modernity that the seducers perhaps can also pretend to represent. Missie May and Sarah, as well as Peterkin's Meta, can thus be said to be pivots "between men."

There is a particular tension in the stories' imagery between breast as home and nature and breast as an erogenous zone susceptible to the modern seducer. Wright's Sarah first offers to breast-feed her baby Ruth; then her breasts are touched sexually by the salesman. Hurston describes the still faithful Missie May in a bathtub with a phrasing that may vaguely foreshadow the ice-cream parlor: "Her stiff young breasts thrust forward aggressively like broad-based cones with the tips lacquered in black" (985). At the end Joe buys so many candy kisses because the baby boy can "suck a sugar tit" (996).

Yet Wright and Hurston conclude their stories in a virtually antithetical fashion. For Hurston, natural time works as a great healer. For Wright, the story steers toward a violent catastrophe. Hurston's seducer is *black*, which gives the whole story an intraracial focus that is characteristic of much of Hurston's oeuvre. Wright's modern tempter is white, which intensifies the dramatic interracial collision: "If it were anybody but a white man," Sarah ponders when she considers pleading with Silas, "it would be different" (348). When Hurston panned *Uncle Tom's Children,* she sarcastically commented that "in 'Long Black Song,' the hero gets the white man most Negro men rail against—the white man who possesses a Negro woman. He gets several of them while he is about the business of choosing to die in a hurricane of bullets and fire because his woman has had a white man. There is lavish killing here, perhaps to satisfy all male black readers."[36]

The killing had been even more lavish in the story's manuscript version. In a fifth section, omitted in publication, Sarah's old lover Tom reappears, together with her brothers Bill and Leroy, and all three black men, uniformed veterans who have just come back from World War I, die fighting at Silas's burning house. The unpublished section is formally distinguished by rapidly alternating Sarah's direct speech, third-person narration, and Bill, Leroy, and Tom's words in an italicized, lowercase language stream, creating the effect as if Sarah heard the words of others only in a swimming blur.

> Hands shook her again. *sarah when this happen sarah tell us whut happened* "They killed 'im!" *where they kill im show us where yuh live sarah* She bent over again and moaned. [. . .]
>
> The car stopped. *Look look that mus be the place its on fire lawd it's a gawddam mob them sonsofbitches them bastards ef ah killed them germans ah kin kill some of them sarah tha you place* "They killed im . . ." *drive on down bill naw not wid sarah in this car hell ah wanna go somebody has t stay here n watch sarah n this baby stay here tom its best we go bill c mon c mon.*[37]

This is a splicing technique that resembles Roth's experimentations. Wright's plotline was the one that Frantz Fanon would later consider the typical Third-World story: the black veteran has fought for a country that denies him his right to live upon his return. Hurston instead incorporates the phrase "bookooing," that black soldiers had picked up in France, from the word "beaucoup."

If for Wright the image of the clock was more traumatic than for Hurston and his salesman brought death rather than knowledge, Wright also took little comfort in the metaphor of the breast as marking happy maternal origins in a community. It is telling that Wright's worst nightmare recorded in *Black Boy* (1945), which occurs after he has been beaten to unconsciousness by his religiously fanatic parents, seems to describe the horrible transformation of what might have been a nourishing breast into a terrifying vehicle of torture and destruction:

> Whenever I tried to sleep I would see huge wobbly white bags, like the full udders of cows, suspended from the ceiling above me. Later, as I grew worse, I could see the bags in the daytime with my eyes open and I was gripped by the fear that they were going to fall and drench me with some horrible liquid. Day and night I begged my mother and father to take the bags away, pointing to them, shaking with terror because no one saw them but me. (9)

If the symbol of the clock spelled doom, that of the breast could be equally deadly. One thinks of such famous autobiographic statements as Wright's line from *Black Boy:* "This was the culture from which I sprang. This was the terror from which I fled" (246). Yet for Wright escape led only to new terror.

There were other ethnic writers in the 1930s and 1940s whose sense of modernity drew on the disciplines of anthropology and sociology. James T. Farrell, who was at the University of Chicago as an undergraduate and wrote a term paper for Ernest Burgess that the famous sociologist saved in his papers, remained so close to a Chicago School of Sociology perspective that he incorporated it quite directly into *Studs Lonigan,* letting a Chicago street orator recite it in the novel. John Connolly, "the King of the Soap Boxers," summarizes, as he puts it, the "plausible ideas presented by members of the Department of Sociology at the University of Chicago," and explains "that the city of Chicago could be divided into three concentric circles." After a differentiated account of these three circles and the city's growth, Connolly proceeds to show that "social and economic forces" created the pressure for black migration into "the white residential districts of the South Side. Blather couldn't halt the process."[38] This is a very close paraphrase of Ernest Burgess's previously cited essay, "The Growth of the City" (1924) which, written at the time when Farrell was a student at Chicago, argued that the "typical processes of that expansion of the city can best be illustrated, perhaps, by a series of concentric circles, which may be numbered to designate both successive zones of urban expansion and the types of areas differentiated in the process of expansion."³⁹ Perhaps for the sake of academic balance, Farrell's next speaker by the Cottage Grove side of the Park, "a small, untidy Jew," invokes the Boasian anthropologists who had "proven that no one race is superior to any other race"—which Studs's buddy Red translates crudely as the Jew's wish to "prove that a Jew was a white man."

Henry Roth was exposed, through the Alfred Kroeber-trained Eda Lou Walton, whose own doctoral work had focused on Navajo poetry, to the anthropological perspective of Frazer's *Golden Bough,* a book Walton admired, that helped Roth understand past folkways *in general* and substitute them for the specific rural family origins that were lost to the urban immigrant, in his version of the "mythical method." Through Walton, Roth also met the anthropologist Margaret Mead.

Mario Suarez, the Mexican-American author who introduced the word "Chicano" to printed literature in 1947 in his modern folk vignettes of life in "El Hoyo" (the ethnic "hole" of Tucson) and his portraits of the section's barber, "Señor Garza." Published in the *Arizona Quarterly,* these sketches strike the familiar anthropological note and fall into the category of ethnic humor, reminiscent of Hurston or Saroyan. Suarez draws a reader, presumed to be an outsider, into an unfamiliar ethnic world. Thus the sketches explain that El Hoyo's "inhabitants are *chicanos* who raise hell on Saturday night, listen to Padre Estanislao on Sunday morning, and then raise more hell on Sunday night. While the term *chicano* is the short way of saying *Mexicano,* it is the long way of referring to everybody." Here Suarez departs from any notion of presenting ethnic homogeneity: "Pablo Gutierrez married the Chinese grocer's daughter and acquired a store; his sons are *chicanos*." Suarez included accounts of parties and suggested a rich folklife, described mixed loyalties and explained folk expressions, but he also stressed that El Hoyo was not a closed, only internally defined universe, for Felipe, for example, came back "from the wars after having killed a score of Germans with his body resembling a patchwork quilt."⁴⁰

In *Out of this Furnace* (1941), Thomas Bell's novel about Slovak-American miners in Braddock, Pennsylvania, there are examples of Wright-like modernist-industrial-urban-gothic prose that was increasingly present in sociologically inspired immigrant writing. Bell attempted to sound both an ominously mystical and a socially conscious note in representing industrial modernity, and he was drawn to the use of *-ing* forms. The following passage is typical of Bell's narrative voice:

A Talbot Avenue streetcar, waiting to begin its long trip through the sleeping towns, the lonely streets, to Pittsburgh, made a yellow glow for the young people to sing by. The voice of the mill was harsher than theirs. It came over the wall like a breathing of a giant at work, like a throb of an engine buried deep in the earth. In it were the piping of whistles and the clash of metal on metal; the chuffing of yard locomotives, the rattle of electric cranes and skip hoists, the bump-bump-bump of a train of cars getting into motion; the wide-mouthed blow of the Bessemers, the thud of five-ton ingots dropping six inches as they were stripped of their moulds, the clean, tenpin crack of billets dropping from a magnet, the solid, unhurried grind of the ore dumper, lifting a whole railroad gondola of iron ore and emptying it, delicately; the high whine of the powerhouse dynamos, the brute growl of the limestone and dolomite crushers, the jolting blows of the steam hammers in the blacksmith shop, the distant, earth-shaking thunder of the blooming mill's giant rolls. A hundred discords merged into harmony, the harsh triumphant song of iron and flame.[41]

Bell, whose father's baptismal surname was Belejcak, was a second-generation immigrant who found his modernist voice not only in the tough tragic-heroic struggle of the men in the brutal industrial world, but also in brief experiments with stream-of-consciousness writing in order to render the feelings of the mother, Mary, who has to raise the children alone after her husband's death.

The differences between two Italian-American prose works, Pietro di Donato's *Christ in Concrete* (1939) and Jerre Mangione's *Mount Allegro* (1943) most specifically resemble those between Wright's and Hurston's oeuvre. Di Donato portrayed immigration as death and a modern industrial crucifixion, Mangione created an immigrant community centered on the culture of the banquet and the tale. Di Donato represented clocks, both setting the rhythm of industrial labor and providing the theme of such Abruzzese songs as "The heart tick-tock alike the clock." He also included an episode in which a phonograph plays twice, and quite incongruously, the American popular song *Indian Love Call,* composed, incidentally by the Czech immigrant Rudolf Friml who had married his Chinese secretary in California. There are also advertisements, radios playing the Billy Rose song *Barney Google,* and there are other reminders of modern commercial culture.[42] Mangione, on the other hand, leaned toward the representation of Sicilians as a "natural" people, part of "culture" rather than of "civilization," a notion which is, however, informed not only by the emotions evoked in going back to one's roots, but also expressly by Mangione's reading of D. H. Lawrence. Lawrence had claimed that Sicilians "never leave off being amorously friendly with almost everybody, emitting a relentless physical familiarity that is quite bewildering."[43] Mangione raises the issue of punctuality in discussions of Mussolini: some relatives tell the narrator not to find fault with Fascism, for did not the American newspapers admit that "Mussolini was a great man who made the trains run on time"? However, when the narrator leaves Realmonte, the Sicilian birthplace of Mangione's mother, he notices and emphasizes with an obvious political intention that in fascist Italy the train arrived half an hour late.[44]

Di Donato's short-story version of "Christ in Concrete" first appeared in *Esquire* in 1937 where it was hyperbolically touted as among the best of forty short stories that *Esquire* had accepted for publication from among 18,000 submissions. Told from the point of view of the construction site foreman Geremio di Alba, an Italian who emigrated from the Abruzzi to the United States in order not to have to fight for "God and Country" in the Italian war against Turkey that ended with the Italian annexation of Libya in 1912, "Christ in Concrete" opens with a description of various immigrant laborers, among them cheery-faced Tomas, the scaffoldman, Old Nick "the Lean" (a war veteran), Snoutnose, Giacomo Sangini, Sandino, Joe Chiappa, and Mike "the Barrelmouth." They all work on a New York construction site which is operated in violation of safety regulations by the Anglo-American boss, "Mister Murdin."

Dorothy Canfield Fisher called attention to the "extraordinary language" in which di Donato's *Christ in Concrete* was written, "the sonorous gift for colorful use of an English which is ringing with memories of Italian."[45] Indeed, there are such literally translated phrases as "I sense badly," for "mi sento male." The workers are largely assumed to be speaking Italian with each other, and when they do speak English it is, as in Roth's *Call It Sleep,* a stereotypically broken idiom. Mike's phrase, "somebodys whose gotta bigga buncha keeds and he alla times talka from somebodys else," is representative (12). There are also Italian words and phrases interspersed into the English text that enhance the translated feeling, though they are not always idiomatic and seem to imply an English rather than an Italian reader, as in "Ah, *bella casa mio*" (14).

The construction workers are seen as objects of forces beyond their control, forces that are like gods and that di Donato capitalizes: "Job" or

"Boss" or "Tenement." Here is an example for the young author's attempt to sound a tough modernist staccato tone—with frequent ellipses marked by "..."—a tone that drives home the violence of labor and the reification of the workers:

> Trowel rang through brick and slashed mortar rivets were machine-gunned fast with angry grind Patsy number one check Patsy number two check the Lean three check Vincenzo four steel bellowed back at hammer donkey engines coughed purple Ashes-ass Pietro fifteen chisel point intoned stone thin steel whirred and wailed through wood liquid stone flowed with dull rasp through iron veins and hoist screamed through space Carmine the Fat twenty-four and Giacomo Sangini check.... The multitudinous voices of a civilization rose from the surroundings and melded with the efforts of the Job. (17)

That the workers live under the rule of secular, not sacred time is made explicit since the gruesome story is set on a cold and snowy Good Friday in March. At a dreamy moment during lunch break (the Catholic Geremio does not eat meat on Fridays) when everything seems unreal to him, Geremio tells Vincenz that he has been thinking "funny! A—yes, what is the time—" and Vincenz tells the time, apparently from a clock on an advertisement: "My American can of tomatoes says ten minutes from two o'clock" (23). Five minutes later, Snoutnose checks the time again, and Geremio "automatically" takes out his watch, rewinds, and sets it. However, "automatic" processes suggest, not aesthetic inspiration, as they did for Stein, but reification and dehumanization; and for di Donato as for Wright, clocked time spells doom, not the impending end of the workday, as Geremio hopes.

Indeed, Murdin has economized too much on the underpinning and ignores Geremio's warning with a simple "Lissenyawopbastard! If you don't like it, you know what you can do!" As a result of the workplace violations, "Job tore down upon them madly" (18). The whole structure collapses, and the men are thrown about in –*ing*-rich sentences: "Walls, floors, beams became whirling, solid, splintering waves crashing with detonations that ground man and material in bonds of death" (25). Several of the workmen die, and some are injured in this immigrant catastrophe caused by an Anglo-American's greed.

The second half of the story is a chilling representation of Geremio's slow and gruesome death, as he is buried alive in construction-site concrete under girders, "the gray concrete gushing from the hopper mouth, and sealing up the mute figure" (26). His agony is more protracted in the original 1937 *Esquire* story. His inside point of view, following Geremio's "train of thought," presented at times in a stream-of-consciousness technique, alternates with third-person narration: "'Ahhh-h, I am not dead yet. I knew it—you have not done with me. Torture away! I cannot believe you, God and Country, no longer!' His body was fast breaking under the concrete's closing wrack. Blood vessels burst like mashed flower stems."[46] Di Donato's interest in the way a violent death may turn human beings into things resembles Toomer's description of Tom Burwell's death in "Blood-Burning Moon.": "The stricken blood surged through a weltering maze of useless pipes and exploded forth from his squelched eyes and formless nose, ears and mouth, seeking life in the indifferent stone." In Geremio's last conscious moment of suffering he moans "the simple songs of barefoot childhood" as if he were returning to culture from the horrors of civilization. His long, very self-consciously Christ-like agony includes prayers, thoughts of his wife Annunziata and their children, memories, curses, and attacks on national and labor exploitation: "they have cheated me with flags, signs and fear."[47] Di Donato also builds upon a contrast to Geremio's vitality and virility: "The strongly shaped body that slept with Annunziata nights and was perfect in all the limitless physical qualities, thudded as a worthless sack among the giant debris that crushed fragile flesh and bone with centrifugal intensity." Before the accident, the men who obviously did not share David Schearl's view of shellfish as "snot" in "rocks," had spoken about going to Mulberry Street for oysters "for the much needed steam they put into the—" but now Geremio's "genitals convulsed. The cold steel rod upon which they were impaled, froze his spine" (28). Di Donato makes Hemingway's Jake Barnes's war wound seem like a mere scratch.

When di Donato made the *Esquire* story the opening chapter of the novel of the same title, he revised and trimmed the death scene, but included some of the phrasings the editors of *Esquire* apparently thought too risky to publish; the chapter now ends with Geremio's son Paul's point of view who hears a Tarantella on his crystal radio at the moment of the father's dying prayer; and the bulk of the novel carries on with the story of the family after the father's death.[48]

Against this grim novel by di Donato stands Jerre Mangione's memoir-novel *Mount Allegro* (1943), a book that evokes the author's experience of growing up in an Italian-American (or more precisely, Sicilian-American) family in a mixed neighborhood of Rochester, New York, and that starts with this passage:

> "WHEN I GROW UP I WANT TO BE AN AMERICAN," Giustina said. We looked at our sister; it was something none of us had ever said.
> "Me too," Maria echoed.
> "Aw, you don't even know what an American is," Joe scoffed.
> "I do so," Giustina said.
> It was more than the rest of us knew.
> "We're Americans right now," I said. "Miss Zimmerman says if you're born here you're an American."
> "Aw, she's nuts," Joe said. He had no use for most teachers. "We're Italians. If y' don't believe me ask Pop."
> But my father wasn't very helpful. "Your children will be *Americani*. But you, my son, are half-and-half. Now stop asking me questions. You should know those things from going to school. What do you learn in school, anyway?" (1)

When Jerre Mangione's *Mount Allegro* was reprinted in 1952 (without a subtitle or genre identification), it carried an introduction by the novelist Dorothy Canfield Fisher who had also introduced the first edition of Wright's *Native Son* and commented on di Donato's language. Fisher praised *Mount Allegro* for its "light-hearted gaiety in the life portrayed," with "none of the sombre tensity which for so long has been a literary fashion" as the book "fortifies the hope in all our hearts that life is not necessarily a martyrdom, but is often a variegated delight."[49] *Mount Allegro* gives the reader a warmly ironic sense of vividly drawn characters who are not victims of circumstances but who spin their tales of old-world memories and new-world mishaps, who celebrate their meals, and who give their American-born descendants a magical sense of a world elsewhere. Like Hurston, Mangione includes fairly precise recipes of particular dishes, jokes, and just story after story. Aunt Giovanna, rejected by immigration officials for the suspicion of suffering from the feared eye disease, trachoma, spent eight days at Ellis Island "looking through iron bars at the Statue of Liberty and the New York skyline, and weeping," before being sent back to Palermo (63). Uncle Luigi, whose anti-Catholicism made him become a Baptist and also go to as many as "three or four services in as many churches of different denominations," would eat two courses of meat on Fridays and attend "a synagogue with some of his Jewish friends" (78). Yet Uncle Luigi notwithstanding, the relatives' Catholicism was a firm part of their lives, and was also "enveloped in a heavy blanket of fatalism" that helped to explain any misfortune as an act of (capitalized) "Destiny" (79, 80).

Both *Mount Allegro* and *Christ in Concrete* include a scene of a séance in which communication with dead relatives is established or at least attempted. Mangione tells the story of a salesman, an Armenian immigrant who was formerly a rug vendor and who now offers to provide the spiritualist contact on a Saturday midnight in the Catholic cemetery. They go there by streetcar, the Armenian ridiculously wearing "plaid golf knickers and a bright yellow sport cap" and displaying "the offensive eagerness of an aggressive salesman" (112). For Mangione, this is an occasion to comment ironically on superstitions, as the narrator's father, unlike two of his Italian-American fellow workers in a candy factory, never believes in the charade. This becomes quite apparent when the "spirits" speak broken Italian in what is recognizably the Armenian's voice. The fraudulent salesman of premodernism escapes, but at least the father is happy not to have paid in advance.

For di Donato, the séance provides an opportunity to create a scene of deep human communication among the poor and oppressed. After the séance, the crippled woman who serves as the medium and Paul's mother Annunziata talk with each other, the medium telling Annunziata "of her two sons killed in the War" and of the bribes she has to pay the police to run her business. Annunziata "felt for her, and in return passionately unburdened to her of Geremio, her Paul, and her children" (156). They drink tea together, the medium charges little, and the night after the séance, both Paul and his mother feel that Geremio's "love surmounted the distance of death" (157).

One motif in which the contrast between di Donato and Mangione becomes apparent is, again, that of the breast. In *Christ in Concrete,* Geremio imagines floating off "to blessed slumber with [his] feet on the chair and the head on the wife's soft full breast" (14), and breasts appear more frequently in their overtly sexual dimensions. Both Mangione and di Donato place at the center a young American-born boy on his way to manhood. In the masculine world of *Christ in Concrete,* following the path toward manhood means giving up being a "titty-drinker" (as the preadolescent Paul is called when he starts working as a bricklayer in his father's place) and feeling, instead, "intoxicating consternation" and "hot blood" sheeting one's face (as the injured Luigi does in his sickbed when Cola swarms her breasts over his face). Cola, Tomas's widow, virtually has the epic epithet "big-titted" accompanying her name throughout the novel; and her comment on Luigi is that she "hugged her breast with one hand and sighed. . . . : 'Even big strong men are like children.'" In an urban melting-pot scene on the New York subway, Paul is pushed against a female subway passenger: "When the train bent around a curve she fell heavily upon him and remained there after the train righted itself. Her body brought him an immediate disturbing message. He shut his eyes. Spongy breasts pulsed against his chest" (225). It is a situation not unlike the one Jim Cowan only fantasized about in Nathan Asch's *Pay Day* (1930).

In *Mount Allegro,* a whole cultural distinction between Sicilian immigrants and Anglo-Americans is derived from attitudes toward breasts:

> [M]y Sicilian relatives had little regard for privacy. They brought all their infants with them on their picnics and the women had no inhibitions about baring their breasts to feed them, no matter where they were or how many Americans might be about to watch them.
>
> Never having seen the exposed breasts of an American mother, I imagined they were never as large and as sprawling as Sicilian breasts, but rather neat and delicate, like the food they packed for picnics. In my prudishness, I was also confident that the breasts of American mothers were purely ornamental and never used for the messy business of hungry brats. (222)

Mangione may here be alluding to, and playing with, the expectation that breast-feeding mothers were a "sight" in immigrant communities, an ambivalent symbol of the immigrants' strange foreign ways as well as of their supposedly natural and admirably premodern qualities. Reports about ethnic communities have included this feature at least since 1898 when E. S. Martin's well-intentioned reportage "East Side Considerations" for *Harper's Monthly Magazine* dwelled on the fact that "you may walk up and down Fifth Avenue for ten years and never see a Fifth Avenue mother nursing her latest born on the doorstep, but in Mott or Mulberry or Cherry Street that is a common sight and always interesting to the respectful observer."[50] At the same time, these examples may be indications of the cultural change from the flat-and-"ornamental"-chested American female ideal of the 1920s toward the busty pinup idols that proliferated after Betty Grable's success and dominated the 1950s, making what used to be an "ethnic" marker a globally exported feature of "American" culture. The women who represented this new ideal were variously referred to in the 1940s as "anatomic bomb" or "sex bomb."

The contrasts that have been drawn out between the different sets of writers resemble each other enough to justify the question addressed to writers of a sociological bent like Wright and di Donato: how, if the world was as oppressive and destructive as they describe it, did anybody ever survive? And to the anthropological camp of Hurston and Mangione: why on earth, if the ethnic world was so wonderful, did their autobiographic projection figures and protagonists choose to leave the community rather than stay in it forever?

Each perspective seems to rest on an assertion as well as a denial, and occasionally the other side comes through: for example, Hurston loved the all-black Florida town of Eatonville enough to claim it as her 1907 birthplace (though she was actually born on January 15, 1891, in Notasulga, Alabama), yet in *Dust Tracks* she once calls Eatonville a "dull village," very much in the way in which Aunt Bertha from *Call It Sleep* looked at her native Veljish; and Jerre Mangione tellingly describes the end of a family party in the 1930s with the adults sitting around "reminiscing about Sicily" while "the youngsters danced and listened to jazz" (237). Mangione also speaks of his determination to "make the break" (227) and leave Mount Allegro—which is a strange description of a departure from paradise. The fact that Hurston invokes a "calling," while Mangione gives as a reason that he was going to college, hardly seems sufficient.

Illustrations of the period reinforced the divergent tendencies in the prose.[51] The *New Masses* (May 1930) self-consciously offered a cartoon that juxtaposed the alternatives of representing black life in the period, William Siegel's two-part illustration, "The white bourgeois version of the Negro" and "—as the white worker knows him." The former image represents singing, comedy, jazz, gamblers, bare-breasted dancers, and so forth, while the latter shows somber scenes of labor and oppression as well as a lynching. It was symptomatic that one of Wright's stories, "Almos' a Man," was fittingly illustrated in the serious WPA style of Thomas Hart Benton, with emaciated and elongated figures and a haggard mule, whereas Hurston had *Mules and Men* cheerily illustrated by the slicker Miguel Covarrubias who had earned his fame as *Vanity Fair* artist. *Esquire*'s art director Eric Lundgren accompanied "Christ in

Concrete" by line drawings depicting sullen workers walking toward the viewer with pickaxes and Geremio praying desperately at the collapsed construction site; the dust jacket for the 1939 hardback featured a pickax and a shovel surrounded by a crown of thorns and a glowing halo; and the 1962 mass market popular library edition also chose an image of workers with shovels and pickaxes against the New York skyline for the front and back cover. Jerre Mangione's *Mount Allegro* was originally illustrated by Peggy Bacon who focused more on the children than the adult characters as subjects of her drawings. In the cases of Mangione/Bacon and Hurston/Covarrubias, the art accompanying ethnic accounts of an all-black hometown and of second-generation immigrant childhood resembled illustrations of children's books or light and comic cartoons. This is also true of William Saroyan's *My Name Is Aram*, which had colored artwork by Don Freeman, whereas Mike Gold's *Jews Without Money* carried stark woodcuts by Howard Simon.

What all of this artwork had in common on either side of the divide and was shared also by much cover art of the period was that it was far more realist and less experimental than modernist art had been since the Armory Show or than were the African-mask-inspired art-deco patterns that were such prevalent book designs in the 1920s. Judging by the images accompanying ethnic literature of the 1930s and early 1940s it would seem that realism (modified only by touches of modernism) had returned in full force.

14

Immigrant Literature and Totalitarianism

For the immigrant and ethnic narratives from *Life Stories, The Promised Land,* and *Giants in the Earth* to *Call It Sleep, Laughing in the Jungle,* and *Mount Allegro* the decisive international connections were those that linked "Americans in the making" with various places of origin. For Antin, it was Polotzk; for Rølvaag, the island of Dønna; for Irvine, Pogue's Entry in Antrim; for Saroyan's parents, Bitlis in eastern Anatolia; and for Roth's Schearls, the village of Veljish. In last two chapters in *Mount Allegro,* Mangione returned to his mother's birthplace Realmonte (or "Munderialli," as the natives called it), his father's original home in Porto Empedocle, and other places in the vicinity of the Sicilian city Agrigento.

The Native's Return: An American Immigrant Visits Yugoslavia and Discovers His Old Country (1934) took Louis Adamic, on a Guggenheim fellowship he received with the help of Sinclair Lewis and H. L. Mencken, back to his birthplace in the Slovenian village of Blato. His first home seemed much smaller than the emigrant had remembered it, for now he had the "consciousness of the Empire State Building and the interior of the Grand Central in New York City." Adamic was impressed, however, by the "bright green of the meadows" with "big splashes of buttercups and purple clover ahum with bees" as well as "forgetmenots in abundance" and "more lilies-of-the-valley in one spot" than he had seen in "nineteen years in America."[1] America seemed to stand for the impressive scale of its man-built environment, while Blato had nostalgic value as pure nature, and Adamic clearly cherished both.

For Stein, Hemingway, Roth, and countless modernist artists, expatriate writers, and musicians, Paris played an important role as the "capital of the arts," a Prohibition-free city that appreciated jazz and was the location of publishers who would dare to bring out works like *Ulysses*. For Toomer, the Château de Prieuré near Fontainebleau may have held meaning as the international headquarter for Gurdjieff's "Institute for the Harmonious Development of Man" whereas the village of Sparta, Georgia, offered artistic inspiration.

Starting in the 1920s, accelerating in the 1930s, and intensifying to its highest pitch in the years of World War II and the beginning Cold War, a new international context emerged that was of some significance not only for individual writers and books but also for the whole trajectory of modernism, ethnic writing, and jazz in the twentieth century. It was the global battle of the ideologies of Fascism (originating in Italy and Germany) and Communism (located in Russia and then expanding to Eastern Europe, China, Korea, and Vietnam) that pulled American writers into these new international constellations. These constituted real lures for some intellectuals in the period, and threats for others. The authoritarian systems of government in which only one political party ruled and which controlled all other institutions and demanded absolute obedience of the individual were called "totalitarian," a term that assumed a generally pejorative meaning only after World War II, notably in Hannah Arendt's widely read work.[2]

Take *My Autobiography* by Benito Mussolini as an example—not exactly a work of "American literature," one might think. Still, written for an American audience and published in 1928 by Hemingway's and Fitzgerald's publisher, Charles Scribner's Sons, it was illustrated with the typical photographs that had accompanied American immigrant autobiographies like S. S. McClure's, ranging from an image of the poor-looking house where the author was born, a stone cottage in Varano di Costa, to one showing him associating with a famous personage—in his case, the Italian king Victor Emmanuel III.[3] The book described the decisive role of World War I, for as a soldier, Mussolini was wounded by a bursting grenade, experienced "indescribable" suffering, and underwent "twenty-seven operations in one month; all except two . . . without anæsthetics" (48). In his disgust for the routine of postwar politicians who "forgot our 600,000 dead and our 1,000,000 wounded," he sounded like a member of another lost generation. But he did something about what he called "the beast of decadence" (63) and the book emphasizes the protagonist's young age at the time of his March on Rome in October of 1922 with which he took power. Mussolini also expressed his admiration for the United States, "now in its golden age," for its discipline, praised the American people for their "sense of organization," and concluded:

> As the reserves of wealth are gone now from the continents to North America, it is right that a large part of the attention of the world should be focused upon the activity of this nation that has men of great value, economists of real wisdom and scholars that are outlining the basis for a new science and a new culture. (26)

In Mussolini's autobiography, "America, the land harboring so many of our emigrants," still called "to the spirit of the new youth" (26). But unlike immigrants, who would at times imagine the American ideal as a fulfillment of childhood dreams from elsewhere in the New World, Mussolini suggested that this ideal was also being fulfilled in fascist Italy, for though he looked to American "youth for her destinies and the preservation of her growing ideals" so did he look "to the youth of Italy for the progress of the Fascist state. It is not easy to remember always the importance of youth. It is not easy to retain the spirit of youth" (27). Was Fascism simply one way of realizing the American ideal, as Mussolini's autobiography seemed to suggest?

That appears to have been the opinion of Richard Washburn Child, the U.S. ambassador to Italy at the time of the March on Rome, who not only introduced the book but also, as was mentioned earlier, actually ghostwrote it and helped to serialize it in the *Saturday Evening Post*. It was a book that was pitched to an American reading public and was, in fact, not available in Italian for the entire duration of fascist rule.[4] Incidentally, S. S. McClure was also trying to sell Mussolini in the United States at the time, but Child had better connections. Child idolized the leader ideal that Mussolini represented and put such sentences in Mussolini's mouth as "I am strict with my most faithful followers" (310), apparently expecting the reader's approbation and applause. Child exemplified an American intellectual so enamored by Fascism that he simply ignored the political terror and repression that had taken command in Italy, and proclaimed from an Olympian distance and extraterritorial safety: "It is absurd to say that Italy groans under discipline. Italy chortles with it! It is victory!" (xiv).

Bigger lights would follow, among them, for example, the archmodernist Ezra Pound who in 1937 wrote in *Germany and You*, a Nazi progaganda publication, about "Totalitarian Scholarship and the New Paideuma"—an early and notably positive American use of the word "totalitarian."[5] Pound's rambling essay argued that "with the march on Rome, which was led not by secluded artists but by men in action, a new phase was initiate[d]" (95). He also criticized those who did not understand the "spirit of the rising Germany," mistaking "the end of demoliberal us[u]rer's Europe for the end of race vigours in Europe" (95). Pound had a longstanding obsession with "Jewish usury" and made English-language propaganda radio broadcasts in fascist Italy during the war years, in which he warned English and American listeners that they were being subjected to Jewish propaganda, or, as he put it in a 1941 broadcast, "clever Kikes runnin' ALL our communication system." In broadcasts of 1942 he argued against pogroms, the "old-style killing of small Jews, for "that system is no good whatsoever." Yet he added: "Of course, if some man had a stroke of genius and could start a pogrom UP AT THE TOP, there might be something to say for it."[6] In 1944, Pound advised Mussolini, now reduced to the Hitler-protected Republic of Saló, that his government should support translations of such a strange array of works as e. e. cummings's *Eimi* (1933), Joyce's *Ulysses*, and Stalin's *Leninism* (1928), and near the very end of the war he wrote the orthodox fascist cantos 72 and 73 (published in 1987). Throughout these years Pound seemed to have believed in the fascist ethos as a version of his American maxim of "making it new." Like Child, he explicitly saw Mussolini as the political leader who would fulfill the American promise—for Pound, most especially Jefferson's project—and he said so in print in his *Jefferson and/or Mussolini*, a book which Pound offered to the British Union of Fascists for publication, which T. S. Eliot (who called it "Jeff & Mutt" in his correspondence with Pound) tried to place, and which in 1936 also appeared in the United States with Horace Liveright, Mike Gold's and Jean Toomer's publisher. In *Jefferson and/or Mussolini*, Pound found that "the fundamental likenesses between these two men are probably greater than their differences" and that the "heritage of Jefferson, Quincy Adams, old John Adams, Jackson, Van Buren, is HERE, NOW *in the Italian peninsula* at the beginning of the second fascist decennio, not in Massachusetts or Delaware."[7]

Among other American authors of the period, Thomas Wolfe cherished sympathies for Nazi Germany and attended the 1936 Berlin Olympics. Zora Neale Hurston's pre-Pearl Harbor manuscript of *Dust*

Tracks on a Road included some chapters which were omitted, at the publisher's suggestion, in the 1942 book publication, among them the concluding "Seeing the World as It Is," which expressed some surprising views on Japan and Hitler. "We Westerners," Hurston commented on the brutal Japanese invasion of China, "wrote that song about keeping a whole hemisphere under your wing. Now the Nipponese are singing our song all over Asia." And with equal sarcasm, she commented on the Nazi military campaigns at the beginning of World War II:

> All around me, bitter tears are being shed over the fate of Holland, Belgium, France, and England. I must confess to being a little dry around the eyes. I hear people shaking with shudders at the thought of Germany collecting taxes in Holland. I have not heard a word against Holland collecting one twelfth of poor people's wages in Asia. Hitler's crime is that he is actually doing a thing like that to his own kind.

Written in 1941, this does not seem to be a very perceptive comment by a writer who was interested in ethnic issues and whose novel *Their Eyes Were Watching God* had been translated into Italian in 1938 by the antifascist Turin intellectual Ada Prospero, the widow of Piero Gobetti, a man who had died after being arrested and tortured by the fascist authorities. Ironically, the back cover of Hurston's published autobiography showed a patriotic Hurston advertising U.S. war bonds.[8]

Gertrude Stein was "encouraged" by her French translator and friend Bernard Faÿ, the Vichy regime director of the Bibliothèque Nationale and Croix de Feu member who also edited anti-Masonic and anti-Semitic reviews, to translate Marshal Pétain's speeches. Stein executed the translation in an intriguingly literal fashion, and she introduced the speeches with the description of Marechal Pétain (a man whom Pound also called, affectionately, "ole Pete Pétain") as a historical figure "who like George Washington, and he is very like George Washington because he too is first in war first in peace and first in the hearts of his countrymen, who like George Washington has given them courage in their darkest moment."[9] Stein, who spent the war years in occupied France, reportedly also recommended Hitler for the Nobel Prize.[10]

By contrast, the clear-sighted W. E. B. Du Bois, who visited Nazi Germany for five months in 1936, stressed in essays published in the *Pittsburgh Courier,* a Negro weekly, that an integral part of Nazi policy "just as prominent now as earlier and perhaps growing in prominence, is world war on Jews. The proof of this is incontrovertible, and must comfort all those in any part of the world who depend on race hate as the salvation of men." He perceptively noticed the power of propaganda, the "greatest single invention" of World War I, which actually made the mass of people believe in what it said:

> Every misfortune of the world is in the whole or in part blamed on Jews—the Spanish rebellion, the obstruction to world trade, etc. One finds cases in the papers: Jews jailed for sex relations with German women; a marriage disallowed because a Jewish justice of the peace witnessed it; Masons excluded from office in the National Socialist Party, because Jews are Masons; advertisements excluding Jews; the total disfranchisement of all Jews; deprivation of civil rights and inability to remain or become German citizens; limited rights of education, and narrowly limited right to work in trades, professions and the civil service; the threat of boycott, loss of work and even mob violence, for any German who trades with a Jew; and, above all, the continued circulation of Julius Streicher's [*Stürmer*], the most shameless, lying advocate of race hate in the world, not excluding Florida. It could not sell a copy without Hitler's consent.[11]

Du Bois thus highlighted the anti-Semitic racism of the National Socialists while also reminding readers of the anti-black racism at home. He stressed that he, a colored man, had been "treated with uniform courtesy and consideration" in Nazi Germany and added: "It would have been impossible for me to have spent a similarly long time in any part of the United States, without some, if not frequent cases of personal insult or discrimination. I cannot record a single instance here."[12]

Far more widespread among American intellectuals, and better studied by scholars, was the lure of Communism, a lure to which Du Bois also succumbed late in his life. For the enticement of Communism grew out of the Marxian interests that were understandably widespread among ethnic intellectuals and among many others who were indignant about the inequalities under capitalism, especially during the years of the Great Depression in the United States. Communism also seemed to present a stronger alternative to Fascism than did the capitalist democracies—at least until the 1939 Stalin-Hitler agreement. The attraction was not only strong in the early revolutionary years symbolized by Trotsky, when the new Soviet Union seemed to be the political home for all sorts of modernist artists and when suprematism and objectivism constituted something like a state art, but it continued well into, and for some, all the way through the Stalinist years of brutal political repression, the kulak liquidation, and the infamous show trials to which many intellectuals and artists fell victim. In Myra Page's novel *Moscow Yankee* (1935), for example, Andy, an incredibly naive cardboard working-class American goes to Russia and becomes an equally unbelievable "new Soviet man" while the novel is blissfully blind to the human costs of collectivization and Stalin's Five Year Plan, the praises of which are sung at the end of the book. The death toll in the Soviet Union for the period 1931–1933 alone has been estimated at around seven million. Was Communism, was Stalinism, twentieth-century Americanism, as American communist Earl Browder's Popular Front slogan had it?

A good number of American intellectuals thought so. Among writers who have been cited or discussed in these pages, Mike Gold remained loyal to the Communist party through all its ideological shifts and changes, and both Henry Roth and Richard Wright remained enthusiastic about the Soviet Union in very dark times. Tellingly, Roth referred to the Soviet Union as his "cherished homeland," and in the statement "Where My Sympathy Lies" (1937), he publicly condoned the Stalinist show trials, for he felt that all defendants had "confessed their guilt." Roth added: "I do not believe together with the Hearst press that these men were under the influence of mesmerism or mysterious narcotics; therefore, I believe them to be, as they themselves acknowledged, guilty."[13] Even at the time of the Hitler-Stalin pact of August 1939 which divided Poland, gave the Baltic states to Stalin, and made possible the beginning of World War II, Richard Wright wrote a brief, unpublished essay that was entitled, "There are still men left" in which he confessed: "The most meaningful moments of experience I have gotten from this world have been in either making an attempt to change the limits of life under which men live, or in watching with *sympathy* the efforts of others to do the same. For that reason I am a card-carrying Communist.... Communism to me is a way of life, ... an unusual mode of existence." This was not a question of rightness or wrongness of the party's position, for Wright stated parenthetically and revealingly: "(sometimes I feel myself most deeply attracted to it when most people are repelled—that is, for instance, when the USSR signed the pact with Nazi Germany)."[14] By implication, Wright spoke not only about Communists but also about Nazis when he concluded: "They are men who are used to seeking, not comfort, security, *individual* happiness, equality, but *meaning*, meaning in terms of feeling and knowing in its most concrete and literal sense." That such convictions approached the level and intensity of a religious experience became clear when Wright, having left the party, participated, together with Ignazio Silone and Arthur Koestler, in Richard Crossman's collection of testimonials entitled *The God That Failed* (1949). Hemingway, who was left-leaning and anti-fascist from the very beginning of that movement and who learned anti-Stalinism from the experience of the Spanish Civil War, never commented in any of his writings or his correspondence on the Nazi-Soviet pact.

The point is neither to idealize nor to vilify cultural participants in hindsight but to show the real attractions and challenges that authoritarian movements presented to modern American writers and intellectuals. One should also not forget that the term "totalitarian" tended to blur important differences among various fascist and communist systems and between Fascism and Communism. Fascism seemed to reestablish and exaggerate—by often very modern means—some traditional forms of authority that modernity had challenged and that seemed to have collapsed in World War I; in its Nazi version, it put "race" at the center of its idea of order. It was a movement that aestheticized power and displayed it as spectacle that was constantly reenacted and amplified with the new means of radio, sound-track-accompanied newsreels, and propaganda films. Fascism appealed to the paradoxical need of some writers for a "forward-looking nostalgia," for a mix of military-style order and ethnic homogeneity, of ritual and "roots." Communism—equally adept at using the modern arts of persuasion—made "class" the central category of human divisions and promised to act on the egalitarian ideal that had been established in the French Revolution, an ideal that was deeply in need of revitalization in the Depression years following the global economic crisis of 1929. However different they were, both the Communist and Fascist revolutions projected youthful images and would thus appeal to a culture that had always emphasized the importance of youth, novelty, and a fresh start. One only has to remember Lee Chew's grandfather's verdict from *Life Stories of Undistinguished Americans* that Americans "were constantly showing disrespect for their ancestors by getting new things to take the place of the old" (178).

How could the by now aged and ancestral political system of democracy, which had attracted little deeply felt cultural enthusiasm after

Antin's World War I writings, become as magnetic as the young –isms with which it was increasingly confronted? Cool and hard-boiled indifference was hardly synonymous with a commitment to democracy: the Italian-American author John Fante, for example, wrote to his editor on May 26, 1940, "They can tear this over-rated civilization apart, they can have their fascism and nazism and bolshevism and democracy. I shall type with one hand, the fingers of the other pinching my nostrils. It will be slower, less convenient, but it will be great writing anyway."[15] In other letters, Fante struck a hedonistic or self-serving note describing himself as an advocate neither of Communism nor of capitalism but of what he actually called "Clitorism." He wrote bluntly: "The only menace I find in poverty is that I can't fuck enough" (134). Fante also thought that "the Italians rushing into this war will cause a lot of Italian-American interest here in this country, and for that reason I give you odds that [Fante's novel] Dago Red will be a success" (168). War could simply be good for the ethnic writer's business and did not compel him to take sides.

Still, perhaps it was the tough Hemingwayesque film-noir style—which Fante often employed but also explicitly satirized in the piece "We Snatch a Frail" (1936) as the ridiculous prose of the "Caldwell-Hemingway-O'Hara school of scribblers" (132)—that exerted the kind of appeal in America that foreign totalitarian leaders commanded abroad. In the absence of an enthusiastically presented and compelling democratic literature, the film-noir style could take on a democratic meaning and ultimately also become one basis of allied self-understanding and propaganda, all the more so since it was often coupled with plotlines centering on apolitical and tough-talking but basically fair-minded existentialist loners who were ultimately forced into political action for democracy because of the aspirations toward global domination that their sinister opponents tried to realize. Michael Curtiz's film *Casablanca* (1942) was only the most famous stylization of existentialists for democratic action.

The confrontation with totalitarianism also generated shriller and more extreme articulations of individualism as the true essence of American capitalist democracy. Perhaps the sharpest opponent of Russian Communism among immigrant writers was Ayn Rand who, born Alissa Zinovievna Rosenbaum in St. Petersburg in 1905, left the Soviet Union in 1926 and came to the United States. She published an autobiographically inspired novel *We the Living* (1936), in which she first developed her idealization of individualism as the ideology of freedom.[16] Her novel is set in communist Russia, and it represents the experiences of the young individualist Kira Argounova enmeshed in a politically charged love triangle in a gloomy world of state terror and collectivism. The novel is interspersed with political headlines and party slogans. When it was reissued in 1958, Rand stressed that this was "not a story about Soviet Russia in 1925" but about "Dictatorship, any dictatorship, anywhere, at any time, whether it be Soviet Russia, Nazi Germany, or—which this novel might do its share in helping to prevent—a socialist America" (vii). Rand also revised *We the Living* stylistically, changing "awkward or confusing lapses" that were the sign of "a particular kind of uncertainty in the use of the English language, which reflected the transitional state of a mind thinking no longer in Russian but not yet fully in English" (viii).

Rand's most famous novel, *The Fountainhead* (1943), extolled the extreme and antialtruistic individual freedom of the idealist modernist architect Howard Roark who defies dominant conventions and mediocre standards, deciding ultimately to destroy the building he had designed rather than to compromise. Roark was apparently inspired by Frank Lloyd Wright. Made into a 1949 movie directed by King Vidor and starring Gary Cooper, this novel helped to propel Rand into national prominence, and her work keeps attracting a following among readers who may not be worried that the extremist endorsement of the strong individual shares features with the fascist ideal of the superman who lives above and beyond the standards of the mass. Though Rand proposes the heroic individual as an answer to totalitarianism, *The Fountainhead* is less an embodiment of the democratic ideal than an expression of contempt for conventions and for people who care about them.

Another possibility for boosting morale and for fleshing out the democratic ideal at a time of threat lay in the notion of the "American dream" that Antin had evoked in *The Promised Land* and the mention of which proliferated in the Depression era. James Truslow Adams is credited with coining this catchphrase in *The Epic of America*: "If the American dream is to come true and to abide with us, it will, at bottom, depend on the people themselves."[17] Michael Foster's novel *American Dream* (1937) helped to popularize the phrase further: Shelby Thrall, the novel's protagonist, ultimately embraces and defines what the narrator calls "that queer phrase, 'the American dream.'"[18]

> Shelby saw suddenly that the dream did live, as it had lived forever through bloody centuries ruled and spoiled by the grabbers and the shouters; as it would live forever, and be seen always by a few men, sometimes by a nation, through slaughter and ruin and loud follies. Because it was not merely the American dream—it was the old, old human faith that somehow, somewhere, a time might come when man would stand on the ruins of an old world and an old self, with the starlight on his shoulders. That a time might come when men would live and deal among themselves with justice. And tenderness. And truth. (499)

Michael Foster's was an all-American story; but the "American dream" also flourished particularly in immigrant writing, as immigrants in the interwar period often brought a comparative understanding of political systems to their appreciation of democracy.

Louis Adamic was instrumental in reviving the tradition that Antin had established in calling attention to the immigrant's story as perfect for the possible realization of the American dream, thereby helping to expand and make more inclusive the term "American" and to give new and multiethnic meaning to American democracy. Antin had made the argument to stem the nativist tide of the 1910s, whereas Adamic developed it further in the 1930s and 1940s in the context of opposition to Fascism; somewhat prophetically, he found the core value of American democracy in its ethnic heterogeneity. In the section "Ellis Island and Plymouth Rock" in a book titled, in the Antin tradition, *My America* (1938), he wished to increase the mutual understanding of "old-stock" and "New Americans" and a better knowledge of the "Dream."[19] In lectures to hundreds of audiences the immigrant Adamic wrote euphorically that Americans must

> work toward an intellectual-emotional synthesis of old and new America; of the Mayflower and the steerage; of the New England wilderness and the social-economic jungle of the city slums and the factory system; of the Liberty Bell and the Statue of Liberty. The old American Dream needs to be interlaced with the immigrants' emotions as they saw the Statue of Liberty. The two must be made into one story.[20]

Adamic hoped for the production of a great encyclopedia that would describe the inspiring ethnic diversity of Whitman's "Nation of Nations," a phrase he adopted for the title of a 1945 book. For Adamic, realizing the American dream meant acknowledging and honoring the country's many diverging origins and its continuing cultural diversity. His journal *Common Ground* was emphatically multiethnic, boasted Mary Antin and Zora Neale Hurston among its contributors, and in 1941, for example, carried one piece about Fante as an all-American writer, the punch line comparing him with Will Rogers, and another by Fante on his Armenian-American friend William Saroyan. In his book programmatically entitled *From Many Lands* (1940) Adamic encouraged both native-born and old-stock Americans to think of a greater diversity when speaking of "Americans" and criticized newcomers for not adopting the term "American" quickly enough:

> I find that most of the new people, when they say "we," don't mean "we Americans" or "we the people in this town," but "we who live in this section and are of Polish or Armenian, etc., origin or background." When they say "Americans," they don't mean themselves.[21]

As has already become clear, immigration created confusing uses of personal pronouns and Adamic wanted immigrants to be entitled to think "we" when they heard the word "Americans."

In her war-effort-sponsored national character study *And Keep Your Powder Dry* (1942) the anthropologist Margaret Mead addressed the problem from the opposite side and asked all Americans, ordinary and "old-stock," to view themselves *as immigrants,* for "however many generations we may actually boast of in this country," she explained, "we are all third generation." Without quoting him, she thus echoed Bourne's universalist position from World War I days as she urged Americans to think "we" when they heard the term "immigrants."[22] It was the effort to define and invigorate the culture of democracy against totalitarianism that gave immigrant narratives a new centrality in the U.S.

The new contexts for the familiar genre of immigrant autobiography are apparent in the case of Salom Rizk, an immigrant from the eastern Mediterranean who had no hesitation to adopt the term "American" and who provided another example of the presence of the notion of the "American dream" in immigrant narratives. Rizk's *Syrian Yankee* (1943)[23] is the life story of an Arabic-speaking Lebanese boy born in 1909 who lived with his paternal grandmother, his only known living relative, in Ain Arab, a little village near Ybose. He describes life on the Christian-Muslim borderline in an *Arabian-Nights*-like drama of a Turkish tax collector, one of whose wives, reputed to be a Christian woman, is rumored to have betrayed her husband. "Mohammedans said [of her], 'She is an untouchable slut who aspires to a place beyond her reach'" (4). Fortunately, the dramatic episode ends happily, merely with a ban on circulating rumors.

When Salom's grandmother dies, he goes to live with an aunt, and refugees from the horrors of World War I massacres in Lebanon reach their village. "They told such wild tales we could hardly believe them. They told how their children had been murdered in cold blood before their very eyes, and their fathers and mothers, too, who were too old to flee. They told of whole villages evacuated, looted, burned and destroyed" (37). Salom has to work as a swineherd and learns to hate pigs "with a deep, passionate, ineradicable, Mohammedan hate" (56). Later a kind and benevolent teacher accepts him to a school where he flourishes. To his surprise, Salom finds out a great secret from the headmaster at age twelve, just when he imagines that he might become a priest: "There are great things ahead for you, my son," the headmaster says, "great things—yes, greater even than you ever dreamed of—for, Salom, you are—a citizen—of America!" (69). Salom has no conception of what that means; and when he asks the schoolmaster, he is told: "No—you don't know what it is. America, Salom," and he sighed deeply, "America is—is heaven." His mother, who died giving birth to Salom, had been an American citizen, he learns; Salom had brothers who were living in America.[24] The grandmother had kept his background a secret because she had lost all of her sons to America, including Salom's father, and did not want to lose her grandson, too. Yet now Salom can really claim American citizenship.

The chapter title "Passport to Heaven" suggests how he feels about this discovery, and from his schoolmaster's account an image of America emerges in Salom's mind in a mildly modernist staccato prose of fragmentary bits: "... the land of hope ... the land of peace ... the land of contentment ... the land of liberty ... the land of brotherhood ... the land of plenty ... where God has poured out wealth ... where the dreams of men come true ... where everything is bigger and grander and more beautiful than it has ever been anywhere else in the world ... where wheat grows waist high, shoulder high, sky high, and as thick as the hair on your head" (71–72). "It sounded like the fairylands my grandmother used to tell about," he writes; and when the teacher explains to him what an American passport is ("a piece of paper that will let you into heaven on earth" [72]), Salom thinks of Aladdin's magic lamp, for his passport, though "just a piece of paper . . . will open the gates of heaven—my passport to paradise" (73).

The thoroughly utopian vision of America his teacher instills in him is carefully delineated as a threefold improvement over Salom's Lebanon. First, it is an extension, an enlargement of what he had liked in his life in Syria so far: the world of learning. Hence America appears to him as a fairy-tale world in which there would be no limit to education: "the marble places of learning, some of them laid out like great cities in a magnificent oasis of green trees, grass, and flowers; . . . where palatial buildings with more rooms than there were houses in Ain Arab were filled with endless rows of books and papers waiting to be read by eager students, scholars, wise men; . . . where every boy and girl, no matter how poor, could learn to read and write and be what he or she wanted to be—teacher, doctor, lawyer, priest" (77).

Second, America is the land of magical plenty with "so much wheat that you could bury all of Mount Hermon and all around in an avalanche of golden kernels; so many cattle that if they were all rolled into one big animal, his nose would be in Beirut and his tail in Damascus" (77–78). The myth of gargantuan abundance is projected onto the familiar landscape in a fairy-tale fashion, with the topos of exaggeration prominently employed.

And third, America is imagined as the land of eternal peace and safety—in sharp contrast to the world Salom had known so far: "villages and cities that were never raided, looted, and terrified by arrogant soldiers and officials; where there were no wars, fears, and hates to keep the people in terror, to wreck their homes, destroy their crops and drive them weeping into the wilderness; where Christians do not sharpen their sword against the Mohammedans, but people of different religions live together in friendliness and peace; where men did not have to walk to the fields or go on journeys armed with rifles, knives, or swords" (78). Salom Rizk spells out the principle of negation: America is "everything that my present life was not" (78).

After five years of waiting and working odd jobs, Rizk finally gets his passport and takes off for America. The arrival scene is appropriate to the genre, complete with the Statue of Liberty:

> [T]he great tall lady with the flaming torch; the immigrants pressing the rail and shouting deliriously, cheering the statue as if it were a liv-

ing thing which heard and responded to their wild and childish greetings. (118)

Yet he also remembers some trepidation at this threshold moment. "Will I be able to make it? Fit in? Act right?" (118), he worries. In Sioux City, Iowa, he is welcomed by an aunt with the phrase *"Ya meet ahla swahla!"* (123) which Rizk translates as "The people and the plains are yours." His brothers are Americanized enough to call him Sam (128).

Yet Salom's heavenly America resembles nothing so much as hell. Like his newfound relatives he works in a mechanized slaughterhouse in which no English-language skills are needed. Once he stays on after the whistle blows and finds himself alone in the nightmarish dark with an army of squealing rats, making the meat-packing plant worse than Dante's *Inferno*. As in the case of the Lithuanian in *Life Stories of Undistinguished Americans*, the mechanized meat-packing plant represents modernity with a vengeance. It seems worse than tending pigs in Syria.

The school of hard knocks continues, but finally the movement is upward, again, as in the Syrian part (and as in Holt's collection or Antin's *Promised Land*), through the magic of education. Mr. Davis, a friendly teacher admits him to ninth-grade English class even though Salom is twenty years old at this point. Learning English now becomes his obsession, and he comments on all the oddities a foreigner encounters who looks for logical rules in the English language: thus he mispronounces "spiced tomato juice" he sees on a menu as "spiked" and is curtly told that the establishment would not serve liquor (177). His English improves so much that he gets to deliver the oration "The Immigrant Speaks," with his accent, and is invited to address the Rotary Club.

Rizk's American dream is fully confirmed, however, only after he takes a trip back to his impoverished homeland, in the course of which he is almost arrested in fascist Italy for making a wisecrack to a border official. (Asked who "Synonyms and Antonyms" are, so the title of his suspicious-looking book, he answers, "They're a couple of revolutionists." [251]). He then travels from Trieste to Syria on a boat (the *Martha Washington*, no less), together with hundreds of Jewish refugees from Nazi Germany headed for Palestine. He notices their bandaged heads and faces, their arms in slings, and hears of the Nazi terror they had been subjected to. Deeply empathizing, Salom asks why they are going to Palestine ("There's nothing for them there—no opportunities, no resources, no anything") and is told: "There's the one hopeful thing about this whole business.

These people don't need opportunities. They make opportunities. . . . They're full of fire, full of hopes, ideas, plans. And what's more, they know how to work" (259). Salom writes an entry in his diary (and this is the only time he quotes from it in the book) in which he contrasts his own anxiety about fitting into the richest country on earth with the courage of these uprooted and exiled Jews who are migrating "to a pale tired land where life will be hard, where they will have to struggle from the bottom up, where they will have to fight and rustle every minute to wrest a few crumbs of existence from stingy Nature, and where they will face the suspicion and hostility of their constantly agitated Arabic neighbors—and they are not afraid. They are brave, inspired, and determined. Since first hearing about it, I have always thought of the resettlement of Palestine as a nice way of disposing of the Jewish problem—creating a national home for these long-wandering exiles of the earth. Now I see in it a hint of an international hope—a way out for democracy and humanity" (261–262).

When Rizk gets to his native land, the size, activity, and mores of America have become the norm by which he measures things (as Adamic did in *The Native's Return*). Beirut seems small after New York, his village Ain Arab "a lifeless skeleton bleaching in the desert" (264), and he is turned off by a Moslem cab driver stopping and praying for twenty minutes and finds it hard to imagine "taxi drivers on Fifth Avenue suddenly halting their cars and hitting the pavement" (265).

Back in the United States after this trip, Salom knows that "bad as things were" in Depression America, "they were infinitely better than in Europe or, for that matter, anywhere else in the world." Rizk finds that his new feelings for America were not merely patriotic,

> for I had an overwhelming wish that the whole world might share in all of it; that the kindly, poverty-stricken people I had so recently visited in Syria, and who had yearned, even begged, so pathetically for passage to America, might have a land like this to live in; that the Jewish exiles returning to the lean and stony ridges of Palestine might have found resources as rich as these, an air to breathe as free of hate and fear as this, and a welcome—yes, a welcome as warm and rousing as the words inscribed to the huddled masses of the Old World on our own Statue of Liberty. (276)

Salom Rizk's wartime articulation of the American Dream as a version of international hope for democracy would not have been complete without his opposition to the totalitarian threat; he is quite explicit about that. Since "racial prejudice, poverty, unemployment, discontent, despair of democracy" might also take root in America, he sees it as his task to warn Americans of the evils that could result from the organization of hatred and intolerance: "Mussolini's brags about Fascismo solving poverty had found welcome lodging in certain American ears. Hitler's maltreatment of the Jews appealed to some of my friends as good common sense. There were those, especially disillusioned young people, who applauded Stalin's arbitrary arrests, killings, and starvation as the future liberation of humanity from the evils of arbitrary arrest, killings, and starvation" (277).

The American dream was, for immigrants like Rizk and for his readers, a hopeful and promising alternative to German Nazism, Italian Fascism, and Soviet Stalinism, an alternative of which Americans themselves, ironically, needed to be convinced by newcomers. Rizk devotes himself to this cause and, sponsored by *Reader's Digest* (306), becomes a lecturer in the service of America.[25] He attacks defeatism in democracy and considers democracy a not-yet-sufficiently recognized success story, the only alternative to "concentration camps and castor oil, purges and pogroms" (311). This is, then, an autobiography with a point, and it can logically end with Rizk's egalitarian view of all Americans, regardless of ancestry:

> Some trace their ancestors through Plymouth Rock and some through Ellis Island. But regardless of origin, they are working quietly, obscurely, and unstintingly to give democracy the victory in one area of life after another, to extend it out to the very last frontier of human aspiration. They are the people who regard every problem as an opportunity. When you meet them and feel their deep, determined resolve, you know that the other kind of people can never defeat the American dream. You can't beat the American people who built and are still building this America. (317)

The autobiography thus ends on a high patriotic note, a moral of sorts that sounds like a national anthem.

Though just about as long as all of the life stories together in Holt's collection, the "Syrian Yankee" also largely remains a social type, defined by the oxymoron in the title. His public life is rendered fully and vividly, but his inner life largely remains hidden from the reader. He accounts for his small flaws from the safe hindsight position of having overcome them. He never falls in love or marries; he has no existential doubts or personal nightmares except such social ones as swineherding or working in an industrial Gothic slaughterhouse. The genre of immigrant autobiography has become an antitotalitarian instrument, as it offers the migrant's fresh and insistent argument for American democracy at the time of World War II as *the* American story, while giving its protagonist little idiosyncratic interiority.

Less ideologically charged and far more individualized, Mangione's *Mount Allegro* also emphasized an immigrant child's "return," in manhood, to a now fascist homeland, a political change which resolves any ambivalence toward ethnic origins in favor of the democratic location of his parents' adopted country. At the end of the book, the narrator wants to leave Sicily for Rochester, as if he were reenacting the original event of the parents' emigration, with the added justification of getting away from Fascism: "I was beginning to get lonely for America and I thought how good it would be to be home again."[26]

In Henry Roth's representation of David Schearl's Lower East Side childhood of 1911 to 1913, the political situation of the early 1930s—the time when the novel was written—made itself felt in some small but telling details. Roth stated explicitly that *Call It Sleep* "violates the truth about what the East Side was" in the 1910s, describing it instead as a "montage of milieus," and specifically suggested the rise of anti-Semitism epitomized by Hitler as an inspiration for the scene in which David Schearl denies his Jewishness to the anti-Semitic boys Pedey and Weasel.[27] In his new preface to the 1935 edition of *Jews Without Money,* Gold reports a friend's account who had heard Nazis laugh hysterically when they saw the book, for they simply could not believe that there were any "Jews without money."[28]

Adamic's *The Native's Return* includes discussions of Mussolini's forced Italianization and suppression of the Slovenian language in the part of the country that Italy received at the end of World War I. He found that opportunistic rulers dangerously played one party leader against the other: "Serbs against Croats, Croats against Serbs, Slovenes against both, Moslems against Orthodox Christians, the latter against Catholics."[29] His conclusion for the American reader appears in italics: Balkan policy *"created a spirit under which the various racial and religious groups became more attentive to their differences than their resemblances"* (342). This was an implicit appeal for multiethnic democratic unity, for finding a "common ground." Adamic was so convinced of the democratic commitment of immigrants to the United States that he proposed in *Two-Way Passage* (1941) that American immigrants from Europe should return to their various countries of origin and help to establish democracies there, educating Europeans in democracy.[30] However, Adamic also held high hopes for Communism as the answer to problems of the Balkans, and of eastern Europe in general; before World War II, he was hopeful that a new war, though "millions of people might die in it," would bring along with it some positive change for the region. "I see now that the salvation of the Yugoslav people and other small backward nations in that part of the world lies, clearly and inescapably, in the direction of Russia."[31] After the war, he supported Tito (with whom he had a correspondence and who awarded Adamic the Yugoslav Order of National Unity) against Stalin; in 1951, Adamic died under suspicious circumstances in his house in New Jersey.

Various forms of cultural opposition to totalitarianism helped to redefine American democracy as totalitarianism's opposite. The American dream might still be incomplete, but the new wisdom seemed to be that the dream was destined to be completed in the multiethnic, nontotalitarian United States and not anywhere else; in Massachusetts and Delaware, and not in Rome, Berlin, or Moscow. American culture was being viewed as vital because it was the culture of democracy, of promise, of process, of mobility, and of plenty.

According to John Kouwenhoven, it was characteristic that an American "invented chewing gum (in 1869) and that it is the Americans who have spread it—in all senses of the verb—throughout the world. A nonconsumable confection, its sole appeal is the process of chewing it."[32] Chewing gum could also appear as a secular equivalent to a communion: thus Toomer's early poem "Gum" (c. 1920) juxtaposed a Christian billboard with the advertisement "WRIGLEYS / eat it / after / every meal / It Does You Good."[33] It was also in a culture that cherished process, that was not "a closed system," in which jazz emerged expressing love for improvisation, or the skyscraper with its arbitrary height, or the serial assembly of parts into a whole, or the aesthetic formula of the soap opera. The changes that took place during the 1930s and 1940s were changes that deeply affected American self-understanding as well as the image of America that it would from now on project abroad.

Yet there were some fairly obvious contradictions. Immigrants turned into typical Americans in Margaret Mead's hands, and Mead also wanted to kindle "the enthusiasm and devotion of every young adult" so as to resist the lure of the "fascist organizer," yet legislation restricting immigration that was enacted in the 1920s remained in full force during much of the period and barred desperate refugees from entering the United States. As the post-Pearl Harbor wartime logic supported Louis Adamic's project of imagining the United States as the nation of immigrants, of giving dominance to Emma Lazarus's view of the Statue of Liberty as a welcome to immigrants and Mary Antin's interpretation of Ellis Island as another name for Plymouth Rock (wholeheartedly endorsed by Salom Rizk), Japanese Americans were called "non-alien Japanese" and put in internment camps, their U.S. citizenship notwithstanding.

The wartime internment of about 120,000 West Coast Japanese Americans was made possible by Roosevelt's executive order 9066, as in the panicked atmosphere after the attack on Pearl Harbor it was possible to subject to forced relocation and detention so many people exclusively on the basis of their ethnic background. Racetracks and stadiums served as temporary centers, while ten concentration camps were being built in usually remote areas of states from California to Wyoming and Arkansas. Many haunting literary works of the 1940s emerged in the context of this traumatic experience. The War Relocation Authority provided mimeographing machines, and nine camps had newsletters or papers, many of which included literary contributions. Toshio Mori, for example, wrote for the Topaz (Utah) *Times*. One representative piece published on January 1, 1943, was simply entitled "A Sketch." It understatedly presented the conversation of two men about a fence that was being erected around the camp. One asks, "What are the fences for? We won't run away." The other quietly replies: "There are two ways of looking at it. It might limit your travels but it also protects you. Don't you think it is meant for protection too? For example, suppose we start a poultry farm. Coyotes roam nearby and the animals need protection. You can never tell when a fence comes in handy." He continues: "We all have fences—within and without. A fence is a symbol of our limited capabilities. And another thing, friend. We have our own fences within ourselves which hinder understanding and cooperation."[34] The critique of fences is thus articulated in the same breath that voices their justification by the somewhat absurd coyote story. Immediately after the war, Miné Okubo published *Citizen 13660* (1946) which, accompanied by drawings, describes her internment, starting at the Santa Anita Racetrack in Tanforan near San Francisco where she was assigned to horse stable 16, stall 50.

Indirection and understatement characterize Hisaye Yamamoto's writing. California-born, she was taken to Poston (Arizona) when she was turning 21, and she started publishing in the Poston *Chronicle*. Her first contribution was a serialized detective story that was set "aboard the last car of the evacuee train," "Death Rides the Rails to Poston." In the middle of a murder mystery, the reader learns about the feelings of the evacuees from Oceanville's Little Tokyo; the solving of the initial murder ultimately seems less important than Pat Nori's recognition "that since evacuation had become a reality her life had somehow taken on the quality of a dream." After the war, Yamamoto returned to the theme of the camp setting as a background to tales of quiet passion.

"The Legend of Miss Sasagawara" (*Kenyon Review*, 1950) is an interesting attempt to represent the fate of a modernist artist in the detention camp. The first sentence of the story seems to take for granted the reader's knowledge of the setting: "Even in that unlikely place of wind, sand, and heat, it was easy to imagine Miss Sasagawara a decorative ingredient of some ballet."[35] Slowly, the precise meaning of the place comes into focus: block 33, "this Japanese evacuation camp in Arizona," or, about Miss Sasagawara and her father: "They were occupying one end of the Block's lone empty barracks, which had not been chopped up yet into the customary four apartments" (20). The first-person narrator is a waitress, and the heroine, who refuses to act normal, remains mysterious, refracted only in the reactions of others; they tend to consider her crazy. Only later does the narrator find a poem by Mari Sasagawara, published in a poetry magazine. "It was a *tour de force,* erratically brilliant and, through the first readings, tantalizingly obscure" (32).

In Yamamoto's story, "Yoneko's Earthquake" (*Furioso*, 1951), another particularly sensitive female internee reacts to the experience with more terror than the others, the crisis here coming with an earthquake.

> The others soon oriented themselves to the catastrophe with philosophy, saying how fortunate they were to live in the country where the peril was less than in the city and going as far as to regard the period as a sort of vacation from work, with their enforced alfresco existence a sort of camping trip. They tried to bring Yoneko to partake of this pleasant outlook, but she, shivering with each new quiver, looked on them as dreamers who refused to see things as they really were.[36]

The situation of Japanese Americans was extreme, calling for later presidential apologies and for the rare case of governmental reparations. Many other ethnic groups were also pitted against each other, making harmonious dreams of a "common ground" somewhat difficult to realize. A 1938 survey, for example, showed that a majority of Americans believed that Jews themselves were at least partly to blame for the treatment they received in Nazi Germany. The African-American *Pittsburgh Courier* warned its readers in 1936 of the many Italian Americans who were secretly Mussolini sympathizers and racists. Many Italian Americans and German Americans were also interned during the War. And while Victory records and the American Forces Network began to use swing—black and white—as if it were the national music, racial segregation was still the dominant ethnic model in place in the United States: interracial marriage was prohibited in more than half of the states and, three quarters of a century after the end of slavery, black voting rights remained severely restricted. In William Gardner Smith's novel *Last of the Conquerors* (1948), which focuses on the interracial love story of the black G.I. Dawkins and the German woman Ilse, a German character says that when he was a prisoner of war in Virginia, the black American soldiers who guarded the white Germans were not permitted to eat in the same restaurant where the Germans ate. During World War II, fought in the name of democracy against an axis of racist, fascist dictatorships, blood banks of the American Red Cross carried separate blood for the black soldiers fighting for democracy, a public health policy that eerily literalized the metaphor of "black" and "white" blood which Toomer had questioned so memorably. "Hitler could hardly desire more," Langston Hughes commented, for the Red Cross had "failed thirteen million Negroes on the home front, and its racial policies [were] a blow in the face of American Negro morale."[37] In 1945 Richard Wright, about to settle permanently in France a year later, cited the existence of separate blood banks in the war as one indication that the United States was not solving its race problem.[38] Such paradoxes led to the "double victory" campaign (at home and abroad), as ethnic intellectuals (like Du Bois) put their finger on prevailing American hypocrisies and helped to provide the momentum for the sea change in American race relations starting with *Brown v. Board of Education* in 1954 and with the end of racially based immigration restrictions in the 1960s.

Delmore Schwartz's short story "A Bitter Farce" (*Kenyon Review,* 1946) vividly portrays some of the ironies that complicated the issues of race and national unity in the situation of teaching during World War II.[39] The story is set in 1943. A young Jewish instructor teaches English composition both to a group of Navy students, some of whom have been in the Pacific war, and to a class of girls. The boys, many of them Southern, talk with their teacher about current events, the existence of a secret weapon, Hitler, the Detroit race riots, and so forth, but the toughest question a student asks the teacher is the sudden, "would you marry a Negro woman?" (248). Mr. Fish is thinking of saying that "he would marry any woman to whom he made love because otherwise his children might be illegitimate," hoping that this might "touch both the sense of honor and the memory of experience in some of them" (248). Yet anticipating the giggles and smirks that might accompany the mentioning of sexual intercourse in class, Fish wonders what to do. Answering in the affirmative would make him lose face with his students; but saying no would mean that he shared their belief in social inequality. After evading the question with the statement that he has not been introduced to any Negroes, he finally answers, and though he appears calm, "his inner being was suddenly full of fear and trembling."

> I would not marry a Negro woman, ... but there are many white women whom I would not marry for the same reasons that I would not marry a Negro woman. Thus it is not a question of discrimination against the Negro race. (249)

Though the answer goes over well, he realizes that his students must think that his reply meant that he "would not marry many white as well as Negro women because he was a Jew" (249).

Teaching in the different ambience of the "passive, polite and docile" girls in which Fish finds conferences with individual students most fruitful, a blonde and blue-eyed student gives him a journal entry in which three girls discuss the question, "If you had to marry one of them, which of these would you choose, a Chinaman, a Jew, or a Negro?" (251). And the deliberation of the question reiterates familiar stereotypes such as "Jews have managed to wangle themselves into good positions and make money" (252) and leads two of the girls to choose the Chinese, allies in the war.

Fish is so amazed that he chooses to talk about form, as he attempted to do when he told the Navy class "we had better return to the difference between the use of the semicolon and the comma. It is possible . . . that the absence of a comma may result in the death of a man—" (247) only to be interrupted. Now, after commending the girl for drawing on her own feelings, he offers her stylistic advice: "You ought not to use such a colloquialism as 'wangled' in a piece of writing" (252). After this formal approach, he states that he need not comment on the content, yet adds that the Chinese also were despised, at least on the Pacific Coast.

Back in the Navy class the topic is Louis Adamic's "Plymouth Rock and Ellis Island" with its hope for the "American Dream" of a "universal culture, a pan-human culture, such as had never before existed on the globe." Fish feels it necessary to offer a criticism of Adamic:

> What Adamic has to say is true, in part; but we ought also to remember that if America has always been the land of liberty, it has also been the land of persecution and the land where everyone feared that he was a stranger or was conscious of a fear of the stranger. (254–255)

Fish expands Adamic's formula to describe America as "the land of liberty and of persecution," using the Los Angeles zoot-suit riots as an example. This encourages an Irish student who disagrees with Adamic to say that "something is wrong with a lot of Jews" (255). In a long dialogue between teacher and student, Fish raises the question that goes to the heart of preconceptions on the basis of ethnicity, "Can a moral act be inherited?" Race prejudice "is a denial of the freedom of the will and of moral responsibility" (257). At the end of the class, the Irish student wants to reassure the Jewish teacher that he has nothing against him personally, but also complains, "They shouldn't have put such essays in the textbook. They're troublemakers" (260).

Schwartz's amusing story illuminates how explosive the topic of intermarriage was and what obstacles Adamic's "nation of nations" faced, even in the middle of the wartime effort of unifying the country.

15

Was Modernism Antitotalitarian?

The confrontation with totalitarianism affected not only American political self-understanding and the new, more positive stress on ethnic pluralism but also the fate of modernism and jazz, which were increasingly presented as prototypically democratic and quintessentially American art forms in the period of the greatest political opposition of the United States to totalitarianism, the years of World War II and of the Cold War.

Juliana Force's 1934 confrontation at the Venice Biennale and Alfred Barr's 1936 MoMA exhibition on *Cubism and Abstract Art* were characterized by the ideological conflicts of the moment. As we saw, Force's Whitney Museum-based and exceptionally modernist display at the American pavilion ran into difficulties with Hearst's scheming and the Italian fascist authorities; while Barr fell foul of New York's customs officials who did not want to accept cubist works as art but merely as matter. Force developed a multiethnic and cosmopolitan rationale for modern American art as the result of "the fusion of different races and nationalities" that made American art the truly international one and also marked an implicit contrast with the fascist ideal of "racial purity."[1] Barr emphasized the term "abstract art," a phrase that had been used occasionally around the time of the Armory Show, but that came into common use only in the 1930s and 1940s. Barr's exhibition catalog defined the term "abstract" as a welcome modernist break with a long artistic tradition characterized by "nature" and "imitation," and praised the "more adventurous and original artists" for being "driven to abandon the imitation of natural appearance."[2]

Yet Barr also included a section on abstract art and politics which mentioned that Lenin dismissed experimental art and literature as "the infantile disorder of Leftism" and that the National Socialists considered art of the Weimar Republic *Kunstbolschewismus;* in short, abstract art was, as Barr put it understatedly, "discouraged" by the two major totalitarian regimes. Hence he concluded that the 1936 cubist "exhibition might well be dedicated to those painters of squares and circles . . . who have suffered at the hands of philistines with political power." Modernism was at odds with totalitarianism.

But was American modernism antitotalitarian? The belief that it was helped the growing official sanctioning of modernism in the United States, but it was a belief difficult to reconcile with the example of such prominent modernists as Ezra Pound. What may have given rise to this notion was nothing inherent in Force's fusion-of-races America or in Barr's squares-and-circles modernism, but the political developments in the two totalitarian countries to which Barr alluded. What ultimately may have proved decisive were not any particular actions undertaken by modernist writers and artists, but rather the aesthetic choices that were made official doctrines by totalitarian governments; and these choices can be described rather simply: in the 1930s, totalitarianism turned antimodernist.

In the 1920s and 1930s, the course of the official aesthetic of the Soviet Union changed to the new antimodernist order signaled by Lenin's dismissal of modernism and cemented by Stalin's official propagation of the exclusive aesthetic of socialist realism and, simultaneously, the banning of jazz, first in the Soviet Union and later in all communist countries. The writer Maxim Gorky was central to both those developments. His essay "On the Music of the Gross," or "the Degenerate," as the English translator put it, was published in 1928 in no lesser an organ than *Pravda* and soon became the backbone of Stalinist repression of jazz music as exploitative, vulgar, sexualized, animalistic, threatening, and degenerate. Gorky heard the music, "a fox-trot executed by a negro-orchestra," as follows:

> One, two, three, ten, twenty strokes, and after them, like a mud ball splashing into clear water, a wild whistle screeches; and then there are rumblings, wails and howls like the snorting of a metal pig, the shriek of a donkey, or the amorous croaking of a monstrous frog. This insulting chaos of insanity pulses to a throbbing rhythm. Listening for a few minutes to these wails, one involuntarily imagines an orchestra of sexually driven madmen conducted by a man-stallion brandishing a huge genital member.[3]

The instruments seemed equally monstrous to Gorky who complained, for example, that "the saxophone emits its quacking nasal sound." Among the effects the music, disseminated by radio, was having on the white middle class were, Gorky actually seemed to believe, obesity and homosexuality of epidemic proportions, as the master class was turning toward the barbarism of jazz that America's oppressed Negroes had been leaving behind. Jazz was "bourgeois," a sign of deep "decadence" from the pinnacle of musical developments such as Mozart or Beethoven. It was an opiate and a tool of capitalist control. It seems hard to believe that such a biased and paranoid little vignette should have formed the theoretical backbone for the official Soviet policy toward jazz; but soon after the publication of this article, its tenets were reiterated by the Commissar for Public Enlightenment Anatoly Lunacharsky, and the prohibition of jazz and much black popular music in communist countries was the ultimate result. Mike Gold's quoted polemic from 1930 against "saxophone clowning" and for the might of classical music was not an idiosyncrasy, but a party-line argument—as was his invective against Stein's or Roth's modernism.

The term "socialist realism" which first appeared in the Soviet Union in 1932 became official doctrine in 1934 after Gorky delivered a programmatic speech to the First All-Union Congress of Soviet Writers in which he envisioned "a new direction essential to us—socialist realism, which can be created only from the data of socialist experience." Realism was the appropriate method of exposing capitalism, affirming, in an optimistic spirit, the advances of socialism, and of educating the proletariat to realize its revolutionary potential. "Socialist realism affirms being as action, as creation, whose aim is the uninterrupted development of each person's most valuable qualities so as to attain victory over the forces of nature, man's health and long life, and the great happiness of living on earth," Gorky proclaimed somewhat mystically.[4] Gorky, the famous author of works like the autobiographical trilogy beginning with *Childhood* (1913) who had early on polemicized against capitalist leisure culture at Coney Island, thus appears to have been the single intellectual who formulated both the attack on jazz and the advocacy of realism as central features of Soviet art policy, features that remained in place until the Gorbachev era.

This did not make Gorky any less popular among writers and intellectuals in the United States. One would expect this from Mike Gold, who liked to be seen as "the American Gorky," but not from the most eminent jazz poet of the period, Langston Hughes. Yet Hughes reported cheerily how, during his train travels through Kazakhstan, he participated in a 1932 celebration honoring the fortieth anniversary of Gorky's literary career, sending "a telegram to Comrade Gorky from the passengers of the train, and another from [Hughes's] Negro group."[5] Hughes may simply not have known Gorky's position on jazz, though Gorky's diatribe was published—without rebuttals—in Marie Budberg's English translation, in the December 1928 issue of the avant-garde *Dial,* a few pages after a contribution by Jean Toomer. In Kunitz's *Twentieth-Century Authors* (1942), Hurston listed Maxim Gorky among her favorite authors; did she—an eager student of black music who in 1941 wrote that while she was not a joiner she saw "many good points" in the Communist Party, but who also was to launch violent attacks on African-American communists in the *American Legion Magazine* of the Cold War years of 1950 and 1951—know that Gorky was one of the Stalinist architects of socialist realism and the intellectual who had laid the cornerstone for the Soviet ban on jazz?

Though it was "racially" sanctioned rather than motivated by political theory, the defining act of the official Nazi aesthetic in the 1930s was surprisingly similar to that which had just emerged in the Soviet Union: a ban of jazz and of modernist art and literature accompanied by an official endorsement of realism. The covers to notorious exhibition guides from the 1930s illustrate this point.

The guidebook for the "Degenerate Music" show in Düsseldorf in 1938 had a specially designed cover page on which a stereotyped saxophone-playing black appears wearing a star of David. "Niggerjazz"—this was the official term—was not permitted to be broadcast on the radio in Nazi Germany, and it was officially dismissed as music stemming from a "sick mental disposition" which could only be "found interesting by snobs who are aloof from the people"; characterized by the "prominence of the saxophone which alone carries the tune while all other instruments grotesquely emphasize the rhythm."[6] The saxophone, the signature instrument of a U.S. president half a century later, thus seems to have enjoyed communist as well as fascist censure.

Although Goebbels, the Nazi minister of propaganda, had published the novel *Michael* (1931) in which great and effusive admiration was voiced for van Gogh's experimental art, the Nazi dismissal of modernist art was comprehensive, unambiguous, and articulated by the highest authority, for it was Hitler who proclaimed at a Nuremberg party rally in 1935 that decades of a "Jewish regime" of modernism would now come to an end:

> What reveals itself to us as the so-called "cult of the primitive" is not the expression of a naïve, uncorrupted soul but of a thoroughly corrupt and sick degeneracy. He who wishes to exculpate the paintings and sculptures—to take only a particularly crass example—of our Dadaists, Cubists, and Futurists or imaginary Impressionists has obviously no comprehension of the task of art, which is not to remind man of the symptoms of his degeneracy but rather to oppose symptoms of degeneracy by showing what is eternally healthy and beautiful.[7]

In Hitler's view, the German people had long outgrown the primitiveness of such artistic barbarians and in the present time did not only "reject this nonsense but consider[ed] its manufacturers to be either charlatans or madmen." And he added authoritatively and menacingly: "we do not intend to let them loose on the people any longer." The ostracizing and banning of "racially inferior, sick, and Jewish-bolshevist art" was the consequence.

The "Degenerate Art" show in Munich 1937 used as cover of the exhibition guide a reproduction of the African-inspired primitivist sculpture *The New Man* by Otto Freundlich. The consequences of this prominent exposure were terrible: Freundlich, one of the pioneering practitioners of abstract art and founders of an international "abstraction-création" group, was killed in the concentration camp Majdanek in 1943. At the opening of the "Degenerate Art" show, Hitler explicitly condemned "Cubism, Dadaism, Futurism, Impressionism, Expressionism" as "completely worthless for the German people."[8] Photographs of the exhibition show men in uniforms inspecting paintings such as Emil Nolde's *Mulattin* (The Mulatto, 1913) under a banner that reads: "The niggerizing of music and theater as well as the niggerizing of the visual arts was intended to uproot the racial instinct of the people and to tear down blood barriers."[9] All Jews were considered *inherently* the producers of "degenerate art," and politically antifascist artists like George Grosz were predictably banned; but too modernist a style or too racially charged a theme could also make apolitical "Aryan" artists "degenerate" in Nazi eyes—including the painter Emil Nolde who had joined the Nazi party as early as 1920 and wanted desperately to be accepted by the party, but who was exhibited as degenerate nonetheless. He simply did not understand why he was expelled from the Prussian Academy of Arts in 1933. Nolde's "Mulatto" painting was undesirable to the Nazis because of its modernist style as well as its theme; the very title seemed to endorse (or at least represent) the racial mingling that, inspired by eugenicists in the United States, the National Socialists so vehemently opposed in the name of "racial purity."[10]

While jazz and modernist art were considered "degenerate" in Nazi Germany and "bourgeois decadent" in the Stalinist Soviet Union, ideologues in both countries espoused realism as the more appropriate art form. In Russia the term "socialist realism" became the catchword for "progressive" art in official terminology as well as in government- (and terror-) sanctioned policy, whereas in Germany realist art was praised as being "healthy" and "close to the beauty ideal of the people"—with equally brutal consequences for those who dared to deviate.

It was the fact that realist doctrine prevailed so virulently and violently in two totalitarian countries that gave an altogether new life and significance to modernism in the United States. In the 1930s one could still observe a turning away from modernism toward realism. Force and Barr were hardly in central positions of cultural authority in the United States; they were merely making arguments then that seemed widely compelling only later. The change came around 1939, as the possibility of a second world war grew.

Ironically, it was one of the employees of the U.S. Customs Service, the agency that had so annoyed Barr when it levied duty on the raw materials of his cubist art exhibit, who developed what was to become perhaps the most widely adopted rationale for modernism in America—though it was only one of many similar interventions. The young intellectual's name was Clement Greenberg, and his 1939 essay "Avant-Garde and Kitsch" was only his second publication.[11] He knew Harold Rosenberg, who was then the art director for the WPA's *American Guide* series and who introduced him to the artists' circle at the Hans Hofmann School. Dwight Macdonald invited Greenberg to write for the initially communist and recently Trotskyist-reborn *Partisan Review,* and Greenberg submitted the essay in 1939, just before he left for a two-month trip to Europe. The piece was at first rejected by Dwight Macdonald who was dissatisfied "because of its unsupported & large generalizations," an assessment that made Greenberg "furious."[12] When it was published after revisions, "Avant-Garde and Kitsch" became a landmark essay that was included in the *Partisan Reader,* reprinted in Britain and the United States, and discussed very widely as a prophetic argument in favor of abstract expressionism. It also established Greenberg as an authority on modern art.

Greenberg's essay began with the serious pronouncement that popular and high art had bifurcated in modern America: "One and the same civilization produces simultaneously two such different things as a poem by T. S. Eliot and a Tin Pan Alley song, or a painting by Braque and a *Saturday Evening Post* cover" (34). Similarly, who could put a poem by Eliot and a poem by once-famous radio poet Eddie Guest "in an enlightening relation to each other"? The poles which Greenberg establishes as opposites ultimately settle around the terms *avant-garde* ("the only form of living culture we now have" though it is endangered) and the "ersatz culture" of *kitsch* ("popular, commercial art and literature with their chromotypes, magazine covers, illustrations, ads, slick and pulp fiction, comic, Tin Pan Alley music, tap dancing, Hollywood movies, etc. etc.") (39). Predictably, the *Saturday Evening Post* is pure kitsch. But there are also stages in-between, for example, "a magazine like the *New Yorker,* which is fundamentally high-class kitsch for the luxury trade, converts and waters down a great deal of avant-garde material for its own uses" (41). And there are borderline authors like Steinbeck. But the situation has reached global proportions so that "the Chinaman, no less than the South American Indian, the Hindu, no less than the Polynesian, have come to prefer to their native art magazine covers, rotogravure sections and calendar girls" (41). As the popular support of kitsch has grown, the opposition to modern art has taken on a decidedly political aspect, too.

> If kitsch is the official tendency of culture in Germany, Italy and Russia, it is not because their respective governments are controlled by philistines, but because kitsch is the culture of the masses in these countries, as it is everywhere else. The encouragement of kitsch is merely another of the inexpensive ways in which totalitarian regimes seek to ingratiate themselves with their subjects. [...] The main trouble with avant-garde art and literature, from the point of view of Fascists and Stalinists, is not that they are too critical, but that they are too "innocent," that it is too difficult to inject effective propaganda into them, that kitsch is more pliable to this end. Kitsch keeps a dictator in closer contact with the "soul" of the people. (46–47)

Hence it was a matter of expediency and not of an inevitable, inner ideological affinity of realism and totalitarianism that made the fit appropriate at the moment, Greenberg argues: "Nevertheless, if the masses were conceivably to ask for avant-garde art and literature, Hitler, Mussolini and Stalin would not hesitate long in attempting to satisfy such a demand" (47).

What Greenberg's essay did was not only to develop a sense of populist-totalitarian conformism associated with mass art of kitsch, but also to suggest the danger that kitsch posed to capitalist America. The strong implication was that given the political context of the period, only the avant-garde art of Eliot, Picasso, and even of the modernist poet and onetime Nazi sympathizer Gottfried Benn, presented hope for resistance. From the point of view of anti-Stalinist socialists as embodied by *Partisan Review*, modernism alone seemed ready to resist the incorporating logic of both totalitarian state art and of capitalist consumer culture.

There were connections between the antipopulists of the *Partisan Review* group and of the Frankfurt School, now in exile as "Institute for Social Research in New York City." Symptomatic was the Institute's 1941 collective research project on "Cultural Aspects of National Socialism" which proposed to determine "the factors that prepared public opinion for authoritarianism prior to the advent of political power," including the "non-political section of the daily press, the illustrated magazines, and the popular biographies," all of which "may play a considerable role in transforming independent men into beings ready to surrender their individual rights." Though focused on Germany, the project rationale emphasized that "American democracy may not be entirely beyond this danger." A part of Theodor W. Adorno's contribution was to undertake

> psychological as well as sociological analysis of the violent reactions voiced by large sections of the German middle classes against features of what they termed "modernism," such as the putative distortion of the human face by radical painters, dissonance in music, the flat roof, and even jazz.[13]

The attempts by Frankfurt School and New York intellectuals to cast modernism in this way—and in addition as an ally in the struggle against racial segregation—were surprisingly successful. Gold had once claimed that "Stein did not care to communicate because essentially there was nothing to communicate"—and in the context of proletarian writing, this had been a devastating critique.[14] Now, in the hands of Greenberg or Adorno, the refusal to communicate could become the central achievement of an artist, and a sign of his or her resistance to the ideologies of the market—and of the ultimate fascist and Stalinist panderers. This was a position that seemed all the more plausible because it mirrored, and was mirrored by, the shriller tone of totalitarian aesthetics.

In 1947, for example, Vladimir Kemenov officially condemned artists like Georgia O'Keeffe as reactionaries, combining an exegesis of Marx with indignation at comparatively mild sexual aspects. Kemenov also specifically excoriated Picasso and Jacques Lipchitz, two artists who had portrayed Stein. "The basic features of decadent bourgeois art," he wrote, "are its falseness, its belligerent anti-realism, its hostility to objective knowledge and to the truthful portrayal of life in art."[15] He contrasted "contemporary mystical and pathological art which reflects the spiritual slough of the contemporary reactionary bourgeoisie" with the "new form of realistic art which is completely popular" that Soviet artists had created. Kemenov also stressed that the focus on "abstract art" was very new, citing a 1943 study of American painting that still concluded that the mass of American artists had been "unaffected by modernism." But by 1947, *Life* and the United States Information Service publication *America* were propagating modernism, a sign that it was advancing to a status of capitalist state art.

The debate had become part of the Cold War, and attacks like Kemenov's only had the effect of strengthening the American resolve to recast modernism as the art of democracy. In that process, the opinions of a small group of intellectuals came to affect government policy and decision-making processes on many levels of the cultural apparatus. The Congress for Cultural Freedom sponsored concerts by modern composers whose work had been banned by Hitler or Stalin, and in some cases, like Alban Berg's, prohibited by both. In 1951, the State Department paid for a production of Gertrude Stein and Virgil Thomson's opera *Four Saints in Three Acts,* the work that had mystified reviewers in 1934. The fact that Stein chose an all-Negro cast in 1934 seemed questionable then, but by 1951 the organizers' official correspondence stressed that "that for psychological reasons the entire cast of *Four Saints* should be American Negro: to counter the 'suppressed race' propaganda and forestall all criticisms to the effect that we had to use foreign negroes because we wouldn't let our own 'out.'" The production starred Leontyne Price.[16]

The official press release for an accompanying modern art exhibition curated by former MoMA director James Johnson Sweeney announced the show (with works by Matisse, Derain, Cézanne, Seurat, Chagall, Kandinsky from American collections) as a self-evident argument for freedom of the arts: "On display will be works that could not have been created nor whose exhibition would be allowed by such totalitarian regimes as Nazi Germany or present-day Soviet Russia and her satellites, as has been evidenced in those governments' labeling as 'degenerate' or 'bourgeois' of many of the paintings and sculptures included."[17] This was quite compatible with the way in which Eisenhower would see things at the twenty-fifth anniversary of MoMA in 1954. Congressman Dondero with his long diatribe against modernism (cited here in the introduction) had no political effect, for he sounded as if he were echoing Hitler or sharing Stalin's artistic taste. In this context, supporting modernism came to seem mere common sense.

Even Hollywood cartoons reflected the change toward modernism and jazz. In 1939, the typical cartoonist working for the Schlesinger studio was described in *Exposure Sheet* as a high school-educated person who "thinks Norman Rockwell" is "tops" and who has "no use for Picasso, van Gogh, Renoir, or any of those 'futuristic guys.'"[18] Yet in 1951, the painter Eyvind Earle joined Disney and received credit for extraordinarily experimental background painting in the ambitious Goofy short *For Whom the Bulls Toil*. Bob Clampett's *Coal Black and the Sebben Dwarfs* (Warner Brothers, 1943), with a black cast, was famously set to the music of Duke Ellington's *Jump for Joy*, but was marred by the employment of controversial black-face stereotypes and drew protests from the NAACP.

Modernism seeped into popular culture (supposedly its kitschy opposite) on many fronts. In 1945 Gertrude Stein traveled to occupied Germany and, in her manner, "covered" her trip for *Life* magazine, kitsch incarnate: The subtitle of her piece read "GERMANS SHOULD LEARN TO BE DISOBEDIENT AND GIS SHOULD NOT LIKE THEM NO THEY SHOULDN'T." Stein expressed great interest in taking Hitler's radiator to use as a flower pot, and included a photograph of her with a group of GIs doing "Hitler's pose on Hitler's balcony at Berchtesgaden."[19] On August 8, 1949, *Life* famously carried an illustrated story on Jackson Pollock. In *Vogue* of March 5, 1951, one could admire fashion models in front of Pollock backdrops. In March 1954 *House and Garden* carried ads for African masks at $5 each, postage paid, by a mail-order company in Ohio.

Modern American authors, including Faulkner and James T. Farrell, were promoted abroad by U.S. government agencies; and their works were exported and translated. The Cold War constellation gave artists and intellectuals a central role in the ideological confrontation. In Richard Wright's novel *The Outsider* (1953) the protagonist Cross Damon

> marveled at the astuteness of both Communist and Fascist politicians who had banned the demonic contagions of jazz. And now, too, he could understand why the Communists, instead of shooting the capitalists and bankers as they had so ardently sworn that they would do when they came to power, made instead with blood in their eyes straight for the school teachers, priests, writers, artists, poets, musicians, and the deposed bourgeois governmental rulers as the men who held for them the deadliest of threats to their keeping and extending their power.[20]

Avant-garde artists and educators, intellectuals mattered in this world. The very fact that works had been banned (or were still banned) meant that they were important; American intellectuals and artists played a state-supported role which they have not regained in later years.

What the story of antitotalitarian modernism omitted was the fact that many artists and much writing developed from modernist emergence toward a new realism: Joseph Stella's *Battle Of Lights, Coney Island* (1913–1914) and his many Brooklyn Bridge paintings were followed by Catholic neorealist (or magical-realist) art representing the Virgin or the Nativity; and Max Weber's famous stage (around 1915) in which he produced the Duchamp-inspired *Rush Hour, New York* and *Grand Central Terminal* as well as his signature Cubist work, the collage-like *Chinese Restaurant,* gave way to a new representational phase in which Weber emphasized Jewish, and especially Hasidic, religious themes in works like *Patriarchs*. In the 1930s and early 1940s, Stein collected now forgotten realist painters, and in 1933, she published her least modernist book, *The Autobiography of Alice B. Toklas*. Richard Wright toned down his modernist strategies in rewriting "Long Black Song," or in moving on from *Lawd Today* to *Native Son*. The tale of modernist emergence notwithstanding, there was a general strengthening of realism in the 1930s and 1940s. What the tale also omitted was the fact that this new American realism of the 1930s had a strong social focus as an art of political opposition—a feature that was confronted indirectly in associating engaged literature with Stalinism or totalitarianism and stylizing modernism as the true art of resistance.

And it is in this aspect that a conflation was successful: it was the mythical fusion of all stories of modernist emergence, according to which van Gogh's movement from *The Potato Eaters* to *Starry Night* or Jackson Pollock's from the Federal Arts Project to abstract expressionism could be seen as one single story of progress, understood both in aesthetic terms and as the political advance of American democracy. Superimposing the older and newer stories of modernism and making them into one single and somewhat timeless modern story carried the advantage that this story helped to cast any realism not only as old-fashioned and obsolete but also as inherently linked to totalitarianism. Imagining realism at best as the mold out of which modernism must always emerge and at worst as the handmaiden of terror helped to make modernism appear as the truly expressive art of antifascist and anti-Stalinist resistance, as the signature expression of American democracy.

The modernist orthodoxy that arose among New York intellectuals and the Frankfurt School in the 1940s avoided a head-on confrontation with some unpleasant facts. Most prominent among the obstacles to the sacralization of modernism was the fact that Italian fascists, German national socialists, and Soviet communists all had modernist phases, and that (as Adorno himself noted) many high modernists were "reactionaries," some of whom had voiced anti-Semitic sentiments and were hardly the stalwarts of democracy. And it removed from view the possibility that modernism was also a failure of nerve. For instead of naming nameable political ills, the modernist aesthetic forced readers to contemplate the disappearance of meaning and to accept that we live in a world of futility and the absurd in which aesthetic form was the only theme that mattered.

16

Facing the Extreme

The film director Joseph Losey once commented on the disillusioning quality of the 1940s and early 1950s: "After Hiroshima, after the death of Roosevelt, after the investigation, only then did one begin to understand the complete unreality of the American dream."[1] How did American writers fictionalize some of the extreme experiences of the 1940s—among them, the Holocaust of the European Jews and the nuclear destruction of the cities of Hiroshima and Nagasaki? How did ethnic writers react at a time when countless people were arrested, tortured, or killed not for what they had done but for who they were and when civilians were killed simply for where they were? Were modernist strategies helpful in representing the world of modernity that the Second World War had so brutally redefined? Did the success of the hard-boiled mode reveal an intentionally uncaring, antisentimental and cynical-seeming response to the modern technologies of death?

World War II seemed to have made true and even surpassed the most nightmarish fears of modernity. The Lithuanian of *Life Stories* described fine lady tourists who came to Chicago's industrial slaughterhouses. Antin gave an account of disinfection at the German border. Mike Gold experienced a subway trip as a cattle-car ride. Saroyan imagined death as the subject of advertising slogans. Roth had a vision that drew on one of the highest sources of energy he could imagine. Now, means of transportation like planes and trains had become means of killing. "Street-cars," in soldier slang going back to World War I, meant "heavy long-range shells."[2]

In her last printed essay, "House of the One Father," published in

Louis Adamic's journal *Common Ground* (1941), Mary Antin reflected on group affiliation in a new time of crisis, for the piece appeared just before the full onslaught of the Holocaust.[3] The SS *Einsatzgruppen* massacred seven thousand Jews in Antin's native Polotzk alone in December 1941. Contemplating Hitler's "object lesson on the fruits of intolerance" Antin reviewed her own attitudes and practices and questioned her own "divorcement" from Jewish life: "Today I find myself pulled by the old forgotten ties, through the violent projection of an immensely magnified Jewish problem. It is one thing to go your separate way, leaving your friends and comrades behind in peace and prosperity; it is another thing to fail to remember them when the world is casting them out" (41). Yet this sense of solidarity did not mean for Antin that it was easy or even possible to return to "her people" or her past.

> I can no more return to the Jewish fold that I can return to my mother's womb; neither can I in decency continue to enjoy my accidental personal immunity from the penalties of being a Jew in a time of virulent anti-Semitism. The least I can do, in my need to share the sufferings of my people, is declare that I am as one of them.
>
> Here, in my own case, is a hint of the historic tragedy of the individual Jew whose nature is to lose himself in universal relationships, but who is driven back into some Ghetto without walls by the action of anti-Semitism. God helping, I shall not let myself be stampeded. (41)

In fact it was on freedom of thought and of association that she now based a broader sense of group loyalty:

> Humbly, respectful of those who feel called to that bitter labor, I shall no more spend myself in defense of the Jew on sectarian or folk lines, except incidentally, as my knowledge of things Jewish may illumine a given situation. Not to dissociate myself from the Jewish lot, but to establish the more unassailable bond, I here declare that the point where I come to life as a member of modern society, where my fullest sense of responsibility is kindled, is deep below the ache and horror of the Jewish dilemma, at the juncture of social forces where I see the persecution or belittlement of a group—*any* group, whether of race, creed, or color—as an attack on democracy. (42)

Antin's wish for responsible, democratic group membership included the individual's right to express solidarity with the persecuted of any group while maintaining a free-thinking person's entitlement to refuse to be stampeded into some "Ghetto without walls." Antin's assertion of bonds was based on past experience with "things Jewish" and a modern sense of democratic humanism and universalism, not on what she termed "sectarian and folk lines" (42). Antin died in 1949, and this was her last published word.

Also in 1949, Jean Toomer who had by then become a Quaker, delivered the William Penn lecture in Philadelphia, titled "The Flavor of Man."[4] In his published address Toomer reflected upon some serious issues of the times. Starting in a light vein, he related a seed catalogue listing for a mysterious "crystal apple," described as an "amazingly attractive cucumber, perfectly round, crystal-white at all stages, with a sweetness and lack of cucumber flavor that is remarkable" (4–5). Toomer considered this "typical of twentieth-century man," ingeniously producing a cucumber that isn't a cucumber. And similarly bread had lost the flavor of bread. That modern America was relatively flavorless had been observed by many immigrant and ethnic writers before, starting with the Greek peddlar from *Life Stories* who complained about American tomatoes. Toomer also struck an environmentalist note when he found that water no longer tasted like water, for American streams had deteriorated. "The air of our cities is becoming smog," and "our literature" is "without the flavor of literature" (5). Commenting on the Cold War and World War II, he continued:

> Outstanding at this time is the fact that we have peace without the flavor of peace. But the wars we wage have the full horrible flavor of war. The bombs we make are not Crystal Apples. (5)

A little later he took a billboard as the point of departure for another commentary:

> As I ride into Philadelphia the train stops at a station near which is a building bearing in large letters this sign: Wrecks Our Specialty. It refers to motor-cars. I am thinking of human beings. (14)

Now Toomer asked his listeners to remember the human wrecks "by the millions" of "so-called peace-time society," in slums, hospitals, and poorhouses, as well as the wrecks of wartime society which abound all over the world as do the "mutilated bodies of countless thousands" that are "buried out of sight" (15). Focusing on the wrecks in a Pennsylvania institution for the insane, Toomer quoted an investigator who compared the patients' grim situation with "the pictures of the Nazi concentration camps at Belsen and Buchenwald" (15). Toomer extended and universalized this strong parallel: "So many of our kinsmen are in asylums so-called, in ghettos, in concentration camps and colonies, and in some high places, critically reduced below the par of man. Does it matter that some have white bodies, some black, that some are Jews, some Gentiles, some Republicans, some Democrats? It matters that they are human." And contemplating the fact that "the rulers of the two most powerful nations of the world are contemplating and preparing for—or, as they would say, preparing against—a war that may indeed end war by ending man," Toomer dramatically described the "desperate race between education and catastrophe." "The alternatives, I am convinced, are starkly these: Transcendence or extinction" (17).

Antin and Toomer exemplify the turn toward universalism that seemed to be the first lesson of World War II drawn by those who did reflect on it. Stressing ethnicity had been part of the problem of fascism, and the time had come to emphasize our common humanity.

Another strategy was indirection, either by a passing reference or by willful omission. Martha Foley's collection *The Best American Short Stories of 1944,* for example, includes contributions by Saul Bellow, Shirley Jackson, Carson McCullers, Vladimir Nabokov, Leon Zurmelian, Lionel Trilling, and others.[5] In a few stories, there are hints of the extremes of World War II. Brooklyn-born Irwin Shaw's "The Veterans Reflect" includes a long interior monologue of a man who is approaching the Swiss border: "Today his name was known in every home on the face of the earth, in every jungle . . . Thirty million people had died earlier than they expected because of him and hundreds of cities were leveled to the ground because of him" (353). What is revealed only a little later is that "he" is Hitler. The events make memories of loud recitals of Longfellow poems ring hollow (349). The narrator of Russian émigré Vladimir Nabokov's story "'That in Aleppo Once . . .'" reports in a single sentence that he heard that those among the Russian refugees in France

> who chanced to have Jewish blood talk of their doomed kinsmen crammed into hell-bound trains; and my own plight, by contrast, acquired a commonplace air of irreality while I sat in some crowded café with the milky blue sea in front of me and a shell-hollow murmur behind telling and retelling the tale of massacre and misery, and the

gray paradise beyond the ocean, and the ways and whims of harsh consuls. (289)

Dorothy Canfield (Fisher)'s "The Knot Hole" is set among prisoners traveling in a crowded boxcar to France only to be returned to Germany. After a frame narrative the account starts in a Kafkaesque manner: "I thought it was probably by accident that I was among those in the boxcar. I never knew why I was. Perhaps there had been room—if you can call it room—for one more" (42).

A good example for a framing of a novel so as to exclude direct representation is Isaac Bashevis Singer's *The Family Moskat*, which appeared in English in 1950 after being serialized in Yiddish in the *Jewish Daily Forward* for two years. It offers a three-generation family story that ends just as World War II has started and the German bombs hit Warsaw. While Singer thus made the choice to stop short just before the Warsaw ghetto years and the Holocaust, the knowledge of what is about to happen after the novel ends informs the whole book, from the topography of the streets that are not yet disrupted by the ghetto wall to the novel's last words, uttered by Hertz Yanovar in clarification of his prophecy, in Polish, that "the Messiah will come soon." "Death is the Messiah. That's the real truth."[6] And here the novel ends.

Singer also draws an analogy between the experience of residential bombing and modernism:

> On Zlota Street they came across a bombed house. From it issued an odor of whitewash, coal, gas, and smoking cinders. The front of the house had collapsed; a ceiling lay sloping above a pile of bricks, plaster, and glass. They made out the interior of rooms, with their beds, tables, and pictures. Asa Heshel was reminded of modernist theater settings. (600)

Had the grim realities of World War II surpassed the wildest modernist nightmares?

The novel starts with the arrival of Reb Meshulam in Warsaw: "From time to time a red-painted tramcar rumbled by, the electric wires overhead giving off crackling blue sparks" (5). The Warsaw streets that the characters traverse in Singer's novel had already become lines of imprisonment; the ghetto streetcar with the Jewish star and the horsedrawn omnibuses in the walled-in ghetto had become associated with the genocide of Warsaw's Jewry. The train station that is the setting for the arrival in the city had become the transfer to the killing center at Treblinka. Yet in 1950 Singer, who had grown up in Warsaw and left it only in the 1930s when he emigrated to New York, chose to be silent about, to imply rather than to represent, what was to follow after the end of his novel.

In this respect Singer's *Family Moskat* is radically different from John Hersey's novel of the same year 1950, *The Wall,* which offers a full-fledged representation of life in Jewish Warsaw from the forced establishment of the Jewish Council by the Nazi occupation authorities to the closing of the ghetto and the mass deportations to Treblinka. Told in the form of a found document, Noach Levinson's archive, and inspired by Emanuel Ringelblum's diary, the novel is written as if it were an English translation from a Yiddish original, with editorial annotations. A day-by-day, dated and annotated account of experiences and reflections in the Warsaw ghetto, *The Wall* is perhaps the first American novel to confront the Holocaust fully and centrally. It is not anachronistic to use the word "Holocaust," for Hersey employs it to describe the genocide of European Jews, perhaps as the first novelist to do so. In a discussion whether or not a baby prematurely born in a hidden basement in 1943 should be circumcised, the father thinks "that circumcision would be folly in the time of an anti-Jewish holocaust," while the mother disagrees and Noach Levinson adds that "at one point Spinoza considered circumcision alone sufficient to keep the Jewish nation alive."[7]

Levinson registers external events and emotions, small details and momentous occurrences in his archive, and the book focuses closely on a small group of individuals who respond variously to the terror of the Warsaw ghetto. Levinson is close to the socialist Hashomer group, but the political divisions as well as the character differences are described in detail. The Communists, for example, have a very hard time making sense of Stalin's policy in 1939–1940. Some figures rise to heroic stature, but one young man, Stefan Mazur, asks his own parents to agree to be deported so that he can save his own life. Before "Jews are barred from trolleys and buses," Rachel Apt takes "long, idle walks and streetcar rides outside the Jewish section—along the Vistula, to Saxon Garden, to Pototzki Palace, past the Bristol and the Europejski Hotels, even to the suburbs, Praga and Zoliborz and Brudno. It was as if she were trying to memorize the Polish parts of her city, the Polish parts of her life" (52). As the wall is being built, Levinson describes it in such precise detail that the official explanation of it being an "epidemicwall" becomes absurd: "This wall is actually intended to keep human beings from passing" (82). Yet his inner reaction puzzles him also: "We will be together, without the constant, sandy rub of life among the Poles and Germans. . . . I *am* glad" (98).

The cumulative effect of different measures is not easily recognizable as part of a plan. When the "resettlements" begin, a pattern emerges: whatever the people around Levinson find out is worse than they could possibly have feared. A chilling turning point is when Slonim undertakes a dangerous mission to ascertain where the cattle trains are going. He discovers the truth about Treblinka, and the underground Socialist broadside *Storm* reports his findings in a way that actually assumes that the reader already knows—but is reluctant to believe. Hersey does not simply reproduce the report, but creates a staccato, a modernist, effect by showing fragments of it as Rachel Apt reads them, for the words "seemed to jump and jerk before her eyes; she could scarcely credit the snatches as she saw them" (323).

> *[T]hree blank-walled rooms, about two meters high, area 25 square meters, with a narrow corridor fronting all three . . . pipes with valves . . . outside, curious scoops reminding one of ship ventilators . . . power room at one end . . . hermetic seals around the doors and at the scoops and valves . . . floors with terra-cotta inlay which moisture renders very slippery. . . .*
>
> *. . . was especially struck by the irony of the classification sign in the first enclosure—Tailors, Hatmakers, Carpenters, Road-builders, and so on—tending to make the Jews believe they were to be sorted for labor farther east . . . kindly speech by a gentle-looking S.S. officer: . . . After the bath and disinfection, this property will be returned to you in accordance with your receipts . . . along the path naked, carrying a small piece of soap and his documents . . . about 15 minutes . . . are carried by the Jewish auxiliary, led by* Kapos *whose identification is a yellow patch at the knee, to the cemetery . . . and this duty, according to the escaped* Kapo *interviewed by our courier in a hut a few kilometers south of Malkinia, is trying in the extreme . . . covered over by bulldozers, the exhausts of whose Diesel motors provide the constant music of Treblinka.* (324)

When Levinson hears the debates "as to whether the Slonim account is 'true,' 'accurate,' 'exaggerated,' 'a calculated attempt by the Socialists to create panic,' and even [. . .] 'totally imaginary—a sick fantasy!,'" he worries, "if there is apathy and incredulity right here, what must there be, what will there not be forever and ever, at the untouched ends of the earth, in Melbourne, in Rio de Janeiro, in Shanghai, in Chicago?" (326–327). He decides to fight to preserve his archive as testimony. As the ghetto is reduced in size, workers like Mordecai have to tear down the wall they had been forced to build, and Mordecai feels as if he were in a trick German slow-motion film played backward. One of Levinson's entries describes the accelerated living on the brink of death in staccato, Hemingway-like sentences: "We want to cram as much as possible into our remaining hours. Appetites are exaggerated. Flirtation is hurried. Courtship is telescoped. In conversation, even, we come quickly to the point. We live as if by telegraphy" (402). When people's names at the Jewish Council are read off, they would say, "*Deported,* or, *Alive,* as the case might be" (433). The German commander enforces ever increasing "resettlement" rates and asks the Jewish Council for "a tax of one million zlotys *to pay,* he said, *for damage done to railroad stock by Jews while being resettled*" (476).

As Singer described Warsaw after the German bombing of 1939, Hersey represented the surrealism of the ruins of the burned-out ghetto in May 1943: "This was some other planet. Nothing was left of the part of the ghetto where we were, it seemed, but fires and trash. Dunes of fallen brick were silhouetted against weird little separate sunsets of flame-touched smoke. The streets were only valleys in the general rubbish-desert. Where parts of walls or frames or chimneys still stood, they were ragged, tapered, and naturalistic; of a stalagmitic architecture. The scene was eerie and unsettling" (589). Miraculously, and unlike Ringelblum who was murdered by the Nazis on March 7, 1944, Levinson is among the few survivors, though he dies of lobar pneumonia within a year after the destruction of the ghetto, due to physical attrition. His archive is saved.

Hersey, having mapped out the novel as a third-person narrative, switched to the first-person singular of Levinson in the process of drafting the book, for the story "could not be told by an all-knowing, all-seeing John Hersey." Levinson's meticulous, even pedantic style, the format of referencing date of event and entry and source at the beginning of each episode, strangely draw in rather than distance the reader. The translated quality of some of the writing creates a similar effect. David Daiches characterized *The Wall* as a "miracle of compassion" when he reviewed it in 1950.[8]

John Hersey, a non-Jewish American author born in China and trained at Groton and Yale, may appear to be a surprising choice in a survey of major American ethnic modernists. He was a realist, though did occasionally employ modernist devices; one does not think of him as "ethnic," though, having spent his formative years in China as the child of American missionaries, his life story had certain similarities with that of an immigrant. Henry Luce, Pearl S. Buck, and Edward F. Haskell had also grown up outside the United States as the children of missionaries. Hersey was an author who made several important contributions to ethnically themed literature. After having worked as secretary for Sinclair Lewis, Hersey served as World War II correspondent for Luce's *Time* and *Life* covering the Pacific theater, the advancing Red Army, and the Italian campaign.

In his Pulitzer prize–winning novel *A Bell for Adano* (1944), he portrayed the familiar ethnic theme of the return of an immigrant to his ancestral homeland. Hersey's novel takes this familiar plotline into the war and presents the arrival of the U.S. major Joppolo, whose parents had emigrated from Florence, in the fictitious town of Adano in Sicily where he helps restore life to normal after Fascism and war. He is an ordinary American hero who has to deal with an insensitive army bureaucracy and the conflicting needs of a poor village. Just when his scheme to procure a new bell for the town has succeeded, he is relieved of his duties due to the meddling of an inane general, modeled on George S. Patton: The ethnic hero is not just an "American" but the better American. Joppolo was inspired by a real man, Frank E. Toscani, who had indeed been in Italy during the allied invasion and provided a bell for the town of Licata. Hersey's popular and rather cheery novel of 1944 was awarded the Pulitzer Prize on VE Day, turned into a Broadway hit starring Fredric March and a Hollywood movie with John Hodiak, had a New York restaurant named after it, and was panned by Diana Trilling as a journalist's novel "for the war effort."

Readers of *A Bell for Adano* were probably glad when they received the *New Yorker* of August 31, 1946, with a happy cover of summer leisure activities, for apart from the "Goings on about Town" section, the entire issue consisted of "A Reporter at Large," a single, long contribution by John Hersey, interrupted only by advertisements.[9] Yet what the reader found was "Hiroshima," a hard-hitting report about the experience of ordinary people who were in Hiroshima when the nuclear bomb was dropped by the American B-29 bomber plane named "Enola Gay" after the pilot's mother. Hersey's writing was considered nonmodernist, even "flat" by some reviewers, as he attempted to create empathy with the people who had faced the extreme and the unimaginably horrifying, and had miraculously survived, for the time being, these new forms of mass annihilation, if not their eerie aftereffects. The editors of the *New Yorker* explained that they undertook this extraordinary publication "in the conviction that few of us have yet comprehended the all but incredible destructive powers of this weapon, and that everyone might well take time to consider the terrible implications of its use" (15).

The wound may have been the symbol of a cool, exceptional Hemingway protagonist or of the inevitable fate that meets Di Donato's hero who is sacrificed as a new Christ, in concrete. In Hiroshima there was nothing exceptional or heroic about the wounds that had become very widespread, and in fact seemed universal. What had happened to empathy, one of the targets of modernist attacks on realism? Was empathy "kitsch," and should one simply shut up about the sufferings of the victims of the twentieth century, in the way in which Gertrude Stein seemed to suggest in what seems a clear trajectory from the deaths of the three women in *Three Lives* to Stein's "Reflections on the Atom Bomb" in 1946?

> They asked me what I thought of the atomic bomb. I said I had not been able to take any interest in it. . . . What is the use, if they are really as destructive as all that there is nothing left and if there is nothing there nobody to be interested and nothing to be interested about. If they are not as destructive as all that then they are just a little more or less destructive than other things and that means that in spite of all destruction there are always lots left on this earth to be interested or to be willing and the thing that destroys is just one of the things that concerns the people inventing it or the people starting it off, but really nobody else can do anything about it so you have to just live along like always, so you see the atomic [bomb] is not at all interesting, not any more interesting than any other machine, and machines are only interesting in being invented or in what they do, so why be interested. I never could take any interest in the atomic bomb.[10]

One would have to be a hard-boiled modernist, indeed, to appreciate Stein even in this articulation, for Stein displayed about as much empathy here as her narrator of *Three Lives* had toward death-bound Melanctha. "A bomb is a bomb is a bomb," as one critic put it.

The atomic destruction of Hiroshima caused an estimated 100,000 immediate human casualties, and many more died later from the burns and the effects of radiation. How could this unimaginable mass death be presented to readers so that they would care, empathize, and identify with the victims—and at a time when newspapers had offered a full coverage of the technical details of the bombing? Hersey begins with the tried old device of creating scenes with which readers anywhere in the modern world could identify—waking up, doing the chores of everyday life, or going somewhere by streetcar—when the extraordinary happens, and his characters have to face the extreme, the full extent of which they begin to realize only slowly. The "noiseless flash" (15) some of them see is far, far worse than Richard Wright's *Brrrrrriiiiiiiiiiiiiiiiiinng!* The moment Hersey chooses is "exactly fifteen minutes past eight in the morning, on August 6, 1945," and his focus is on six survivors who are spared the fate of an instant death at that moment:

> Each of them counts many small items of chance or volition—a step taken in time, a decision to go indoors, catching one streetcar instead of the next—that spared him. And now each knows that in the act of survival he lived a dozen lives and saw more death than he ever thought he would see. (15)

The witnesses he interviewed were a German Jesuit, Father Wilhelm Kleinsorge; the Methodist Reverend Mr. Kiyoshi Tanimoto; Dr. Terufumi Sasaki, a Red Cross Hospital surgeon; Miss Toshiko Sasaki, a clerk not related to Dr. Sasaki; another physician, Dr. Masakazu Fujii; and a tailor's widow with three small children, Mrs. Hatsuyo Nakamura.

It is Dr. Sasaki who "caught a streetcar at once" on his way to work. "He later calculated," Hersey adds, that "if he had had to wait a few minutes for the streetcar, as often happened, he would have been close to the center at the time of the explosion and would surely have perished" (17). The trams also served as part of one of the postexplosion myths that offered to explain the extraordinary to people who could not possibly comprehend what had happened: "The bomb was not a bomb at all; it was a kind of fine magnesium powder sprayed over the whole city by a single plane, and it exploded when it came into contact with the live wires of the city power system," something that was only possible to do to "big cities and only in the daytime, when the tram lines and so forth are in operation" (39). Hiroshima certainly fit the bill for that story, for it boasted a fleet of 123 tramcars—out of which only three were in working condition after the attack. Some cars remained only as shadows that the gigantic light of the explosion left on streets and some stone walls.

The creation of these permanent shadows helped experts figure out where the hypocenter of the explosion, named "ground zero" in an Americanism of 1945, must have been by triangulating various shadows of buildings.[11] The shadows themselves seemed like another violent parody of surrealist art.

> A few vague human silhouettes were found, and these gave rise to stories that eventually included fancy and precise details. One story told how a painter on a ladder was monumentalized in a kind of bas-relief on the stone façade of a bank building on which he was at work, in the act of dipping his brush into the paint can; another, how a man and his cart on the bridge near the Museum of Science and Industry, almost under the center of the explosion, were cast down in an embossed shadow which made it clear that the man was about to whip his horse. (46)

Modern forms of destruction seemed to make a mockery of modern art. The shadows were not the only strange pseudomodernist creations brought about by the sudden change "from a busy city of two hundred and forty-five thousand that morning to a mere pattern of residue in the afternoon" (26). The strangeness of so much destruction caused, without warning, by only one single plane flying in a clear sky remains unmitigated even after the scientists' explanations. Nature was changed. Father Kleinsorge sees a pumpkin "roasted on the vine" and "potatoes that were nicely baked under the ground" (26). Miss Sasaki notices that "wild flowers were in bloom among the city's bones. The bomb had not only left the underground organs of plants intact; it had stimulated them." Ground zero was so quickly covered by sickle senna that it seemed "as if a load of sickle-senna seed had been dropped along with the bomb" (44–45).

Hersey is strong in describing the horrors of human destruction and deformation; he writes about a group of Japanese soldiers:

> Their faces were wholly burned, their eyesockets were hollow, the fluid from their melted eyes had run down their cheeks. (They must have

had their faces upturned when the bomb went off; perhaps they were anti-aircraft personnel.) Their mouths were mere swollen, pus-covered wounds, which they could not bear to stretch enough to admit the spout of the teapot. (34)

Hersey is careful to universalize reactions of stoicism: the phrase used was "'*Shikata ga nai,*' a Japanese expression as common as, and corresponding to, the Russian word '*nichevo*': 'It can't be helped. Oh well. Too bad'" (59). While staying closely to the points of view of the people he interviewed, he lets moral points emerge only in an understated manner, for example by Dr. Sasaki:

> I see . . . that they are holding a trial for war criminals in Tokyo just now. I think they ought to try the men who decided to use the bomb and they should hang them all." The atomic bomb was part of war action—but was mass killing and was maiming of so many civilians justifiable, as the Vatican asked? (59–60)

The interruptions of the *New Yorker* ads were eerie at times and a reminder of the impassiveness of the world of market and commerce to even the most extreme human atrocities. Opposite the page on which Hersey describes the change "from a busy city of two hundred and forty-five thousand that morning to a mere pattern of residue in the afternoon" (26), RCA Victor promoted "Sniperscope," an infrared telescope that, mounted on a carbine, enabled a soldier in total darkness to hit a target the size of a man at seventy-five yards, an invention that was, the full-page ad announced proudly, responsible for "thirty percent of the Japanese casualties during the first three weeks of the Okinawa campaign" (27). When Hersey describes the analysis of the bombing by Japanese scientists, an ad for a "federal union" warns readers that "now—in this atomic age . . . a bomb could destroy the statue . . . and Liberty, too. We can no longer afford to leave it to a statue to carry that torch" (41). Another ad for "Hair Pieces FOR PARTLY OR ALL BALD SCALPS" seemed pasted, as if intentionally by a perverse editor at the *New Yorker*, precisely next to the passage in which Hersey gives a harrowing account of the many ailments of the survivor-victims who had been exposed to radiation; and at the level between the words "Hair" and "Pieces" in the ad, Hersey's text reads: "the main symptom was falling hair" (48). Next to Hersey's information that the city of Hiroshima "authorized and built four hundred one-family 'barracks'" a Honeywell ad informed readers under the slogan "Modern Art, eh, Gertie?" (perhaps alluding to Stein) that a Honeywell "M-H 'Personalized' Heating Control" thermostat was a "little object more important... than a collection of Dali originals" (53). The fact that modernism was on its way toward becoming a safe part of the commercial culture and a commodity was also visible in an ad for a lowercase and all-in-one-word "modernage" shop on 34th Street (48). And a New York Stock Exchange ad that represented all-white customers on a train platform at a suburban station looking for their own names as investors and co-owners of the company that were written on a Pullman car out of which a happily smiling black porter was looking on suggested the extent to which the double victory campaign and the sense of an "American dilemma" had reached the country (54).

Hersey's reportage was immensely successful, as readers seemed to look at what had happened as if for the first time. The cumulative effect of the stories of individual survivors was more powerful than many other, more "objective" accounts which had been published before. The *New Yorker* was quickly sold out, the book publication that followed has never since gone out of print, and the government felt obliged to develop a more full-fledged rationale for the employment of the weapon than it had offered before Hersey's *Hiroshima*.

New York intellectuals may have looked at Hersey's work as what Greenberg called "kitsch." Dwight Macdonald complained that in *Hiroshima*, Hersey's "suave, toned-down, underplayed kind of naturalism" was "no longer adequate, either esthetically or morally, to cope with the modern horrors." According to Macdonald, Hersey had "no eye for the one detail that imaginatively creates a whole." And worse: "the 'little people' of Hiroshima whose sufferings Hersey records in antiseptic *New Yorker* prose might just as well be white mice, for all the pity, horror, or indignation the reader—or at least this reader—is made to feel for them."[12] Mary McCarthy thought that the "human interest" method of *Hiroshima* constituted an "insipid falsification of the truth of atomic warfare." She added a demand that was impossible to fulfill by anyone (unless he were an Odysseus or a Dante): "To have done the atom bomb justice, Mr. Hersey would have had to interview the dead."[13]

Lacking the quality of being "difficult" for readers, of being very self-consciously concerned with formal experimentation, Hersey certainly would not qualify as a full-blown modernist, even though Harry Levin, in his introduction to the 1947 *Portable James Joyce* (a companion to

Cowley's *Portable Faulkner*) asked: "How many of those who read John Hersey's *Hiroshima* recognize its literary obligation to *Ulysses*?"[14] This may have been hyperbole, for Hersey appears to have received more formal inspiration from the search for transcendence in the coincidence of a handful of characters who share an accidental death in Thornton Wilder's novel *The Bridge of San Luis Rey* (1927) than from any of Joyce's stylistic devices. The point is not to claim Hersey as an ethnic modernist, but to suggest by the discussion of some of his works in the 1940s what American modernists and ethnic writers stayed away from in the same period: a full-fledged confrontation with the horrors of World War II.

James Agee left only a strange novel fragment, entitled "Dedication Day," in which a nuclear scientist commits suicide to atone for his participation in the building of the bomb. In his Simple tale "Here to Yonder: Simple and the Atom Bomb" (August 18, 1945) Langston Hughes seems to start seriously but then make light of the subject. Simple is worried that the bomb may end all human relations: "The way it kills people for miles around, all my relations and—me, too—is liable to be wiped out in no time." The narrator assures him:

> "Nobody is dropping that bomb on you . . . We are dropping it way over in Asia."
>
> "And what is to keep Asia from dropping it back on us?" asked Simple.
>
> "The Japanese probably do not have any atomic bomb to drop," I said.[15]

From there, the conversation drifts to why the bomb was not used in Germany, to the cost of the bomb and better ways to spend the money and to the Mississippi election. This little sketch still makes Hughes exceptionally engaged, for Hurston and Wright, for example, barely mentioned the Holocaust or Hiroshima in their writing, published or unpublished.

John Hersey's report *Hiroshima* and his novel *The Wall* both address the very issue of genocide that came to matter so much to the many writers who would *later* invoke the legacy of Hiroshima and the *univers concentrationnaire* of Auschwitz. The very fact that a young writer, an outsider trained as a journalist, wrote and published such works at a time of much silence about these themes points to the remarkable absence of those issues in American modernist and ethnic fiction right after World War II. Perhaps the time has come to think of modernism not as an inherently redemptive, progressive, or resistant category but merely as a set of stylistic conventions—not unlike realism or neoclassicism—that helped artists achieve some extraordinary aesthetic accomplishments but that also could, and did, serve many different ideological purposes, some good and some bad.

17

Grand Central Terminal

A short story by the Hungarian émigré Leo Szilard, entitled "Report on 'Grand Central Terminal,'" written in 1948 and first published in the *University of Chicago Magazine* in 1952, engages the reader as an interpreter of the meaning of artifacts—against an unusual background.[1] A research team of extraterrestrial scientists investigates Manhattan after a neutron bomb war has destroyed all human, animal, and plant life on earth (hence all subjects of empathy), but has left buildings intact. The story develops a tension between the conservative narrator and the radical scientist Xram. Their conflicting views come to the fore as they investigate Grand Central Terminal, the New York train station that had been the subject of a 1915 Max Weber oil canvas and of several Berenice Abbott photographs, and that made Louis Adamic's Slovenian birthplace seem so small. Szilard's narrator explains:

> What its name "Grand Central Terminal" meant we do not know, but there is little doubt as to the general purpose which this building served. It was part of a primitive transportation system based on clumsy engines which ran on rails and dragged cars mounted on wheels behind them. (117)

The narrator concludes that there must have been two kinds of people in the city of Grand Central Terminal, those with a "smoky" and those with a "fair or 'nonsmoky'" complexion; he theorizes that in this primitive transportation system they were probably segregated as "Smokers" and "Nonsmokers" (118). A third strain of earth-dwellers, endowed with wings, appears to have died out earlier, since none of the numerous skeletons belonged to this winged strain and since their images "are *much more frequently found among the older paintings than among the more recent paintings*" (118).

The scientists are puzzled by the public toilets at the station, "small cubicles which served as temporary shelter for earth-dwellers while they were depositing their excrements" (119). Here is one of the investigators' problem:

> [T]he door of each and every cubicle in the depository was locked by a rather complicated gadget. Upon investigation of these gadgets it was found that they contained a number of round metal disks. By now we know that these ingenious gadgets barred entrance to the cubicle until an additional disk was introduced into them through a slot; at that very moment the door became unlocked, permitting access to the cubicle.
>
> These disks bear different images and also different inscriptions which, however, all have in common the word "Liberty." What is the significance of these gadgets, the disks in the gadgets and the word "Liberty" on the disks? (119–120)

A scholarly consensus emerges that these disks suggest "a ceremonial act accompanying the act of deposition" and that "the word 'Liberty' must designate some virtue which was held in high esteem by the earth-dwellers or their ancestors" (120). But why the gadgets at the locks? The scientists assume that "earth-dwellers [. . .] were perhaps driven by a certain sense of urgency, that in the absence of the gadgets they might have occasionally forgotten to make the disk sacrifice and would have consequently suffered pangs of remorse afterward" (120). Xram disagrees, however, and we hear his opinion filtered through the skeptical narrator:

> [Xram] believes that these disks were given out to earth-dwellers as rewards for services. He says that the earth-dwellers were not rational beings and that they would not have collaborated in co-operative enterprises without some special incentive.
>
> He says that, by barring earth-dwellers from depositing their excrements unless they sacrificed a disk on each occasion, they were made eager to acquire such disks [. . .].
>
> He thinks that the disks found in the depositories represent only a special case of a more general principle and that the earth-dwellers probably had to deliver such disks not only prior to being given access to the depository but also prior to being given access to food, etc. (121)

Xram is now in a state of excitement as he develops a larger theory, with which the condescending narrator clearly does not sympathize:

> [H]e had made some elaborate calculations which show that a system of production and distribution of goods based on a system of exchanging disks cannot be stable, but is necessarily subject to great fluctuations vaguely reminiscent of the manic-depressive cycle in the insane. He goes so far as to say that in such a depressive phase war becomes psychologically possible even within the same species. (121)

The narrator has no difficulty disproving Xram's obviously "nonsensical ideas," for "a spot check of ten different lodging houses of the city, selected at random" (121) reveals "a number of depositories but not a single one that was equipped with a gadget containing disks." This leaves only the assumption that disks in the "Grand Central Terminal" depositories "had been placed there as a ceremonial act. Apparently such ceremonial acts were connected with the act of deposition in *public* places, and in public places only" (122).

The thoroughly ironic Jewish author of the story was the same Budapest-born Leo Szilard who, after emigrating to the United States in 1938, was among the "Manhattan project" pioneers in the development of nuclear chain reactions that made possible the building and use of the first atomic bombs. He once reported that, having read H. G. Wells's "The World Set Free," a visionary science fiction story about atomic energy, he had a sudden burst of inspiration (while he was waiting for a traffic light to change at the corner of Southampton Row in London) that a neutron chain reaction could release energy from fissioning atoms. Szilard was an adventurer in the world of modernity who filed a patent for an electron microscope and, with Albert Einstein, for a refrigerator pump; and who devised his own advertising copy for the book which included "Report on 'Grand Central Terminal'": "In Philadelphia almost everybody reads *The Voice of the Dolphins*. . . . On sale in the Harvard Coop. If you do not buy it to-day you will forget it."

Szilard also had a strong sense of political responsibility. In 1932 he tried to organize a boycott of Japan in protest against the brutal war Japan was waging against China. And in 1945 Szilard vehemently opposed the use of the atomic bomb in Hiroshima and Nagasaki on moral grounds. After trying unsuccessfully to appeal directly to Roosevelt and then Truman, Szilard circulated a "Petition to the President" among

Manhattan Project scientists (dated July 17, 1945) which argued that while the use of an atomic bomb would have been justified had the United States been attacked with such a weapon by Germany, "such attacks on Japan could not be justified, at least not unless the terms which will be imposed after the war on Japan were made public in detail and Japan were given an opportunity to surrender." Worrying about the moral responsibilities involved in such a step, the scientists warned that "a nation which sets the precedent of using these newly liberated forces of nature for purposes of destruction may have to bear the responsibility of opening the door to an era of devastation on an unimaginable scale." Anticipating the arms race of "rival powers," the petition to the U.S. Commander-in-Chief argued that the lead in the field of atomic power gave the United States "the obligation of restraint and if we were to violate this obligation our moral position would be weakened in the eyes of the world and in our own eyes."[2] Szilard's appeal, although it was signed by sixty-nine other atomic scientists, had no effect on Truman's decision making. Szilard made his efforts the point of departure of another sarcastic tale, "My Trial as a War Criminal" (1947), in which Russians, having taken control of the United States after a biological weapons attack on New Jersey, were rounding up those Americans who were involved in the development and employment of the atomic bomb, in order to prosecute them for Nuremberg-trial-defined crimes such as "violation of the customs of war" and "planning a war in violation of international agreements."[3]

In "Report on 'Grand Central Terminal'" Szilard presented a model case for a minority view held by Xram (an inversion of the name of a famous theorist) that is infuriatingly dismissed by the narrator of the story. Could the "Liberty" disks have something to do with peace and war? Szilard's question is all the more haunting since he defamiliarizes such fixtures of modern life as pay toilets in a postwar, and also chillingly posthuman, setting. An extraordinary example of immigrant writing in the post-Hiroshima mode, this subtle tale suggests that modernity, the wish to acquire disks in "manic-depressive" market cycles, and moral irresponsibility had taken mankind to the last stop of a "Grand Central Terminal," indeed.

The period from 1910 to 1950 had a certain four-decade-long unity. But it was also marked by deep ruptures. The teens were both prewar and war years, and the war marked a deep caesura: the international republic of letters generally gave way to nationalized intellectuals who supported or opposed war efforts—though there was a good amount of neutralism, pacifism, and new internationalism as well. World War I developed political propaganda to a new high pitch, and, after the war, its target could be redirected from "Huns" (the term inadvertently launched by Kaiser Wilhelm himself in a pep talk to German soldiers departing for China in 1900) to "Reds" or Jews or "Japs" or social equality or to any other enemy construction throughout the period up into the Cold War. On the home front, the Americanization movement and assimilation drives set out to Anglicize immigrants: the hyphen was a minus sign and English the language of the Declaration. World War I had a deep effect on the marginalization and demonization of languages other than English—a process of which Spanish was ultimately to become the main target. The color line was being drawn more and more sharply, and eugenicist research offered the most comprehensive rationale for racism in the war years and the subsequent two decades.

The years from the end of World War I to 1929 were boom years, with isolationism growing, and they were deeply conservative. At the same time ethnic autobiography and literature became more modernist, self-reflexive, and somber. The stock exchange crash of 1929, another event marking a deep rupture in the period, may or may not have affected literary production, but some social themes moved to the foreground in literature during the Great Depression of the 1930s. Perhaps more important, there was a return of the realist aesthetic on many political fronts; and the victory of Hemingway's compromise modernism might also be understood in this context.

The next big caesura was World War II. The war years, with their multiethnic platoon stories and Roosevelt's articulation of the four liberties, popularly illustrated by Norman Rockwell, ushered in a double victory campaign over Fascism abroad and racism at home, and an intensified effort toward intercultural education as a safeguard against the genocidal danger stemming from group hostilities and stereotyping. Yet American modernist and ethnic writers—with very few exceptions—did not confront the "concentration camp universe" until the Beat Generation came along. Nineteen forty-five to 1950 marked the transformation from war alliance to new anti-Communism and Cold War; 1940 to 1950 also brought the ultimate acceptance of modernism as the art of democracy.

As the period ended, the civil rights movement was about to get going, and it accelerated from the 1954 *Brown v. Board of Education* decision to the civil rights movement legislation of the 1960s. In 1967, the Supreme Court in the *Loving v. Virginia* case also declared unconstitutional one of the oldest and most widespread racist set of laws prohibiting interracial marriage.

In the period from 1930 to 1950 economic mobility prevailed in the United States: whereas the richest 1 percent of American households controlled more than 40 percent of the nation's wealth in 1930, the figure had declined to under 30 percent by 1949 (only to rise again to nearly 40 percent by 1990). This means that the economic developments from 1930 to 1950 gave mobility narratives a certain plausibility whereas by the end of the twentieth century economic mobility rates in the United States were actually lower than those in other democratic countries.

The acceptance of modernism as the art of democracy and of resistance could become more widespread because the totalitarian opposition made such an acceptance plausible—despite the continued populist resistance to art that wasn't about anything. Yet this populism (embodied by Dondero's congressional appearance) could not find effective political expression during the Cold War years.

As modernism became more what one could call normal practice in the 1950s, it stabilized the story line of its own emergence as its central myth. Retold in the shape of so many biographically informed narratives (from Cézanne, van Gogh, Ensor, Monet, and Picasso to American immigrant artists Joseph Stella, Emmanuel Radnitsky—who became better known as Man Ray—and Max Weber), the story always moved from a premodern, Victorian, realist code to the formal explosion of style and color that marked the achievement of each modern artist. Stein's story could be told in similar terms as a development from *Q.E.D.* to *Three Lives* and *The Making of Americans* and toward the world of Picasso, Cézanne, and Matisse. It was a very powerful story of emergence and it may still dominate much of the landscape of modernism. Yet it was also a selective story that was based on omissions and conflation. It was a story that may now have run its course.

Chronology
Notes
Bibliography
Acknowledgments
Index

Chronology

1890	William James (1842–1910) employs term "stream of thought" in *Principles of Psychology*
May 8, 1894	Antin family arrives in Boston on the *Polynesia*
1896	Abraham Cahan (1860–1951), *Yekl: A Tale of the New York Ghetto*
	Leon M. Solomons and Gertrude Stein publish "Normal Motor Automatism" in *Harvard Psychological Review*
1901	Jacob Riis (1849–1914), *The Making of an American*
	Booker T. Washington (1856–1915), *Up from Slavery*
October 18, 1901	Booker T. Washington has lunch at White House with President Theodore Roosevelt (1858–1919)
1901–1910	8,795,386 immigrants arrive in the US
1902	Hutchins Hapgood (1869–1944), *The Spirit of the Ghetto*
September 25, 1902	Sadie Frowne, "The Story of a Sweatshop Girl" published in Hamilton Holt's *Independent,* leading to a series of about seventy published life stories
1903	Gertrude Stein (1874–1946) writes "Q.E.D." (published posthumously)
March 17, 1904	*Independent* runs "The Race Problem—An Autobiography by a Southern Colored Woman"
1905	William James, "The Stream of Consciousness"
	Joseph Stella (1877–1946), "Americans in the Rough" published in *Outlook*
1906	Hamilton Holt (1872–1951), *The Life Stories of Undistinguished Americans As Told by Themselves*
1907	Henry James (1843–1916), *The American Scene*
	Peak year of immigration: more than 1.25 million arrive
August 8, 1907	Maxim Gorky (1868–1936), essay "Boredom," on Coney Island, appears in *Independent*
1908	Sigmund Freud (1856–1939), "Der Familienroman der Neurotiker" (Family Romance)
1908–1917	Alfred Stieglitz (1864–1946), exhibitions in gallery 291
1909	Gertrude Stein, *Three Lives*
	Sui Sin Far (1865–1914), "Leaves from the Mental Portfolio of an Eurasian"
	Dafydd Rhys Williams, *Llyfr y Dyn Pren ac Eraill*

1910	Total U.S. population 91,972,266 Negro 9,827,763 Foreign-born 13,345,545 (104,481 *not* born in Europe or the Americas) Foreign white stock 32,243,382 More than one in seven Americans is foreign-born, more than one in three is born of at least one foreign-born parent
1910	Alexander Irvine (1863–1941), *From the Bottom Up: The Life Story of Alexander Irvine* Leon Kobrin (1872–1946), "Di shprakh fun elnt" (The language of misery) Ernest Poole (1880–1950), "A Mixing Bowl of All Nations," illustrated by Joseph Stella
December 1910	W. E. B. Du Bois (1868–1963) includes Stein's *Three Lives* in list for "What to Read?" in *Crisis* magazine
1912	Mary Antin (1881–1946), *The Promised Land* and "First Aid to the Alien" James Weldon Johnson (1871–1938), *The Autobiography of an Ex-Colored Man* Johan Person (1868–1921), "Ett missförstådt folk" (A Misunderstood People) Sui Sin Far, *Mrs. Spring Fragrance*
February 15 to March 15, 1913	"International Exhibition of Modern Art" at 69th Infantry Regiment Armory, Lexington Avenue at 25th Street, New York
March 22, 1913	Theodore Roosevelt publishes "A Layman's View of an Art Exhibition"
September 1913	Joseph Stella takes a bus ride to Coney Island during a post-Labor Day "Mardi Gras" celebration at the amusement park
1913–1914	Joseph Stella, *Coney Island: Battle of Lights*
1914	Mary Antin, *They Who Knock at Our Gates: A Complete Gospel of Immigration,* illustrated by Joseph Stella Vachel Lindsay (1879–1931), *The Congo* S.S. McClure (1857–1949) [and Willa Cather (1873–1947)], *My Autobiography* Edward Steiner (1866–1956), *From Alien to Citizen*
1914–1918	World War I
1915	Van Wyck Brooks (1886–1963) introduces "highbrow"/"lowbrow" distinction in *America's Coming-of-Age* Ole Buslett (1855–1924), *Veien til Golden Gate* (The Road to the Golden Gate)

	Horace M. Kallen (1882–1974), "Democracy Versus the Melting-Pot" in the *Nation*
1916	Randolph S. Bourne (1886–1918), "Trans-National America" in *Atlantic Monthly*
	Agnes Repplier (1855–1950), "The Modest Immigrant" in *Atlantic Monthly*
	Carl Sandburg (1878–1967), *Chicago Poems*
1917	Waldemar Ager (1869–1941), *Paa veien til smeltepotten* (On the Way to the Melting Pot)
	Abraham Cahan, *The Rise of David Levinsky*
	Marcus E. Ravage (1884–1965), *An American in the Making*
	Barrett Wendell wonders about Antin's claim to be an American
	Johannes B. Wist (1864–1923), *Jonasville: Et kulturbillede* (The Rise of Jonas Olsen: A Norwegian Immigrant's Saga)
1917ff.	*The Cambridge History of American Literature,* ed. William Peterfield Trent et al.
1918	Willa Cather, *My Antonia*
	The Education of Henry Adams (1838–1918) (public printing)
	Mike Gold (1893–1967), "Surveys of the Promised Land," calling Antin a "bright slum parvenu"
1919	Horace Bridges (1880–1955), *On Becoming an American*
	Waldo Frank (1889–1967), *Our America*
	John Cournos (1881–1966), *The Mask*
	H. L. Mencken (1880–1956), *The American Language*
1920	Edward Bok (1863–1930), *The Americanization of Edward Bok: The Autobiography of a Dutch Boy Fifty Years After*
	Edward Hopper (1882–1967), *Night on the El Train*
	Anzia Yezierska (1880–1970), *Hungry Hearts*
June 1920	John Dewey (1859–1952), "Americanism and Localism" published in *The Dial*
1921	John Cournos (1881–1966), *The Wall*
	John Dos Passos (1896–1970), *Three Soldiers*
	Constantine Panunzio (1884–1964), *The Soul of an Immigrant*
	Julia Peterkin "The Merry-Go-Round" in *Smart Set*
	Feri Felix Weiss, *The Sieve; or, Revelations of the Man Mill*
1922	John Cournos (1881–1966), *Babel*
	T. S. Eliot (1888–1965), *The Waste Land*
	James Joyce (1882–1941), *Ulysses*
	Ludwig Lewisohn (1882–1955), *Up Stream*
	Walter Lippmann (1889–1974) draws attention to "stereotypes"
	Harold Stearns (1891–1943), *Civilization in the United States*
	Anzia Yezierska, *Salome of the Tenements*

October 27–29, 1922	Mussolini marches on Rome
Thanksgiving 1922	Anzia Yezierska' novel *Salome of the Tenements* released to coincide with moving picture based on her *Hungry Hearts*
1923	Michael Pupin (1858–1935), *From Immigrant to Inventor*
	Jean Toomer (1894–1967), *Cane* published, selling a total of 429 copies
1924	Konrad Bercovici (1882–1960), *Around the World in New York*
	Felipe Maximiliano Chacón (1873–1949), *Obras*
	Pascal D'Angelo (1894–1932), *Son of Italy*
	F. Scott Fitzgerald (1896–1940, "How to Live on $36,000 a Year" published in *Saturday Evening Post*
	Ernest Hemingway (1899–1961), *In Our Time*
	Horace M. Kallen coins term "cultural pluralism"
	Virginia *Act to Preserve Racial Purity* is passed
1925	Sherwood Anderson (1876–1941), *Dark Laughter*
	Konrad Bercovici, *On New Shores*
	Johan Bojer (1872–1959), *The Emigrants*
	Edward Bok, *Twice Thirty: Some Short and Simple Annals of the Road*
	Giuseppe Cautela (1883–?), *Moon Harvest*
	Theodore Dreiser (1871–1945), *An American Tragedy*
	F. Scott Fitzgerald, *The Great Gatsby*
	Alain Locke (1886–1954), *The New Negro*
	Martha Ostenso (1900–1963), *Wild Geese*
	Anzia Yezierska, *The Bread Givers*
1926	William Faulkner (1897–1962), *Soldier's Pay*
	Ernest Hemingway, *The Sun Also Rises* and *The Torrents of Spring*
	Luigi Sturzo (1879–1959), *Italy and Fascismo,* uses term "totalitarianism" in a positive sense
	Ladies' Home Journal uses word "hard-boiled"
	Carl Van Vechten (1880–1964), *Nigger Heaven*
April 1926	Jean Toomer has a mystical conversion experience at the platform of the 66th Street L stop in Manhattan
1927	Edward Hopper writes letter about Hemingway's "The Killers" to *Scribner's*
	Mourning Dove (1888–1936), *Cogewea, the Half-Blood*
	Ole E. Rølvaag (1876–1931), *Giants in the Earth*
August 23, 1927	Sacco and Vanzetti executed; day on which Nathan Asch's novel *Pay Day* is set
1928	Nella Larsen (1891–1964) writes letter of praise to Stein
	Ludwig Lewisohn (1882–1955), *The Island Within*

	Claude McKay (1890–1948), *Home to Harlem*
	Benito Mussolini (1883–1945) [Richard Washburn Child (1881–1935)], *My Autobiography*
	Paul Rosenfeld (1890–1946), *A Boy in the Sun*
April 17, 1928	*New York Times* criticizes jazz
December 1928	English translation of Maxim Gorky's diatribe against jazz, "The Music of the Degenerate," published in *The Dial* (served as theoretical backbone for banning jazz in Soviet Union)
1929	William Faulkner, *The Sound and the Fury*
	Jessie Fauset (1882–1961), *Plum Bun*
	Ernest Hemingway, *A Farewell to Arms*
	Oliver LaFarge (1901–1963), *Laughing Boy*
	Ole E. Rølvaag, *Peder Victorious*
	Jean Toomer, "Race Problems and Modern Society"
1930	Nathan Asch (1902–1964), *Pay Day*
	Dorthea Dahl (1881–1958), "Kopper-kjelen" (The Copper Kettle)
	Mike Gold, *Jews Without Money*
	Dashiel Hammett (1894–1961), *The Maltese Falcon*
	Ludwig Lewisohn, *Stephen Escott* (repr. as *The Vehement Flame: The Story of Stephen Escott,* 1948)
	Nathanael West (1903–1940), *Miss Lonelyhearts*
1931	Louis Adamic (1899–1951), *Laughing in the Jungle: The Autobiography of an Immigrant in America*
	James Truslow Adams uses the term "American dream" in *The Epic of America*
	Konrad Bercovici, *Manhattan Side-Show*
	Emma Goldman (1869–1940), *Living My Life*
	Ole E. Rølvaag, *Their Fathers' God*
	Lincoln Steffens (1866–1936), *Autobiography*
	Nathanael West, *The Dream Life of Balso Snell*
1931–1952	*Story Magazine,* edited by Whit Burnett and Martha Foley
1932	Raymond Chandler (1888–1959), "Beer in the Sergeant Major's Hat (or The Sun Also Sneezes)"
	William Faulkner, *Light in August*
	Dashiel Hammett (1894–1961), *The Thin Man*
1933	Duke Ellington (1899–1974) records *Daybreak Express*
	Granville Hicks (1901–1982), *The Great Tradition: An Interpretation of American Literature Since the Civil War*
	Zora Neale Hurston (1891–1960), "The Gilded Six-Bits" in *Story*
	Gertrude Stein, *The Autobiography of Alice B. Toklas*

Fall 1933	*Esquire* is launched
1934	Indian Reorganization Act
	Propagation of "Socialist realism" in Soviet Union after Maxim Gorky delivers programmatic speech at First All-Union Congress of Soviet Writers
	Louis Adamic, *The Native's Return: An American Immigrant Visits Yugoslavia and Discovers His Old Country*
	Daniel Fuchs (1909–1993), *Summer in Williamsburg*
	Mike Gold, "Gertrude Stein: A Literary Idiot"
	John Joseph Mathews (1894–1979), *Sundown*
	Henry Roth (1906–1995), *Call It Sleep*; sells approx. 4,000 copies in 1930s
	William Saroyan (1908–1981), "Aspirin Is a Member of the N.R.A" in *American Mercury* and *The Daring Young Man on the Flying Trapeze and Other Stories*
	Nathanael West, *A Cool Million*
	American pavilion at Venice Biennale organized by Juliana Force, with emphasis on modernist works
February 9, 1934	New York Times reviews Stein's opera *Four Saints in Three Acts*
1935	Hitler denounces modernist art at Nuremberg Party rally
	James T. Farrell (1904–1979), *Studs Lonigan* (trilogy completed)
	Lin Yutang (1895–1976), *My Country and My People*
1935–1943	Federal Writers' Project
1936	Alfred H. Barr, Jr. exhibits "Cubism and Abstract Art" at Museum of Modern Art
	William Faulkner, *Absalom, Absalom!*
	Joseph Freeman (1897–1965), *An American Testament*
	Daniel Fuchs, *Homage to Blenholt*
	D'Arcy McNickle (1904–1977), *The Surrounded*
	Ezra Pound (1885–1972), *Jefferson and/or Mussolini*
	Ayn Rand (1905–1982), *We the Living*
	Sophus Keith Winther (1893–1983), *Take All to Nebraska*
February 12, 1936	Lincoln's Birthday holiday and date on which Richard Wright's novel *Lawd Today* is set
1937	Nazi "Degenerate Art" show opens in Munich
	John Fante (1909–1983), *Wait until Spring, Bandini*
	Michael Foster (1904–1956), *American Dream*
	Daniel Fuchs, *Low Company*
	Zora Neale Hurston (1891–1960), *Their Eyes Were Watching God*
	Younghill Kang (1903–1972), *East Goes West: The Making of an Oriental Yankee*

	Claude McKay, *A Long Way from Home*
	Sophus Keith Winther (1893–1983), *Mortgage Your Heart*
	Richard Wright (1908–1960), *Lawd Today* (ms. "Cesspool" finished)
March 1937	*Esquire* publishes "Christ in Concrete" by Pietro di Donato (1911–1992)
1938	Nazi "Degenerate Music" show in Düsseldorf
	Gertrude Stein reputedly recommends Hitler to the Nobel Prize Committee
	Louis Adamic, *My America*
	John Dos Passos (1896–1970), *U.S.A.*
	José Rodrigues Miguéis (1901–1980), *Gente da terceira classe* (Steerage)
	Harold Stearns (1891–1943), *America Now: An Inquiry into Civilization in the United States*
	Sophus Keith Winther (1893–1983), *This Passion Never Dies*
	Richard Wright, *Uncle Tom's Children*
1939	Raymond Chandler, *The Big Sleep*
	Pietro di Donato, *Christ in Concrete*
	Ludwig Lewisohn, *The Story of American Literature*
	Nathanael West, *Day of the Locust*
June 14, 1939	Ralph Ellison hears in Harlem bar and transcribes tale of Sweet-the-monkey who "could make hisself invisible"
August 1939	Hitler-Stalin agreement
September 1939	Germany attacks Poland; beginning World War II
Fall 1939	Clement Greenberg (1909–1994), "Avant-Garde and Kitsch," *Partisan Review*
December 12, 1939	Delmore Schwartz (1913–1966) writes in diary that he read Stein's "The Good Anna," but "not with the proper attention"
1940	Louis Adamic, *From Many Lands*
	Raymond Chandler, *Farewell, My Lovely*
	Fray Angélico Chávez (1910–1996), *New Mexico Triptych*
	Michael DeCapite (1915–1958), *Maria*
	John Fante, *Dago Red*
	Ernest Hemingway, *For Whom the Bell Tolls*
	William Saroyan, *My Name Is Aram*
	Gertrude Stein, *What Are Masterpieces*
	Richard Wright, *Native Son*
1940–1949	Louis Adamic's, *Common Ground*
1941	Mary Antin, "House of the One Father," *Common Ground*
	Thomas Bell (1903–1961), *Out of this Furnace*
	Edward F. Haskell (1906–1986) publishes *Lance: A Novel about Multicultural Men,* launching word "multicultural"

	Vladimir Nabokov (1899–1977), *The Real Life of Sebastian Knight*
	W. Lloyd Warner (1898–1970) introduces the word "ethnicity" in his *Yankee City Series*
	Richard Wright, *12 Million Black Voices*
December 1941	SS-Einsatzgruppen massacre seven thousand Jews in Polotzk, Antin's native town
1942	William Faulkner, *Go Down, Moses*
	Zora Neale Hurston, *Dust Tracks on a Road: An Autobiography*
	Pardee Lowe (1904–1996), *Father and Glorious Descendant*
	Margaret Mead (1901–1978), *And Keep Your Powder Dry*
February 19, 1942	President Roosevelt signs executive order 9066 providing for the internment of all Japanese Americans residing west of the Mississippi
May 30, 1942	Lionel Trilling (1905–1975), "The McCaslins of Mississippi," review of Faulkner's *Go Down, Moses* in the *Nation*
1943	Jerre Mangione (1909–1998), *Mount Allegro*
	Toshio Mori (1910–1980), "A Sketch," *Topaz Times*
	Salom Rizk, *Syrian Yankee*
	Ayn Rand, *The Fountainhead*
	Hisaye Yamamoto (1921–), "Death Rides the Rails to Poston," *Poston Chronicle*
January 23, 1943	Duke Ellington's *Black, Brown, and Beige* at Carnegie Hall
1944	John Hersey (1914–1993), *A Bell for Adano*
	Saul Bellow (1915–2005), *Dangling Man*
	Martha Foley's *The Best Short Stories of 1944* includes Saul Bellow, Dorothy Canfield (Fisher), Vladimir Nabokov, and Irwin Shaw
	Raphaël Lemkin (1900–1959), *Axis Rule in Occupied Europe: Laws of Occupation, Analysis of Government, Proposals for Redress* coins the word "genocide"
	Double Indemnity, directed by Billy Wilder (1906–2002)
1944–1948	Edwin Seaver, *Cross Section*
1945	St. Clair Drake (1911–1990) and Horace R. Cayton (1903–1970), *Black Metropolis: A Study of Negro Life in a Northern City*
	Josephina Niggli (1910–1983), *Mexican Village*
	Gertrude Stein, *Wars I Have Seen*
	Jade Snow Wong (1922–2006), *Fifth Chinese Daughter*
	Richard Wright, *Black Boy*
July 17, 1945	Leo Szilard (1898–1964) circulates a "Petition to the President" among Manhattan Project scientists imploring Truman not to use an atomic bomb against Japan

August 6, 1945	Atomic bomb in Hiroshima
	Gertrude Stein, "Off We All Went to See Germany," in *Life*, with photograph of her doing "Hitler's pose on Hitler's balcony"
August 9, 1945	Atomic bomb in Nagasaki
August 18, 1945	Langston Hughes (1902–1967), "Here to Yonder: Simple and the Atom Bomb"
1946	Carlos Bulosan (1913–1956), *America Is in the Heart: A Personal History*
	Miné Okubo (1912–2001), *Citizen 13660*
	Isaac Rosenfeld (1918–1956), *Passage from Home*
	Delmore Schwartz, "A Bitter Farce," *Kenyon Review*
	Gertrude Stein, "Reflections on the Atom Bomb"
	The Big Sleep, directed by Howard Hawks (1896–1977)
August 31, 1946	John Hersey (1914–1993), "Hiroshima" issue of *New Yorker*
1947	Saul Bellow (1915–2005), *The Victim*
	Vladimir Nabokov (1899–1977), *Bend Sinister*
	The Portable Faulkner, ed. Malcolm Cowley (after proposal was first rebuffed by Viking Press)
	The Portable James Joyce, ed. Harry Levin
	Mario Suarez (1925–1998), stories "El Hoyo" and "Señor Garza" appear in *Arizona Quarterly* (early use of word "Chicanos," short for *mexicanos*)
	Leo Szilard writes "My Trial as a War Criminal"
	Lionel Trilling (1905–1975), *The Middle of the Journey*
1948	Sinclair Lewis (1885–1951), *Kingsblood Royal*
	Norman Mailer (1923–2007), *The Naked and the Dead*
	William Gardner Smith (1927–1974), *Last of the Conquerors*
	Leo Szilard, "Report on 'Grand Central Terminal'" (published 1952)
	Lin Yutang (1895–1976), *Chinatown Family*
1949	Nelson Algren (1901–1981), *The Man with the Golden Arm*
	David P. Boder (1886–1961), *I Did Not Interview the Dead*
	Mary Doyle Curran (1917–1981), *The Parish and the Hill*
	Toshio Mori, *Yokohama, California*
	Jean Toomer, *The Flavor of Man*
	Hisaye Yamamoto, "Seventeen Syllables" (*Partisan Review*)
August 8, 1949	*Life* runs illustrated story on Jackson Pollock (1912–1956)
August 16, 1949	George A. Dondero launches attack on modern art in Congress
1950	U.S. population total 150,697,361
	Negroes 15,042,286

	Foreign-born white 10,158,854 (includes approx. 125,000 from Near East and 50,000 from South and East Asia)
1950	Erik Erikson (1902–1994), in *Childhood and Society*, introduces term "identity"
	Faulkner wins Nobel Prize
	John Hersey, *The Wall* uses word "holocaust"
	Isaac Bashevis Singer (1904–1991), *The Family Moskat* published in English
	Jade Snow Wong, *Fifth Chinese Daughter*
	Hisaye Yamamoto, "The Legend of Miss Sasagawara" in *Kenyon Review*
1951	Hannah Arendt (1906–1975), *Origins of Totalitarianism*
	Stein's *Four Saints in Three Acts* produced with State Department support
	Eyvind Earle (1916–2000) does experimental background painting for ambitious Goofy short *For Whom the Bulls Toil* (released 1953)
	Hisaye Yamamoto, "Yoneko's Earthquake"
March 5, 1951	Fashion models appear in front of Jackson Pollock backdrop in *Vogue*
1952	Ralph Ellison (1914–1994), *Invisible Man*
1953	Saul Bellow, *The Adventures of Augie March*
	Monica Sone (1919–), *Nisei Daughter*
1954	Hemingway is awarded the Nobel Prize
	Brown v. Board of Education
February 19, 1954	President Dwight D. Eisenhower sends tape-recorded greetings on the twenty-fifth anniversary of the Museum of Modern Art.
1956	State Department sends Dizzy Gillespie (1917–1993) on a tour of the Middle East
1962	Warner Brothers releases animated art musical *Gay Purr-ee* designed by Victor Haboush (1924–)
January 13, 1962	Norman Rockwell (1894–1978), "The Connoisseur" is cover of *Saturday Evening Post*

Notes

1. Introduction

1. Gertrude Stein, "Sacred Emily" (1913), first published in *Geography and Plays* (1922; repr. Madison: University of Wisconsin Press, 1993), 187; Richard Wright, *Lawd Today,* in Richard Wright, *Early Works,* ed. Arnold Rampersad (New York: Library of America, 1991), 174.
2. William Carlos Williams, "Recollections," *Art in America* LI, 1 (February 1963): 52. Cited in Bram Dijkstra, *Cubism, Stieglitz, and the Early Poetry of William Carlos Williams* (Princeton, N.J.: Princeton University Press, 1978), 9.
3. "A Layman's View of an Art Exhibition," *Outlook* (March 22, 1913), reprinted, together with other contemporary reactions and with cartoons, in *1913 Armory Show: 50th Anniversary Exhibition 1963* (New York: Henry Street Settlement, and Utica, N.Y.: Munson-Williams-Proctor Institute, 1963), 155–175.
4. *XIXa Esposizione Biennale Internazionale d'Arte 1934: Catalogo* (First ed., Venice: Carlo Ferrari, 1934); *La Biennale di Venezia: Le Esposizioni Internazionali d'Arte 1895–1995* (Venice: Electa, 1996). "Rules Davies Picture Must Stay In Place: Head of Venice Exposition Keeps Film Star's Portrait in American Pavilion," *New York Times* (June 28, 1934). See also Fred Lawrence Guiles, *Marion Davies: A Biography* (New York: McGraw Hill, 1972), 274–275, and Avis Berman, *Rebels on Eighth Street: Juliana Force and the Whitney Museum of American Art* (New York: Atheneum, 1990), 362–366.
5. Alfred H. Barr, Jr., *Cubism and Abstract Art* (1936), repr., with an introd. by Robert Rosenblum (Cambridge, Mass.: Harvard University Press, 1986); Edward Alden Jewell, "Shock Troops in Review: Museum of Modern Art Opens a Pageant of the Cubists and Abstractionists," *New York Times* (March 8, 1936).
6. *New York Times* (April 17, 1928): 26.
7. Harold Stearns, ed., *America Now: An Inquiry into Civilization in the United States* (New York and London: Charles Scribner's Sons, 1938), 6.

8. John Bassett, ed., *William Faulkner: The Critical Heritage* (London and Boston: Routledge & Kegan Paul, 1975) includes a number of positive reviews but stresses that the "two dominant issues in Faulkner commentary" of the 1930s were "his obscurity and his morbidity" (1) and that near the end of World War II only *Sanctuary* had sold more than a few thousand copies.
9. Ludwig Lewisohn, *Expression in America* (1932); repr., with an appendix as *The Story of American Literature* (New York: The Modern Library, 1938), 521.
10. *On Native Grounds* (1942; repr. New York: Harcourt Brace Jovanovitch, 1982), 465.
11. "The McCaslins of Mississippi," *Nation* (May 30, 1942): 632; in Bassett, 296–298.
12. Bassett, 26.
13. Bassett mentions that Viking at first rebuffed Cowley's proposal for a "Portable Faulkner" edition (26) and writes that the years from 1948–1952 "witnessed the most significant transition in Faulkner studies" (30).
14. George A. Dondero, address to Congress on August 16, 1949, *Congressional Record* 95.9 (Washington, D.C.: United States Government Printing Office, 1949), 11584–11587.
15. Sanka Knox, "Eisenhower Links Art and Freedom: Salutes Modern Museum on Its 25th Year," *New York Times* (February 20, 1954). See also the full text of "Freedom of the Arts" in *The Museum of Modern Art Bulletin* 22.1 (Fall-Winter, 1954).
16. Harold Rosenberg, *The Tradition of the New* (1959; repr. New York and Toronto: McGraw-Hill, 1965), 20.
17. "The Situation in American Writing," *Partisan Review,* 6.5 (Fall 1939): 103–113.
18. John Dewey, "Americanism and Localism," *The Dial* (June 1920), 686.
19. "Thoughts of a Great Thinker," *Liberator* (April 1922), quoted in Daniel Aaron, *Writers on the Left: Episodes in American Literary Communism* (1961; repr. New York: Avon Library Book, 1965), 107; "O Californians! O Ladies and Gentlemen!" *Gently, Brother* (March 1924), reprinted in *Mike Gold: A Literary Anthology,* ed. Michael Folsom (New York: International Publishers, 1972), 123.
20. Frank Durham, ed., *The Merrill Studies in Cane* (Columbus, Ohio: Charles E. Merrill, 1971) speaks of "only a very few reviewers" of *Cane* (iii), and Charles R. Larson's *Invisible Darkness: Jean Toomer and Nella Larsen* (Iowa City: University of Iowa Press, 1993), 27, gives the sales figure of 429 copies for the 1923 edition. Robert Bone, who had referred to *Cane* as "by far the most impressive product of the Negro Renaissance" as early as

1958, reviewed the reprint of *Cane* in the *New York Times Book Review* (January 19, 1969), 3, to which the editor gave the heading "The Black Classic That Discovered 'Soul' Is Rediscovered After 45 Years." According to Walter Allen's afterword to the thirtieth printing of the Avon edition of Henry Roth's *Call It Sleep*, the novel sold about 4,000 copies in the 1930s before slipping out of print. The front-page review by Irving Howe, "Life Never Let Up," *New York Times Book Review* (October 25, 1964), 1, stimulated a revival and a sales figure of over one million copies by the twentieth printing.
21. Waldo Frank, *Our America* (New York: Boni and Liveright, 1919), 97; cited by Daniel Terris, "Waldo Frank and the Rediscovery of America, 1889–1929," dissertation, Harvard University, 1992, 306.
22. Walt Whitman, "Preface to 1855 Edition," *Leaves of Grass;* "Specimen Days" (New York: Doubleday, Page & Company, Inc., 1927), 488; "The Spanish Element in our Nationality," *Complete Prose Works* (Boston: Small, Maynard, and Company, 1898), 388; "Preface to 1855 Edition," 506; editorial cited in David S. Reynolds, *A Historical Guide to Walt Whitman* (New York and Oxford: Oxford University Press, 2000), 76.
23. Erik Erikson, *Childhood and Society* (1950; second ed., repr. New York: W. W. Norton, 1963), 281, with reference to the phrase "Heimlichkeit der gleichen inneren Konstruktion" in Freud's "Ansprache an die Mitglieder des Vereins B'nai B'rith (1926)," *Gesammelte Werke*, vol. XVI. See Philip Gleason, "Identifying Identity: A Semantic History," in *Theories of Ethnicity*, ed. Werner Sollors (New York: New York University Press, 1997), 460–487.
24. Raphaël Lemkin, *Axis Rule in Occupied Europe: Laws of Occupation, Analysis of Government, Proposals for Redress* (Washington, D.C.: Carnegie Endowment for International Peace, 1944), 79.

2. Gertrude Stein and "Negro Sunshine"

1. Gertrude Stein, *Three Lives* (1909; repr. New York: Penguin Books, 1990, ed. Ann Charters), 167. Further page references to this edition, which includes a reprint of *Q.E.D.*, will be made parenthetically.
2. Gertrude Stein, *The Autobiography of Alice B. Toklas* (New York: Harcourt, Brace and Company, 1933), 50. Further page references in parentheses.
3. Gertrude Stein, *The Making of Americans Being a History of a Family's Progress* (New York: Something Else Press, 1966), 221.
4. Carl Van Doren, *The American Novel, 1789–1939* (New York: The Macmillan Company), 339. Van Doren continued: "Gertrude Stein's importance, so far as literature was concerned, lay less in her actual writings than in her reforming influence on the tones and cadences of prose."

5. Edmund Wilson, *Axel's Castle: A Study in the Imaginative Literature of 1870–1930* (New York: Charles Scribner's Sons, 1931), 239.
6. Leon M. Solomons and Gertrude Stein, "Normal Motor Automatism," *Harvard Psychological Laboratory* 3.5 (September 1896): 492–512, esp. 506; see also Gertrude Stein, "Cultivated Motor Automatism: A Study of Character in Relation to Attention," *Psychological Review* 5 (May 1898): 295–306.
7. William James, *The Principles of Psychology* (New York: Hamilton Holt and Company, 1890), 224; and "The Hidden Self," *Scribner's* (March 1890), 861–873, here 873.
8. William James, *Talks to Teachers on Psychology and to Students on Some of Life's Ideals* (1905; repr. Cambridge, Mass.: Harvard University Press, 1983), 19.
9. Gertrude Stein, "Poetry and Grammar," *How to Write* (1931; repr. New York: Dover Publications, Inc., 1975), 18.
10. Gertrude Stein, *As a Wife Has a Cow: A Love Story* (1926; repr. Barton, Vt.: Something Else Press, Inc., 1973), 20.
11. William James, letter to Gertrude Stein, quoted in *William James, Philosopher and Man: Quotations and References in 652 Books,* ed. Charles Herrick Compton (New York: Scarecrow Press, 1957), 189. In a similar vein, the twenty-six-year-old Delmore Schwartz confided in his journal on December 14, 1939: "I read Gertrude Stein's 'The Good Anna' before going to bed, but not with the proper attention." *Portrait of Delmore: Journals and Notes of Delmore Schwartz, 1939–1959,* ed. Elizabeth Pollet (New York: Farrar, Straus, Giroux, 1986), 7.
12. Mabel Dodge, "Speculations, or Post-Impressionism in Prose," *Arts and Decoration* (March 1913); repr. *The Critical Response to Gertrude Stein,* ed. Kirk Curnutt (Westport, Conn.: Greenwood Press, 2000), 151.
13. "A Futurist Novel," Philadelphia Public Ledger (April 10, 1915); repr. *The Critical Response to Gertrude Stein,* ed. Kirk Curnutt (Westport, Conn.: Greenwood Press, 2000), 12–13.
14. Gertrude Stein, *Lectures in America* (1935; repr. New York: Vintage Books, 1975), 177.
15. "Four Saints's Acts Is Acts in 30 Acts," *New York Times* (February 9, 1934). The edition used for the electronic version carries a different title and subtitle.
16. Delmore Schwartz, "The Grapes of Crisis," *Partisan Review* 18 (January/February 1951), 7–16, here 12.
17. *Beatitude Anthology* (San Francisco: City Lights Books, 1960), 4.
18. William Faulkner, *Absalom, Absalom!,* in *William Faulkner: Novels 1936–1940,* ed. Joseph Blotner and Noel Polk (New York: The Library of America, 1990), 182.

19. Claude McKay, *Home to Harlem* (1928; repr. Boston: Northeastern University Press, 1987), 228.
20. Hutchins Hapgood, April 22, 1906, *The Flowers of Friendship: Letters Written to Gertrude Stein,* ed. Donald Gallup (New York: Knopf, 1953), 32.
21. Introduction to Gertrude Stein, *Three Lives* (Norfolk, Conn.: New Directions, 1933), x.
22. Wyndham Lewis, *Time and Western Man* (New York: Harcourt, Brace, 1927), 61–62.
23. Mike Gold, "Gertrude Stein: A Literary Idiot" in *Change the World!* (1934); repr. in *The Critical Response to Gertrude Stein,* ed. Kirk Curnutt (Westport, Conn.: Greenwood Press, 2000), 209. Further references in parentheses.
24. Richard Wright, "Review: *Wars I Have Seen,* Gertrude Stein" in *Richard Wright Reader,* ed. Ellen Wright and Michael Fabre (New York: Harper & Row, 1978), 76. For a full account of the relationship between Wright and Stein see M. Lynn Weiss, *Gertrude Stein and Richard Wright: The Poetics and Politics of Modernism* (Jackson University Press of Mississippi, 1998).
25. Quoted in *The Selected Writings of Gertrude Stein,* ed. Carl Van Vechten (New York: Random House, 1946 [repr. Vintage Books, 1962]), 338.
26. Richard Wright, "Memories of My Grandmother," unpublished manuscript, Beinecke Rare Book and Manuscript Library, Yale University.
27. Wright, "Review: *Wars I Have Seen,*" 75.
28. Wright, "Memories of My Grandmother."
29. Richard Wright, "The Horror and the Glory," *Black Boy,* in *Richard Wright: Later Works,* ed. Arnold Rampersad (New York: The Library of America, 1991), 267.
30. Robert Haas, "A Transatlantic Interview, 1946" in *A Primer for the Gradual Understanding of Gertrude Stein,* ed. Robert Haas (Los Angeles: Black Sparrow Press, 1971), 32.
31. James T. Farrell, *Studs Lonigan: A Trilogy* (New York: The Modern Library, 1938), "Judgment Day," 169.
32. Jerre Mangione, "Finale" (1981), in *Mount Allegro* (1943; repr. New York: Columbia University Press, 1981), 287.
33. Nona Balakian, *The World of William Saroyan* (Lewisburg, Penn.: Bucknell University Press, 1988), 32–33.
34. Jack Dunphy, *John Fury* (New York and London: Harper & Brothers, 1946), 165, and dust jacket text of first edition.
35. Claude McKay, *A Long Way from Home* (1937; repr. New York: Harcourt Brace, 1970), 248.
36. *The Letters of Gertrude Stein and Carl Van Vechten 1913–1946,* ed. Edward Burns (New York: Columbia University Press, 1986), 281.
37. George Hutchinson, *In Search of Nella Larsen: A Biography of the Color Line* (Cambridge, Mass.: Belknap Press of Harvard University Press, 2006), 313.

38. Sterling Brown, *The Negro in American Fiction* (1937; repr. together with *Negro Poetry and Drama,* introd. Robert Bone, New York: Atheneum, 1969), 112. Brown quotes Van Vechten and proceeds to assess "Melanctha" quite critically, but arrives at his positive general assessment.
39. Clarence Major, "*Three Lives* and Gertrude Stein," *Par Rapport* 2 (1979): [53–66; unpaginated essay].
40. John A. Kouwenhoven, *The Beer Can by the Highway: Essays on What's "American" about America,* introd. Ralph Ellison (Baltimore: Johns Hopkins University Press, 1988).
41. Melvin B. Tolson, "Mu," *Harlem Gallery* (1965; repr. New York: Collier Books, 1969), 67.
42. Stein, *Autobiography,* 292.
43. Brown, *The Negro in American Fiction,* 111.
44. Ludwig Lewisohn, *The Story of American Literature* (1932; repr. New York: The Modern Library, 1939), 486.
45. McKay, *A Long Way,* 248.
46. Ernest Hemingway, *A Moveable Feast* (1964; repr. New York: Simon & Schuster, 1983), 14, 20.
47. Hemingway, letter to Harvey Breit, July 3, 1956. *Selected Letters 1917–1961,* ed. Carlos Baker (New York: Charles Scribner's Sons, 1981), 862.

3. Ethnic Lives and Lifelets

1. Henry James, *The American Scene* (1907; repr. Bloomington and London: Indiana University Press, 1968), 125. James also perceived the electric cars as part of an "assault of the street": "The electric cars, with their double track, are everywhere almost as tight a fit in the narrow channel of the roadway as the projectile in the bore of a gun" (101).
2. John Dewey, "Americanism and Localism," *The Dial* (June 1920): 686.
3. Hamilton Holt, ed. *The Life Stories of Undistinguished Americans As Told by Themselves* (1906; repr. and enlarged, New York: Routledge, 1990), 220. Further page references in parenthesis.
4. U.S. Census figures drawn from appendices to *The Harvard Encyclopedia of American Ethnic Groups,* ed. Oscar Handlin, Stephan Thernstrom, and Ann Orlov (Cambridge, Mass., and London: Harvard University Press, 1980) and from *The Social and Economic Status of the Black Population in the United States: An Historical Overview, 1790–1978* (Washington, D.C.: U.S. Department of Commerce, Bureau of the Census, Current Population Reports, Special Studies Series P-23, No. 80, 1979). See also http://www.census.gov/.
5. Walter Lippmann, "The Acids of Modernity," *A Preface to Morals* (1929; repr. New Brunswick, N.J.: Transaction Publishers, 1982), 63.

6. Mike Gold, *Jews Without Money* (1930; repr. New York: Bard Books/Avon, 1972), 23.
7. Myra Kelly, *Little Citizens: The Humour of School Life* (New York: Grosset & Dunlap, 1904), 226.
8. Claude McKay, *A Long Way From Home* (1937; repr. New York: Harcourt Brace & World, 1970), 187.
9. David P. Demarest, Jr., "Afterword," Thomas Bell, *Out of this Furnace* (1941; repr. Pittsburgh: University of Pittsburgh Press, 1976), 418, 419.
10. Jerre Mangione, *Mount Allegro* (1943; repr. New York: Columbia University Press, 1981), 211–217, and 7.
11. John Fante, "The Odyssey of a Wop," first published in H. L. Mencken's *American Mercury* (September 1933), and then in Fante's *Dago Red*, 1940); repr. in *A Gathering of Ghetto Writers: Irish, Italian, Jewish, Black, and Puerto Rican*, ed. Wayne Charles Miller (New York: New York University Press, 1972), 182–195, here 185, 191.
12. Orm Øverland launched, defined, and fleshed out the helpful term "homemaking myths" in his excellent book *Immigrant Minds, American Identities: Making the United States Home, 1870–1930* (Urbana: University of Illinois Press, 2000).
13. Anzia Yezierska, *Salome of the Tenements* (1922; repr. Urbana: University of Illinois Press, 1995), 157, 160.
14. Henry Roth, *Call It Sleep* (New York: Robert O. Ballou, 1934), 328.
15. Feri Felix Weiss, *The Sieve; or, Revelations of the Man Mill* (Boston: The Page Company, 1921), 237–242 (with explicit discussion of Edward Everett Hale's "Man Without a Country," 109–118, 187–209, 297, 306).
16. Edward Bok, *The Americanization of Edward Bok: The Autobiography of a Dutch Boy Fifty Years After* (1920; 50th edition, New York: Charles Scribner's Sons, 1930), 434–447, here 435 and 436. Further page references in parentheses. See Aviva Taubenfeld, *Rough Writing: Ethnic Authorship in Theodore Roosevelt's America* (New York: New York University Press, 2008), for an excellent discussion of Roosevelt's relationship with Edward Bok.
17. Abraham Cahan, *Yekl: A Tale of the New York Ghetto* (New York: Appleton, 1896), 44.
18. Holt, *Life Stories*.
19. Maxim Gorky, "Boredom," *Independent* (August 8, 1907): 309–317, here 314.
20. Jessie Fauset, *Plum Bun: A Novel Without a Moral* (1929; repr. Boston: Beacon Press, 1990), 240.
21. Stuart P. Sherman, "The Naturalism of Mr. Dreiser," *The Nation* (December 2, 1915); repr. as "The Barbaric Naturalism of Theodore Dreiser," in *On Con-*

temporary Literature (New York: Holt, 1917), 85–101. See also Sherman's book *The Main Stream* (New York: Charles Scribner's Sons, 1927).
22. Mary Antin, *The Promised Land* (1912; repr. New York: Penguin, 1997), 1.
23. Gertrude Stein, *The Autobiography of Alice B. Toklas* (New York: Harcourt, Brace and Company, 1933), 310.
24. Carl Van Doren, *Contemporary American Novelists, 1900–1920* (New York: Macmillan, 1927), 144.
25. Horace M. Kallen, *Culture and Democracy in the United States* (New York: Boni and Liveright, 1924), 155n1.
26. Framing material for "Christ in Concrete," *Esquire* (March 1937).
27. For a discussion of Elizabeth Stern, see Taubenfeld, *Rough Writing*.
28. Henry James, *The American Scene*, 120.

4. Ethnic Themes, Modern Themes

1. Mary Antin, *The Promised Land* (1912; repr. New York: Penguin, 1997), 2–3.
2. Alain Locke, ed., *The New Negro* (1925; repr. New York: Atheneum, 1970), 6.
3. Zora Neale Hurston, "Story in Harlem Slang," *American Mercury* (1942), repr. in *Zora Neale Hurston, Novels and Stories,* ed. Cheryl A. Wall (New York: The Library of America, 1995), 1001–1010, here 1005.
4. Henry Roth, *Call It Sleep* (New York: Robert O. Ballou, 1934), 332.
5. Edward Bok, *The Americanization of Edward Bok: The Autobiography of a Dutch Boy Fifty Years After* (1920; 50th edition, New York: Charles Scribner's Sons, 1930), 273.

5. Mary Antin: Progressive Optimism against Odds

1. Mary Antin, "First Aid to the Alien," *Outlook*, 101 (June 29, 1912): 481–485.
2. Mary Antin, *The Promised Land* (1912; repr. New York: Penguin, 1997). Further page references in parentheses.
3. Mary Antin, *From Plotzk to Boston* (1899; repr. Upper Saddle River, N.J.: Literature House, 1970), 43.
4. Mary Antin, letter to Ellery Sedgwick, July 19, 1911, Massachusetts Historical Society, published in Evelyn Salz, ed. *The Selected Letters of Mary Antin* (Syracuse, N.Y.: Syracuse University Press, 2000), 52–54.
5. Estelle M. Hart, "Trolley-Car Ornithology," *Atlantic Monthly* 101.6 (June 1908): 784.
6. Randolph Bourne, "Trans-National America," *Atlantic Monthly* 118.7 (July 1916): 86–97.

7. Quoted in [Maimie Pinzer,] *The Maimie Papers,* ed. Ruth Rosen and Sue Davidson (Old Westbury, N.Y.: Feminist Press, 1977), 149.
8. *Outlook* 101 (June 29, 1912): 502.
9. Irwin Granich [Mike Gold], "Surveys of the Promised Land," *Liberator* (July 1918): 32–33.
10. Elizabeth Woodbridge, *Yale Review* n.s. 2 (1912): 175–176; and William H. Maxwell, *Literary Digest* 44 (June 15, 1912): 1261–1262.
11. Mary Antin, "A Woman to her Fellow Citizens," *Outlook* 102 (November 2, 1912): 482–486. Antin's correspondence with Roosevelt was published in Salz, ed. *Letters,* 72–73, 75, and 151–152.
12. Barbara Haskell, *Joseph Stella* (New York: Whitney Museum of American Art and Harry N. Abrams, 1994), 42–43. Haskell, 16, reproduces samples from *Americans in the Rough,* and, 192n96 notes parallels between Gorky's and Stella's reactions to Coney Island.
13. Mary Antin, *They Who Knock at Our Gates: A Complete Gospel of Immigration* (Boston: Houghton Mifflin, 1914), 14, 28, and 40.
14. Antin, *They Who Knock,* 63, 98.
15. Mike Gold, *Jews Without Money* (1930; repr. New York: Bard Books/Avon, 1972), 49.
16. Antin, *They Who Knock,* 19.
17. Edward Steiner, *From Alien to Citizen* (New York: Fleming H. Revell Co., 1914), 167.

6. Who Is "American"?

1. Edward Bok, *Twice Thirty: Some Short and Simple Annals of the Road* (New York: Charles Scribner's Sons, 1925), 256.
2. M. A. DeWolfe Howe, *Barrett Wendell in His Letters* (Boston: The Atlantic Monthly Press, 1924), 281–282.
3. Agnes Repplier, "The Modest Immigrant," *Counter-Currents* (Boston: Houghton Mifflin, 1916), 197–232; esp. 226–227, 213, 202.
4. Letter to F. C. S. Schiller, July 15, 1907, in William James, *Selected Unpublished Correspondence: 1885–1910,* ed. Frederick J. Down Scott. (Columbus: Ohio State University Press, 1986), 443.
5. Horace M. Kallen, "Democracy Versus the Melting-Pot," *The Nation* (February 18 and 25, 1915); repr. in *Theories of Ethnicity: A Classical Reader,* ed. Werner Sollors (New York: New York University Press, 1996), 67–92.
6. Mike Gold, "America Needs a Critic," *New Masses,* 1.6 (October 1926): 7.
7. Randolph Bourne, "Trans-National America," *Atlantic Monthly* 118 (July

1916): 86–97; repr. in *Theories of Ethnicity: A Classical Reader,* ed. Werner Sollors (New York: New York University Press, 1996), 93–108.
8. Ellery Sedgwick, letter to Randolph Bourne, March 30, 1916, Randolph Bourne Papers, Columbia University Library, and Thomas Bender, *New York Intellect: A History of Intellectual Life in New York City, from 1750 to the Beginnings of Our Own Time* (Baltimore: Johns Hopkins University Press, 1987), 247–248.
9. Mary Antin, "The Lie," *Atlantic Monthly* 112 (August 1913): 177–190.
10. Bourne, "Trans-National America," in *Theories of Ethnicity,* 94. Further page references in parentheses.
11. Allan Mazur, *A Romance in Natural History: The Lives and Works of Amadeus Grabau and Mary Antin* (Syracuse, N.Y.: Garret, 2004).
12. Mary Antin, letter to Ellery Sedgwick, August 13, 1911, Massachusetts Historical Society, publ. in Evelyn Salz, ed., *The Selected Letters of Mary Antin* (Syracuse: Syracuse University Press, 2000), 60.
13. Mary Antin letter to Mary Austin, March 11, 1925, Henry Huntington Library, in *Letters,* ed. Salz, 100–105; see also her letter to Thomas A. Watson, September 11, 1920, Boston Public Library, in *Letters,* ed. Salz, 95–98.
14. Mary Antin, letter Antin to Dale Warren, December 17, 1926, Boston Public Library, in *Letters,* ed. Salz, 107–108.

7. American Languages

1. H. L. Mencken, *The American Language: Supplement Two* (New York: Alfred A. Knopf, 1948), 717.
2. Mencken, *The American Language: An Inquiry into the Development of English in the United States* (1919; repr. New York: Alfred A. Knopf, 1948), 393.
3. Zora Neale Hurston, *Novels and Stories,* ed. Cheryl A. Wall (New York: The Library of America, 1995), 1009.
4. Louis Adamic, "The Yugoslav Speech in America," *American Mercury* (November 1927): 319–321. John Fante's "Odyssey of a Wop" also first appeared in Mencken's *American Mercury* (September 1933).
5. Jerre Mangione, *Mount Allegro* (1943; repr. New York: Columbia University Press, 1981), 51–52.
6. Konrad Bercovici, *Manhattan Side-Show* (New York and London: The Century Co., 1931), 12.
7. Kurt M. Stein, *Die schönste Lengevitch* (Chicago: P. Covici, 1925), 18.
8. *The Multilingual Anthology of American Literature,* ed. Marc Shell and Werner Sollors (New York: New York University Press, 2000).
9. Leon Kobrin, "Di shprakh fun elnt" (The language of misery), in *Der*

farloirener nigun: roman un zeks dertseylungen (New York: YKUF, 1948), 245–262. Translated as "A Common Language" in Max Rosenfeld, ed. and transl., *Pushcarts and Dreamers and Other Stories of Jewish Life in America* (South Brunswick, N.Y., and London: Thomas Yoseloff, 1967), 29–46, esp. 43.

10. José Rodrigues Miguéis, *Gente da terceira classe* (Lisbon: Editorial Estúdios Cor, 1971); *Steerage and Ten Other Stories,* transl. George Monteiro and Carolina Matos (Providence, R.I.: Gavea-Brown, 1983).

11. Marcus Lee Hansen, "Immigration and American Culture," in *The Immigrant in American History,* ed. and introd. Arthur M. Schlesinger (1940; repr. New York: Harper & Row, 1964), 129–153, here 138.

8. "All the past we leave behind"?

1. *Giants in the Earth: A Saga of the Prairie* (New York: Harper & Brothers, 1927) was originally published in Norwegian as two separate novels *I de dage: fortelling om norske nykommere i Amerika* (Kristiania: H. Aschehoug & Co. [W. Nygaard], 1924), and *Riket grundlægges* (Oslo: H. Aschehoug & Co. [W. Nygaard], 1925). *Peder Victorious: A Tale of the Pioneers Twenty Years Later,* transl. Nora O. Solum (New York: Harper & Brothers, 1929) was the English version of *Peder Seier* (Oslo: H. Aschehoug & Co., 1928). *Their Fathers' God* (New York: Harper & Brothers, 1931) was the English translation by Trygve M. Ager of *Den signede dag* (Oslo: H. Aschehoug, 1931). The author's surname was spelled "Rølvaag" in the Norwegian publications, but Rölvaag in English.

2. Drude Krog Janson, *A Saloonkeeper's Daughter,* transl. Gerald Thorson, ed. and introd. Orm Øverland (Baltimore and London: Johns Hopkins University Press, 2002).

3. Waldemar Ager, "The Melting Pot," *Cultural Pluralism versus Assimilation,* ed. Odd S. Lovell (Northfield, Minn.: The Norwegian-American Historical Association, 1977), 85.

4. Johannes B. Wist, *The Rise of Jonas Olsen: A Norwegian Immigrant's Saga,* transl. and introd. Orm Øverland, foreword by Todd W. Nichol (Minneapolis: University of Minnesota Press, 2006).

5. Solveig Zempel, "Rølvaag as Translator: Translations of Rølvaag," *Norwegian-American Essays,* Knut Djupedal, et al., eds. (NAHA-Norway: Stavanger, 1993), 40–50. Zempel is also Rølvaag's granddaughter.

6. Horace Kallen, "Americanization," in *Culture and Democracy in the United States* (New York: Boni and Liveright, 1924), 146–147.

7. James T. Farrell, Preface to *The Short Stories of James T. Farrell* (New York: The Vanguard Press, 1934), xix.

9. Modernism, Ethnic Labeling, and the Quest for Wholeness

1. Jean Toomer, *Cane* (1923; repr. New York: Harper & Row, Harper Perennial Classic, 1969), 71–72. Further page references in parentheses.
2. See Henry F. May, *The End of American Innocence: A Study of the First Years of Our Own Time 1912–1917* (London: Jonathan Cape, 1960).
3. "The Experience," in Frederik L. Rusch, ed., *A Jean Toomer Reader: Selected Unpublished Writings* (New York and Oxford: Oxford University Press, 1993), 33–76, here 33, 34, and 37–39 in section "Transport."
4. Waldo Frank, *Our America* (New York: Boni and Liveright, 1919), cited in the context of the Frank–Toomer correspondence by Daniel Terris, "Waldo Frank and the Rediscovery of America, 1889–1929," dissertation, Harvard University, 1992, 306.
5. From an autobiographical sketch cited by Darwin T. Turner in the Norton Critical Edition of *Cane* (New York: W.W. Norton, 1988), 141–142, henceforth Turner, *Cane*. A larger excerpt appears in Darwin T. Turner, ed., *The Wayward and the Seeking: A Collection of Writings by Jean Toomer* (Washington, D.C.: Howard University Press, 1983), 121.
6. Turner, *Wayward*, 129. Cynthia Kerman and Richard Eldridge, *The Lives of Jean Toomer: A Hunger for Wholeness* (Baton Rouge, LA., and London, 1987), 116, also call attention to this passage.
7. Excerpted in Turner, *Cane*, 152.
8. The play was published in Turner, *Wayward*, 243–325. See also the discussions by Nellie Y. McKay, *Jean Toomer, Artist* (Chapel Hill, N.C.: University of North Carolina Press, 1984), 68–81, and Rudolph P. Byrd, *Jean Toomer's Years with Gurdjieff* (Athens, Ga., and London, 1990) as well as Daniel Terris, "Waldo Frank."
9. Mike Gold, "Notes of the Month," *New Masses* 5 (February 1930): 3. This essay is quoted at length and analyzed by George Hutchinson, *The Harlem Renaissance in Black and White* (Cambridge, Mass., and London: Harvard University Press, 1995), 272.
10. Flint's and Pound's maxims are cited in William Pratt, ed., *The Imagist Poem* (New York: Dutton, 1963), 18.
11. The description continues in drawing out tree imagery—which takes on a sinister undertone in view of the lynching that is about to occur as well the brutal murder of the pregnant Mame Lamkins in "Kabnis" (*Cane*, 92 and 111), based on the Mary Turner lynching. See Walter White, *Rope and Faggot* (1929; repr. New York: Arno Press, 1969), 28–29.
12. Rusch, *Toomer Reader*, 280–281. See also Martha J. Nadell, *Enter the New Negroes: Images of Race in American Culture* (Cambridge, Mass., and London: Harvard University Press, 2004).
13. "Race Problems and Modern Society," in *Man and His World*, ed. Baker

Brownell (New York: Van Nostrand, 1929), 98–99; repr. in *Theories of Ethnicity: A Classical Reader*, ed. Werner Sollors (New York: New York University Press, 1996), 168–190.
14. In *Interracialism: Black-White Intermarriage in American History, Literature, and Law,* ed. Werner Sollors (New York and Oxford: Oxford University Press, 2000), 23–24. See also George Hutchinson, "Jean Toomer and American Racial Discourse" (1993; repr. in *Interracialism*), 369–390.
15. Rusch, *Toomer Reader,* 107.
16. Ibid., 109.
17. Jean Toomer, *Essentials* (Chicago, 1931; repr. ed. with introd. by Rudolph P. Byrd, Athens, Ga., and London, 1991), XXIV.
18. Turner, *Wayward,* 121.
19. Jean Toomer to Samuel Pessin, cited in Kerman and Eldridge, *Lives,* 99.
20. Arna Bontemps, "Introduction" to Toomer, *Cane,* viii-ix; henceforth Bontemps, "Introduction." The latter part of this important letter is included in Turner, *Cane,* 128–129, and cited in Kerman and Eldridge, *Lives,* 96.
21. Rusch, *Toomer Reader,* 105.
22. See Kerman and Eldridge, *Lives,* 202.
23. See McKay, *Toomer,* 46–50; Byrd, *Years,* 97; Kerman and Eldridge, *Lives,* 97.
24. Jean Toomer to Waldo Frank, April 26, 1922; cited in Kerman and Eldridge, *Lives,* 87.
25. Rusch, *Toomer Reader,* 222.
26. Robert B. Jones, *Jean Toomer and the Prison-House of Thought: A Phenomenology of the Spirit* (Amherst: University of Massachusetts Press, 1993), 24.
27. Jean Toomer to John McClure, July 22, 1922, cited in Kerman and Eldridge, *Lives,* 96.

10. Freud, Marx, Hard-Boiled

1. Freud's blurb appears on front cover of *The Case of Mr. Crump* (1926; repr. New York: Noonday Press of Farrar, Straus & Giroux, 1965), with a preface by Thomas Mann, vii-viii, that is partly excerpted on the back cover.
2. Ludwig Lewisohn, *Stephen Escott* (1930; repr. as *The Vehement Flame: The Story of Stephen Escott,* New York: Farrar, Straus & Giroux, 1948), 239–240. Further references to this edition appear in the text.
3. Mike Gold, *Jews Without Money* (1930; repr. New York: Bard Books/Avon, 1972), 224. Parenthetic pages refer to this edition.
4. Nathan Asch, *Pay Day* (1930; repr. with an introd. by Warner Berthoff, Detroit, Mich.: Omnigraphics, 1990), 66. Further page numbers refer to this edition.

5. Granville Hicks, *The Great Tradition* (1935: repr. New York: Biblo and Tannen, 1967), 311.
6. William Faulkner, *The Sound and the Fury* in *William Faulkner: Novels 1926–1929*, ed. Joseph Blotner and Noel Polk (New York: The Library of America, 2006), 956–957. Further page references appear in the text.
7. Jean-Paul Sartre, "American Novelists in French Eyes," *Atlantic Monthly* 178 (August 1946): 114–118.
8. Ernest Hemingway, letter to Harvey Breit, July 3, 1956. *Selected Letters 1917–1961*, ed. Carlos Baker (New York: Charles Scribner's Sons, 1981), 862.
9. Ernest Hemingway, letter to Mr. Rider, July 29, 1956, cited in *Selected Letters*, 864n2.
10. Ernest Hemingway, *The Sun Also Rises* (1926; repr. New York: Charles Scribner's Sons, 1954), 224. References to this edition will be incorporated into the text.
11. Ernest Hemingway, *A Moveable Feast* (New York: Charles Scribner's Sons, 1964), 12.
12. Ernest Hemingway, *Green Hills of Africa* (New York: Charles Scribner's Sons, 1935), 21.
13. Cited in Carlos Baker, *Ernest Hemingway, A Life Story* (New York: Charles Scribner's Sons, 1969), 90.
14. Ernest Hemingway, *A Farewell to Arms* (1929; repr. New York: Charles Scribner's Sons, 1969), 185.
15. Carl Van Doren, *The American Novel, 1789–1939* (New York: The Macmillan Company, 1940), 341.
16. Matthew J. Bruccoli, ed., *The Sun Also Rises: A Facsimile Edition* (Ann Arbor, Mich.: Omnigraphics, 1990), reproduced from the manuscript of the novel in the John F. Kennedy Presidential Library and Museum, Ernest Hemingway Collection.
17. Stuart P. Sherman, *The Main Stream* (New York: Charles Scribner's Sons, 1927), v.
18. Edward Hopper, letter to editors of *Scribner's*, in response to March 1927 publication of "The Killers" by Ernest Hemingway. Quoted in Gail Levin, *Edward Hopper as Illustrator* (New York: Norton, 1979), 7.
19. Joseph Warren Beach, *American Fiction, 1920–1940* (New York: The Macmillan Company, 1941), 101.
20. Ernest Hemingway, "The Snows of Kilimanjaro," in *The Snows of Kilimanjaro and Other Stories* (New York: Charles Scribner's Sons, 1961), 9.
21. Beach, *American Fiction*, 101.
22. Hemingway, *The Sun Also Rises*, 11. Compare this and the following manuscript passages in Bruccoli ed., *The Sun Also Rises: A Facsimile Edition*.

23. Hemingway, *The Sun Also Rises*, 247.
24. Ernest Hemingway to Maxwell Perkins, May 4, 1927, *Selected Letters*, 250–251.
25. Hemingway, *Green Hills of Africa*, 18.
26. Ernest Hemingway, *The Complete Short Stories: The Finca Vigía Edition* (1987; repr. New York: Scribner Paperback Fiction, 1998), 356.
27. Harry Levin, "Observations on the Style of Ernest Hemingway," *Memories of the Moderns* (1980; repr. New York: New Directions, 1982), 81–104, here 91; Ernest Hemingway, *For Whom the Bell Tolls* (1940; repr. New York: Charles Scribner's Sons, n.d.), 313.
28. The Spanish translation could not render this other than by using the word "jerez" twice and italicizing the second *jerez*, and by a footnote indicating that all terms that appear in Spanish in the English original are italicized in the translation. Ernest Hemingway, *Fiesta*, transl. Joaquín Adsuar (1983; repr. Barcelona: DeBols, 2006), 183, 132n.

11. Hemingway Spoken Here

1. Delmore Schwartz, "The Fiction of Ernest Hemingway: Moral Historian of the American Dream," in *Selected Essays of Delmore Schwartz*, ed. Donald Dike and David Zucker (Chicago: University of Chicago Press, 1970), 259.
2. Meyer Levin, *Frankie and Johnnie* (New York: John Day Company, 1930), 212. In his autobiography, *In Search* (New York: Horizon Press, 1950), Levin associates the Hemingway influence with his desire that his writing "be considered American" (39).
3. Claude McKay, *A Long Way From Home* (1937; repr. New York: Harcourt Brace & World, 1970), 249–252.
4. James T. Farrell, *The League of Frightened Philistines and Other Papers* (New York: The Vanguard Press, 1945), 21–22. The beginning of Farrell's "Young Lonigan" in the *Studs Lonigan* trilogy (1935) offers some good examples of following the Hemingway mode. For example: "He took a last drag at his cigarette, tossed the butt down the toilet, and let the water run in the sink to wash the ashes down" (9).
5. Ludwig Lewisohn, *The Story of American Literature* (New York: Harper and Brothers, 1939), 518–519.
6. Alfred Kazin, *On Native Grounds: An Interpretation of Modern American Prose Literature* (1942; repr. New York: Harcourt Brace Jovanovich, 1982), 340–341.
7. "Hemingway—White Collar Poet," in *Mike Gold: A Literary Anthology*, ed. Michael Folsom (New York: International Publishers, 1972), 159–160.

8. Richard Wright, "How 'Uncle Tom's Children' Grew," *The Writers' Book Club Bulletin* (Columbia University) vol. 2 (1938): 16–18, here 17.
9. Raymond Chandler, "Notes (Very Brief, Please) on English and American Style" in *Later Works and Other Writings*, ed. Frank MacShane (New York: Library of America, 1995), 1013.
10. Ibid.
11. Raymond Chandler, "Beer in the Sergeant Major's Hat (or The Sun Also Sneezes)," 1932. In *The Notebooks of Raymond Chandler and English Summer: A Gothic Romance*, ed. Frank MacShane (New York: Ecco Press, 1976), 23–24.
12. André Gide, "The New American Novelists" (1949), in *Transatlantic Mirrors: Essays in Franco-American Literary Relations*, ed. Sidney D. Braun and Seymour Lainoff (Boston: Twayne, 1978), 256.
13. Lucy Fischer, "The Savage Eye: Edward Hopper and the Cinema," in Townsend Ludington, ed., *A Modern Mosaic: Art and Modernism in the United States* (Chapel Hill: University of North Carolina Press, 2000), 342.
14. Stanley Cavell, "The Same and the Different: *The Awful Truth*," in *Pursuits of Happiness: The Hollywood Comedy of Remarriage* (Cambridge, Mass.: Harvard University Press, 1981), 257. I am deeply indebted to Stanley Cavell for calling attention to, transcribing, and analyzing this remarkable scene.
15. *Double Indemnity*, directed by Billy Wilder, Paramount, 1944.
16. *The Big Sleep*, directed by Howard Hawks, Warner Brothers, 1946.
17. James T. Farrell, "The Language of Hollywood," *Saturday Review of Literature* 5 (August 1944), 29–32.
18. James Agee, *Agee on Film: Reviews and Comments*, ed. Tomi Ungerer (Boston, Mass.: Beacon Press, 1958), 131, 217.
19. "Books in Brief," *Christian Century* 51.44 (October 31, 1934): 1378.
20. William Saroyan, "Myself Upon the Earth: A Story," *The American Mercury Reader*, ed. Lawrence E. Spivak and Charles Angoff (Philadelphia, Penn.: The Blakiston Company, 1944), 280.
21. William Saroyan, "Aspirin Is a Member of the N.R.A.," *The American Mercury* 32.125 (May 1934), 87–90, here 89–90; *Subway Circus;* in *The Best One-Act Plays of 1940* (New York: Dodd, Mead & Company, 1941), 77–135.
22. William Saroyan, "Seventy Thousand Assyrians," in *The Daring Young Man on the Flying Trapeze and Other Stories* (New York: Random House, 1934), 34.
23. Ernest Hemingway, "Notes on Life and Letters," *Esquire* 3.1 (January 1935): 21, 159.

24. William Saroyan, letter to Ernest Hemingway, December 16, 1934, San Francisco, 5pp. Held at John F. Kennedy Presidential Library and Museum, Ernest Hemingway Collection.
25. Back cover of paperback edition of *The Neon Wilderness* (n.p.: Writers and Readers Publishing Inc., 1986).
26. Nelson Algren, *The Man with the Golden Arm* (1949; repr. New York: Seven Stories Press, 1999), 258.
27. Ernest Hemingway, letter to Harvey Breit, July 3, 1956. *Selected Letters 1917–1961*, ed. Carlos Baker (New York: Charles Scribner's Sons, 1981), 862, 863.
28. Toni Morrison, *Playing in the Dark: Whiteness and the Literary Imagination* (Cambridge, Mass.: Harvard University Press, 1992), 69.

12. Henry Roth: Ethnicity, Modernity, and Modernism

1. Henry Roth, *Call It Sleep* (New York: Robert O. Ballou, 1934; second printing, January 1935), 570. Further references in parenthesis.
2. "Brief Review," *New Masses* (February 12, 1935): 27.
3. Kenneth Burke, "More about Roth's *Call It Sleep.*" *New Masses* (February 26, 1935): 21, and Edwin Seaver, "Caesar or Nothing," *New Masses* (March 5, 1935): 21.
4. Sigmund Freud, "Family Romances" (orig. "Der Familienroman der Neurotiker," 1908), *Standard Edition of the Complete Psychological Works*, ed. James Strachey, vol. 9 (1906–1908) (London: Hogarth Press, 1959), 236–241.
5. Sigmund Freud, "Beyond the Pleasure Principle" (orig. "Jenseits des Lustprinzips," 1920), *Standard Edition of the Complete Psychological Works*, trans. James Strachey, vol. 18 (1920–1922; repr. London: Hogarth, 1955), 7–64; here 14–15.
6. "I don't know much about Freud and I never did. . . . If I'd known about things like Oedipus complexes I probably never would have written the book at all. I'd have said, 'Shucks, why bother? Sounds just like a case history.'" Henry Roth, cited in Jane Howard, "The Belated Success of Henry Roth," *Life* 53 (January 8, 1965): 75–76.
7. It is a collection in which Roth is understatedly thanked for "assistance in proofreading and other clerical help" (vii) and is divided in three parts, following the times of day. It includes samplings from T. S. Eliot, e. e. cummings, Langston Hughes, Amy Lowell, Hart Crane, William Carlos Williams, and many other modern poets in a city world.
8. The phrase "a hura mezda" does not yet appear in the manuscript, "A bath-tub is a bath-tub" was inserted into it later, replacing the earlier

answer, "What is a suitor?" (3?E), and in one of many notes and additions Roth wrote to himself at the composition stage of the novel, he associates the "jug a jug jug" with the "bed spring rhythm" during "copulation" (Notes additions IV, items 56 and 57; Berg Collection, New York Public Library).

9. William Butler Yeats, *The Winding Stair and Other Poems* (New York: Macmillan, 1933), 47, 51–52.
10. Franz Kafka, *Amerika*, trans. Edwin Muir (New York: New Directions, 1946), 1. Kafka's work appeared in *transition* in the 1920s, and *Amerika* was first published in 1927.
11. Alter Brody, "Lowing in the Night," *Lamentations* (New York: Coward-McCann, Inc., 1928), 4, 13.
12. Judah Leib Lazerow, "The Staff of Judah" (1921), in *The Multilingual Anthology of American Literature,* ed. Marc Shell and Werner Sollors (New York: New York University Press, 2000), 503.
13. Eda Lou Walton, *The City Day: An Anthology of Recent American Poetry* (New York: The Ronald Press Company, 1929), 3.
14. Roth interview in Bonnie Lyons, *Henry Roth: The Man and His Work* (New York: Cooper Square Publishers, Inc., 1976), 167.
15. See Thomas J. Ferraro, *Ethnic Passages: Literary Immigrants in Twentieth-Century America* (Chicago: University of Chicago Press, 1993), 113–118, for an illuminating analysis of Roth's crosscutting technique, and booklet 59 of the manuscript, New York Public Library.
16. Sir James George Frazer, *The Golden Bough* (1890; repr. abr. ed. New York: Criterion Books, 1959), 581; and, in the unabridged edition, vol. VII: Baldur the Beautiful; ch. i: Between Heaven and Earth; § 1: Not to touch the Earth; pp. 6–7.
17. Roth interview in Irit Manskleid-Makowsky, "The 'Jewishness' of Jewish American Literature: The Examples of Ludwig Lewisohn and Henry Roth," M.A. thesis, John F. Kennedy-Institut, Freie Universität Berlin, 1978, 114.
18. Henry Roth, *Shifting Landscape: A Composite, 1925–1987,* ed. and introd. Mario Materassi (Philadelphia: Jewish Publication Society, 1987), 197.

13. *Brrrrrrriiiiiiiiiiiiiiiiiiiinng!*

1. Richard Wright, *Lawd Today,* in Richard Wright, *Early Works,* ed. Arnold Rampersad (New York: The Library of America, 1991), 173. Further page references in parentheses.

2. Hamilton Holt, *The Life Stories of Undistinguished Americans As Told by Themselves* (1906; repr. and enlarged, New York: Routledge, 1990), 26.
3. "Impressions of a Plumber," *Lavender* (1925), repr. in Henry Roth, *Shifting Landscape: A Composite, 1925–1987*, ed. and introd. Mario Materassi (Philadelphia, Penn.: Jewish Publication Society, 1987), 5.
4. Richard Wright, *Lawd Today*, in *Richard Wright: Early Works*, ed. Rampersad, 1; "Native Son," typescript, Schomburg Collection, New York Public Library, 1.
5. Richard Wright, *Native Son*, in *Richard Wright: Early Works*, ed. Rampersad, 447. Further page references in parentheses. See Cristina Lombardi, "Native Son: Genesi di un romanzo," thesis, Dipartimento di Anglistica, Università degli Studi di Roma, 1989, and Keneth Kinnamon, ed., *New Essays on Native Son* (New York and Cambridge: Cambridge University Press, 1990).
6. Ernest W. Burgess, "The Growth of the City: An Introduction to a Research Project." *Publications of the American Sociological Society* 18, 1924, 85–97. Repr. in Robert E. Park, Ernest W. Burgess, and Roderick D. McKenzie, ed., *The City* (Chicago: University of Chicago Press, 1984), 47–62.
7. Louis Wirth, "Urban Society and Civilization," *American Journal of Sociology* 45 (March 1940): 743–755.
8. Robert E. Park, "The City: Suggestions for the Investigation of Human Behavior in the Urban Environment," in *The City*.
9. Robert Redfield, *Tepoztlàn: A Mexican Village* (Chicago: University of Chicago Press, 1930), 1–6.
10. Richard Wright, "Introduction," in St. Clair Drake and Horace R. Cayton, *Black Metropolis: A Study of Negro Life in a Northern City* (1945; repr. New York: Harper Torchbooks, 1962), xxii, xvii-xviii.
11. Richard Wright, *Black Boy (American Hunger)*, in *Richard Wright: Later Works*, ed. Arnold Rampersad, 249. Further page references in parentheses.
12. "Blueprint for Negro Literature" (1937), *Amistad* 2, ed. John A. Williams and Charles F. Harris (New York: Vintage, 1971), 3–20, here 10. The passage does not appear in the shorter version of "Blueprint" reprinted from *New Challenge* 1937 in *The Richard Wright Reader*, ed. Ellen Wright and Michel Fabre (New York: Harper and Row, 1978). See Ralph Ellison, *Invisible Man* (1952; repr. New York: The Modern Library, n.d.), 268: "Stephen's problem, like ours, was not actually one of creating the uncreated conscience of his race, but of creating the *uncreated features of his face*."
13. Keneth Kinnamon, *The Emergence of Richard Wright: A Study in Literature and Society* (Urbana: University of Illinois Press, 1972), 116.

14. William James, *Principles of Psychology* (New York: Holt, 1890), 293; cited in "Introduction," *Black Metropolis*, xxxii.
15. "Introduction," *Black Metropolis*, xxxiii.
16. Richard Wright, *12 Million Black Voices* (1941; repr. Boston: Thunder's Mouth Press, 1988), 146. Compare the ending of Ellison's *Invisible Man*, "Who knows but that, on the lower frequencies, I speak for you?" (439).
17. Unpublished manuscript, James Weldon Johnson Collection, Beinecke Library, Yale University, JWJ Wright Misc. #281. This blurb parallels Bigger's lawyer Boris Max's effort to interpret his client in *Native Son:* "Let me, Your Honor, explain further the meaning of Bigger Thomas' life. In him and men like him is what was in our forefathers when they first came to these strange shores hundreds of years ago. We were lucky. They are not" (814).
18. Richard Wright, "Between Laughter and Tears," *New Masses* (October 5, 1937): 22.
19. Zora Neale Hurston, "Stories of Conflict," *Saturday Review of Literature* (April 2, 1938): 32.
20. *New York World Telegram* (February 6, 1935), cited by Robert E. Hemenway, *Zora Neale Hurston: A Literary Biography* (Urbana, Chicago, and London: University of Illinois Press, 1977), 215.
21. Hurston, *Mules and Men* (1935), in Zora Neale Hurston, *Folklore, Memoirs, and Other Writings,* ed. Cheryl A. Wall (New York: The Library of America, 1995), 9.
22. Hurston's most famous novel, *Their Eyes Were Watching God* (1937), suggests that her strategies of universalizing were shaped by her familiarity with anthropology and folklore. Janie Mae Crawford's growth, in the course of the novel, is enmeshed in myth and folk beliefs and takes place in rural settings—the all-black town of Eatonville and the wilder world of the muck. Tree images abound, from Nanny's "branches without roots" to Logan's "stump in the middle of the woods where nobody had ever been," Jodie Starks's "new lumber [. . .] rattling off the wagon," and Tea Cake ("Vergible Woods") going out to the lemon tree, picking some lemons, and squeezing them for Janie. Characters seem defined by nature and belief, and modernity, in the shape of Sears and Roebuck streetlights, for example, is readily integrated. Truly notable is Hurston's elegance in employing a folk-inspired idiom (that she also catalogued and described in such essays as "Characteristics of Negro Expression") that avoids the nineteenth-century dialect-writing problems and that is audible in the voices of characters as well as the narrator.
23. Hurston, "My People, My People!," in *Folklore, Memoirs, and Other Writings,* ed. Wall, 773–774.

24. Hurston, "Seeing the World as It Is," in *Folklore, Memoirs, and Other Writings*, ed. Wall, 783.
25. Hurston, *Dust Tracks on a Road* (1942), in *Folklore, Memoirs, and Other Writings*, ed. Wall, 713.
26. Hurston, "What White Publishers Won't Print" (1950), in *Folklore, Memoirs, and Other Writings*, ed. Wall, 952.
27. Hurston, *Folklore, Memoirs, and Other Writings*, ed. Wall, 40.
28. Ibid., 86.
29. Wright, *12 Million Black Voices*, 41.
30. Hurston, "Court Order Can't Make Races Mix," in *Folklore, Memoirs, and Other Writings*, ed. Wall, 956–958.
31. Julia Peterkin, "The Merry-Go-Round," *Smart Set* 56 (December 1921): 69–72; repr. in *Collected Stories of Julia Peterkin*, ed. Frank Durham (Columbia: University of South Carolina Press, 1970), 75–81, here 75.
32. Zora Neale Hurston, *Novels and Stories*, ed. Cheryl A. Wall (New York: The Library of America, 1995), 985–996.
33. Wright, "How 'Uncle Tom's Children' Grew," *The Writers' Book Club Bulletin* (Columbia University) vol. 2 (1938): 16–18; here 17.
34. Richard Wright, *Early Works*, ed. Rampersad, 329–354.
35. Peterkin, "The Merry-Go-Round." 75. Perhaps Peterkin means the folksy narrative voice to be recognizable as biased, as in the description of the village policeman: "He was black, but he upheld the law whenever it was possible" (79).
36. Hurston, "Stories of Conflict," *Saturday Review* (April 2, 1938): 32.
37. Wright, typescript of "Long Black Song," JWJ Wright #964, 35, Wright Papers, James Weldon Johnson Collection, Beinecke Library, Yale University.
38. James T. Farrell, "The Young Manhood of Studs Lonigan," in *Studs Lonigan: A Trilogy* (New York: The Modern Library, 1938), 312–313. I am indebted to Carla Cappetti, *Writing Chicago: Modernism, Ethnography, and the Novel* (New York: Columbia University Press, 1993) for this connection and for many other links between American literature and the Chicago School of Sociology.
39. Burgess, 50.
40. Mario Suarez, "El Hoyo," *Arizona Quarterly* 3.2 (Summer 1947): 112, 114.
41. Thomas Bell, *Out of this Furnace* (1941; repr. Pittsburgh: University of Pittsburgh Press, 1976), 195.
42. Pietro di Donato, *Christ in Concrete* (Indianapolis: Bobbs-Merrill Co., 1939). Further page references in parentheses.
43. D. H. Lawrence, *Sea and Sardinia* (1921); repr. in *D. H. Lawrence and Italy*, ed. Simonetta De Filippis et al. (Harmondsworth, England: Penguin Books, 1997), 8.

44. Jerre Mangione, *Mount Allegro* (1943; repr. with illustr. Peggy Bacon and introd. Dorothy Canfield, New York: Knopf, 1952), 232–292, esp. 271.
45. Dust jacket, inside front flap, of the 1939 Bobbs-Merrill edition.
46. Pietro di Donato, "Christ in Concrete," *Esquire* 7:3 (March 1937), 40–41, 194–196, here 196.
47. "Christ in Concrete," *Esquire,* 196.
48. Thomas J. Ferraro, *Feeling Italian: The Art of Ethnicity in America* (New York: New York University Press, 2005) has noted that there are three versions of "Christ in Concrete" and analyzed them: the 1937 magazine publication in *Esquire* 7, a previously little-known separate book *Christ in Concrete* (Chicago: Esquire Inc, 1937) that is less cleaned up than the magazine version, and the 1939 Bobbs-Merrill novel.
49. "Introduction," Mangione, *Mount Allegro,* viii. The parenthetic page references follow the 1981 reprint by Columbia University Press.
50. E. S. Martin, "East Side Considerations," *Harper's Monthly* 96 (May 1898): 859.
51. See Martha J. Nadell, *Enter the New Negroes: Images of Race in American Culture* (Cambridge, Mass., and London: Harvard University Press, 2004).

14. Immigrant Literature and Totalitarianism

1. Louis Adamic, *The Native's Return: An American Immigrant Visits Yugoslavia and Discovers His Old Country* (New York and London: Harper and Brothers, 1934), 21, 19–20. Further page references in parentheses.
2. Hannah Arendt, *The Origins of Totalitarianism* (New York: Harcourt Brace, 1951).
3. Benito Mussolini, *My Autobiography,* with a foreword by Richard Washburn Child (New York, C. Scribner's Sons, 1928). Further page references in parentheses.
4. The Italian typescript, with autograph revisions (unsigned), written at Rome, 1927–1928, is available at Houghton Library, Harvard University.
5. Ezra Pound, "Totalitarian Scholarship and the New Paideuma," *Germany and You: Our Age* 7.4 (Berlin: Wiking Verlag, 1937), 95–96.
6. Leonard W. Doob, ed., *"Ezra Pound Speaking": Radio Speeches of World War II* (Westport, Conn.: Greenwood Press, 1978), 388, 115. See also Tim Redman, *Ezra Pound and Italian Fascism* (Cambridge: Cambridge University Press, 1991).
7. Ezra Pound, *Jefferson and/or Mussolini; L'idea statale; Fascism as I Have Seen It* (New York: Liveright, 1936), 11–12.
8. Zora Neale Hurston, *Folklore, Memoirs, and Other Writings,* ed. Cheryl A.

Wall (New York: The Library of America, 1995), 792. Antonella Ghiotto, "The Italian Translation of Zora Neale Hurston's *Their Eyes Were Watching God*" (tesi di laurea, Venice, 1996).

9. Barbara Will, "Lost in Translation: Stein's Vichy Collaboration," *Modernism/modernity* 11:4 (November 2004): 1–18. Will's excellent essay refers to Gertrude Stein's unpublished manuscript "Translation and Introduction to Pétain's *Paroles aux français*," Gertrude Stein and Alice B. Toklas Papers, Yale Collection of American Literature, Beinecke Rare Book and Manuscript Library, Yale University.

10. These (rather questionable) reports go back to Gustav Hendrikksen, a former member of the Nobel Prize Committee. See Jonathan Mahler, "How Gertrude Stein Sought Nobel Prize for Hitler," *Forward,* Issue 3106 (New York, N.Y.: February 2, 1996): 1. Mahler also mentions Stein's friendship with Bernard Faÿ. A statement that Stein made in 1934 has been read as an ironic expression of black humor: "I say that Hitler ought to have the peace prize, because he is removing all elements of contest and of struggle from Germany. By driving out the Jews and the democratic and Left elements, he is driving out everything that conduces to activity. That means peace." See *The Letters of Gertrude Stein and Thornton Wilder,* ed. Edward Burns and Ulla E. Dydo, with William Rice (New Haven, Conn. and London: Yale University Press, 1996), 414.

11. *Pittsburgh Courier* (December 19, 1936). My essay "W. E. B. Du Bois in Nazi Germany, 1936," *Amerikastudien/American Studies* 44.2 (1999): 207–222, provides a more detailed discussion.

12. *Pittsburgh Courier* (December 5, 1936).

13. Henry Roth, *Shifting Landscape: A Composite, 1925–1987,* ed. and introd. Mario Materassi (Philadelphia, Penn.: Jewish Publication Society, 1987), 48–51, here 50.

14. Richard Wright, "There are still men left," James Weldon Johnson Collection, Beinecke Library, Yale University, JWJ Wright Misc. 771. As Arnold Rampersad writes, Ralph Ellison also supported the Soviet Union after the Hitler–Stalin agreement: "A week after the signing of the pact he was unmoved when German armies overwhelmed Poland, just as he would be unmoved in November when Soviet armies entered Finland. 'None of the people who are so hot about Finland,' he noted even as he questioned fund-raising for the Finns, 'are saying a word about the 3,000,000 homeless, foodless, sharecroppers we have in this country, let alone the millions of us who don't have decent jobs." *Ralph Ellison: A Biography* (New York: Alfred A. Knopf, 2007), 128.

15. John Fante, *Selected Letters, 1932 to 1981,* ed. Seamus Cooney (Santa Rosa, Calif.: Black Sparrow Press, 1991), 166. Further page references in parentheses.

16. Ayn Rand, *We the Living* (1936; repr. New York: Signet Books, n.d.). Further page references in parentheses.
17. James Truslow Adams, *The Epic of America* (Boston: Little, Brown and Co., 1931), 410. Cited as source in *Oxford English Dictionary,* 3rd edition. Adams further defines this notion as "that dream of a land in which life should be better and richer and fuller for everyone, with opportunity for each according to ability or achievement. It is a difficult dream for the European upper classes to interpret adequately, and too many of us ourselves have grown weary and mistrustful of it. It is not a dream of motor cars and high wages merely, but a dream of social order in which each man and each woman shall be able to attain to the fullest stature of which they are innately capable, and be recognized by others for what they are, regardless of the fortuitous circumstances of birth or position" (214–215).
18. Michael Foster, *American Dream: A Novel* (New York: The Literary Guild of America, 1937), 498. (See also 28.) Further page references in parentheses.
19. Louis Adamic, "Ellis Island and Plymouth Rock," *My America* (1938; repr. New York: Da Capo Press, 1976), 185–259, here 258.
20. Louis Adamic, "Plymouth Rock and Ellis Island," *From Many Lands* (New York: Harper & Brothers, 1940), 289–301, here 299. This book includes polyethnic photographs and writing by and about immigrants and other minorities, among them Charles Kikuchi, who is merely identified as "A Young American with a Japanese Face." See Matthew Manuel Briones, "An American Type: The Kikuchi Diaries, a Cultural Biography (1941–1947)," Ph. D. dissertation, Harvard University, 2005.
21. Adamic, *From Many Lands,* 297.
22. Margaret Mead, "We Are All Third Generation," orig. publ. in *And Keep Your Powder Dry* (1942), repr. in *Theories of Ethnicity: A Classical Reader* (New York: New York University Press, 1996), 216–231, here 218.
23. Salom Rizk, *Syrian Yankee* (Garden City, N.Y.: Doubleday, Doran, & Co., 1943). Further references are to this edition. The introduction to the first edition by DeWitt Wallace describes the book as "Salom's own story—. . . told in his own way" (ix); and Doubleday printed a biographical sketch on the flyleaf. Rizk dedicated his book "To THE REV. HAROLD E. SCHMIDT without whose inspiring friendship, constant encouragements, and help there could have been no *Syrian Yankee.*" Strangely, the book was republished in 2000 under the title *America, More than a Country* (Beverly Hills, Calif.: Laredo Publishing Co.). It is an enlarged edition with some new chapters added and old chapters augmented in the second half of the book, while the ending of the last chapter is identical with that of the first edition. In the new parts, all told in Salom's first-person singular, there are several additional dialogues with "Harold," his benevolent religious helper in the

Americanization process. On the copyright pages, there is an explanation for the presence of these new passages: "Out of love for America and his long time friendship with Salom Rizk, Rev. Schmidt has revised his autobiography, capturing the essence of the original and added thoughts about his personal experience. Every effort has been made by Rev. Schmidt to locate the rightful heirs of Mr. Rizk." I found little secondary literature about Salom Rizk, and perhaps a riddle remains to be solved.

24. His American brothers learn, to their surprise, that Salom is alive, since so many had died in Lebanon; he almost has a sense of survivor's guilt, for while Turkey had "a prohibition against new ideas, against ideas which did not suit the regime" (82) and had killed those who stood up for peace and freedom and independence, Salom was "just a boy. I never made any speeches. I never protested. I meekly, ignorantly accepted the oppression and injustice, the poverty and misery. I really was not worth killing" (82).

25. My edition of *Syrian Yankee* has a handwritten dedication: "To my good friend who 'discovered' me for The Reader's Digest, Charles Ferguson, with sincere and lasting appreciation, Salom Rizk"—thus identifying the benevolent editor who remains anonymous in the published text (306).

26. Jerre Mangione, *Mount Allegro* (1943; repr. New York: Columbia University Press, 1981) 285.

27. Henry Roth, *Call It Sleep* (New York: Robert O. Ballou, 1934), 336; and David Bronsen, "A Conversation with Henry Roth," *Partisan Review* 36 (1969): 265–280, here 267–268.

28. "Author's Note" (1935); repr. in *Jews Without Money*, introd. Alfred Kazin (New York: Carroll and Graf, 2004), 9–12; here 9.

29. Adamic, *Native's Return*, 341–342.

30. Louis Adamic, *Two-Way Passage* (New York: Harper & Brothers, 1941).

31. Adamic, *Native's Return*, 361.

32. John A. Kouwenhoven, *The Beer Can by the Highway: Essays on What's "American" about America* (1961; repr. Baltimore: Johns Hopkins University Press, 1988), 69.

33. Quoted in Robert B. Jones, *Jean Toomer and the Prison-House of Thought: A Phenomenology of the Spirit* (Amherst: University of Massachusetts Press, 1993), 26.

34. Toshio Mori, "A Sketch," *Topaz Times*, New Year Edition (January 1, 1943): II, 1.

35. Hisaye Yamamoto, "The Legend of Miss Sasagawara," repr. in *Seventeen Syllables and Other Stories*, ed. King-Kok Cheung (Latham, N.Y.: Kitchen Table Press, 1988), 20–33, here 20. Further page references in parentheses.

36. Hisaye Yamamoto, "Yoneko's Earthquake," repr. in *Seventeen Syllables*, 46–56, here 51.

37. Letter to Carl Van Doren, March 18, 1943, cited in Arnold Rampersad, *The Life of Langston Hughes,* vol. 2, *I Dream a World* (New York and Oxford: Oxford University Press, 1988), 71.
38. Richard Wright, "No" (Answer to question "Is America Solving Its Race Problem,") *Negro Digest,* vol. 3, n. 10 (August 1945), 43.
39. Delmore Schwartz, "A Bitter Farce," *Kenyon Review* 8 (Spring 1946): 245–261. Further references in parentheses.

15. Was Modernism Antitotalitarian?

1. *XIXa Esposizione Biennale Internazionale d'Arte 1934: Catalogo* (First ed., Venice: Carlo Ferrari, 1934).
2. Alfred H. Barr, Jr., *Cubism and Abstract Art* (1936), repr., with an introd. by Robert Rosenblum (Cambridge, Mass.: Harvard University Press, 1986).
3. Quoted in S. Frederick Starr, *Red and Hot: The Fate of Jazz in the Soviet Union, 1917–1980* (New York and Oxford: Oxford University Press, 1983), 89–90. A different English translation of Gorky's "O muzyke tolstych" by Marie Budberg, "The Music of the Degenerate," appeared in *Dial* (1928).
4. See http://members.surfeu.at/horvath/realism.htm. Accessed June 2, 2007.
5. Langston Hughes, *A Negro Looks at Soviet Central Asia* (Moscow: Co-Operative Publishing Society of Foreign Workers in the U.S.S.R., 1934), repr. in *The Collected Works of Langston Hughes, Vol. 9: Essays on Art Race, Politics, and World Affairs,* ed. Christopher C. De Santis (Columbia: University of Missouri Press, 2002), 76.
6. "Was ist Niggerjazz?" reproduced in Mike Zwerin, *La Tristesse de Saint Louis: Swing under the Nazis* (New York: Quartet Books, 1985), 15. (My translation.)
7. *Völkischer Beobachter* (September 13, 1935): 4. (My translation.)
8. *Völkischer Beobachter* (July 19, 1937), 2. (My translation.)
9. Photograph reproduced in Peter Adam, *Art of the Third Reich* (New York: Harry Abrams, 1992), 127. (My translation.)
10. As George Hutchinson has shown in his study *In Search of Nella Larsen: A Biography of the Color Line* (Cambridge, Mass.: Harvard University Press, 2006), 71–72, Nella Larsen visited Denmark from 1908–1912, an experience that informed her novel *Quicksand.* Hutchinson found no artist in Copenhagen like Larsen's figure of Axel Olsen, but offers as "the most likely model . . . the expressionist Emil Nolde, born Emil Hansen in the North Schleswig border town whose name he later took. [. . .] Nolde was fascinated by 'exotic' races and most forms of dance, which he felt exemplified a primitive vitality and participation in the divinity of nature. [. . .] [I]n 1912 he was planning a book on primitive art. [. . .] He would certainly have been interested in meeting, and painting, a young, intelli-

gent 'mulatto' in Copenhagen at a time when such 'types' were rare in Scandinavia."
11. Clement Greenberg, "Avant-Garde and Kitsch," *Partisan Review* (Fall 1939): 34–49. Further references in the text. For excellent discussions of the Cold War politics surrounding the ascent of New York abstract expressionism and of the relationship of avant-garde and mass culture, see Serge Guilbaut, *How New York Stole the Idea of Modern Art: Abstract Expressionism, Freedom, and the Cold War,* transl. Arthur Goldhammer (Chicago: University of Chicago Press, c1983) and Thomas E. Crow, *Modern Art in the Common Culture* (New Haven, Conn.: Yale University Press, 1996).
12. Clement Greenberg, letter to Harold Lazarus, June 27, 1939, in *The Harold Letters 1928–1943: The Making of an American Intellectual,* ed. Janice Van Horne (Washington, D.C.: Counterpoint, 2000), 203.
13. Application for a Guggenheim fellowship, ms. Columbia University Library.
14. Mike Gold, "Gertrude Stein: A Literary Idiot," *Change the World!* (1934); repr. in *The Critical Response to Gertrude Stein,* ed. Kirk Curnutt (Westport, Conn.: Greenwood Press, 2000), 210.
15. Vladimir Kemenov, "Aspects of Two Cultures," in *Theories of Modern Art,* ed. Herschel B. Chipp (Berkeley: University of California Press, 1968), 490, excerpted from the article in *VOKS Bulletin* (Moscow), U.S.S.R. Society for Cultural Relations with Foreign Countries, 1947, 20–36.
16. Frances Stonor Saunders, *The Cultural Cold War: The CIA and the World of Arts and Letters* (New York: New Press, 1999), 118–119. I am deeply indebted to Saunders's rich account of the cultural cold war throughout this book.
17. James Johnson Sweeney, press release, April 18, 1952 (ACCF/NYU), quoted in Saunders, *Cultural Cold War,* 268.
18. Anonymous, "The Typical Schlesinger Employee," *The Exposure Sheet,* January 20, 1939.
19. Gertrude Stein, "Off We All Went to See Germany," *Life* (August 6, 1945): 54–58.
20. Richard Wright, *The Outsider,* in *Richard Wright: Later Works,* ed. Arnold Rampersad (New York: The Library of America, 1991), 585.

16. Facing the Extreme

1. Quoted in Michael Denning, *The Cultural Front: The Laboring of American Culture in the Twentieth Century* (London: Verso, 1996), 421.
2. The *Oxford English Dictionary,* third edition, cites one instance from 1920 as well as a letter by Raymond Chandler of May 18, 1950 in which Chan-

dler mentions that among "the most commonly used words of soldier-slang" are "'street cars' or 'tram cars' for heavy long range shells." See *Selected Letters of Raymond Chandler*, ed. Frank MacShane (New York: Columbia University Press, 1981), 217.

3. Mary Antin, "House of the One Father," *Common Ground* 1 (Spring 1941): 36–42. Further page references in parentheses.
4. Jean Toomer, *The Flavor of Man* (Philadelphia: Young Friends Movement of the Philadelphia Yearly Meetings, 1949).
5. Martha Foley, ed., *The Best American Short Stories of 1944* (Boston: Houghton Mifflin, 1944). Page references to this yearbook, dedicated to Dorothy Canfield Fisher, will be given parenthetically.
6. Isaac Bashevis Singer, *The Family Moskat*, transl. A. H. Gross (1950; repr. New York: Farrar, Straus & Giroux, 1973), 611. I am indebted to, and following closely, Hana Wirth-Nesher's analysis of Singer's novel in her study *City Codes: Reading the Modern Urban Novel* (Cambridge and New York: Cambridge University Press, 1996).
7. John Hersey, *The Wall* (New York: Alfred A. Knopf, 1950), 503. Further page references appear in parentheses. I am indebted to Alan Rosen, *Sounds of Defiance: The Holocaust, Multilingualism and the Problem of English* (Lincoln, Neb. and London: University of Nebraska Press, 2005). *Notes from the Warsaw Ghetto: The Journal of Emmanuel Ringelblum*, Jacob Sloan's English edition and translation of Ringelblum's *Notitsn fun Varshever geto* was published in New York by McGraw-Hill in 1958.
8. David Daiches, "Record and Testament," *Commentary* (April 1950), 385–388.
9. John Hersey, "Hiroshima," *New Yorker* (August 31, 1946): 15–60. Further page references are to this first edition of "Hiroshima."
10. Gertrude Stein, "Reflection on the Atomic Bomb," *The Previously Uncollected Writings of Gertrude Stein*, ed. Robert Bartlett Haas, vol. 1 (Los Angeles: Black Sparrow Press, 1973), 161.
11. Although the *Oxford English Dictionary*, 3rd edition, defines "ground zero," as "that part of the ground situated immediately under an exploding bomb, esp. an atomic one" and cites a July 7, 1946 *New York Times* article as the first use, the term (that Hersey did not use in his "Hiroshima") appeared as early as July 1945 in reference to the Alamogordo atomic test site in New Mexico. See Paul Boyer, *By the Bomb's Early Light: American Thought and Culture at the Dawn of the Atomic Age* (New York: Pantheon, 1985), 244; Michael B. Stoff, Jonathan F. Fanton, and R. Hal Williams, eds., *The Manhattan Project: A Documentary Introduction to the Atomic Age* (Philadelphia: Temple University Press, 1991), 1, specifies that "ground zero" originally referred to the tower that held the bomb.

12. Dwight Macdonald, "Hersey's *Hiroshima*," *Politics* 3 (October 1946): 308.
13. Mary McCarthy, "The Hiroshima *New Yorker*," *Politics* 3 (October 1946): 367. This quip may have inspired the psychologist David P. Boder to give his collection of interviews with concentration camp survivors the title *I Did Not Interview the Dead* (Urbana: University of Illinois Press, 1949).
14. Harry Levin, ed., *The Portable James Joyce* (New York: The Viking Press, 1947), 1.
15. Langston Hughes, "Here to Yonder: Simple and the Atom Bomb," *Chicago Defender* (August 18, 1945).

17. Grand Central Terminal

1. Leo Szilard, "Report on 'Grand Central Terminal.'" *The Voice of the Dolphins* (New York: Simon and Schuster, 1961), 115–122. Further page references in parentheses.
2. *A Petition to the President of the United States,* United States National Archives, Record Group 77, Records of the Chief of Engineers, Manhattan Engineer District, Harrison-Bundy File, folder 76. Ed. Gene Dannen. Accessed June 2, 2007 at http://www.dannen.com/decision/45-07-17.html.
3. Szilard, *Voice of the Dolphins*, 75–86.

Bibliography

Aaron, Daniel. *Writers on the Left: Episodes in American Literary Communism.* 1961; repr. New York: Avon Library Book, 1965.
Adamic, Louis. *From Many Lands.* New York: Harper & Brothers, 1940.
———. *My America: 1928–1938.* New York: Harper & Brothers, 1938.
———. *The Native's Return: An American Immigrant Visits Yugoslavia and Discovers His Old Country.* New York and London: Harper & Brothers, 1934.
———. *Two-Way Passage.* New York: Harper & Brothers, 1941.
———. "The Yugoslav Speech in America." *American Mercury* 12 (November 1927): 319–321.
Adam, Peter. *Art of the Third Reich.* New York: Harry Abrams, 1992.
Adams, James Truslow. *The Epic of America.* Boston: Little, Brown and Co., 1931.
Agee, James. *Agee on Film: Reviews and Comments.* 1958; repr. Boston: Beacon Press, 1966.
Ager, Waldemar. *Cultural Pluralism versus Assimilation.* Odd Lovell, ed. Northfield, Minn.: The Norwegian-American Historical Association, 1977.
Algren, Nelson. *The Man with the Golden Arm.* 1949; repr. New York: Seven Stories Press, 1999.
———. *The Neon Wilderness.* 1947; repr. n.p.: Writers and Readers Publishing, Inc., 1986.
Antin, Mary. "First Aid to the Alien." *Outlook* 101 (June 29, 1912): 481–485.
———. *From Plotzk to Boston.* Boston: W. B. Clarke, 1899.
———. "House of the One Father." *Common Ground* 1 (Spring 1941): 36–42.
———. "The Lie." *Atlantic Monthly* 112 (August 1913): 177–190.
———. *The Promised Land.* 1912; repr. New York: Penguin, 1997.
———. *They Who Knock at Our Gates: A Complete Gospel of Immigration.* Boston: Houghton Mifflin, 1914.
———. "A Woman to Her Fellow Citizens." *Outlook* 102 (November 2, 1912): 482–486.
Arendt, Hannah. *The Origins of Totalitarianism.* New York: Harcourt, Brace, 1951.
Asch, Nathan. *Pay Day.* 1930; repr. Detroit, Mich.: Omnigraphics, 1990.
Baker, Carlos. *Ernest Hemingway: A Life Story.* New York: Charles Scribner's Sons, 1969.

Balakian, Nona. *The World of William Saroyan*. Lewisburg, Penn.: Bucknell University Press, 1988.
Barr, Alfred H., Jr. *Cubism and Abstract Art*. 1936; repr., with an introd. by Robert Rosenblum. Cambridge, Mass.: Harvard University Press, 1986.
Barrier, Michael. *Hollywood Cartoons: American Animation in Its Golden Age*. New York and Oxford: Oxford University Press, 1999.
Bassett, John, ed. *William Faulkner: The Critical Heritage*. London and Boston: Routledge & Kegan Paul, 1975.
Beach, Joseph Warren. *American Fiction, 1920–1940*. 1941; repr. New York: Russell & Russell, 1960.
Beatitude Anthology. San Francisco: City Lights Books, 1960.
Bell, Thomas. *Out of this Furnace*. 1941; repr. Pittsburgh, Penn.: University of Pittsburgh Press, 1976.
Bender, Thomas, *New York Intellect: A History of Intellectual Life in New York City, from 1750 to the Beginnings of Our Own Time*. Baltimore, Md.: Johns Hopkins University Press, 1987.
Bercovici, Konrad. *Around the World in New York*. New York and London: The Century Co., 1924.
———. *Manhattan Side-Show*. New York and London: The Century Co., 1931.
Berman, Avis. *Rebels on Eighth Street: Juliana Force and the Whitney Museum of American Art*. New York: Atheneum, 1990.
Berman, Patricia Gray and Martin Brody, curators. *Cold War Modern: The Domestic Avantgarde*. Chandler Gallery, Wellesley College, September 15, 2000–June 17, 2001.
Biennale di Venezia, La. *La Biennale di Venezia: Le Esposizioni Internationali d'Arte 1895–1995*. Venezia: Electa, 1996.
Biennale Internazionale d'Arte. XIXa Esposizione. Catalogo. First ed., Venice: Carlo Ferrari, 1934.
Boder, David P. *I Did Not Interview the Dead*. Urbana: University of Illinois Press, 1949.
Boelhower, William, ed. *The Future of American Modernism: Ethnic Writing Between the Wars*. Amsterdam: VU University Press, 1990 (European Contributions to American Studies 17).
Bok, Edward. *The Americanization of Edward Bok: The Autobiography of a Dutch Boy Fifty Years After*. New York: Charles Scribner's Sons, 1930.
———. *Twice Thirty: Some Short and Simple Annals of the Road*. New York: Charles Scribner's Sons, 1925.
Bone, Robert. "The Black Classic That Discovered 'Soul' Is Rediscovered After 45 Years." (Review of Jean Toomer's *Cane*) *New York Times Book Review* (January 19, 1969): 3, 34.
———. *Down Home: A History of African American Short Fiction from Its Beginnings to the Harlem Renaissance*. New York: Putnam, 1975.

Bourne, Randolph S. "Trans-National America." *Atlantic Monthly* 118 (July 1916): 86–97.
Boyer, Paul. *By the Bomb's Early Light: American Thought and Culture at the Dawn of the Atomic Age.* New York: Pantheon, 1985.
Brinnin, John Malcolm. *The Third Rose: Gertrude Stein and Her World.* New York: Grove Press, 1959.
Briones, Matthew Manuel. "An American Type: The Kikuchi Diaries, a Cultural Biography." Ph.D. dissertation, Harvard University, 2005.
Brody, Alter. "Lowing in the Night." In *Lamentations.* New York: Coward-McCann, Inc., 1928.
Brooks, Van Wyck, Alfred Kreymborg, Lewis Mumford, and Paul Rosenfeld, ed. *The American Caravan: A Yearbook of American Literature.* New York: Literary Guild, 1927.
Browder, Laura. *Slippery Characters: Ethnic Impersonators and American Identities.* Chapel Hill and London: University of North Carolina Press, 2000.
Brown, Sterling. *The Negro in American Fiction.* 1937; repr. with *Negro Poetry and Drama,* introd. Robert Bone, New York: Atheneum, 1969.
Brüderlin, Markus. *Ornament und Abstraktion. Kunst der Kulturen, Moderne und Gegenwart im Dialog.* (Catalogue of an exhibition at Fondation Beyeler, Riehen, Switzerland) Cologne: DuMont, 2001.
Bureau of the Census. *Social and Economic Status of the Black Population in the United States: An Historical Overview.* Washington, D.C.: U.S. Department of Commerce, 1979. Current Population reports, Special Studies Series P-23.
Burgess, Ernest W. "The Growth of the City." In Robert Park and Ernest Burgess, ed. *The City.* Chicago, Ill.: University of Chicago Press, 1984.
Burke, Kenneth. "More about Roth's *Call It Sleep.*" *New Masses* 14 (February 26, 1935): 21.
Burns, Edward, ed. *The Letters of Gertrude Stein and Carl Van Vechten 1913–1946.* New York: Columbia University Press, 1986.
———, et al. ed. *The Letters of Gertrude Stein and Thornton Wilder.* New Haven, Conn., and London: Yale University Press, 1996.
Byrd, Rudolph P. *Jean Toomer's Years with Gurdjieff.* Athens, Ga., and London: University of Georgia Press, 1990.
Cahan, Abraham. *Yekl: A Tale of the New York Ghetto.* New York: Appleton, 1896.
Cappetti, Carla. *Writing Chicago: Modernism, Ethnography, and the Novel.* New York: Columbia University Press, 1993.
Carpenter, Humphrey. *A Serious Character: The Life of Ezra Pound.* 1988; repr. New York: Delta, 1990.
Cavell, Stanley. *Pursuits of Happiness: The Hollywood Comedy of Remarriage.* Cambridge, Mass.: Harvard University Press, 1981.
Chametzky, Jules. *Our Decentralized Literature: Cultural Mediations in Selected Jewish and Southern Writers.* Amherst: University of Massachusetts Press, 1986.

Chandler, Raymond. *Chandler before Marlowe: Raymond Chandler's Early Prose and Poetry, 1908–1912*. Matthew J. Bruccoli, ed. Columbia: University of South Carolina Press, 1973.

———. *The Notebooks of Raymond Chandler and English Summer: A Gothic Romance*. Frank MacShane, ed. New York: Ecco Press, 1976.

———. "Notes (Very Brief, Please) on English and American Style." In *Later Works and Other Writings*. Frank MacShane, ed. New York: Library of America, 1995.

———. *The Selected Letters of Raymond Chandler*. Frank Macshane, ed. New York: Columbia University Press, 1981.

Chipp, Herschel B., ed. *Theories of Modern Art: A Source Book by Artists and Critics*. Berkeley and Los Angeles: University of California Press, 1968.

Cohn, Jan. *Creating America: George Horace Latimer and the Saturday Evening Post*. Pittsburgh, Penn.: University of Pittsburgh Press, 1989.

Corn, Wanda M. *The Great American Thing: Modern Art and National Identity, 1915–1935*. Berkeley and Los Angeles: University of California Press, 1999.

Crow, Thomas E. *Modern Art in the Common Culture*. New Haven, Conn.: Yale University Press, 1996.

Curnutt, Kirk, ed. *The Critical Response to Gertrude Stein*. Westport, Conn.: Greenwood Press, 2000.

Daiches, David. "Record and Testament." *Commentary* 9 (April 1950): 385–388.

Dearborn, Mary V. *Pocahontas's Daughters: Gender and Ethnicity in American Culture*. New York: Oxford University Press, 1986.

Degering, Thomas. *Raymond Chandler*. Hamburg: Rowohlt, 1985.

Demarest, David P. *Out of this Furnace*. Pittsburgh, University of Pittsburgh Press, 1976.

Denning, Michael. *The Cultural Front: The Laboring of American Culture in the Twentieth Century*. London and New York: Verso, 1996.

Dewey, John. "Americanism and Localism." *The Dial* 68 (June 1920): 684–688.

Dijkstra, Bram. *Cubism, Stieglitz, and the Early Poetry of William Carlos Williams*. Princeton, N.J.: Princeton University Press, 1978.

Di Donato, Pietro. "Christ in Concrete." *Esquire* 7.3 (March 1937): 40–41, 194–196.

———. *Christ in Concrete*. Indianapolis: Bobbs-Merrill Co., 1939.

Dodge, Mabel. "Speculations, or Post-Impressionism in Prose." *Arts and Decoration* 3 (March 1913): 172–174.

Dolan, Marc. *Modern Lives: A Cultural Re-reading of "The Lost Generation."* West Lafayette, Ind.: Purdue University Press, 1996.

Dondero, George A. Address to Congress on August 16, 1949. Washington, D.C.: United States Government Printing Office, 1949.

Doob, Leonard W., ed. *"Ezra Pound Speaking": Radio Speeches of World War II*. Westport, Conn.: Greenwood Press, 1978.

Drake, St. Clair, and Horace R. Cayton. *Black Metropolis: A Study of Negro Life in a Northern City.* 1945; repr. New York: Harper Torchbooks, 1962.
Dunphy, Jack. *John Fury.* New York and London: Harper and Brothers, 1946.
Durham, Frank, ed. *The Merrill Studies in Cane.* Columbus, Ohio: Charles E. Merrill, 1971.
Eisenhower, Dwight D. "Freedom of the Arts." *The Museum of Modern Art Bulletin* 22.1 (Fall-Winter 1954).
Ellison, Ralph. *Invisible Man.* 1952; repr. New York: Modern Library, n.d.
Erikson, Erik. *Childhood and Society.* 1950; 2nd. ed. New York: W. W. Norton, 1963.
Fabre, Michel. *Richard Wright: Books and Writers.* Jackson and London: University of Mississippi Press, 1990.
Fante, John. "The Odyssey of a Wop." *American Mercury* 30 (September 1933): 89–97.
———. *Selected Letters, 1923–1981.* Seamus Cooney, ed. Santa Rosa, Calif.: Black Sparrow Press, 1991.
Farrell, James T. "The Language of Hollywood." *Saturday Review of Literature* 27 (August 5, 1944): 29–32.
———. *The League of Frightened Philistines and Other Papers.* New York: Vanguard Press, 1945.
———. *The Short Stories of James T, Farrell.* New York: The Vanguard Press, 1934.
———. *Studs Lonigan: A Triology.* New York: The Modern Library, 1938.
Faulkner, William. *Novels 1926–1929.* Joseph Blotner and Noel Polk, ed. New York: The Library of America, 2006.
———. *Novels 1930–1935.* Joseph Blotner and Noel Polk ed. New York: The Library of America, 1985.
———. *Novels 1936–1940.* Joseph Blotner and Noel Polk ed. New York: The Library of America, 1990.
———. *Novels 1942–1954.* Joseph Blotner and Noel Polk ed. New York: The Library of America, 1994.
Fauset, Jessie. *Plum Bun: A Novel Without a Moral.* 1929; repr. Boston: Beacon Press, 1990.
Ferraro, Thomas J. *Ethnic Passages: Literary Immigrants in Twentieth-Century America.* Chicago and London: University of Chicago Press, 1993.
———. *Feeling Italian: The Art of Ethnicity in America.* New York: New York University Press, 2005.
Fine, David M. *The City, the Immigrant and American Fiction, 1880–1920.* Metuchen, N.J., and London: Scarecrow Press, 1977.
Floan, Howard R. *William Saroyan.* New York: Twayne, 1966.
Foley, Martha, ed. *The Best American Short Stories of 1944.* Boston: Houghton Mifflin, 1944.

Foster, Michael. *American Dream: A Novel.* New York: The Library Guild of America, 1937.
Frank, Waldo. *Our America.* New York: Boni and Liveright, 1919.
Frazer, Sir James George. *The Golden Bough.* 1890; repr. abr. ed. New York: Criterion Books, 1959.
Freud, Sigmund. *The Standard Edition of the Complete Psychological Works.* James Strachey ed. London: Hogarth Press, 1957–1974.
Gelfant, Blanche H., ed. *The Columbia Companion to the Twentieth-Century American Short Story.* New York: Columbia University Press, 2000.
Ghiotto, Antonella. "The 1938 Italian Translation of Zora Neale Hurston's *Their Eyes Were Watching God.*" Tesi di laurea, Universitá degli Studi di Venezia, 1996.
Gide, André. "The New American Novelists." In *Transatlantic Mirrors: Essays in Franco-American Literary Relations.* Sidney D. Braun and Seymour Lainoff, ed. Boston: Twayne, 1978.
Gilbert, Felix. *The End of the European Era, 1890 to the Present.* New York: W. W. Norton, 1970.
Gilmore, Michael T. *Differences in the Dark: American Movies and English Theater.* New York: Columbia University Press, 1998.
Gold, Mike. "America Needs a Critic." *New Masses* 1 (October 1926): 7.
———. "Gertrude Stein: A Literary Idiot." In *Change the World!* 1934; repr. Westport, Conn.: Greenwood Press, 2000.
———. *Jews Without Money.* 1930; repr. New York: Bard Books/Avon, 1972.
———. *A Literary Anthology.* Michael Folsom, ed. New York: International Publishers, 1972.
———. "Notes of the Month." *New Masses* 5 (February 1930): 3.
———. "Surveys of the Promised Land." *Liberator* (July 1918): 32–33.
Gorky, Maxim. "Boredom." *Independent* (August 8, 1907): 309–317.
———. "The Music of the Degenerate." *The Dial* 6 (1928): 480–494.
Greenberg, Clement. "Avant-Garde and Kitsch." *Partisan Review* 6 (Fall 1939): 34–49.
———. *The Collected Essays and Criticism.* John O'Brien, ed. 4 vols. Chicago and London: University of Chicago Press, 1986.
———. *The Harold Letters. 1928–1943: The Making of an American Intellectual.* Janice Van Horne, ed. Washington D.C.: Counterpoint, 2000.
Griffin, Farah Jasmine. *"Who Set You Flowin'?": The African-American Migration Narrative.* New York: Oxford University Press, 1995.
Guilbaut, Serge. *How New York Stole the Idea of Modern Art: Abstract Expressionism, Freedom, and the Cold War.* Transl. Arthur Goldhammer. Chicago: University of Chicago Press, 1983.
Guiles, Fred Lawrence. *Marion Davies: A Biography.* New York: McGraw Hill, 1972.

Haas, Robert, ed. *A Primer for the Gradual Understanding of Gertrude Stein*. Los Angeles: Black Sparrow Press, 1971.
Handlin, Oscar, et al., ed. *Harvard Encyclopedia of American Ethnic Groups*. Cambridge, Mass., and London: Harvard University Press, 1980.
Hansen, Marcus Lee. "Immigration and American Culture." In *The Immigrant in American History*. 1940. Arthur M. Schlesinger, ed. and introd. New York, Evanston, Ill., and London: Harper, 1964.
Hapgood, Hutchins. *The Flowers of Friendship: Letters Written to Gertrude Stein*. New York: Knopf, 1953.
Hart, Estelle M. "Trolley-Car Ornithology." *Atlantic Monthly* 101 (1908): 784–787.
Haskell, Barbara. *Joseph Stella*. New York: Whitney Museum of American Art and Harry N. Abrams, 1994.
Hathaway, Heather. *Caribbean Waves: Relocating Claude McKay and Paule Marshall*. Bloomington and Indianapolis: University of Indiana Press, 1999.
Heilbut, Anthony. *Exile in Paradise: German Refugee Artists and Intellectuals in America from the 1930s to the Present*. 2nd. ed. Berkeley and Los Angeles: University of California Press, 1997.
Hemenway, Robert. *Zora Neale Hurston: A Literary Biography*. Urbana, Chicago, and London: University of Illinois Press, 1977.
Hemingway, Ernest. *The Complete Short Stories: The Finca Vigía Edition*. New York: Scribner Paperback Fiction, 1998.
———. *A Farewell to Arms*. 1929; repr. New York: Charles Scribner's Sons, 1969.
———. *Fiesta*. Spanish trans. by Joaquín Adsuar. 1983; repr. Barcelona: DeBols, 2006.
———. *For Whom the Bell Tolls*. 1940; repr. New York: Charles Scribner's Sons, n.d.
———. *Green Hills of Africa*. New York: Charles Scribner's Sons, 1935.
———. *A Moveable Feast*. New York: Charles Scribner's Sons, 1964.
———. "Notes on Life and Letters." *Esquire* 3.1 (January 1931): 21, 159.
———. *Selected Letters, 1917–1961*. Carlos Baker, ed. New York: Charles Scribner's Sons, 1981.
———. *The Snows of Kilimanjaro and Other Stories*. New York: Charles Scribner's Sons, 1961.
———. *The Sun Also Rises*. New York: Charles Scribner's Sons, 1954.
———. *The Sun Also Rises: A Facsimile Edition*. Matthew J. Bruccoli, ed. Ann Arbor, Mich.: Omnigraphics, 1990.
Hersey, John. *A Bell for Adano*. New York: Alfred A. Knopf, 1944.
———. "Hiroshima." *New Yorker* (August 31, 1946): 15–60.
———. *The Wall*. New York: Alfred A. Knopf, 1950.
Hicks, Granville. *The Great Tradition: An Interpretation of American Literature Since the Civil War.* 1933; repr. Biblo and Tannen, 1967.

Holt, Hamilton, ed. *The Life Stories of Undistinguished Americans As Told by Themselves*. 1906; repr. New York: Routledge, 1990.
Howard, Jane. "The Belated Success of Henry Roth." *Life* 53 (January 8, 1965): 75–76.
Howe, Irving. "Life Never Let Up." (Review of Henry Roth's *Call it Sleep*.) *New York Times Book Review* (October 25, 1964): 1, 60.
Howe, M.A. DeWolfe, ed. *Barrett Wendell in His Letters*. Boston: The Atlantic Monthly Press, 1924.
Huggins, Nathan Irvin. *Harlem Renaissance: The Afro-American Ordeal in Slavery*. New York: Pantheon Books, 1977.
Hughes, Langston. *A Negro Looks at Soviet Central Asia*. Moscow: Co-Operative Publishing Society of Foreign workers in the U.S.S.R., 1934; repr. in *The Collected Works of Langston Hughes*. C. De Santis, ed. Columbia: University of Missouri Press, 2002.
———. "Here to Yonder: Simple and the Atom Bomb." *Chicago Defender* (August 18, 1945): 12.
Hurston, Zora Neale. *Folklore, Memoirs, and Other Writings*. Cheryl A. Wall, ed. New York: The Library of America, 1995.
———. *Novels and Stories*. Cheryl A. Wall, ed. New York: The Library of America, 1995.
———. "Stories of Conflict." *Saturday Review of Literature* 17 (April 2, 1938): 32.
Hutchinson, George. *In Search of Nella Larsen: A Biography of the Color Line*. Cambridge, Mass.: Belknap Press of Harvard University Press, 2006.
———. *The Harlem Renaissance in Black and White*. Cambridge, Mass.: Belknap Press of Harvard University Press, 1995.
Ickringill, Steve, ed. *Looking Inward, Looking Outward: From the 1930s through the 1940s*. Amsterdam: VU University Press, 1990 (European Contributions to American Studies 18).
Ickstadt, Heinz, ed. *The Thirties: Politics and Culture in a Time of Broken Dreams*. Amsterdam: VU University Press, 1987 (European Contributions to American Studies 12).
Inglehart, Babette F., and Anthony R. Mangione. *The Image of Pluralism in American Literature: The American Experience of European Ethnic Groups*. New York: The Institute on Pluralism and Group Identity of the American Jewish Committee, 1974.
James, Henry. *The American Scene*. Bloomington and London: Indiana University Press, 1968.
James, William. "The Hidden Self." *Scribner's* 7 (March 1890): 861–873.
———. Letter to Gertrude Stein. In Charles Herrick Compson. *William James, Philosopher and Man: Quotations and References in 652 Books*. New York: Scarecrow Press, 1957.

———. *The Principles of Psychology.* New York: H. Holt, 1890.

———. *Selected Unpublished Correspondence, 1885–1910.* Frederick Down Scott, ed. Columbus: Ohio State University Press, 1986.

———. *Talks to Teachers on Psychology and to Students on Some of Life's Ideals.* New York: H. Holt, 1899

Janson, Drude Krog. *A Saloonkeeper's Daughter.* Baltimore and London: Johns Hopkins University Press, 2002.

Joachimides, Christos M., and Norman Rosenthal, ed. *American Art in the 20th Century.* Munich: Prestel, 1993. Royal Academy of Arts and ZEITGEIST-Gesellschaft.

Jones, Robert B. *Jean Toomer and the Prison-House of Thought: A Phenomenology of the Spirit.* Amherst: University of Massachusetts Press, 1993.

Juliana Force and American Art: A Memorial Exhibition September 24–October 30, 1949. New York: Whitney Museum of American Art, n.d. [1949].

Kafka, Franz. *Amerika.* Edwin Muir trans. New York: New Directions, 1946.

Kalaidjian, Walter. *American Culture Between the Wars: Revisionary Modernism and Postmodern Critique.* New York: Columbia University Press, 1993.

Kallen, Horace M. *Culture and Democracy in the United States.* New York: Boni and Liveright, 1924.

Kazin, Alfred. *On Native Grounds: An Interpretation of Modern American Prose Literature.* New York: Reynal & Hitchcock, 1942.

Kelly, Myra. *Little Citizens: The Humour of School Life.* New York: Grosset & Dunlap, 1904.

Kerman, Cynthia, and Richard Eldridge. *The Lives of Jean Toomer: A Hunger for Wholeness.* Baton Rouge, La., and London, 1987.

Kinnamon, Keneth. *The Emergence of Richard Wright: A Study in Literature and Society.* Urbana: University of Illinois Press, 1972.

———, ed. *New Essays on Native Son.* New York and Cambridge, England: Cambridge University Press, 1990.

Klein, Marcus. *Foreigners: The Making of American Literature 1900–1940.* Chicago and London: University of Chicago Press, 1981.

Knox, Sanka. "Eisenhower Links Art and Freedom: Salutes Modern Museum on Its 25th. Year." *New York Times* (October 20, 1954): 30.

Kobrin, Leon. "Di shprakh fun elnt." In *Der farloirener nigun: roman un zeks dertseylungen.* [New York:] YKUF farlag, 1948. In *Pushcarts and Dreamers and Other Stories of Jewish Life in America.* Max Rosenfeld, ed. and transl. South Brunswick, N.Y., and London: Thomas Yoseloff, 1967.

Kouwenhoven, John A. *The Beer Can by the Highway: Essays on What's "American" about America.* Introd. Ralph Ellison. Baltimore, Md.: Johns Hopkins University Press, 1988.

Larson, Charles R. *Invisible Darkness: Jean Toomer and Nella Larsen*. Iowa City: University of Iowa Press, 1993.
Lawrence, D. H. *Sea and Sardinia*. 1921; repr. in *D. H. Lawrence and Italy*. Simonetta De Filippis et al. ed. Harmondsworth, England: Penguin Books, 1997.
Lazerow, Judah Leib. "The Staff of Judah." In *The Multilingual Anthology of American Literature*. Marc Shell and Werner Sollors, ed. New York: New York University Press, 2000.
Lemkin, Raphaël. *Axis Rule in Occupied Europe: Laws of Occupation, Analysis of Government, Proposals for Redress*. Washington, D.C.: Carnegie Endowment for International Peace, 1944.
Levin, Gail. *Edward Hopper as Illustrator*. New York: Norton, 1979.
Levin, Harry. "Observations on the Style of Ernest Hemingway." In *Memories of the Moderns*. New York: New Directions, 1982.
———, ed. *The Portable James Joyce*. New York: The Viking Press, 1947.
Levin, Meyer. *Frankie and Johnnie*. New York: John Day Company, 1930.
———. *In Search: An Autobiography*. New York: Horizon Press, 1950.
Lewis, Wyndham. *Time and Western Man*. New York: Harcourt, Brace, 1927.
Lewisohn, Ludwig. *The Case of Mr. Crump*. 1926; repr. New York: Noonday Press of Farrar, Straus & Giroux, 1965.
———. *Stephen Escott*. 1930; repr. *The Vehement Flame: The Story of Stephen Escott*. New York: Farrar, Straus & Giroux, 1948.
———. *Expression in America*. New York: The Modern Library, 1931.
———. *The Story of American Literature*. New York: The Modern Library, 1939.
Lippmann, Walter. "The Acids of Modernity." In *A Preface to Morals*. 1929; repr. New Brunswick: Transaction Publishers, 1982.
Locke, Alain, ed. *The New Negro*. 1925; repr. New York: Atheneum, 1970.
Lombardi, Cristina. "*Native Son:* Genesi di un romanzo." Thesis, Dipartimento di Anglistica, Università degli Studi di Roma, 1989.
Ludington, Townsend, ed. *A Modern Mosaic: Art and Modernism in the United States*. Chapel Hill and London: University of North Carolina Press, 2000.
Lynn, Kenneth S. *Hemingway*. New York: Fawcett, 1987.
Lyons, Bonnie. *Henry Roth: The Man and His Work*. New York: Cooper Square Publishers, Inc., 1976.
Macdonald, Dwight. "Hersey's *Hiroshima*." *Politics* 3 (October 1946): 308.
Mahler, Jonathan. "How Gertrude Stein Sought Nobel Prize for Hitler." *Forward* 3106 (February 2, 1996): 1.
Major, Clarence. "*Three Lives* and Gertrude Stein." *Par Rapport* 2, 1979, [53–66].
Mangione, Jerre. *Mount Allegro*. Illustrated by Peggy Bacon. Boston: Houghton Mifflin, 1943.

---. "Finale." In *Mount Allegro: A Memoir of Italian American Life.* New York: Columbia University Press, 1981.

---, and Ben Morreale. *La Storia: Five Centuries of the Italian American Experience.* New York: HarperCollins, 1992.

Manskleid-Makowsky, Irit. "The 'Jewishness' of Jewish American Literature: The Examples of Ludwig Lewisohn and Henry Roth." M.A. Thesis (with an interview), John F. Kennedy-Institut, Freie Universität Berlin, 1978.

Martin, E. S. "East Side Considerations." *Harper's Monthly* 96 (May 1898): 853–863.

May, Henry F. *The End of American Innocence: A Study of the First Years of Our Own Time 1912–1916.* London: Jonathan Cape, 1960.

Mazur, Allan. *A Romance in Natural History: The Lives and Works of Amadeus Grabau and Mary Antin.* Syracuse, N.Y.: Garret, 2004.

McCarthy, Mary. "The Hiroshima *New Yorker.*" *Politics* 3 (October 1946): 367.

McKay, Claude. *A Long Way from Home.* 1937; repr. New York: Harcourt, Brace & World, 1970.

---. *Home to Harlem.* 1928; repr. Boston: Northeastern University Press, 1987.

McKay, Nellie Y. *Jean Toomer, Artist.* Chapel Hill: University of North Carolina Press, 1984.

Melnick, Jeff. *A Right to Sing the Blues: African Americans, Jews, and American Popular Song.* Cambridge, Mass.: Harvard University Press, 1999.

Mencken, H. L. *The American Language.* 1919; repr. New York: Alfred A. Knopf, 1948.

Middleton, William D. *The Time of the Trolley.* Milwaukee: Kalmbach Publishing, 1967.

Migueis, José Rodrigues. *Gente de terceira classe.* Lisbon: Editorial Estúdios Cor, 1971.

---. *Steerage and Ten Other Stories.* Transl. George Monteiro and Carolina Matos. Providence, R.I.: Gavea-Brown, 1983.

Mori, Toshio. "A Sketch." *Topaz Times.* New Year edition (January 1, 1943): II, 1.

Morrison, Toni. *Playing in the Dark: Whiteness and the Literary Imagination.* Cambridge, Mass. and London: Harvard University Press, 1992.

Mussolini, Benito. *My Autobiography.* Foreword by Richard Washburn Child. New York: Charles Scribner's Sons, 1928.

Nadell, Martha J. *Enter the New Negroes: Images of Race in American Culture.* Cambridge, Mass.: Harvard University Press, 2004.

North, Michael. *The Dialect of Modernism: Race, Language, and Twentieth-Century Literature.* New York: Oxford University Press, 1994.

Nyman, Jopi. *Men Alone: Masculinity, Individualism, and Hard-Boiled Fiction.* Amsterdam: Rodopi, 1997.

Øverland, Orm. *Immigrant Minds, American Identities: Making the United States Home, 1870–1930*. Urbana & Chicago: University of Illinois Press, 2000.

———. *The Western Home: A Literary History of Norwegian America*. Northfield, Minn.: Norwegian-American Historical Association, 1996.

Pattee, Fred Lewis. *The New American Literature, 1890–1930*. New York and London: The Century Co., 1930.

Peretti, Burton W. *The Creation of Jazz: Music, Race, and Culture in Urban America*. Urbana and Chicago: University of Illinois Press, 1992.

Peterkin, Julia. *Collected Stories of Julia Peterkin*. Frank Durham, ed. Columbia: University of South Carolina Press, 1970.

Peterson, Carla. "The Remaking of Americans: Gertrude Stein's 'Melanctha' and African-American Musical Tradition." In *Criticism and the Color Line: Desegregating American Literary Studies*. Henry B. Wonham, ed. New Brunswick, N.J.: Rutgers University Press, 1995.

Poirier, Richard. *A World Elsewhere: The Place of Style in American Literature*. New York: Oxford University Press, 1966.

Pollet, Elizabeth, ed. *Portrait of Delmore: Journals and Notes of Delmore Schwartz, 1939–1959*. New York: Farrar, Straus, Giroux, 1986.

Pound, Ezra. *Jefferson and/or Mussolini; L'idea statale; Fascism as I Have Seen It*. New York: Liveright, 1936.

———. "Totalitarian Scholarship and the New Paideuma." *Germany and You: Our Age* 7.4 (Berlin: Wiking Verlag, 1937): 95–96.

Pronzini, Bill, and Jack Adrian, ed. *Hard-Boiled: An Anthology of American Crime Stories*. New York and Oxford: Oxford University Press, 1995.

Rampersad, Arnold. *The Life of Langston Hughes*. Vol. 2, *I Dream a World*. New York and Oxford: Oxford University Press, 1988.

———. *Ralph Ellison: A Biography*. New York: Alfred A. Knopf, 2007.

Rand, Ayn. *We the Living*. 1936; repr. New York: Signet Books, n.d.

Redfield, Robert. *Tepoztlàn: A Mexican Village*. Chicago: University of Chicago Press, 1930.

Redman, Tim. *Ezra Pound and Italian Fascism*. Cambridge, Mass.: Cambridge University Pressm 1991.

Repplier, Agnes. "The Modest Immigrant." In *Counter-Currents*. Boston: Houghton Mifflin, 1916.

Reynolds, David S. *A Historical Guide to Walt Whitman*. New York and Oxford: Oxford University Press, 2000.

Ringelblum, Emmanuel. *Notes from the Warsaw Ghetto: The Journal of Emmanuel Ringelblum*. Jacob Sloan, ed. and transl. New York: McGraw-Hill, 1958.

Rizk, Salom. *Syrian Yankee*. Garden City, N.Y.: Doubleday, Doran & Co., 1943.

Rølvaag, Ole E. *Giants in the Earth: A Saga of the Prairie*. Trans. Lincoln Colcord and Ole E. Rølvaag. New York: Harper & Brothers, 1927.

———. *Peder Victorious: A Tale of the Pioneers Twenty Years Later.* Trans. Nora O. Solum and Ole E. Rølvaag. New York: Harper & Brothers, 1929.

———. *Their Father's God.* Trans. Trygve M. Ager. New York: Harper & Brothers, 1931.

Rosen, Alan. *Sounds of Defiance: The Holocaust, Multilingualism, and the Problem of English.* Lincoln, Neb., and London: University of Nebraska Press, 2005.

Rosen, Ruth, and Sue Davidson, ed. *The Maimie Papers.* Old Westbury, N.Y.: Feminist Press, 1977.

Rosenberg, Harold. *The Tradition of the New.*. 1959; repr. New York and Toronto: McGraw-Hill, 1965.

Roth, Henry. *Call It Sleep.* New York: Robert O. Ballou, 1934.

———. *Shifting Landscape: A Composite, 1925–1987.* Mario Materassi, ed. Philadelphia: Jewish Publication Society, 1987.

Rubenfeld, Florence. *Clement Greenberg: A Life.* New York: Scribner, 1997.

Rusch, Frederick L., ed. *A Jean Toomer Reader: Selected Unpublished Writings.* New York and Oxford: Oxford University Press, 1993.

Ryland, Philip, and Enzo Di Martino. *Flying the Flag for Art: The United States and the Venice Biennale, 1895–1991.* Richmond, Va.: Wyldbore and Wolferstan, 1993.

Salz, Evelyn, ed. *The Selected Letters of Mary Antin.* Syracuse, N.Y.: Syracuse University Press, 2000.

Sanders, David. *John Hersey Revisited.* Boston: Twayne, 1990.

Saroyan, Aram. *William Saroyan.* New York: Harcourt, Brace, Jovanovitch, 1983.

Saroyan, William. "Aspirin Is a Member of the N.R.A." *American Mercury* 32 (May 1934): 87–90.

———. *The Daring Young Man on the Flying Trapeze and Other Stories.* New York: Random House, 1934.

———. "Myself Upon the Earth: A Story." In *The American Mercury Reader.* Philadelphia, Penn.: The Blakiston Company, 1944.

———. "Seventy Thousand Assyrians." In *The Daring Young Man on the Flying Trapeze and Other Stories.* New York: Random House, 1934.

———. "Subway Circus." In *The Best One-Act Plays of 1940.* New York: Dodd, Mead & Company, 1941, 77–135.

Sartre, Jean-Paul. "American Novelists in French Eyes." *Atlantic Monthly* 178 (August 1946): 114–118.

Saunders, Frances Stonor. *The Cultural Cold War: The CIA and the World of Arts and Letters.* New York: New Press, 1999.

Schwartz, Delmore. "A Bitter Farce." *Kenyon Review* 8 (Spring 1946): 245–261.

———. "The Grapes of Crisis." *Partisan Review* 18 (January-February 1951): 7–15.

---. *Selected Essays of Delmore Schwartz*. Donald Dike and David Zucker, ed. Chicago: University of Chicago Press, 1970.
Seaver, Edwin. "Caesar or Nothing." *New Masses* 14 (March 5, 1935): 21.
Shell, Marc and Werner Sollors, ed. *The Multilingual Anthology of American Literature: A Reader of Original Texts with English Translations*. New York: New York University Press, 2000.
Sherman, Stuart P. "The Barbaric Naturalism of Mr. Dreiser." *Nation* 101 (December 2, 1915): 648–650.
---. *The Main Stream*. New York: Charles Scribner's Sons, 1927.
Silva, Umberto. *Ideologia e arte del fascismo*. Milan: Mazzotta, 1973.
Singer, Isaac Bashevis. *The Family Moskat*. Cambridge and New York: Cambridge University Press, 1996.
Sollors, Werner, ed. *Interracialism: Black-White Intermarriage in American History, Literature, and Law*. New York and Oxford: Oxford University Press, 2000.
---, ed. *Theories of Ethnicity: A Classical Reader*. New York: New York University Press, 1996.
Solomons, Leon M. and Gertrude Stein. "Normal Motor Automatism." *Harvard Psychological Laboratory* 3.5 (September 1896): 492–512.
Soto, Mike. *The Modernist Nation: Generation, Renaissance, and Twentieth-Century American Literature*. Tuscaloosa: University of Alabama Press, 2004.
Spiller, Robert E. et al. ed. *Literary History of the United States*. New York: Macmillan, 1948.
Squires, Nancy Elam. "Back to the Blanket: The Indian Fiction of Oliver La Farge, John Joseph Mathews, D'Arcy McNickle, Ruth Underhill and Frank Waters, 1927–1944." Ph. D. dissertation, Harvard University, 2004.
Starr, S. Frederick. *Red and Hot: The Fate of Jazz in the Soviet Union, 1917–1980*. New York and Oxford: Oxford University Press, 1983.
Stearns, Harold, ed. *America Now: An Inquiry into Civilization in the United States*. New York and London: Charles Scribner's Sons, 1938.
Stein, Kurt M. *Die Schönste Lengevitch*. Chicago: P. Covici, 1925.
Stein, Gertrude. *As a Wife Has a Cow: A Love Story*. 1926; repr. Barton, Vt.: Something Else Press, 1973.
---. *The Autobiography of Alice B. Toklas*. New York: Harcourt, Brace and Company, 1933.
---. "Cultivated Motor Automatism: A Study of Character in Relation to Attention." *Psychological Review* 5 (May 1898): 295–306.
---. *Lectures in America*. 1935; repr. New York: Vintage Books, 1975.
---. *The Making of Americans; Being a History of a Family's Progress*. New York: Something Else Press, 1966.
---. "Off We All Went to See Germany." *Life* (August 6, 1945): 54–58.

———. "Poetry and Grammar." In *How to Write*. New York: Dover Publications, Inc., 1975.
———. *Three Lives*. Ann Charters, ed. New York: Penguin Books, 1990.
Steinberg, Salme Harju. *Reformer in the Marketplace: Edward W. Bok and The Ladies' Home Journal*. Baton Rouge and London: Louisiana State University Press, 1979.
Steiner, Edward. *From Alien to Citizen*. New York: Fleming H. Revell Co., 1914.
Stoff, Michael B., Jonathan F. Fanton, and R. Hal Williams, ed. *The Manhattan Project: A Documentary Introduction*. Philadelphia, Penn.: Temple University Press, 1991.
Sturzo, Luigi. *Italy and Fascismo*. Barbara Barclay Carter, trans. London: Faber & Gwyer, 1926.
Suárez, Mario. "El Hoyo." *Arizona Quarterly* 3.2 (Summer 1947): 112–115.
———. "Señor Garza." *Arizona Quarterly* 3.2 (Summer 1947): 115–121.
Szilard, Leo. *A Petition to the President of the United States*. United States National Archives RG 77. Records of the Chief of Engineers, Manhattan Engineer District, Harrison-Bundy File, folder 76. At *http://www.dannen.com/decision/45-07-17.html*; accessed June 2, 2007.
———. *The Voice of the Dolphins*. New York: Simon and Schuster, 1961.
Taubenfeld, Aviva. *Rough Writing: Ethnic Authorship in Theodore Roosevelt's America*. New York: New York University Press, 2008.
Tedeschini Lalli, Biancamaria, and Maurizio Vaudagna, ed. *Brave New Words: Strategies of Language and Communication in the United States of the 1930s*. Amsterdam: VU University Press, 1999. (European Contributions to American Studies 36.)
Terris, Daniel. "Waldo Frank and the Rediscovery of America, 1889–1929." Ph. D. dissertation, Harvard University, 1992.
Tolson, Melvin B. "Mu." In *Harlem Gallery*. New York: Collier Books, 1969.
Toomer, Jean. *Cane*. 1923; repr. New York: New York: Harper & Row, 1969.
———. *Essentials*. 1931; repr. Rudolph P. Byrd, ed. Athens, Ga., and London: University of Georgia Press, 1991.
———. *The Flavor of Man*. Philadelphia: Young Friends Movement of the Philadelphia Yearly Meetings, 1949.
Trilling, Diana. "Fiction in Review." *Nation* (February 12, 1944): 194–195.
Trilling, Lionel. *The Liberal Imagination: Essays on Literature and Society*. New York: Viking Press, 1950.
———. "The McCaslins of Mississippi." *Nation* (May 30, 1942): 632–633.
Turner, Darwin T., ed. *Cane*. New York: W. W. Norton, 1988. Norton Critical Edition.
———, ed. *The Wayward and the Seeking: A Collection of Writings by Jean Toomer*. Washington, D.C.: Howard University Press, 1983.

Van Doren, Carl. *The American Novel 1789–1939*. New York: Macmillan, 1940.

———. *Contemporary American Novelists, 1900–1920*. New York: Macmillan, 1927.

Van Vechten, Carl, ed. *The Selected Writings of Gertrude Stein*. New York: Random House, 1946.

Wald, Priscilla. *Constituting Americans: Cultural Anxiety and Narrative Form*. Durham, N.C., and London: Duke University Press, 1995.

Walton, Eda Lou, ed. *The City Day: An Anthology of Recent American Poetry*. New York: The Ronald Press Company, 1929.

Weiss, Feri Felix. *The Sieve; or, Revelations of the Man Mill*. Boston: The Page Company, 1921.

Weiss, M. Lynn. *Gertrude Stein and Richard Wright: The Poetics and Politics of Modernism*. Jackson: University Press of Mississippi, 1998.

Weston, Richard. *Modernism*. London: Phaidon Press, 1996.

White, Newman I. *American Negro Folk-Songs*. Cambridge, Mass.: Harvard University Press, 1928.

Whitman, Walt. *Complete Prose Works*. Boston: Small, Maynard, and Company, 1898.

———. "Preface to 1855 Edition." In *Leaves of Grass*. New York: Doubleday, Page & Company, Inc., 1927.

Will, Barbara. "Lost in Translation: Stein's Vichy Collaboration." *Modernism/modernity* 11.4 (November 2004): 651–668.

Williams, William Carlos. "Recollections." In *Art in America*. Princeton, N.J.: Princeton University Press, 1978.

Wilson, Edmund. *Axel's Castle: A Study in the Imaginative Literature of 1870–1930*. New York: Charles Scribner's Sons, 1931.

Wirth, Louis. "Urban Society and Civilization." *American Journal of Sociology* 45 (March 1940): 743–755.

Wirth-Nesher, Hana. *Call It English: The Languages of Jewish American Literature*. Princeton, N.J.: Princeton University Press, 2006.

———. *City Codes: Reading the Modern Urban Novel*. New York and Cambridge, Mass.: Cambridge University Press, 1996.

———. ed. *New Essays on Call It Sleep*. New York and Cambridge, Mass.: Cambridge University Press, 1996.

Wist, Johannes B. *The Rise of Jonas Olsen: A Norwegian Immigrant's Saga*. Minneapolis: University of Minnesota Press, 2006.

Wolff, Edward N. *Top Heavy: A Study of the Increasing Inequality of Wealth in America*. New York: Twentieth Century Fund, 1995.

Wright, Richard. "Between Laughter and Tears." *New Masses* 25 (October 5, 1937): 2.

———. *Early Works*. Arnold Rampersad, ed. New York: The Library of America, 1991.

———. "How 'Uncle Tom's Children' Grew." *The Writers' Club Bulletin,* New York, Columbia University, 2, 1938, 16–18.
———. *Later Works.* Arnold Rampersad, ed. New York: The Library of America, 1991.
———. "Memories of My Grandmother." Beinecke Rare Books and Manuscript Library, Yale University.
———. *The Richard Wright Reader.* Ellen Wright and Michel Fabre, ed. New York: Harper & Row, 1978.
———. *12 Million Black Voices.* 1941; repr. Boston, Mass.: Thunder's Mouth Press, 1988.
Yamamoto, Hisaye. *Seventeen Syllables.* Latham, N.Y.: Kitchen Table Women of Color Press, 1988.
Yeats, William Butler. *The Winding Stair and Other Poems.* New York: Macmillan, 1933.
Yezierska, Anzia. *Salome of the Tenements.* 1922; repr. Urbana: University of Illinois Press, 1995.
Yin, Xiao-huang. *Chinese American Literature since the 1850s.* Urbana: University of Illinois Press, 2000.
Zempel, Solveig. "Rølvaag as Translator: Translations of Rølvaag." In *Norwegian-American Essays.* Knut Djupedal, et al. ed. Oslo: The Norwegian Emigrant Museum, 1993, 40–50.
Zwerin, Mike. *La Tristesse de Saint Louis: Swing under the Nazis.* London: Quartet Books, 1985.
Zyla, Wolodomyr T., and Wendell M. Aycock, ed. *Ethnic Literatures since 1776: The Many Voices of America.* Lubbock: Texas Tech Press, 1978, 2 vols.

Acknowledgments

I am grateful to Sacvan Bercovitch for asking me to write these pages, for encouraging me and being remarkably patient along the way, as well as for making many helpful comments. Instead of aiming for "coverage," which would be an impossible goal to achieve, I have chosen to place emphasis on certain works and moments that were particularly important for the story of American ethnic prose literature from 1910 to 1950. Though occasionally plots are "summarized," there is a continued focus on single sentences and paragraphs as the representative units of prose works. Analogous developments in the visual arts are examined throughout, and a recurrent concern is for examples of modernity, especially in representations of means of transportation such as the trolley and the train.

The final writing was facilitated by a senior fellowship from the National Endowment for the Humanities. I am indebted to Jesse Matz for reading some sections and making excellent suggestions; and I profited enormously from presenting the introductory sections at a Harvard English Department faculty colloquium and other parts of this work at conferences and lectures in various parts of the world. "Ethnic Modernism" first appeared as a contribution to volume six of *The Cambridge History of American Literature,* and I thank Ray Ryan at Cambridge University Press for his support.

Lindsay Waters at Harvard University Press encouraged me to bring this essay out as an independent book publication, and I am ever as grateful for his enthusiasm as I am impressed by his boundless energies. His imaginative assistant Phoebe Kosman addressed all issues in the process quickly, expertly, and with good cheer. The anonymous readers provided helpful and encouraging comments for the process of revision. The brief and generally positive comments on my contribution to the *The Cambridge History of American Literature* made by reviewers in *American Studies International* and the *Journal of American Studies* were also appreciated. Changes have been made sparingly, the most dramatic among them being the addition of footnotes. The chronology offers a quick temporal orientation, and the bibliography refers to selected primary sources and to the scholarship that has been most influential in giving shape to this book.

I wish to acknowledge the research assistance of Breda O'Keeffe, Jessica Hook, and, in the last stages of writing, Erica Michelstein—who also proofread the whole manuscript and made many valuable suggestions; Marques Redd assisted in putting together the initial chronology; and Francesca Petrosini Gamber helped with loose ends and the double-checking of sources. For the publication as a separate monograph, Lisa Sanchez tracked down references, caught some errors, and drafted notes. Thomas Dichter, Katharine Waterman, and Kelsey LeBuffe helped prepare the manuscript at various stages; Tonnya Norwood provided expert copyediting; and Fatin Abbas proofread everything carefully, helped revise footnotes, chronology, and bibliography, and created the index.

More than three decades of teaching courses on African American literature, on "Ethnicity, Modernity, and Modernism," and "Literature of Migration" at the Freie Universität Berlin, at Columbia and Harvard Universities as well as at the Unversità degli Studi di Venezia Ca' Foscari have helped me shape the argument that is developed here, and I am grateful to the graduate students who taught sections as well as to the undergraduates who took my courses and wrote many excellent term papers. I have also benefited from student work in many other courses, and I would like to acknowledge that my interest in Japanese-American newspapers from the detention camps was first aroused by Karen Sekiguchi's 1977 term paper "Perceptions of an Ethnic-American Identity" for a course at Columbia College. Over the years, I have presented versions of various sections of this book to many audiences, and have published talks and essays.

Among the most relevant related publications, some of which include extensive additional documentation and notes, are the following: "Anthropological and Sociological Tendencies in American Literature of the 1930s and 1940s: Richard Wright, Zora Neale Hurston, and American Culture." *Looking Inward, Looking Outward: From the 1920s through the 1940s,* ed. Steve Ickringill. Amsterdam: VU University Press, 1990 (European Contributions to American Studies 18), 22–75; Introduction to expanded edition of *The Life Stories of Undistinguished Americans as Told by Themselves* (New York and London: Routledge, 1990); "Of Plymouth Rock and Jamestown and Ellis Island: Ethnic Literature and Some Redefinitions of 'America,' " *Immigrants in Two Democracies: French and American Experience,* ed. Donald Horowitz and Gérard Noiriel (New York: New York University Press, 1992), 205–244; Introduction to Jean Toomer, *Cane* (bilingual edition with annotations, Venice: Marsilio, 1993); "Polyethnic Panorama: The Life Stories of Undistinguished Americans as Told by Themselves," *Swedes in America: Intercultural and Interethnic Perspectives on Contemporary Research,* ed. Ulf Beijbom (Växjö: The Swedish Emigrant Institute Series 6, 1993), 203–217; Introduction to *Theories of Ethnicity: A Classical Reader* (London: Macmillan and New York: New York University Press, 1996); " 'A world somewhere, somewhere else': Language, Nostalgic Mournfulness, and Urban Immigrant Family Romance in *Call It Sleep,*" *New Essays on Call It Sleep,* ed. Hana Wirth-Nesher (Cambridge and New York: Cambridge

University Press, 1996), 127–188; Introduction to Mary Antin, *The Promised Land* (New York and Harmondsworth, England: Penguin, 1997); Introduction to *Multilingual America: Transnationalism, Ethnicity, and the Languages of America* (New York: New York University Press, 1998); "W. E. B. Du Bois in Nazi Germany, 1936," *Amerikastudien/American Studies* 44.2 (1999): 207–222; "Jean Toomer's *Cane*: Modernism and Race in Interwar America," in *Dream-Fluted Cane: Essays on Jean Toomer and the Harlem Renaissance,* ed. Geneviève Fabre and Michel Feith (New Brunswick, N.J.: Rutgers University Press, 2001), 18–37; "Non-English Short Stories," in *The Columbia Companion to Twentieth-Century American Short Fiction,* ed. Blanche H. Gelfant (New York: Columbia University Press, 2001), 72–80; "How German Is It? Multilingual America Reconsidered," in *Not English Only: Redefining "American" in American Studies,* ed. Orm Øverland (Amsterdam: VU Press, 2001. European Contributions to American Studies 48), 148–155; " 'Eager to acquire disks?' American Studies in War and Peace," in *American Studies and Peace,* ed. Dorothea Steiner and Thomas Hartl (Frankfurt: Peter Lang, 2001), 23–40; "Holocaust and Hiroshima: American Ethnic Prose Writers Face the Extreme," *Publications of the Modern Language Association* 118.1 (Spring, 2003): 1–11; "Four Types of Writing under Modern Conditions; or, Black Writers and 'Populist Modernism,'" in *Race and the Modern Artist,* ed. Heather Hathaway, Josef Jařab, and Jeffrey Melnick (New York: Oxford University Press, 2003), 42–68; "African American Intellectuals and Europe between the Two World Wars," *Regards Croises sur les Afro-Americains: Hommage à Michel Fabre,* ed. Claude Julien (GRAAT No. 27, Tours: Presses Universitaires François Rabelais, 2003), 41–57; "Hemingway, Film Noir, and the Emergence of a Twentieth-Century American Style," *REAL: Yearbook of Research in English and American Literature 21: Literature, Literary History, and Cultural Memory,* ed. Herbert Grabes (Tübingen: Gunter Narr, 2005), 45–55; "Ethnic Modernism" in *Vox Litterarum: Kultura, Komunikazia, Kritika* 4 (2005): 62–70. (Bulgarian translation of a lecture given in Plovdiv, Bulgaria).

The author and publisher wish to thank the following for permission to reproduce copyrighted material: William Saroyan, letter to Ernest Hemingway, December 16, 1934, San Francisco, 5pp. Held at John F. Kennedy Presidential Library and Museum, Ernest Hemingway Collection. By permission of the John F. Kennedy Presidential Library and Museum, the William Saroyan Foundation and the Stanford University Library. If any copyright-holders have been inadvertently overlooked the publishers will be pleased to make the necessary arrangement at the first opportunity.

***

As always in the past decades, Alide Cagidemetrio has again helped me think through and strengthen my argument in this project. I dedicate this book to her.

Index

Abbott, Berenice, 235
Abbott, Jacob, 67
Act to Preserve Racial Purity, 39, 110
Adamic, Louis, 13, 40, 76–77, 202; *My America,* 42, 193; *Laughing in the Jungle: The Autobiography of an Immigrant in America,* 57, 85, 183; "The Yugoslav Speech in America," 86; *The Native's Return: An American Immigrant Visits Yugoslavia and Discovers, His Old Country,* 183, 198, 200; *From Many Lands,* 194; "Plymouth Rock and Ellis Island," 193–194, 206; *Two-Way Passage,* 201. See also *Common Ground*
Adams, Henry, 61, 119
Adams, James Truslow: *The Epic of America,* 192
Adorno, Theodor W., 88, 214, 215, 218
Agee, James: *Let Us Now Praise Famous Men,* 11; and "hard-boiled" prose, 134, 135; "Dedication Day," 233
Ager, Waldemar, 93
Agrigento, 183
Ain Arab, 194, 196, 198
Albers, Josef, 12
Aleichem, Sholem, 83
Algren, Nelson, 40, 167; *The Neon Wilderness,* 137–138; *The Man with the Golden Arm,* 138
"American dream," Antin and 68; origin of phrase, 192–193; Adamic and, 193–194; Rizk and, 194, 197, 198, 199; and totalitarianism, 201; Schwartz and, 206; Losey on, 219
American Forces Network, 204
American Legion Magazine, 210
American Red Cross, 204
Anderson, Sherwood, 25, 26, 30, 33; and Stein, 25, 30, 33; and McKay, 26; Lewisohn on, 33; and Toomer, 101–102, 112; and Faulkner, 120; and Hemingway, 123
Antin, Mary, 13, 43, 60, 61, 65–84, 100, 144, 157, 190–191, 193, 194, 202, 219–221, 222; *The Promised Land,* 42, 55, 66, 67–74, 76, 82–84, 99, 118, 183, 192, 197; "First Aid to the Alien," 65; *From Plotzk to Boston,* 66, 70, 87, 98; *They Who Knock at Our Gates: A Complete Gospel of Immigration,* 75–77, 84; "The Lie," 81; "Malinke's Atonement," 83; "House of the One Father," 219–221

Anti-Semitism, 115, 188, 200, 218, 220
Antrim, 183
Arbus, Diane, 8
Arendt, Hannah, 15, 184
Arizona Quarterly, 173
Arlen, Michael, 137
Armory Show, 23, 75, 78, 103, 182, 207
Armstrong, Louis, 8, 12
Asch, Nathan, 118–119, 150; *Pay Day,* 118–119, 180; and Hemingway, 119, 135
Asch, Sholem, 87–88, 119
Assimilation, 13, 14, 16, 38, 39, 46, 59, 67, 89, 90, 91, 120, 239; Antin and, 80, 82; Bourne and, 81; Dahl and, 90, 91; Ager on, 93; Rølvaag on, 95, 97, 99. *See also* Ethnicity; Melting Pot; Pluralism
Atherton, Gertrude, 62
Atlantic Monthly, 67, 73, 79, 81, 83–84, 135
Aufbau, 88
Auschwitz, 233

Baba, Meher, 84
Bacon, Peggy, 182
Baldwin, James, 121, 166
Baltimore Sun, 37
Barbusse, Henri, 26
Barr, Alfred H., Jr., 3, 207–208, 212
Bartholdt, Richard: *From Steerage to Congress,* 43
Beach, Joseph Warren, 125–126
Beat Generation, 25, 239
Beirut, 196, 198
Bell, Thomas, 40; *Out of this Furnace,* 44, 173–174
Bellow, Saul, 40, 167, 222
Benedict, Ruth, 165
Benn, Gottfried, 214

Benton, Thomas Hart, 181
Bérard, Christian, 1
Bercovici, Konrad, 40, 86; *Manhattan Side-Show,* 86
Berenson, Bernard, 22
Berg, Alban, 215
Bible, 67, 68, 69, 73, 97; Exodus, 69; Esther, 73; Song of Songs, 97; Corinthians, 104, 141; John, 115; Isaiah, 141, 143, 152, 153
Bitlis, 183
Bjørnson, Bjørnstjerne, 93, 97
Black Mask, 132
Black Mountain College, 12, 47
Blane, Ralph: "Trolley Song," 140
Blato, 183
Boas, Franz, 165, 166
Boccioni, Umberto, 3
Boder, David P., 281n13
Bok, Edward, 43, 64; *Ladies' Home Journal,* 10, 46, 47, 62, 124; *The Americanization of Edward Bok,* 42, 46–47, 55, 99; *Twice Thirty: Some Short and Simple Annals of the Road,* 78
Bontemps, Arna, 167; *Black Thunder,* 53
Bourne, Randolph, 14, 73, 80–81, 83, 194; "Trans-National America," 14, 73, 80–82
Bradstreet, Anne, 111
"Brahmin," 73; origin of term, 80
Brandeis, Louis D., 74
Brand names, 61–62
Braque, Georges, 4, 213
Braun, Nikolaus, 36
Breast, 112, 170, 171–172, 179–181
Brecht, Bertolt, 88
Breit, Harvey, 34
Breuer, Bessie, 117
Bridges, Horace: *On Becoming an American,* 42

Briones, Matthew Manuel, 276n20
Brittain, Miller Gore: *Two Waitresses on a Streetcar Crossing the Reversing Falls*, 36
Brody, Alter: "Lowing in the Night," 145
Brooks, Van Wyck, 6, 83, 159
Broom, 20, 102
Browder, Earl, 189
Brown v. Board of Education, 167, 204, 240
Brown, Sterling, 30, 32, 33, 167
Buck, Pearl S., 227
Budberg, Marie, 210
Bulosan, Carlos, 40: *America Is in the Heart: A Personal History*, 41
Bulwer-Lytton, Sir Edward G. D., 97
Burgess, Ernest W.: "The Growth of the City: An Introduction to a Research Project," 159–160, 172
Burke, Kenneth, 141
Burnett, Whit, 40, 135, 167
Burroughs, Edgar Rice, 135
Burroughs, William, 22
Buslett, Ole Amundsen, 89, 92; "Veien til *Golden Gate*," 89

Cahan, Abraham, 13, 40, 74, 98, 100; *Yekl: A Tale of the New York Ghetto*, 46, 98; *The Rise of David Levinsky*, 56, 100
Cain, James M., 117, 132, 136; "Three of a Kind," 134
Caldwell, Erskine, 5, 90, 117
Calloway, Cab, 2
Canfield, Dorothy. *See* Fisher, Dorothy Canfield
Cappetti, Carla, 273n3
Carrà, Carlo: *What the Street-Car Told Me*, 36
Cassatt, Mary Stevenson: *In the Omnibus (The Tramway)*, 36

Cather, Willa, 18, 57, 96
Cavell, Stanley, 268n14
Cayton, Horace R., 159–160, 167; *Black Metropolis*, 160, 163
Les Cenelles, 87
Cézanne, Paul, 4, 23, 216, 240
Chacón, Eusebio, 87
Chagall, Marc, 216
Chamberlain, John, 5
Chandler, Raymond: "Notes (very brief, please) on English and American style," 131; "Beer in the Sergeant Major's Hat (or The Sun Also Sneezes)," 131; *The Big Sleep*, 132; *The High Window*, 132; *The Lady in the Lake*, 132; *Farewell, My Lovely*, 132, 134
Château de Prieuré, 184
Chekhov, Anton, 26, 67
Chesnutt, Charles W.: "The Future American," 110
Chicago: in *Life Stories*, 47, 219; Wright and, 61, 130, 157, 158, 160, 161, 163, 164; School of Sociology, 62, 159–160, 172; Dahl and, 89; Toomer and, 106, 107; Hemingway and, 124, 127; Meyer Levin and, 128; Chandler and, 131; Algren and, 138; Renaissance, 159; Hurston and, 168; Farrell and, 172; in Hersey, 226; Szilard and, 235
Chicano: origin of word, 41, 173; literary movement, 41–42; Daniel James and, 55
Child, Richard Washburn, 6, 185, 186
China, 48, 52, 84, 88, 184, 187, 227, 237
Christian Century, 135
City Lights Books, 25
Civil War, 38, 53, 106, 120
Clampett, Bob: *Coal Black and the Sebben Dwarfs*, 216

Clock, 48, 121, 123, 148, 159–161, 167, 169, 171, 172, 174, 176
Colcord, Lincoln, 41, 98–99; *Visions of War,* 98
Cold War, 7, 184, 207, 210, 215, 217, 221, 239–240
Coleridge, Samuel Taylor, 67
Common Ground, 40, 194, 220
Communism/Communist, 16, 189, 190, 210, 217, 218, 239; organizations, 7; art, 7; modern art and, 7, 215; characters, 117, 224; intellectuals and Communism, 119, 141, 184, 188–190, 191, 201; Party, 189, 210; systems, 190; Revolution, 190; countries, 192, 208, 209; music and censure, 210; publications, 212
Cone, Etta, 12, 23
Congress for Cultural Freedom, 8, 215
Conrad, Joseph, 143
Conroy, Jack, 167
Content, Marjorie, 102, 156
Cooper, Gary, 192
Cooper, James Fenimore, 97
Cosmopolitanism, 3, 13, 72, 76, 81, 207
Covarrubias, Miguel, 181, 182
Cowley, Malcolm: *The Portable Faulkner,* 6, 233
Crane, Hart, 101, 102
Croix de Feu, 187
Cronbach, Abraham, 83
Crossman, Richard: *The God That Failed,* 190
Cross Section, 40
cummings, e. e., 186
Cunard, Nancy, 112
Curran, Mary Doyle, 40
Curtiz, Michael, 191

Dahl, Dorthea, 89–91, 92; "Kopperkjelen," 89–91
Dahlberg, Edward, 117
Daiches, David, 226
Damrosch, Walter, 4
Davies, Marion, 3
Davis, Allison, 167
de Beauvoir, Simone, 138
Defoe, Daniel, 55, 67
"Degenerate Art" exhibition, 211
"Degenerate Music" exhibition, 210
Delmar, Viña, 132
Democracy, 190–191, 218; and Communism, 16; and fascism, 16; and literature, 27, 126, 194, 200; Antin on, 76, 220; Fante on, 191; Adamic and, 193, 201; Rizk on, 198–199; film-noir style and, 191; and totalitarianism, 194, 201; and World War II, 204; and Frankfurt School, 214; and modernism, 215, 218, 239–240
Derain, André, 216
Dewey, John, 11, 36
Dial, 102, 210
Dickinson, Emily, 9
di Donato, Pietro, 117, 135, 167, 178, 228; "Christ in Concrete," 56, 175–177, 181 182; *Christ in Concrete,* 61, 62, 174–177, 179–180, 182
Disney, Walt, 216
Dodge, Mabel. *See* Luhan, Mabel Dodge
Dondero, George A., 6–7, 8, 216, 240
Dønna, 183
Dos Passos, John, 62, 80, 120, 124, 135–136; *U.S.A.,* 62; *Nineteen Nineteen,* 80
Dostoyevsky, Fyodor, 67, 102
Double consciousness, 60
Douglass, Frederick, 87

Drake, St. Clair: *Black Metropolis,* 160
Dreiser, Theodore, 18, 54, 136
Du Bois, W. E. B., 30, 74, 94, 187–188, 204; *The Souls of Black Folk,* 94
Duchamp, Marcel, 2, 12, 217; *Nude Descending a Staircase, No. 2,* 2, 23, 135
Dunphy, Jack: *John Fury,* 29–30
Durham, Robert Lee: *The Call of the South,* 37
Dvořák, Antonín, 4

Earle, Eyvind: *For Whom the Bulls Toil,* 216
Eaton sisters. *See* Far, Sui Sin; Watanna, Onoto
Eatonville, 181
Eighth Street, 23, 144, 155–156, 157
Einstein, Albert, 237
Eisenhower, Dwight D., 7–8, 77, 216
Elevated train: in Marsh, 3, 36; in Hopper, 36; in Toomer, 102–103; in Gold, 118; in Roth, 147, 154. *See also* Streetcar/Tram/Trolley; Subway
Eliot, George, 67
Eliot, T. S., 24, 64, 97, 121, 141, 159, 186, 213, 214; *The Waste Land,* 1, 36; Roth and, 141, 143, 146, 150, 155; Wright and, 159, 163; and Pound, 186; versus Tin Pan Alley, 213
Ellington, Duke, 1, 4, 12; "Daybreak Express," 4; *Black, Brown, and Beige: A Tone Parallel to the History of the American Negro,* 8; *Jump for Joy,* 216
Ellis Island, 75, 76–77, 79, 143–144, 178, 193, 199, 202, 206
Ellison, Ralph, 31, 40, 104, 135, 163, 167; *Invisible Man,* 39, 121
Emerson, Ralph Waldo, 67, 104

Engels, Friedrich, 119
"Enola Gay," 228
Ensor, James, 240
Erikson, Erik: and term "identity," 14
Esquire, 56, 136–137, 175, 177, 181
Ethnicity: origin of term, 14; reading for an author's, 54; characters' responses to, 59; preconceptions on the basis of, 206; stressing, 222. *See also* Race Ethnic
Exposure Sheet, 216

Fanon, Frantz, 171
Fante, John, 40, 44, 85, 191, 194; "The Odyssey of a Wop," 44; "We Snatch a Frail," 191
Far, Sui Sin, 41, 55–56; *Mrs. Spring Fragrance,* 41; "Leaves from the Mental Portfolio of an Eurasian," 55
Farrell, James T., 40, 61, 99–100, 129, 135–136, 159, 166, 217; *Studs Lonigan,* 29, 99, 117, 172 -173; "The Language of Hollywood," 134
Fascism/Fascist, 15, 222, 239; fascist realism, 3; fascists, 54; March on Rome, 6, 184, 185, 186; Europe, 12; use of term "racism," 15; and democracy, 16; and German-language exile literature, 88; in Wright, 161, 217; in Italy, 185, 186, 197; in Mangione, 175, 200; and writers, 184; and Mussolini, 184–185; and Pound, 185–186; British Union of, 186; Communism as alternative to, 188; systems, 190; revolution, 190; Fante on, 191; ideals, 192, 207; and Adamic, 193; and Rizk, 199; Mead and, 202; dictatorships, 204; modern art and, 207; music and, 210; antifascist artists, 211; Clement Greenberg

Fascism/Fascist, *(continued)* and, 213, 215; avant-garde and, 213; modernism and, 218; and Hersey, 227. *See also* Hitler; Mussolini; National Socialism/Nazi
Faulkner, William, 29, 101, 120–23, 134–135, 217; *Sanctuary,* 5; *Go Down, Moses,* 5, 121; *Absalom, Absalom!,* 5, 25, 121; *Soldier's Pay,* 120; *Light in August,* 121; *The Sound and the Fury,* 121–122
Fauset, Jessie: *Plum Bun,* 50
Faÿ, Bernard, 187
Federal Writers' Project, 40–41, 85, 130, 167; "Lexicon of Trade Jargon," 85; *Writers Guide Series,* 138, 212
Ferber, Edna: *American Beauty,* 45
Ferraro, Thomas J., 270n15, 274n48
Feuchtwanger, Lion, 88
Fingernails as racial sign, 62
First All-Union Congress of Soviet Writers, 209
Fisher, Dorothy Canfield, 175, 178; "The Knot Hole," 223
Fiske, John, 68
Fitzgerald, F. Scott, 10, 62, 90, 120, 124; *The Great Gatsby,* 62, 120; "How to Live on $36,000 a Year," 10
Flaubert, Gustave, 18, 102
Flint, F. S., 108–109
Foley, Martha, 40, 135, 168, 222
Fontainebleau, 184
Force, Juliana, 3, 12, 155, 207, 208, 212
Foster, Michael: *American Dream,* 192–193
Fox, Paul S., 132
France, 49, 81, 115, 122, 129, 171, 187, 204, 222, 223
Frank, Anne: *Diary of a Young Girl,* 128

Frank, Waldo, 13, 101, 103, 105, 112, 159; *Our America,* 13, 101, 105, 112; "Hope," 103; *Holiday,* 103
Frankfurt School, 214, 218; "Cultural Aspects of National Socialism," 214
Franklin, Benjamin, 74
Frazer, Sir James: *The Golden Bough,* 150, 155, 173
Freeman, Don, 182
French Revolution, 190
Freud, Sigmund, 14, 113, 116, 117, 119, 163; *Beyond the Pleasure Principle,* 142; "family romance," 142, 151, 153
Freundlich, Otto: *The New Man,* 211
Friml, Rudolf: *Indian Love Call,* 174
Fuchs, Daniel, 40; *Homage to Blenholt,* 61; *Williamsburg Trilogy,* 99
Fujii, Masakazu, 229
Furioso, 203

Gardner, Burleigh B., 167
Gardner, Mary R., 167
Garland, Judy, 8
Gay Purr-ee, 8
Genocide: origin of term, 15
Germany: immigrants from, 38, 69; German-Americans and, 79. *See also* National Socialism/Nazi
Germany and You, 185–186
Gershwin, George, 125
Ghiotto, Antonella, 274n8
Ghostwriting, 57
Giacometti, Alberto, 4
Gide, André, 132
Gillespie, Dizzy, 8
Gleason, Philip, 255n23
Gobetti, Piero, 187
Goebbels, Joseph, 210
Gogol, Nikolai, 67
Gold, Mike, 23, 186, 189; *Jews Without Money,* 27, 43, 45, 57, 76, 86,

117–118, 182, 200, 219; on *Saturday Evening Post,* 11; on Stein, 27–28, 74, 119, 214–215; on Antin, 74, 76; on Bourne, 80; on Jazz, 107–108, 209; on Hemingway, 130, 135; on Proust and Roth, 141
Goldman, Emma, 23, 143
Goodman, Paul, 10
Gorky, Maxim, 49, 208–210; "On the Music of the Degenerate," 208–209
Grabau, Amadeus William, 79, 83–84
Grable, Betty, 180
Grass, Günter, 121
Great Depression, 117, 188, 190, 192, 198, 239
Greenberg, Clement, 156, 212–215, 232; "Avant-Garde and Kitsch," 212–214
Grosz, George, 211
"Ground Zero," 230
Guest, Eddie, 213
Guggenheim, Peggy, 12
Gurdjieff, George, 102, 103, 184

Hale, Edward Everett, 43, 67, 68, 82; "The Man Without a Country," 45, 67, 215n15
Halper, Albert: *The Foundry,* 118
Hammett, Dashiell, 132
Hamsun, Knut, 97
Hansen, Marcus Lee, 91
Hapgood, Hutchins, 26
"Hard-boiled": Lewisohn on, 115, 125, 129; Hemingway and, 124, 129–130, 139; Twain and, 124; *Ladies' Home Journal* and, 124–125; Sherman and, 125; Chandler and, 131, 132; Hollywood movies and, 132, 134; Farrell and, 134; Agee and, 134; Wright and, 158; Motley and, 166; indifference and democracy, 191; and modern technologies of death, 219; modernists, 228
Harland, Henry, 55
Harlem Renaissance, 27, 39, 102, 159
Harper's, 135, 180
Hart, Estelle M.: "Trolley-Car Ornithology," 73
Harvard University, 78
Haskell, Edward F., 14, 227; *Lance: A Novel about Multicultural Men,* 14; and term "multicultural," 14
Hathaway, Henry, 132
Hawks, Howard: *The Big Sleep,* 134
Hawthorne, Nathaniel, 104
Hearst, William Randolph, 3, 189, 207
Hemingway, Ernest, 10, 101, 113, 122–139, 183, 228, 239; *The Sun Also Rises,* 25, 34, 61–62, 102, 122–124, 127, 129, 138; *A Moveable Feast,* 34, 123; *The Torrents of Spring,* 123; *Paris 1922,* 123; *A Farewell to Arms,* 124, 129; "The Killers," 125, 134; "The Snows of Kilimanjaro," 125–126; *Green Hills of Africa,* 126; "The Gambler, the Nun and the Radio," 127; *For Whom the Bell Tolls,* 127; and Stein, 25, 34, 123, 124; and brand names, 61–62; and Lewisohn, 114, 129–130; and Asch, 119, 135; on Faulkner, 122; and parody, 122–123; Van Doren on, 124; and "hard-boiled," 124–125; as compromise modernist, 124–125, 239; and revision, 124–125, 126; Sherman on, 125; Hopper on, 125; Beach on, 125–126; Schwartz on, 127, 128; and translation, 127, 267n28; Harry Levin on, 127; Meyer Levin on, 128–129, 267n2; McKay on, 129; Farrell on, 129, 134; Kazin on, 130; Gold on, 130; and Wright, 130, 158,

Hemingway, Ernest, *(continued)* 160, 163; Chandler and, 131–132; Gide on, 132; film noir and, 134; Agee on, 134–135; and Saroyan, 135–137; and Algren, 137–138; and Roth, 143; di Donato and, 177; Fante and, 191; Hersey and, 226

Henderson, Fletcher, 12

Hendrikksen, Gustav, 275n10

Hersey, John, 224–233; *The Wall,* 224–226, 233; *A Bell for Adano,* 227; "Hiroshima," 227–233

Herskovits, Melville, 165

Hicks, Granville, 159: *The Great Tradition: An Interpretation of American Literature since the Civil War,* 118–119

Hildreth, Richard: *The Slave; or, Memoirs of Archy Moore,* 54

Hiroshima, 11, 138, 219, 227–233, 237–238

Hirschfeld, Magnus: *Racism,* 15

Hitler, Adolf: Hearst and, 3; Schwartz on, 25; Wright and, 158; Mussolini and, 186; Hurston on, 187; Stein and, 187, 216, 251; Du Bois on, 188; Rizk on, 199; Roth and, 200; Hughes on, 204; Schwartz and, 205; and modernism, 211, 216; Greenberg on, 214; Congress for Cultural Freedom and, 215; Antin and, 220; Shaw and, 222. *See also* National Socialists; Nazi Germany

Hitler-Stalin pact, 188, 189, 190, 275n14

Hodiak, John, 227

Hoffman, Hans, 12; School, 156, 212

Hollywood, 56, 132, 134, 166, 213, 216, 227

Holmes, Oliver Wendell: *Elsie Venner,* 80

Holocaust, 15, 219–220, 213, 219, 220, 223–224, 233

Holt, Hamilton, 56, 199; *The Life Stories of Undistinguished Americans as Told by Themselves,* 47–54, 55, 57, 58, 63, 66, 75, 143, 183, 190 197, 219, 221

"Homemaking myth," 44, 45, 71, 77, 153. *See also* Øverland, Orm

Hopper, Edward, 3, 36, 125, 154, 132, 154; *Early Sunday Morning,* 3; *Night on the El Train,* 36

House and Garden, 216

Howe, Fanny, 83

Hughes, Langston: "The Cat and the Saxophone (2 A.M.)," 107; "A Good Job Gone," 136; and American Red Cross, 204; and Gorky, 210; "Here to Yonder: Simple and the Atom Bomb," 233

Hurston, Zora Neale, 40, 165–166, 173, 174, 178, 181, 182, 233; *Dust Tracks on a Road: An Autobiography,* 29, 166, 181, 186–187; "Story in Harlem Slang," 61, 85; *Their Eyes Were Watching God,* 163–164, 272n22; *Seraph on the Suwanee,* 166; *Mules and Men,* 167, 181; "The Gilded Six-Bits," 168–169, 170; and Wright, 164–165, 171; and the Federal Writers' Project, 167; and *Brown v. Board of Education,* 167; and phrase "bookooing," 171; and Eatonville, 181; Italian translation of *Their Eyes Were Watching God,* 187; and *Common Ground,* 194; and Gorky, 210

Hutchinson, George, 257n37, 264n9, 265n14, 278n10

Ibsen, Henrik, 93, 97, 102

Identity: launching of term, 14; ethnic, 15, 52, 55, 60, 72; American,

80, 82, 92, 97; Brahmin, 80; Freud on, 255n3
Immigrant autobiography, 27, 66, 99, 184, 194, 200
Immigration: Child and, 3; policy 13, 38–39; restriction, 43; liberal reformers and, 43; debate, 45, 53, 66, 71, 75–77, 84, 99, 143, 174, 178, 194, 202, 204, 243; *Saturday Evening Post* and, 54
Independent, 36, 37, 47, 49, 56; "The Race Problem - An Autobiography by a Southern Colored Woman," 36–37, 52, 53, 65. See also Holt, Hamilton
Indian Reorganization Act, 39
Individualism, 42, 191–192
Intermarriage, 37, 39, 96, 111–112, 204, 206, 240
Irvine, Alexander, 43, 47, 183; *From the Bottom Up: The Life Story of Alexander Irvine*, 43
Italy, 185, 197

Jackson, Shirley, 222
James, Daniel, 55
James, Henry, 35, 58, 61, 68, 73, 128, 131; *The American Scene*, 35
James, William, 14, 21, 163–164; *Principles of Psychology*, 21–22, 79–80, 163–164; *Talks to Teachers on Psychology: and to Students on Some of Life's Ideals*, 21; and Stein, 21, 22
Janson, Drude Krog: *En saloonkeepers datter*, 92–93
Japan, 187, 237–238
Jazz, 6; criticism of, 4; government sponsored tours, 8; Van Vechten and, 9; Stein and, 24; McKay and, 44; songs, 101; Toomer's *Cane* and, 106–107; Mangione and, 181;
Siegel and, 181; Paris and, 183–184; international context and, 184; American culture and, 201; totalitarianism and, 207; Soviet Union and, 208, 210; Gorky and, 208–209; Hughes and, 210; Nazi Germany and, 210, 212; Adorno on, 214; Hollywood cartoons and, 216; Wright and, 217
Jefferson, Thomas, 186
Jewish Daily Forward, 223
Johnson, James Weldon, 30, 56, 74; *Autobiography of an Ex-Colored Man*, 56
Joyce, James, 4, 24, 26, 97, 119, 163, 233; *Ulysses*, 1, 2, 22, 155, 184; *Dubliners*, 101; and Toomer, 107, 108; *Portrait of the Artist as a Young Man*, 108; and Asch, 119; Saroyan and, 135; and Roth, 141, 143, 144, 147, 148; Wright and, 158, 163; "The Dead," 163; Pound and, 186; *The Portable James Joyce*, 232–233

Kafka, Franz, 106, 223; *Amerika*, 144
Kahnweiler, Daniel-Henry, 22
Kaiser, Wilhelm, 239
Kallen, Horace M., 14, 56, 78, 79–80, 82, 83, 99, 134; and term "cultural pluralism," 14, 78; *Culture and Democracy in the United States*, 78; "Democracy Versus the Melting-Pot," 80
Kandinsky, Wassily, 216
Kang, Younghill: *East Goes West: The Making of an Oriental Yankee*, 41
Kato, Saburo, 88
Kazin, Alfred: *On Native Grounds*, 5, 130
Kelly, Myra: *Little Citizens: The Humour of School Life*, 43–44

Kemenov, Vladimir, 215
Kenyon Review, 203
Kerouac, Jack, 25
Kikuchi, Charles, 276n20
King Victor Emmanuel III, 184
Kingston, Maxine Hong Kingston, 96
Kipling, Rudyard, 43
Kleinsorge, Wilhelm, 229–230
Kobrin, Leon, 61; "Di shprakh fun elnt," 89
Koestler, Arthur, 190
Kouwenhoven, John, 201; *The Beer Can by the Highway,* 31
Kroeber, Alfred, 173
Kuhn, Walt: *Blue Clown,* 3
Kunitz, Stanley, 210

"L." *See* Elevated train
Ladies' Home Journal, 10, 46, 47, 62, 124–125
LaFarge, Oliver: *Laughing Boy,* 41
Lang, Fritz: *Scarlet Street,* 132
Languages, mixed, 85–86
Lardner, Ring, 125
Larsen, Nella: *Quicksand,* 30; *Passing,* 30; and Stein, 30
Latimer, Margery: "Confession," 111
Lawrence, D. H., 26, 163, 175; *Lady Chatterley's Lover,* 22
Lazarus, Emma, 67, 202; "The New Colossus," 49, 76
Lazarus, Josephine, 67
Lazerow, Rabbi Judah Leib: *The Staff of Judah,* 147
Lebanon, 195, 196
Lemkin, Raphaël, 15; and term "genocide," 15
Lenin, Vladimir, 207–208
Levin, Harry, 1; on Hemingway, 127; *The Portable James Joyce,* 232
Levin, Meyer, 56, 128–129, 135–136; *The Old Bunch,* 128; *Reporter,* 128;

Frankie and Johnnie, 128; on Hemingway, 267n2
Lewis, Sinclair, 183, 222
Lewis, Wyndham, 27–28, 122–123
Lewisohn, Ludwig, 99; *Expression in America,* 5; *The Case of Mr. Crump,* 113; *The Vehement Flame: The Story of Stephen Escott,* 113–116, 145; *Up Stream,* 113; *The Island Within,* 113; *The Story of American Literature,* 116–117; on Stein, 33; and Adams, 119; and term "hard-boiled," 115, 125, 129; on Hemingway, 129–130
"Lexicon of Trade Jargon," 85
Liberator, 74, 102
Liberty Magazine, 134
Life, 215, 216, 227
Life Stories of Undistinguished Americans as Told by Themselves. See Holt, Hamilton
Lincoln, Abraham, 158, 159
Lipchitz, Jacques, 215
Lippmann, Walter, 14, 38–39; and term "stereotype," 14
Little, Thomas, 132
Liveright, Horace, 186
Lloyd, Harold, 57
Locke, Alain: *The New Negro,* 60, 102
Lockridge, Ross, 121
Loeb, Harold, 20, 102, 156
Lombardi, Cristina, 271n5
London, Jack, 18, 43
Long, Sylvester C.: *Long Lance,* 56
Longfellow, Henry Wadsworth, 9, 67, 222
Lorimer, George Horace, 10
Losey, Joseph, 219
"Lost Generation," 25
Loving v. Virginia, 240
Lowe, Pardee: *Father and Glorious Descendant,* 41
Lowell, James Rusell, 9

Luce, Henry, 227
Luhan, Mabel Dodge, 23, 102, 156
Lunacharsky, Anatoly, 209
Lundgren, Eric, 181–182

Macdonald, Dwight, 212, 232
Majdanek, 211
Major, Clarence, 30
Malevich, Kazimir: *Lady in a Tram*, 36
Mangione, Jerre, 45, 167, 175, 181; *Mount Allegro*, 29, 44, 57, 63, 86, 174, 177–179, 180, 182, 183, 200
Manhattan Project, 237–238
Mann, Thomas, 88, 113
March, Fredric, 227
March on Rome, 184–185
"Marginal men," 62–63
Marquez, Gabriel García, 121
Marsh, Reginald: *Why Not Use the "L"?*, 3, 36
Martin, E. S.: "East Side Considerations," 180
Martin, George Madden: *Emmy Lou: Her Book & Heart*, 67
Martin, Hugh: "Trolley Song," 140
Marx, Karl, 113, 119, 215; Marxists, 27, 105, 107; Marxian themes, 117–118, 119; Marxian interests, 188. *See also* Communism/Communist; Soviet Union
Mathews, John Joseph: *Sundown*, 41
Matisse, Henri, 4, 23, 216, 240
Matthews, Brander: "Making America a Racial Crazy-Quilt," 78
Mayflower, 76, 80, 81, 193
McCarey, Leo: *The Awful Truth*, 132–133
McCarthy, Mary, 232
McClure, S. S., 43, 57, 184, 185; *My Autobiography*, 57
McClure's Magazine, 56
McCullers, Carson, 90, 222

McKay, Claude, 40, 67, 85, 67, 167; *Home to Harlem*, 10, 25–26, 61, 129; *A Long Way from Home*, 30, 44, 129; and Stein, 30, 31, 32, 33; and Mencken, 85; on Hemingway, 129
McNickle, D'Arcy: *The Surrounded*, 41
Mead, Margaret, 165, 173, 194, 202; *And Keep Your Powder Dry*, 194
Meet Me in St. Louis, 140
Melting Pot: and Zangwill, 10, 67; Repplier on, 79; Kallen on, 80; Ager, on 93; Rølvaag on, 93, 97; Farrell on, 100; encounters, 119, 180; Roth's surrealistic, 140
Melville, Herman, 9, 30, 102
Mencken, H. L., 85–86, 132, 183; *American Mercury*, 85–86, 135; *The American Language*, 86; *Black Mask*, 132
Miguéis, José Rodrigues, 90–91, 120; "Gente da Terceira Classe," 90–91
Miller, Henry, 116; "The Tailor Shop," 116
Miró, Joan, 4
Modernism/Modernist, 1–2, 6, 8–10, 15, 20, 216, 217, 218, 232, 234, 239, 240; music, 4, 24; literature, 5, 25, 36; and totalitarianism, 7, 8, 184, 207–208, 212, 240; and modernity, 10, 63, 64, 219; and ethnic groups, 12, 26; and ethnic literature, 12–13, 16, 100, 239; and Stein, 17, 26, 28, 34, 124, 209; antimodernist literary form, 63; Rølvaag and, 97; Toomer and, 101, 102, 104, 109; Hemingway and, 124, 125, 239; Saroyan and, 135; Roth and, 140, 156, 209; and nostalgia, 150; Wright and, 158, 163; Soviet Union and, 208, 212; Nazis and, 210–212; art and Greenberg,

Modernism/Modernist, *(continued)* 213, 214; Kemenov and, 215; Singer and, 223; Hersey and, 232

Modernity: and modernism, 10, 63, 64, 219; ethnic groups and, 12; "The Race Problem—An Autobiography by a Southern Colored Woman" and, 37; ethnic literature and, 60–61, 62, 64; literature and, 63, 168; Gold and, 118; Redfield and, 160; Wright and, 160–161; Bell and, 173; fascism and, 190; Szilard and, 237, 238

Modern Review, 102

Momaday, N. Scott: *House Made of Dawn,* 41

Monet, Claude, 240

Mori, Toshio: *Yokohama, California,* 41; "A Sketch," 202

Morrison, Toni, 121, 138–39

Motley, Willard: *Knock on Any Door,* 61, 166

Münsterberg, Hugo, 20–21, 23

Multiculturalism, 13–15, 41, 82, 86, 91, 138; origin of term "multicultural," 14

Multilingual literature, 85–91, 141

Museum of Modern Art (MoMA), 3, 7, 216

Mussolini, Benito, 3, 6, 175, 184–186, 199–200, 204; *My Autobiography,* 184–185

Nabokov, Vladimir, 40, 87, 222; "'That in Aleppo Once . . . ,'" 222–223

Nadell, Martha J., 264n12, 274n51

Nagasaki, 11, 219, 237

Nakamura, Hatsuyo, 229

National Association for the Advancement of Colored People (NAACP), 216

National Socialism/Nazi: Nazi leaders and genocide, 15; fascism and, 184; *Germany and You,* 185; Pound and, 185–186; Wolfe and, 186; Hurston and, 187; Du Bois and, 187–188; Wright on, 189; USSR and, 189; Hitler-Stalin pact, 190; "race" and, 190; Fante on, 191; Rand on, 192; Rizk and, 197; American Dream and, 199; Gold and, 200; Americans and, 204; art of the Weimar Republic and, 208; aesthetic, 210; and Jazz, 210, 212; Goebbels, 210; and modernist art, 210–211, 212; realist art and, 212; and "racial purity," 212; Greenberg on, 213; "Cultural Aspects of National Socialism," 214; Benn and, 214; Stein and, 216; modern art exhibition and, 216; modernism and, 218; concentration camps, 222; Dorothy Canfield Fisher and, 223; Hersey and, 224, 226; Agee and, 233; Manhattan Project and, 238

Nazi Germany. *See* Fascism/Fascist; Hitler; National Socialism/Nazi

New Masses, 107, 141, 164, 181

New York, 1, 2, 3, 8, 9, 14, 26, 43, 88, 207, 214, 218, 224; *Times,* 4, 6, 8, 13, 24, 280n11; streetcars in, 35; Irvine and, 43; Poole and, 47; *Life Stories* and, 48–50; in Kobrin, 61, 89; Stella and, 75; Antin and, 83; Adorno and, 88; in Miguéis, 90; in Lewisohn, 113, 115; in Asch, 119; Dos Passos and, 136; in Roth, 140, 148, 151, 155, 156; in Hurston, 165, 167; *Panorama,* 167; in di Donato, 175, 180, 182; in Adamic, 183, 235; in Rizk, 198; in Weber, 217, 235; Hersey and, 227, 232; in Szilard, 235–237

New Yorker, 145, 213, 227–228, 231–232
Nobel Prize, 6, 40, 187
Nolde, Emil: *Mulattin* (The Mulatto), 211–212
Norden, 89
Notasulga, 181
Nursery rhymes: in Toomer, 107, 108; in Roth, 148

Oakland, 22, 29
O'Brien, Edward J., 135
O'Hara, John, 117
O'Keeffe, Georgia, 101–102, 109, 215; *Mountains, New Mexico,* 3; *Birch and Pine Trees-Pink,* 109
Okina, Kyuin: "Boss," 88
Okubo, Miné: *Citizen 13660,* 202–203
O'Neill, Eugene: "The Emperor Jones," 102
Ornitz, Samuel, 40, 99; *Haunch, Paunch and Jowl,* 56
Outlook, 2, 36, 65, 74–75
Øverland, Orm, 93, 259n12

Page, Myra: *Moscow Yankee,* 189
Palestine, 197–198
Paris, 2, 3, 8, 22–23, 25, 27, 34, 48, 51, 123, 136, 139, 183–184
Park, Robert E., 62, 159, 160
Parker, Charlie, 12
Partisan Reader, 213
Partisan Review, 11, 212, 214
Patton, George S., 227
Pearl Harbor, 186, 202
Pétain, Marshal Philippe, 187
Peterkin, Julia: "The Merry-Go-Round," 168–170
Petry, Ann: *The Narrows,* 121; *Country Place,* 166

Picasso, Pablo 1, 4, 7, 22–23, 25, 212, 214–215, 240
Pluralism, 13, 15; cultural, term coined, 14, 78; Bourne and, 81, 82; and totalitarianism, 207
Pinzer, Maimie, 83
Pittsburgh: Stella "Types," 75; in Thomas Bell, 173–174
Pittsburgh Courier, 187, 204
Plymouth Rock, 46; and Ellis Island, 76–77, 79, 193, 199, 202, 206; as mythic point of origin, 80
Poe, Edgar Allan, 9
Pollock, Jackson, 216, 218
Polotzk, 43, 66–69, 70, 71, 82, 183, 220
Poole, Ernest, 47, 54, 75; *The Voice of the Street,* 47, 75; *The Harbor,* 47; *Millions,* 47; "Up from the Ghetto: From a Dweller to a Speculator in the Slums," 54; "Getting That Home: Told by Jan, the Big Polish Laborer," 54; "A Mixing Bowl of All Nations," 75
Porto Empedocle, 183
The Postman Always Rings Twice, 134
Poston, 203
Poston *Chronicle,* 203
Pound, Ezra, 24, 108–109, 187, 208; "In a Station of the Metro," 36, 108; *Germany and You,* 185–186; "Totalitarian Scholarship and the New Paideuma," 186; *Jefferson and/or Mussolini,* 186
Pravda, 208
Price, Leontyne, 215
Pronoun use, 5, 52, 55, 72, 77, 194
Prospero, Ada, 187
Prussian Academy of Arts, 212
Pulitzer Prize, 227
Pupin, Michael: *From Immigrant to Inventor,* 43

Race: substitution of "ethnicity" for, 14; and dialect, 33; problem, 36, 166, 204; and dining 37; riots, 39, 205; debit to the, 42; Yezierska on Jewish, 45; typification and, 53; relations, 56, 121, 204; of scholars, 80; Toomer on, 109–112; hatred, 165, 188; "raceless" novels, 166; Pound on, 186; centrality for fascists of, 190; and national unity, 205; prejudice, 206; Antin on, 220

Race ethnic: literature defined, 12; literature and modernism, 12–13; writers and America, 13, 15, 16, 39, 42, 46; heterogeneity, 37–38, 43, 81, 193; authenticity, 54, 55–57; themes, 59–60; literature and modernity, 62–64; glossary, 70; loyalty and treason, 72, 89, 146; embarrassment, 90, 95; scapegoating, 114, 116, 188; writers and Hemingway, 128–139; humor, 43–44, 173–174; homogeneity and fascism, 190. *See also* Ethnicity

Racism: origin of term, 15; and Hirschfeld, 15; racial segregation, 39, 110, 157, 204; Wright and, 42, 163, 167; attacks on, 45; Du Bois and, 188; eugenicist research and, 239; modernism and racial segregation, 214

Radnitsky, Emmanuel. *See* Ray, Man

Ragtime, 4

Rand, Ayn: *We The Living*, 191–192; *The Fountainhead*, 192

Ravage, Marcus: *An American in the Making*, 42

Ray, Man, 12, 23, 240

Realism: nineteenth-century, 1; fascist, 3; Rockwell and, 6; Stein and, 21, 22; and sexuality, 22; American ethnic authors and, 26; Rølvaag and, 97; Gold and, 117; Farrell on hard-boiled, 134; Wright and, 163; and modernist art, 182; and literature, 182; Socialist, 208, 209; and Soviet art policy, 209; Nazi endorsement of, 210, 212; Soviet endorsement of, 210, 212; and modernism, 212; and totalitarianism, 214, 218; Stella and, 217–218, 228, 234; Gorky and, 209, 210

Realmonte, 183

Rechy, John: "El Paso del Norte," 42

Redfield, Robert: *Tepoztlán*, 160

Reid, Louis, 4

Reid, Sydney, 47

Reiss, Winold, 102

Reizenstein, Ludwig von: *Die Geheimnisse von New-Orleans*, 87

Renoir, Auguste, 23, 216

Repplier, Agnes, 79, 82

Richman, Arthur, 133

Riis, Jacob, 43, 74; *The Making of an American*, 42

Ringelblum, Emanuel, 224, 226

Rizk, Salom, 40, 42, 194–200, 202; *Syrian Yankee*, 42, 194–200; and Harold E. Schmidt, 276n23; and Charles Ferguson, 277n5

Robeson, Paul, 31–32

Rochester, 29, 178, 200

Rockwell, Norman, 6, 8, 63, 216, 239; "The Connoisseur," 8–9

Rogers, Will, 194

Rollins College, 47

Rølvaag, Ole E., 41, 45, 87, 92–100, 107, 183; *I de dage*, 41, 98; *Riket grundlægges*, 41; *Giants in the Earth: A Saga of the Prairie*, 41, 45, 92, 94, 95–96, 97–98, 99, 183; *Peder Victorious*, 92, 94, 95, 96–97, 99, 107; *Their Fathers' God*, 92, 94–95, 99; *Omkring fædrearven*, 93; *Amerika-*

Breve, 93; *To tullinger,* 93; *Pure Gold,* 93–94
Roosevelt, Franklin Delano, 202, 237, 239
Roosevelt, Nicholas, 78
Roosevelt, Theodore, 37, 43, 47, 62, 83; "A Layman's View of an Art Exhibition," 2
Rose, Billy: *Barney Google,* 174
Rose, Francis, 1
Rosenbaum, Alissa Zinovievna, 191
Rosenberg, Harold, 9, 212
Rosenfeld, Isaac: *Passage from Home,* 104–105
Rosenfeld, Max, 89
Rosten, Leo, 132, 145; *The Education of H*y*m*a*n K*a*p*l*a*n,* 145
Roth, Henry, 53, 61, 100, 104, 120, 140–157, 167, 171, 173, 189, 209, 219; *Call It Sleep,* 12–13, 45, 63, 75, 82, 140–156, 175, 181, 183, 200; "Impressions of a Plumber," 159; "Where My Sympathy Lies," 189

Said, Omar Ibn, 87
St. Olaf's College, 93
St. Petersburg, 191
Salon art, 3
Sandburg, Carl, 97
San Francisco, 29, 203
Santa Anita Racetrack, 203
Saroyan, William, 40, 173, 194, 219; *The Daring Young Man on the Flying Trapeze and Other Stories,* 135, 136; *Subway Circus,* 136; *Three Times Three,* 135; *My Name is Aram,* 182; "Aspirin Is a Member of the N.R.A," 135; and Stein, 29; and Hemingway, 136–137
Sartre, Jean-Paul, 122, 130, 138
Sasaki, Terufumi, 229

Sasaki, Toshiko, 229–230
Saturday Evening Post: and Mussolini's autobiography, 6, 185; and Rockwell's "The Connoisseur," 9; and Fitzgerald, 10, 62; and advertisement, 11; and Dewey, 11; and Gold, 11; and "lifelets," 54, 57; and traditional literary forms, 63; and Saroyan's "Aspirin Is a Member of the N.R.A, 136; and kitsch, 213
Saturday Review, 165
Saunders, Frances Stonor, 279n16
Schneider, Isidor: *From the Kingdom on Necessity,* 118
Schönberg, Arnold, 1, 8, 12, 88
Schurz, Carl, 74
Schwartz, Delmore: "Grapes of Crisis," 25; "A Bitter Farce," 204–206; and Hemingway, 127, 128; on reading Stein, 256n11
Scott, Sir Walter, 97
Seaver, Edwin, 40, 141
Sedgwick, Ellery, 67, 73, 79, 80–81
Séjour, Victor: "Le Mulâtre," 87
Seligmann, Kurt, 7
Seurat, Georges, 9, 216
Sewell, Anna: *Black Beauty,* 67
Sexual themes, 22, 24, 34, 97, 106, 113, 114–117, 152, 153, 154, 169, 170, 179, 205, 208, 209, 215
Shahn, Ben, 8, 12
Shakespeare, William: *Coriolanus,* 154
Shaw, Bernard, 102
Shaw, Irwin: "The Veterans Reflect," 222
Sheeler, Charles, 8
Sherman, Stuart P., 54; *The Main Stream,* 125
Shriver, William P.: *Immigrant Forces: Factors in the New Democracy,* 68
Sicily, 53, 86, 181, 200

Siegel, William, 181
Silone, Ignazio, 190
Simmel, Georg, 62–63
Simon, Howard, 182
Sinclair, Upton: *The Jungle*, 47
Singer, Isaac Bashevis, 40, 88, 226; *The Family Moskat*, 223–224
Slosson, Edwin E., 47
Smart Set, 168
Smith, William Gardner: *Anger at Innocence*, 166; *Last of the Conquerors*, 204
Solger, Reinhold: *Anton in Amerika*, 88
Solomons, Leon M., 21
Song of Songs, 97. *See also* Bible
Soviet Union, 8, 188–189, 191–192, 208–210, 212, 216. *See also* Communism/Communist
Spanish Civil War, 139, 190
Sparta, Georgia, 184
Stalin, Joseph, 186, 188–189, 199, 201, 208, 214–216, 224; *Leninism*, 186; Stalinism, 199, 210, 212, 214–215, 218. *See also* Communism/Communist; Hitler-Stalin pact
Starr, S. Frederick, 278n3
Statue of Liberty: in *Life Stories*, 49; as symbol, 60; and Emma Lazarus, 67, 76, 202; and Antin, 67, 76; in Roth, 143–144; in Kafka, 144; in Mangione, 178; in Adamic, 193; in Rizk, 196–197, 198
Stearns, Harold, 4, 5
Stein, Gertrude, 1, 2, 17–36, 62, 68, 71, 109, 119, 157, 176, 183, 209, 217, 240; *Three Lives*, 17–36, 101, 108, 228, 229, 240; "Melanctha: Each One as She May," 17–18, 19, 24, 26–27, 28, 30–31, 32–33, 105; "The Good Anna," 18; "The Gentle Lena," 18, 31, 35, 37, 65; *Q.E.D.; or, Things as They Are*, 18, 24, 32, 35, 240; *The Autobiography of Alice B. Toklas*, 19, 20, 21, 23, 26, 31, 55, 217; *The Making of Americans*, 19–20, 21, 30, 42, 240; "As Fine as Melanctha," 20, 31, 112; *Everybody's Autobiography*, 22; *As a Wife Has a Cow: A Love Story*, 22–23; *Lectures in America*, 23, 24; *Four Saints in Three Acts*, 24, 31, 215; *Wars I Have Seen*, 28; *What Are Masterpieces*, 28; *Brewsie and Willie*, 28; "Off We All Went to See Germany," 216; "Reflections on the Atom Bomb," 228–229; and advertisement, 2, 232; style, 19–20, 22; and Loeb, 20, 102; and psychology, 20–21, 22; William James on reading, 22; and "erotic" writing, 22; and modernist painting, 22–23, 215; and modern photography, 23; and film, 23; and modern music, 24; and phrase "Lost Generation," 25; Faulkner and, 25, 121; McKay and, 26, 30; Hapgood and, 26; Van Vechten and, 26–27, 31; Wyndham Lewis and, 27; Gold and, 27, 28, 74, 119, 214; Wright and, 28–29, 31, 33, 158, 163; Farrell and, 29; Mangione and, 29; Hurston and, 29; Saroyan and, 29, 135; Dunphy and, 29–30; Du Bois and, 30; Johnson and, 30; Toomer and, 30, 101, 102, 105, 108, 109; Larsen to, 30; Sterling Brown on, 30, 32; Major and, 30; and stereotypes, 31, 33–34; Ellison and, 31; Tolson and, 31; Robeson and, 31–32; Lewisohn on, 33; Hemingway and, 34, 123, 124; and Sedgwick, 73; and Hollywood movies, 132–133; Roth and, 142, 143, 146; and Pétain, 187; and Hitler, 187, 216

Stein, Kurt M.: "Streetcar Song, Gay '90's," 87; *Die schönste Lengevitch,* 87
Stein, Leo, 12
Steinbeck, John, 117, 213
Steiner, Edward: *From Alien to Citizen,* 42, 77
Steiner, Rudolph, 84
Stella, Joseph, 12, 75–76, 240; "Americans in the Rough: Character Studies at Ellis Island," 75; *Battle of Lights, Coney Island,* 217
Stereotypes: use of word, 14, 15; Stein and, 26, 31–33; and ethnic writing, 43–45, 50; Antin and, 65–66; Toomer on, 109, 114, 118; Schwartz on, 205; in Nazi propaganda, 210; in cartoons, 216
Stern, Elizabeth, 56
Stevenson, Robert Louis, 43, 67
Stieglitz, Alfred, 4, 23, 101–102, 109–110; Gallery 291, 4; *Camera Work,* 4, 23; "Equivalents," 109–110
Story Magazine, 40, 135, 168
Stowe, Harriet Beecher, 19, 71, 105, 161; *Uncle Tom's Cabin,* 17, 161
Strauss, Richard: *Electra,* 24
Streetcar/Tram/Trolley, 35–37, 61; business, 22; in Dunphy, 29; in Stein, 35; Henry James on, 35, 258n1; in Eliot, 36; in painting, 36; Dewey on, 36; "Southern Colored Woman" on, 36–37; Theodore Roosevelt on, 62; in Antin, 65, 69, 157; in *Atlantic Monthly,* 73; in Mencken, 85, 280n2; in Kurt M. Stein, 87; in Toomer, 112, 157; in Faulkner, 121–122; in Hemingway, 124; in Algren, 138; in Roth, 140, 141, 143, 146, 148, 153, 154–156, 157; in *Meet Me in St. Louis,* 140; in Wright, 157–158, 164; in Park, 160; in Bell, 174; in Mangione, 179; in Singer, 223; in Warsaw ghetto, 223; Jews barred from, 224; in Hersey, 229; for explanation of atomic bomb, 229–230; as permanent shadow in Hiroshima, 230. *See also* Elevated train; Subway
Sturzo, Luigi: *Italy and Fascismo,* 15
Styka, Tadé, 3
Suarez, Mario: "El Hoyo," 173; "Señor Garza," 41, 173; and term "Chicano," 41, 173
Subway: in caricature, 2; settings, 35, 36; in Pound, 36; in Motley, 61; in Asch, 119; in Saroyan, 135–136; Burgess on, 160; in Hurston, 165; in di Donato, 180, in Weber, 217; in Gold, 219. *See also* Elevated train; Streetcar/Tram/Trolley
Sue, Eugène: *Wandering Jew,* 67
Surmelian, Leo, 40
Sweeney, James Johnson, 216
Syria, 196–198
Szilard, Leo, 235, 237–238, 251; "My Trial as a War Criminal," 238; Petition to the President," 237–238; "Report on 'Grand Central Terminal,'" 235–238; *The Voice of the Dolphins,* 237

"Take out," 132
Tanforan, 203
Tanimoto, Kiyoshi, 229
Tate, Allen, 124
Taubenfeld, Aviva, 259n16, 260n27
Taylor, Deems, 4
Tcheletchew, Pavel, 1
Tennyson, Alfred, 67, 68
Thomas, W. I., 159
Thomson, Virgil: *Four Saints in Three Acts,* 24, 31, 215

Thrasher, Max Bennett, 43
Time, 227
Tito, Josip Broz, 201
Tolson, Melvin B., 31
Tolstoy, Leo, 26, 67, 102
Tooker, George: *The Subway,* 36
Toomer, Jean, 23, 61, 100–112, 156, 157, 184, 186, 204, 210; *Cane,* 12,13, 30, 101 102, 103–109, 111, 112; "Blood-Burning Moon," 177; "Gum," 201; *Natalie Mann,* 105; "The Americans," 110; "Race Problems and Modern Society," 110; "Blue Meridian," 111; "On Being an American," 111; *Essentials,* 111; "The Flavor of Man," 221–222; and O'Keeffe, 109
Topaz Times, 202
Toscani, Frank E., 227
Totalitarianism/Totalitarian, 15; and Congress for Cultural Freedom, 8; and modern art, 7, 208, 216; regimes, 25, 184; origin of term "totalitarian," 186; and individualism, 191, 192; and democracy, 194, 201; Rizk and, 199; opposition to, 200, 207, 208, 217, 240; and modernism, 208, 212, 217, 218; and realism, 212, 214; and kitsch, 213; aesthetics, 215
Treblinka, 223–224, 225
Trieste, 197
Trilling, Diana, 227
Trilling, Lionel, 1, 5, 40, 222
Trotsky, Leon, 188
Truman, Harry, 237, 238
Turgenyev, Ivan, 67
Twain, Mark, 30, 62, 67; *A Connecticut Yankee in King Arthur's Court,* 62; "General Grant's Grammar," 124; and "hard-boiled," 124

Universalism, 84, 165–166, 221–222

Van Doren, Carl, 20, 56, 124
Van Gogh, Vincent, 8, 210, 216, 218, 240
Vanity Fair, 181
Van Vechten, Carl, 9, 26–28, 30–32, 61; *Nigger Heaven,* 27, 61
Veljish, 183
Venice Biennale, 3, 8, 207
Ventura, Luigi: *Peppino,* 98
Vidor, King, 192
Villareal, José Antonio, 42

Walker, Margaret, 167
Walton, Eda Lou, 2, 149–150, 155, 173; *The City Day,* 143
Warner, W. Lloyd, 14, 167
Warsaw, 223–224, 226
Washington, Booker T., 37, 43, 74; *Up from Slavery,* 43, 74
Watanna, Onoto: *Miss Nume of Japan: A Japanese-American Romance,* 56
Weber, Max, 3, 12, 36, 217, 235, 240; *Chinese Restaurant,* 3, 217; *Grand Central Terminal,* 36, 217; *Rush Hour, New York,* 217; *Patriarchs,* 217
Weill, Kurt, 12
Weiss, Feri Felix: *The Sieve; or, Revelations of the Man Mill,* 45–46
Weiss, M. Lynn, 257n24
Wellesley College, 3
Wells, H. G.: "The World Set Free," 237
Welty, Eudora: "Death of a Traveling Salesman," 62
Wendell, Barrett, 78–79
Whitman, Walt, 9, 13–14, 96–97, 105–106, 111–112, 193; "Nation of Nations," 13, 193, 206

Whitney, Gertrude Vanderbilt, 155
Whitney Museum, 3, 155, 207
Whittier, John Greenleaf, 9, 67
Wilder, Billy: *Double Indemnity,* 134
Wilder, Thornton, 233
Will, Barbara, 275n9
Williams, Dafydd Rhys, 88
Williams, William Carlos, 2
Wilson, Edmund, 9, 137; *Axel's Castle,* 9; on reading Stein, 20
Winther, Sophus Keith, 99
Wirth, Louis, 159, 160; "Urban Society and Civilization," 160
Wise, Rabbi Stephen S., 74
Wist, Johannes B., 93
Wolfe, Thomas, 186
Woolf, Virginia, 24
Works Progress Administration, 40, 167, 181, 212; Federal Arts Project, 218. *See also* Federal Writers' Project
World War I: and the United States, 11–12, 38; and modern writers, 25; McKay and, 26, 129; and languages other than English, 41, 87; and life stories, 47; Antin and, 82, 83–84, 100, 191; Colcord and, 98; Rølvaag and, 99; Toomer's "Seventh Street" and, 101, 106; Miller and, 116; Faulkner and, 120; Hemingway and, 139; Wright and, 169, 171; Du Bois and, 188; and fascism, 190; Bourne and, 194; Rizk and, 195; Adamic and, 200; and soldier slang, 219; and political propaganda, 239
World War II: and U.S. cultural products, 9–10; and the United States, 11–12; cultural pluralism after, 15; Schwartz and, 25, 204–205; Wright and, 28; and racism in the United States, 29, 204, 239; ethnic modernist authors and, 121, 233, 234; and fascism, 184, 239; and Communism, 184; Hurston and, 187; and Hitler-Stalin pact, 189; and American democracy, 200; Adamic and, 201; and U.S. opposition to totalitarianism, 207; and modernity, 219; Toomer's "The Flavor of Man" and, 221; and universalism, 222; Singer's *The Family Moskat* and, 223; Hersey and, 227
Wright, Frank Lloyd, 192
Wright, Richard, 40, 61, 62, 85, 117, 168, 174, 176, 181, 204, 229, 233; *Lawd Today,* 2, 157–159, 163, 217; *Black Boy,* 28, 29, 42, 85, 164, 172; *Native Son,* 39, 116, 159, 160–163, 164, 178, 217; *Uncle Tom's Children,* 131, 161, 165, 171; "Long Black Song," 131, 169–171, 217; "Bright and Morning Star," 163; "Blueprint for Negro Writing," 163; "The Man Who Lived Underground," 163; *12 Million Black Voices,* 164, 166, 167; *Savage Holiday,* 166; "Almos' a Man," 181; *The Outsider,* 217; and Stein, 28–29, 30, 31, 33, 163; and Hemingway, 130, 135, 163; and Chicago School of Sociology, 159–160; and Eliot, 163; and Joyce, 163; and Lawrence, 163; and William James, 163–164; and Hurston, 164–165; and the Federal Writers' Project, 167; and Communism, 189–190; and Nazis, 189–190

Yamamoto, Hisaye, 41, 203–204; "Seventeen Syllables," 41;

Yamamoto, Hisaye, *(continued)* "Death Rides the Rails to Poston," 203; "The Legend of Miss Sasagawara," 203; "Yoneko's Earthquake," 203–204

Yeats, William Butler: "Vacillation," 143

Yerby, Frank, 166–167

Yezierska, Anzia, 10, 40, 45, 61, 64; *Salome of the Tenements,* 10, 45, 61; *Hungry Hearts,* 10

Yutang, Lin, 88

Zangwill, Israel, 10, 66–67; *The Melting-Pot,* 10, 66–67

Zurmelian, Leon, 222

www.ingramcontent.com/pod-product-compliance
Lightning Source LLC
Chambersburg PA
CBHW031406290426
44110CB00011B/281